COMEDY
★ CLASSICS ★

COMEDY
★ CLASSICS ★

TREASURE PRESS

First published in Great Britain in 1984 by
Octopus Books Limited under the title
Laughter On Parade

This edition published in 1987 by
Treasure Press
59 Grosvenor Street
London W1

Illustration by Angela Barrett

ISBN 1 85051 192 6

Printed in Czechoslovakia

50556/2

Contents

Special Delivery

RICHARD GORDON

As a young medical student in 1950s London Richard Gordon encountered many extraordinary characters and unexpected situations. None was more uncomfortable or more testing of his vocation than the following wintry adventure....

IN ORDER TO TEACH THE students midwifery St Swithin's supervised the reproductive activities of the few thousand people who lived in the overcrowded area surrounding the hospital. In return, they cooperated by refusing to water down the demands of Nature with the less pressing requests of the Family Planning Association.

The midwifery course is of more value to the student than a piece of instruction on delivering babies. It takes him out of the hospital, where everything is clean and convenient and rolled up on sterile trollies, to the environment he will be working in when he goes into practice – a place of dirty floors, bed-bugs, no hot water, and lights in the most inconvenient places; somewhere without nurses but with bands of inquisitive children and morbid relatives; a world of broken stairs, unfindable addresses, and cups of tea in the kitchen afterwards.

It was fortunate that I was plunged into the practice of midwifery shortly after my unfruitful love life, for it is a subject which usually produces a sharp reactionary attack of misogyny in its students. Tony Benskin, Grimsdyke, and myself started 'on the district' together. We had to live in the hospital while we were midwifery clerks, in rooms the size of isolation cubicles on the top floor of the resident doctors' quarters. My predecessor, a tall, fair-haired, romantic-looking man called Lamont, had been so moved by his experiences he was on the point of breaking off his engagement.

'The frightful women!' he said heatedly, as he tried to cram a pile of textbooks into his case. 'I can't understand that anyone would ever want to sleep with them. That someone obviously has done so in the near past is quite beyond me.'

'How many babies have you had?' I asked.

'Forty-nine. That includes a couple of Caesars. I'd have made a half-century if I hadn't missed a B.B.A.'

'B.B.A.?'

'Born before arrival. Terrible disgrace for the midder clerk, of course. I reckoned I'd have time for my lunch first, and when I got there the blasted thing was in the bed. However, mother and child did well, so I suppose no real harm was done. Don't try and open the window, it's stuck. I'm going out to get drunk. Best of luck.'

Picking up his bag he left, the latest penitent for the sin of Adam.

I sat on the bed, feeling depressed. It was an unusually raw afternoon in November and the sky hung over the roof-tops in an unbroken dirty grey sheet. There was no fire in the room and the pipes emitted flatulent noises but no heat. The only decoration was a large black-and-white map of the district on which some former student had helpfully added the pubs in red ink. I looked out of the window and saw a few flakes of snow – ominous, like the first spots of a smallpox rash. I wished women would go away and bud, like the flowers.

The three of us reported to the senior resident obstetrical officer, a worried-looking young man whom we found in the ante-natal clinic. This clinic was part of the St Swithin's service. Every Thursday afternoon the mothers came and sat on the benches outside the clinic door, looking like rows of over-ripe poppy-heads. The obstetrical officer was absently running his hands over an abdomen like the dome of St Paul's to find which way up the baby was.

'You the new clerks?' he asked, without interest.

We each nodded modestly.

'Well, make sure you're always within call. When you go out on a case a midwife will be sent separately by the local maternity service, so you've got nothing to worry about. Don't forget to carry two pennies in your pocket.'

'To phone, of course,' he said when I asked why. 'If you get into trouble dash for the nearest box and call me, and I'll come out in a police car. Don't wait till it's too late, either.'

He dismissed us and bent over to listen to the foetal heart rate with a stethoscope shaped like a small flower-vase.

Our next call was on the Extern Sister, who controlled all the midwifery students. I found her a most interesting woman. She was so ugly she could never have had much expectation of fulfilling her normal biological function; now she had been overtaken by the sad menopause and was left no chance of doing so at all. As she had not been offered the opportunity of bearing children she had thrown herself into midwifery like a novice into religion. She knew more about it than the obstetrical officer. She could talk only about mothers and babies and thought of everyone solely as a reproductive element. In her room was a gold medal she had won in her examinations, which she proudly displayed in a small glass-covered frame between two prints of Peter Scott's ducks. She talked of the anatomy involved in the birth of a baby as other women described their favourite shopping street. She had, however, the unfortunate trick of awarding the parts of the birth canal to the listener.

'When your cervix is fully dilated,' she told us gravely, 'you must decide whether to apply your forceps to your baby. You must feel to see if your head or your breech is presenting.'

'Supposing it's your shoulder or your left ear?' asked Benskin.

'Then you put your hand in your uterus and rotate your child,' she replied without hesitation.

She gave us a rough idea of delivering babies and demonstrated the two instrument bags we had to take on our cases. They were long leather affairs, like the luggage of a dressy cricketer, containing sufficient material to restore the biggest disaster it was likely a student could pull down on himself. There were bottles of antiseptic, ether and chloroform, needles and catgut in tins of Lysol, a pair of obstetrical forceps, a peculiar folding canvas arrangement for holding up the mother's legs, enamel bowls, rubber gloves, and a number of unidentifiable packages.

'You must check your bags before you go to your mother,' Sister said.

We chalked our room-numbers on the board in the hall and went out for a drink in the King George. The snow was falling thickly, swirling round the lamp-posts and clinging to the hospital walls, giving the old building a more sinister appearance than ever.

'What a night to start stork-chasing!' Grimsdyke exclaimed.

'What happens when we get out there?' I asked.

'Getting nervous, old boy?'

'I am a bit. I haven't seen a baby born before. I might faint or something.'

'There's nothing to worry about,' Benskin told me cheerfully. 'I was talking to one of the chaps we're relieving. The midwife always gets there first and tells you what to do under her breath. They're a good crowd. They let the patient think you're the doctor, which is good for the morale of both of you.'

We went back to the hospital for dinner. Afterwards Benskin asked the duty porter if everything was still quiet.

'Not a thing, sir,' he replied. 'It's a bad sign, all right. After it's been as quiet as this for a bit they start popping out like rabbits from their warrens.'

We sat in Grimsdyke's room and played poker for matches for a couple of hours. It was difficult to concentrate on the game. Every time the phone bell rang in the distance we jumped up nervously together. Grimsdyke suggested bed at ten, predicting we would be roused as soon as we dropped off to sleep. We cut for who should be on first call: I lost.

It was four when the porter woke me up. He cheerily pulled off the bedclothes and handed me a slip of paper with an address scribbled on it in pencil.

'You'd better hurry, sir,' he said. 'They sounded proper worried over the phone.'

11

I rolled out of bed and dressed with the enthusiasm of a prisoner on his execution morning. The night outside was as thick and white as a rice pudding. After a glance through the curtains I pulled a green-and-yellow hooped rugby jersey over my shirt and a dirty cricket sweater over that. I tucked the ends of my trousers into football stockings, wrapped a long woollen scarf round my neck and hid the lot under a duffle coat. I looked as if I was going to take the middle watch on an Arctic fishing vessel.

The reason for this conscientious protection against the weather was the form of transport allotted to the students to reach their cases. It was obviously impossible to provide such inconsequential people with a car and we were nearly all too poor to own one ourselves. On the other hand, if the students had been forced to walk to their patients the race would have gone to the storks. A compromise had therefore been effected some ten years ago and the young obstetricians had the loan of the midwifery bicycle.

This vehicle had unfortunately not worn well in the service of the obstetrical department. It had originally been equipped with such necessaries as brakes, mudguards, lights, and rubber blocks on the pedals, but, as human beings sadly lose their hair, teeth, and firm subcutaneous fat in the degeneration of age, the machine had similarly been reduced to its bare comfortless bones. The saddle had the trick of slipping unexpectedly and throwing the rider either backwards or forwards, it was impossible to anticipate which. The only way to stop the machine was by falling off. It was the most dangerous complication of midwifery in the practice of the hospital.

I searched for the address on the map. It was on the other side of the district, a short, narrow, coy street hiding between a brewery and a goods yard. It seemed as remote as Peru.

I waddled down to the out-patient hall to collect the instrument bags. The place was cold and deserted; the porter who had called me was yawning in the corner over the telephone, and the two night nurses huddled in their cloaks round their tiny electric fire, sewing their way through a stack of gauze dressings. They took no notice of the globular figure coming down the stairs: an insignificant midwifery clerk wasn't worth dropping a stitch for. For the houseman, or, if they were lucky, one of the registrars come to open an emergency appendix – to them they would give a cup of coffee and a flutter of the eyelids. But what good were the junior students?

The bicycle was kept in a small shed in the hospital courtyard, and had for its stablemate the long trolley used for moving unlucky patients to the mortuary. I saw that the first problem of the case was balancing myself and my equipment on the machine. As well as the two leather bags I had a couple of drums the size of biscuit barrels containing the sterilized

12

dressings. There was a piece of thick string attached to the bicycle, which I felt was probably part of its structure, but I removed it and suspended the two drums round my neck like a yoke. Carefully mounting the machine, I clung to the bags and the handlebars with both hands and pedalled uncertainly towards the front gate. The snowflakes fell upon me eagerly, like a crowd of mosquitoes, leaping for my face, the back of my neck, and my ankles.

The few yards across the courtyard were far enough to indicate the back tyre was flat and the direction of the front wheel had no constant relationship to the way the handlebars were pointing. I crunched to a stop by the closed iron gates and waited for the porter to leave his cosy cabin and let me out.

'You all right, sir?' he asked with anxiety.

'Fine,' I said. 'I love it like this. It makes me feel like a real doctor.'

'Well,' he said dubiously, 'good luck, sir.'

'Thank you.'

The porter turned the key in the lock and pulled one of the gates open against the resisting snow.

'Your back light isn't working, sir,' he shouted.

I called back I thought it didn't matter and pedalled away into the thick night feeling like Captain Oakes. I had gone about twenty yards when the chain came off.

After replacing the chain I managed to wobble along the main road leading away from the hospital in the direction of the brewery. The buildings looked as hostile as polar ice-cliffs. Everything appeared so different from the kindly daytime, which gave life to the cold, dead streets with the brisk circulation of traffic. Fortunately my thorough knowledge of the local public houses provided a few finger-posts, and I might have done tolerably well as a flying angel of mercy if the front wheel hadn't dropped off.

I fell into the snow in the gutter and wished I had gone in for the law. As I got to my feet I reflected that the piece of string might have been something important to do with the attachment of the front wheel; but now the lesion was inoperable. Picking up my luggage, I left the machine to be covered by the snow like a dead husky and trudged on. By now I was fighting mad. I told myself I would damn well deliver that baby. If it dared to precipitate itself into the world ungraciously without waiting for me I decided I would strangle it.

I turned off the main road towards the brewery, but after a few hundred yards I had to admit I was lost. Even the pubs were unfamiliar. I now offered no resistance to my environment and submissively felt the moisture seeping through my shoes. I leant against a sheltering doorpost, preparing to meet death in as gentlemanly a way as possible.

At that moment a police car, forced like myself into the snow, stopped in front of me. The driver swung his light on my load and on myself, and had no alternative than to decide I was a suspicious character. He asked for my identity card.

'Quick!' I said dramatically. 'I am going to a woman in childbirth.'

'Swithin's?' asked the policeman.

'Yes. It may be too late. I am the doctor.'

'Hop in the back!'

There is nothing that delights policemen more than being thrown into a midwifery case. There is a chance they might have to assist in the performance, which means a picture in the evening papers and congratulatory beer in the local. The constable who walked into St Swithin's one afternoon with an infant born on the lower deck of a trolley bus looked as pleased as if he were the father.

The warm police car took me to the address, and the crew abandoned me with reluctance. It was a tall, dead-looking tenement for ever saturated with the smells of brewing and shunting. I banged on the knocker and waited.

A thin female child of about five opened the door.

'I'm the doctor,' I announced.

The arrival of the obstetrician in such a briskly multiplying area caused no more stir than the visit of the milkman.

'Upstairs, mate,' she said and scuttled away into the darkness like a rat.

The house breathed the sweet stench of bed-bugs; inside it was dark, wet, and rotting. I fumbled my way to the stairs and creaked upwards. On the second floor a door opened a foot, a face peered through, and as the shaft of light caught me it was slammed shut. It was on the fifth and top floor that the accouchement seemed to be taking place, as there was noise and light coming from under one of the doors. I pushed it open and lumbered in.

'Don't worry!' I said. 'I have come.'

I took a look round the room. It wasn't small, but a lot was going on in it. In the centre, three or four children were fighting on the pockmarked linoleum for possession of their plaything, a piece of boxwood with a nail through it. A fat woman was unconcernedly making a cup of tea on a gas-ring in one corner, and in the other a girl of about seventeen with long yellow hair was reading last Sunday's *News of the World*. A cat, sympathetic to the excited atmosphere, leapt hysterically among the children. Behind the door was a bed beside which was grandma – who always appears on these occasions, irrespective of the social standing of the participants. Grandma was giving encouragement tempered with warning to the mother, a thin, pale, fragile woman on the bed, and it was obvious that the affair had advanced alarmingly. A tightly-packed fire roared in the grate and above the mantelpiece Field-Marshal Montgomery, of all people, looked at the scene quizzically.

'Her time is near, Doctor,' said grandma with satisfaction.

'You have no need to worry any longer, missus,' I said brightly.

I dropped the kit on the floor and removed my duffle coat, which wept dirty streams on to the lino. The first step was to get elbow room and clear out the non-playing members of the team.

'Who are you?' I asked the woman making tea.

'From next door,' she replied. 'I thought she'd like a cup of tea, poor thing.'

'I want some hot water,' I said sternly. 'Lots of hot water. Fill basins with it. Or anything you like. Now you all go off and make me some hot water. Take the children as well. Isn't it past their bedtime?'

'They sleep in 'ere, Doctor,' said grandma.

'Oh. Well – they can give you a hand. And take the cat with you. Come on – all of you. Lots of water, now.'

They left unwillingly, in disappointment. They liked their entertainment to be fundamental.

'Now, mother,' I started, when we were alone. A thought struck me – hard, in the pit of the stomach. The midwife – the cool, practised, confident midwife. Where was she? Tonight – this memorable night to the two of us in the room – what had happened to her? Snowbound, of course. I felt like an actor who had forgotten his lines and finds the prompter has gone out for a drink.

'Mother,' I said earnestly. 'How many children have you?'

'Five, Doctor,' she groaned.

Well, that was something. At least one of us knew a bit about it.

She began a frightening increase in activity.

'I think it's coming, Doctor!' she gasped, between pains. I grasped her hand vigorously.

'You'll be right as rain in a minute,' I said, as confidently as possible. 'Leave it to me.'

'I feel sick,' she cried miserably.

'So do I,' I said.

I wondered what on earth I was going to do.

There was, however, one standby that I had thoughtfully taken the trouble to carry. I turned into the corner furthest away from the mother and looked as if I was waiting confidently for the precise time to intervene. Out of my hip pocket I drew a small but valuable volume in a limp red cover – *The Student's Friend in Obstetrical Difficulties*. It was written by a hard-headed obstetrician on the staff of a Scottish hospital who was under no illusions about what the students would find difficult. It started off with 'The Normal Delivery'. The text was written without argument, directly, in short numbered paragraphs, like a cookery book. I glanced at the first page.

'Sterility,' it said. 'The student must try to achieve sterile surroundings for the delivery, and scrub-up himself as for a surgical operation. Newspapers may be used if sterile towels are unobtainable, as they are often bacteria-free.'

Newspaper, that was it! There was a pile of them in the corner, and I scattered the sheets over the floor and the bed. This was a common practice in the district, and if he knew how many babies were born yearly straight on to the *Daily Herald* Mr Percy Cudlip would be most surprised.

There was a knock on the door, and grandma passed through an enamel bowl of boiling water.

'Is it come yet, Doctor?' she asked.

'Almost,' I told her. 'I shall need lots more water.'

I put the bowl down on the table, took some soap and a brush from the bag, and started scrubbing.

'Oh, Doctor, Doctor ... !' cried the mother.

'Don't get alarmed,' I said airily.

'It's coming Doctor!'

I scrubbed furiously. The mother groaned. Grandma shouted through the door she had more hot water. I shouted back at her to keep out. The cat, which had not been removed as ordered, jumped in the middle of the newspaper and started tearing at it with its claws.

Suddenly I become aware of a new note in the mother's cries – a higher, wailing, muffled squeal. I dropped the soap and tore back the bedclothes.

The baby was washed and tucked up in one of the drawers from the wardrobe, which did a turn of duty as a cot about once a year. The mother was delighted and said she had never had such a comfortable delivery. The spectators were readmitted, and cooed over the infant. There were cups of tea all round. I had the best one, with sugar in it. I felt the name of the medical profession never stood higher.

'Do you do a lot of babies, Doctor?' asked the mother.

'Hundreds,' I said. 'Every day.'

'What's your name, Doctor, if you don't mind?' she said.

I told her.

'I'll call 'im after you. I always call them after the doctor or the nurse, according.'

I beamed and bowed graciously. I was genuinely proud of the child. It was my first baby, born through my own skill and care. I had already forgotten in the flattering atmosphere that my single manoeuvre in effecting the delivery was pulling back the eiderdown.

Packing the instruments up, I climbed into my soggy duffle coat and, all smiles, withdrew. At the front door I found to my contentment that the snow had stopped and the roads shone attractively in the lamplight. I began to whistle as I walked away. At that moment the midwife turned the corner on her bicycle.

'Sorry, old chap,' she said, as she drew up. 'I was snowed under. Have you been in?'

'In! It's all over.'

'Did you have any trouble?' she asked dubiously.

'Trouble!' I said with contempt. 'Not a bit of it! It went splendidly.'

'I supposed you remembered to remove the afterbirth?'

'Of course.'

'Well, I might as well go home then. How much did it weigh?'

'Nine pounds on the kitchen scales.'

'You students are terrible liars.'

I walked back to the hospital over the slush as if it were a thick pile carpet. The time was getting on. A hot bath, I thought, then a good breakfast ... and a day's work already behind me. I glowed in anticipation as I suddenly became aware that I was extremely hungry.

At the hospital gate the porter jumped up from his seat.

''Urry up, sir,' he said, 'and you'll just make it.'

'What's all this?' I asked with alarm.

'Another case, sir. Been waiting two hours. The other gentlemen are out already.'

'But what about my breakfast?'

'Sorry, sir. Not allowed to go to meals if there's a case. Orders of the Dean.'

'Oh, hell!' I said. I took the grubby slip of paper bearing another address. 'So this is midwifery,' I added gloomily.

'That's right, sir,' said the porter cheerfully. 'It gets 'em all down in the end.'

The O'Conors of Castle Conor, County Mayo

ANTHONY TROLLOPE

I SHALL NEVER FORGET my first introduction to country life in Ireland, my first day's hunting there, or the manner in which I passed the evening afterwards. Nor shall I ever cease to be grateful for the hospitality which I received from the O'Conors of Castle Conor. My acquaintance with the family was first made in the following manner. But before I begin my story, let me inform my reader that my name is Archibald Green.

I had been for a fortnight in Dublin, and was about to proceed into County Mayo on business which would occupy me there for some weeks. My headquarters would, I found, be at the town of Ballyglass; and I soon learned that Ballyglass was not a place in which I should find hotel accommodation of a luxurious kind, or much congenial society indigenous to the place itself.

'But you are a hunting man, you say,' said old Sir P—— C——; 'and in that case you will soon know Tom O'Conor. Tom won't let you be dull. I'd write you a letter to Tom, only he'll certainly make you out without my taking the trouble.'

I did think at the time that the old baronet might have written the letter for me, as he had been a friend of my father's in former days; but he did not, and I started for Ballyglass with no other introduction to anyone in the county than that contained in Sir P——'s promise that I should soon know Mr Thomas O'Conor.

I had already provided myself with a horse, groom, saddle and bridle, and these I sent down, *en avant*, that the Ballyglassians might know that I was somebody. Perhaps, before I arrived, Tom O'Conor might learn that a hunting man was coming into the neighbourhood, and I might find at the inn a polite note intimating that a bed was at my service at Castle Conor. I had heard so much of the free hospitality of the Irish gentry as to imagine that such a thing might be possible.

But I found nothing of the kind. Hunting gentlemen in those days were very common in County Mayo, and one horse was no great evidence of a man's standing in the world. Men there, as I learnt afterwards, are sought for themselves quite as much as they are elsewhere; and though my groom's top-boots were neat, and my horse a very tidy animal, my entry into Ballyglass created no sensation whatever.

18

In about four days after my arrival, when I was already infinitely disgusted with the little pothouse in which I was forced to stay, and had made up my mind that the people in County Mayo were a churlish set, I sent my horse on to a meet of the foxhounds, and followed after myself on an open car.

No one but an erratic foxhunter such as I am – a foxhunter, I mean, whose lot it has been to wander about from one pack of hounds to another – can understand the melancholy feeling which a man has when he first intrudes himself, unknown by any one, among an entirely new set of sportsmen. When a stranger falls thus as it were out of the moon into a hunt, it is impossible that men should not stare at him and ask who he is. And it is so disagreeable to be stared at, and to have such questions asked! This feeling does not come upon a man in Leicestershire or Gloucestershire, where the numbers are large, and a stranger or two will always be overlooked, but in small hunting fields it is so painful that a man has to pluck up much courage before he encounters it.

We met on the morning in question at Bingham's Grove. There were not above twelve or fifteen men out, all of whom, or nearly all, were cousins to each other. They seemed to be all Toms, and Pats, and Larrys, and Micks. I was done up very knowingly in pink, and thought that I looked quite the thing; but for two or three hours nobody noticed me.

I had my eyes about me, however, and soon found out which of them was Tom O'Conor. He was a fine-looking fellow, thin and tall, but not largely made, with a piercing grey eye, and a beautiful voice for speaking to a hound. He had two sons there also, short, slight fellows, but exquisite horsemen. I already felt that I had a kind of acquaintance with the father, but I hardly knew on what ground to put in my claim.

We had no sport early in the morning. It was a cold, bleak February day, with occasional storms of sleet. We rode from cover to cover, but all in vain. 'I am sorry, sir, that we are to have such a bad day, as you are a stranger here,' said one gentleman to me. This was Jack O'Conor, Tom's eldest son, my bosom friend for many a year after. Poor Jack! I fear that the Encumbered Estates Court sent him altogether adrift upon the world.

'We may still have a run from Poulnaroe, if the gentleman chooses to come on,' said a voice coming from behind with a sharp trot. It was Tom O'Conor.

'Wherever the hounds go, I'll follow,' said I.

'Then come on to Poulnaroe,' said Mr O'Conor. I trotted on quickly by his side, and before we reached the cover had managed to slip in something about Sir P—— C——.

'What the deuce!' said he. 'What! a friend of Sir P——'s? Why the deuce didn't you tell me so? What are you doing down here? Where are you staying?' etc., etc., etc.

At Poulnaroe we found a fox, but before we did so Mr O'Conor had asked me over to Castle Conor. And this he did in such a way that there was no possibility of refusing him – or, I should rather say, of disobeying him. For his invitation came quite in the tone of a command.

'You'll come to us of course when the day is over – and let me see; we're near Ballyglass now, but the run will be right away in our direction. Just send word for them to send your things to Castle Conor.'

'But they're all about, and unpacked,' said I.

'Never mind. Write a note and say what you want now, and go and get the rest tomorrow yourself. Here, Patsey! – Patsey! run into Ballyglass for this gentleman at once. Now don't be long, for the chances are we shall find here.' And then, after giving some further hurried instructions, he left me to write a line in pencil to the innkeeper's wife on the back of a ditch.

This I accordingly did. 'Send my small portmanteau,' I said, 'and all my black dress clothes, and shirts, and socks, and all that, and above all my dressing things, which are on the little table, and the satin neck-handkerchief, and whatever you do, mind you send my *pumps*'; and I underscored the latter word; for Jack O'Conor, when his father left me, went on pressing the invitation. 'My sisters are going to get up a dance,' said he; 'and if you are fond of that kind of thing perhaps we can amuse you.' Now in those days I was very fond of dancing – and very fond of young ladies too, and therefore glad enough to learn that Tom O'Conor had daughters as well as sons. On this account I was very particular in underscoring the word pumps.

'And hurry, you young divil,' Jack O'Conor said to Patsey.

'I have told him to take the portmanteau over on a car,' said I.

'All right; then you'll find it there on our arrival.'

We had an excellent run, in which I may make bold to say that I did not acquit myself badly. I stuck very close to the hounds, as did the whole of the O'Conor brood; and when the fellow contrived to earth himself, as he did, I received those compliments on my horse, which is the most approved praise which one foxhunter ever gives to another.

'We'll buy that fellow off you before we let you go,' said Peter, the youngest son.

'I advise you to look sharp after your money if you sell him to my brother,' said Jack.

And then we trotted slowly off to Castle Conor, which, however, was by no means near to us. 'We have ten miles to go – good Irish miles,' said the father. 'I don't know that I ever remember a fox from Poulnaroe taking that line before.'

'He wasn't a Poulnaroe fox,' said Peter.

'I don't know that,' said Jack; and then they debated that question hotly.

Our horses were very tired, and it was late before we reached Mr

O'Conor's house. That getting home from hunting with a thoroughly weary animal, who has no longer sympathy or example to carry him on, is a very tedious work. In the present instance I had company with me; but when a man is alone, when his horse toes at every ten steps, when the night is dark and the rain pouring, and there are yet eight miles of road to be conquered – at such times a man is almost apt to swear that he will give up hunting.

At last we were in the Castle Conor stablcyard – for we had approached the house by some back way; and as we entered the house by a door leading through a wilderness of back passages, Mr O'Conor said out loud, 'Now, boys, remember I sit down to dinner in twenty minutes.' And then turning expressly to me, he laid his hand kindly upon my shoulder and said, 'I hope you will make yourself quite at home at Castle Conor – and whatever you do, don't keep us waiting for dinner. You can dress in twenty minutes, I suppose?'

'In ten!' said I, glibly.

'That's well. Jack and Peter will show you to your room,' and so he turned away and left us.

My two young friends made their way into the great hall, and thence into the drawing-room, and I followed them. We were all dressed in pink, and had waded deep through bog and mud. I did not exactly know whither I was being led in this guise, but I soon found myself in the presence of two young ladies, and of a girl about thirteen years of age.

'My sisters,' said Jack, introducing me very laconically; 'Miss O'Conor, Miss Kate O'Conor, Miss Tizzy O'Conor.'

'My name is not Tizzy,' said the younger; 'it's Eliza. How do you do, sir? I hope you had a fine hunt! Was papa well up, Jack?'

Jack did not condescend to answer this question, but asked one of the elder girls whether anything had come, and whether a room had been made ready for me.

'Oh, yes!' said Miss O'Conor; 'they came, I know, for I saw them brought into the house; and I hope Mr Green will find everything comfortable.' As she said this I thought I saw a slight smile steal across her remarkably pretty mouth.

They were both exceedingly pretty girls. Fanny, the elder, wore long glossy curls – for I write, oh, reader, of bygone days, as long ago as that, when ladies wore curls if it pleased them so to do, and gentlemen danced in pumps, with black handkerchiefs round their necks – yes, long black, or nearly black silken curls; and then she had such eyes – I never knew whether they were most wicked or most bright; and her face was all dimples, and each dimple was laden with laughter and laden with love. Kate was probably the prettier girl of the two, but on the whole not so attractive. She was fairer than her sister, and wore her hair in braids; and was also somewhat more demure in her manner.

In spite of the special injunctions of Mr O'Conor senior, it was impossible not to loiter for five minutes over the drawing-room fire talking to these houris – more especially as I seemed to know them intimately by intuition before half of the five minutes was over. They were so easy, so pretty, so graceful, so kind, they seemed to take it so much as a matter of course that I should stand there talking in my red coat and muddy boots.

'Well; do go and dress yourselves,' at last said Fanny, pretending to speak to her brothers but looking more especially at me. 'You know how mad papa will be. And remember, Mr Green, we expect great things from your dancing tonight. You coming just at this time is such a Godsend.' And again that *soupçon* of a smile passed over her face.

I hurried up to my room, Peter and Jack coming with me to the door. 'Is everything right?' said Peter, looking among the towels and water-jugs. 'They've given you a decent fire for a wonder,' said Jack, stirring up the red hot turf which blazed in the grate. 'All right as a trivet,' said I. 'And look alive like a good fellow,' said Jack. We had scowled at each other in the morning as very young men do when they are strangers; and now, after a few hours, we were intimate friends.

I immediately turned to my work, and was gratified to find that all my things were laid out ready for dressing; my portmanteau had of course come open, as my keys were in my pocket, and therefore some of the excellent servants of the house had been able to save me all the trouble of unpacking. There was my shirt hanging before the fire; my black clothes were spread upon the bed, my socks and collar and handkerchief beside them; my brushes were on the toilet table, and everything prepared exactly as though my own man had been there. How nice!

I immediately went to work at getting off my spurs and boots, and then proceeded to loosen the buttons at my knees. In doing this I sat down in the armchair which had been drawn up for me, opposite the fire. But what was the object on which my eyes then fell – the objects I should rather say!

Immediately in front of my chair was placed, just ready for my feet, an enormous pair of shootingboots – halfboots, made to lace up around the ankles, with thick double leather soles, and each bearing half a stone of iron in the shape of nails and heelpieces. I had superintended the making of these shoes in Burlington Arcade with the greatest diligence. I was never a good shot; and, like some other sportsmen, intended to make up for my deficiency in performance by the excellence of my shooting apparel. 'Those nails are not large enough,' I had said; 'nor nearly large enough.' But when the boots came home they struck even me as being too heavy, too metalsome. 'He, he, he,' laughed the boot boy as he turned them up for me to look at. It may therefore be imagined of what nature were the articles which were thus set out for the evening's dancing.

And then the way in which they were placed! When I saw this the conviction flew across my mind like a flash of lightning that the preparation had been made under other eyes than those of the servant. The heavy big boots were placed so prettily before the chair, and the strings of each were made ready to dangle down at the sides, as though just ready for tying! They seemed to say, the boots did, 'Now, make haste. We at any rate are ready – you cannot say that you were kept waiting for us.' No mere servant's hand had ever enabled a pair of boots to laugh at one so completely.

But what was I to do? I rushed at the small portmanteau, thinking that my pumps also might be there. The woman surely could not have been such a fool as to send me those tons of iron for my evening wear! But alas, alas! no pumps were there. There was nothing else in the way of covering for my feet; not even a pair of slippers.

And now what was I to do? The absolute magnitude of my misfortune only loomed upon me by degrees. The twenty minutes allowed by that stern old paterfamilias were already gone and I had done nothing towards dressing. And indeed it was impossible that I should do anything that would be of avail. I could not go down to dinner in my stocking feet, nor could I put on my black dress trousers over a pair of mud-painted topboots. As for those iron-soled horrors – and then I gave one of them a kick with the side of my bare foot which sent it halfway under the bed.

But what was I to do? I began washing myself and brushing my hair with this horrid weight upon my mind. My first plan was to go to bed, and send down word that I had been suddenly taken ill in the stomach; then to rise early in the morning and get away unobserved. But by such a course of action I should lose all chance of any further acquaintance with those pretty girls! That they were already aware of the extent of my predicament, and were now enjoying it – of that I was quite sure.

What if I boldly put on the shootingboots, and clattered down to dinner in them? What if I took the bull by the horns, and made, myself, the most of the joke? This might be very well for the dinner, but it would be a bad joke for me when the hour for dancing came. And, alas! I felt that I lacked the courage. It is not every man that can walk down to dinner, in a strange house full of ladies, wearing such boots as those I have described.

Should I not attempt to borrow a pair? This, all the world will say, should have been my first idea. But I have not yet mentioned that I am myself a large-boned man, and that my feet are especially well developed. I had never for a moment entertained a hope that I should find anyone in the house whose boot I could wear. But at last I rang the bell. I would send for Jack, and if everything failed, I would communicate my grief to him.

I had to ring twice before anybody came. The servants, I well knew, were putting the dinner on the table. At last a man entered the room, dressed in rather shabby black, whom I afterwards learned to be the butler.

'What is your name, my friend?' said I, determined to make an ally of the man.

'My name? Why, Larry sure, yer honer. And the masther is out of his sinses in a hurry, becase yer honer don't come down.'

'Is he though? Well, now, Larry; tell me this; which of all the gentlemen in the house has got the largest foot?'

'Is it the largest foot, yer honer?' said Larry, altogether surprised by my question.

'Yes; the largest foot,' and then I proceeded to explain to him my misfortune. He took up first my topboot, and then the shootingboot – in looking at which he gazed with wonder at the nails – and then he glanced at my feet, measuring them with his eye; and after this he pronounced his opinion.

'Yer honer couldn't wear a morsel of leather belonging to ere a one of 'em, young or ould. There niver was a foot like that yet among the O'Conors.'

'But are there no strangers staying here?'

'There's three or four on 'em come in to dinner; but they'll be wanting their own boots I'm thinking. And there's young Misther Dillon; he's come to stay. But Lord love you——' and he again looked at the enormous extent which lay between the heel and the toe of the shooting apparatus which he still held in his hand. 'I niver see such a foot as that in the whole barony,' he said, 'barring my own.'

Now Larry was a large man, much larger altogether than myself, and as he said this I looked down involuntarily at his feet; or rather at his foot, for as he stood I could only see one. And then a sudden hope filled my heart. On that foot there glittered a shoe – not indeed such as were my own which were now resting ingloriously at Ballyglass while they were so sorely needed at Castle Conor; but one which I could wear before ladies, without shame – and in my present frame of mind with infinite contentment.

'Let me look at that one of your own,' said I to the man, as though it were merely a subject for experimental inquiry. Larry, accustomed to obedience, took off the shoe, and handed it to me. My own foot was immediately in it, and I found that it fitted me like a glove.

'And now the other,' said I – not smiling, for a smile would have put him on his guard; but somewhat sternly, so that that habit of obedience should not desert him at this perilous moment. And then I stretched out my hand.

'But yer honer can't keep 'em you know,' said he. 'I haven't the ghost of another shoe to my feet.' But I only looked more sternly than before, and still held out my hand. Custom prevailed. Larry stooped down slowly, looking at me the while, and pulling off the other slipper handed it to me with much hesitation. Alas; as I put it to my foot I found that it was old, and worn, and irredeemably down at heel – that it was in fact no counterpart at all to that other one which was to do duty as its fellow. But nevertheless I put my foot into it, and felt that a descent to the drawing-room was now possible.

'But yer honer will give 'em back to a poor man?' said Larry, almost crying. 'The masther's mad this minute becase the dinner's not up. Glory to God, only listhen to that!' And as he spoke a tremendous peal rang out from some bell downstairs that had evidently been shaken by an angry hand.

'Larry,' said I – and I endeavoured to assume a look of very grave importance as I spoke – 'I look to you to assist me in this matter.'

'Och – wirra sthrue then, and will you let me go? just listhen to that,' and another angry peal rang out, loud and repeated.

'If you do as I ask you,' I continued, 'you shall be well rewarded. Look here; look at these boots,' and I held up the shooting-shoes new from Burlington Arcade. 'They cost thirty shillings – thirty shillings! and I will give them to you for the loan of this pair of slippers.'

'They'd be no use at all to me, yer honer; not the laist use in life.'

'You could do with them very well for tonight, and then you could sell them. And here are ten shillings besides,' and I held out half a sovereign which the poor fellow took into his hand.

I waited no further parley but immediately walked out of the room. With one foot I was sufficiently pleased. As regarded that I felt that I had overcome my difficulty. But the other was not so satisfactory. Whenever I attempted to lift it from the ground the horrid slipper would fall off, or only just hang by the toe. As for dancing, that would be out of the question.

'Och, murther, murther,' sang out Larry, as he heard me going downstairs. 'What will I do at all? Tare and 'ounds; there, he's at it agin, as mad as blazes.' This last exclamation had reference to another peal which was evidently the work of the master's hand.

I confess I was not quite comfortable as I walked downstairs. In the first place I was nearly half an hour late, and I knew from the vigour of the peals that had sounded that my slowness had already been made the subject of strong remarks. And then my left shoe went flop, flop, on every alternate step of the stairs. By no exertion of my foot in the drawing up of my toe could I induce it to remain permanently fixed upon my foot. But over and above and worse than all this was the conviction strong upon my mind that I should become a subject of merriment to the girls as soon as I entered the room. They would understand the cause of my distress, and probably at this moment were expecting to hear me clatter through the stone hall with those odious metal boots.

However, I hurried down and entered the drawing-room, determined to keep my position near the door, so that I might have as little as possible to do on entering and as little as possible in going out. But I had other difficulties in store for me. I had not as yet been introduced to Mrs O'Conor; nor to Miss O'Conor, the squire's unmarried sister.

'Upon my word I thought you were never coming,' said Mr O'Conor as soon as he saw me. 'It is just one hour since we entered the house. Jack, I wish you would find out what has come to that fellow Larry,' and again he rang the bell. He was too angry, or it might be too impatient, to go through the ceremony of introducing me to anybody.

I saw that the two girls looked at me very sharply, but I stood at the back of an armchair so that no one could see my feet. But that little imp Tizzy walked round deliberately, looked at my heels, and then walked back again. It was clear that she was in the secret.

There were eight or ten people in the room, but I was too much fluttered to notice well who they were.

'Mamma,' said Miss O'Conor, 'let me introduce Mr Green to you.'

It luckily happened that Mrs O'Conor was on the same side of the fire as myself, and I was able to take the hand which she offered me without coming round into the middle of the circle. Mrs O'Conor was a little woman, apparently not of much importance in the world, but, if one might judge from first appearance, very good-natured.

'And my aunt Die, Mr Green,' said Kate, pointing to a very straight-backed, grim-looking lady, who occupied a corner of a sofa, on the opposite side of the hearth. I knew that politeness required that I should walk across the room and make acquaintance with her. But under the existing circumstances how was I to obey the dictates of my politeness? I was determined therefore to stand my ground, and merely bowed across the room at Miss O'Conor. In so doing I made an enemy who never deserted me during the whole of my intercourse with the family. But for her, who knows who might have been sitting opposite to me as I now write?

'Upon my word, Mr Green, the ladies will expect much from an Adonis who takes so long over his toilet,' said Tom O'Conor in that cruel tone of banter which he knew so well how to use.

'You forget, father, that men in London can't jump in and out of their clothes as quick as we wild Irishmen,' said Jack.

'Mr Green knows that we expect a great deal from him this evening. I hope you polka well, Mr Green,' said Kate.

I muttered something about never dancing, but I knew that that which I said was inaudible.

'I don't think Mr Green will dance,' said Tizzy; 'at least not much.' The impudence of that child was, I think, unparalleled by any that I have ever witnessed.

'But in the name of all that's holy, why don't we have dinner?' And Mr O'Conor thundered at the door. 'Larry, Larry, Larry!' he screamed.

'Yes, yer honer, it'll be all right in two seconds,' answered Larry, from some bottomless abyss. 'Tare an' ages; what'll I do at all,' I heard him continuing, as he made his way into the hall. Oh, what a clatter he made upon the pavement – for it was all stone! And how the drops of perspiration stood upon my brow as I listened to him!

And there was a pause, for the man had gone into the dining-room. I could see now that Mr O'Conor was becoming very angry, and Jack the eldest son – oh, how often he and I have laughed over all this since – left the drawing-room for the second time. Immediately afterwards Larry's footsteps were again heard, hurrying across the hall, and then there was a great slither, and an exclamation, and the noise of a fall – and I could plainly hear poor Larry's head strike against the stone floor.

'Ochone, ochone!' he cried at the top of his voice, 'I'm murthered with 'em now intirely; and d—— 'em for boots – St Peter be good to me.'

There was a general rush into the hall, and I was carried with the stream. The poor fellow, who had broken his head, would be sure to tell how I had robbed him of his shoes. The coachman was already helping him up, and Peter good-naturedly lent a hand.

'What on earth is the matter?' said Mr O'Conor.

'He must be tipsy,' whispered Miss O'Conor, the maiden sister.

'I ain't tipsy at all thin,' said Larry, getting up and rubbing the back of his head, and sundry other parts of his body. 'Tipsy indeed!' And then he added when he was quite upright, 'The dinner is sarved – at last.'

And he bore it all without telling! 'I'll give that fellow a guinea tomorrow morning,' said I to myself, 'if it's the last that I have in the world.'

I shall never forget the countenance of the Miss O'Conors as Larry scrambled up, cursing the unfortunate boots. 'What on earth has he got on?' said Mr O'Conor.

'Sorrow take 'em for shoes,' ejaculated Larry. But his spirit was good and he said not a word to betray me. We all then went in to dinner how we best could. It was useless for us to go back into the drawing-room, that each might seek his own partner. Mr O'Conor, 'the masther,' nor caring much for the girls who were around him, and being already half beside himself with the confusion and delay, led the way by himself. I as a stranger should have given my arm to Mrs O'Conor; but as it was I took her eldest daughter instead, and contrived to shuffle along into the dining-room without exciting much attention, and when there I found myself happily placed between Kate and Fanny.

'I never knew anything so awkward,' said Fanny; 'I declare I can't conceive what has come to our old servant Larry. He's generally the most precise person in the world, and now he is nearly an hour late – and then he tumbles down in the hall.'

'I am afraid I am responsible for the delay,' said I.

'But not for the tumble, I suppose,' said Kate from the other side. I felt that I blushed up to the eyes, but I did not dare to enter into explanations.

'Tom,' said Tizzy, addressing her father across the table, 'I hope you had a good run today.' It did seem odd to me that a young lady should call her father Tom, but such was the fact.

'Well; pretty well,' said Mr O'Conor.

'And I hope you were up with the hounds.'

'You may ask Mr Green that. He at any rate was with them, and therefore he can tell you.'

'Oh, he wasn't before you, I know. No Englishman could get before you – I am quite sure of that.'

'Don't you be impertinent, miss,' said Kate. 'You can easily see, Mr Green, that papa spoils my sister Eliza.'

'Do you hunt in topboots, Mr Green?' said Tizzy.

To this I made no answer. She would have drawn me into a conversation about my feet in half a minute, and the slightest allusion to the subject threw me into a fit of perspiration.

'Are you fond of hunting, Miss O'Conor?' asked I, blindly hurrying into any other subject of conversation.

Miss O'Conor owned that she was fond of hunting – just a little; only papa would not allow it. When the hounds met anywhere within reach of Castle Conor, she and Kate would ride out to look at them; and if papa were not there that day – an omission of rare occurrence – they would ride a few fields with the hounds.

'But he lets Tizzy keep with them the whole day,' said she, whispering.

'And has Tizzy a pony of her own?'

'Oh, yes, Tizzy has everything. She's papa's pet, you know.'

'And whose pet are you?' I asked.

'Oh – I am nobody's pet, unless sometimes Jack makes a pet of me when he's in a good humour. Do you make pets of your sisters, Mr Green?'

'I have none. But if I had I should not make pets of them.'

'Not of your own sisters?'

'No. As for myself, I'd sooner make a pet of my friend's sister, a great deal.'

'How very unnatural,' said Miss O'Conor, with the prettiest look of surprise imaginable.

'Not at all unnatural, I think,' said I, looking tenderly and lovingly into her face. Where does one find girls so pretty, so easy, so sweet, so talkative as the Irish girls? And then with all their talking and all their ease who ever hears of their misbehaving? They certainly love flirting as they also love dancing. But they flirt without mischief and without malice.

I had now quite forgotten my misfortune, and was beginning to think how well I should like to have Fanny O'Conor for my wife. In this frame of mind I was bending over towards her as a servant took away a plate from the other side, when a sepulchral note sounded in my ear. It was like the *memento mori* of the old Roman – as though some one pointed in the midst of my bliss to the sword hung over my head by a thread. It was the voice of Larry, whispering in his agony just above my head:

'They's disthroying my poor feet intirely, intirely, so they is! I can't bear it much longer, yer honer.' I had committed murder like Macbeth; and now my Banquo had come to disturb me at my feast.

'What is it he says to you?' asked Fanny.

'Oh, nothing,' I answered, once more in my misery.

'There seems to be some point of confidence between you and our Larry,' she remarked.

'Oh, no,' said I, quite confused; 'not at all.'

'You need not be ashamed of it. Half the gentlemen in the county have their confidences with Larry – and some of the ladies too, I can tell you. He was born in this house, and never lived anywhere else; and I am sure he has a larger circle of acquaintances than anyone else in it.'

I could not recover my self-possession for the next ten minutes. Whenever Larry was on our side of the table I was afraid he was coming to me with another agonized whisper. When he was opposite, I could not but watch him as he hobbled in his misery. It was evident that the boots were too tight for him, and had they been made throughout of iron they could not have been less capable of yielding to the feet. I pitied him from the bottom of my heart. And I pitied myself also, wishing that I was well in bed with some feigned malady, so that Larry might have had his own again.

And then for a moment I missed him from the room. He had doubtless gone to relieve his tortured feet in the servant's hall, and as he did so was cursing my cruelty. But what mattered it? Let him curse. If he would only stay away and do that, I would appease his wrath when we were alone together with pecuniary satisfaction.

But there was no such rest in store for me. 'Larry, Larry,' shouted Mr O'Conor, 'where on earth has the fellow gone to?' They were all cousins at the table except myself, and Mr O'Conor was not therefore restrained by any feeling of ceremony. 'There is something wrong with that fellow today; what is it, Jack?'

'Upon my word, sir, I don't know,' said Jack.

'I think he must be tipsy,' whispered Miss O'Conor, the maiden sister, who always sat at her brother's left hand. But a whisper though it was, it was audible all down the table.

'No, ma'am; it ain't dhrink at all,' said the coachman. 'It is his feet as does it.'

'His feet!' shouted Tom O'Conor.

'Yes; I know it's his feet,' said that horrid Tizzy. 'He's got on great thick nailed shoes. It was that that made him tumble down in the hall.'

I glanced at each side of me, and could see that there was a certain consciousness expressed in the face of each of my two neighbours – on Kate's mouth there was decidedly a smile, or rather, perhaps, the slightest possible inclination that way; whereas on Fanny's part I thought I saw something like a rising sorrow at my distress. So at least I flattered myself.

'Send him back into the room immediately,' said Tom, who looked at me as though he had some consciousness that I had introduced all this confusion into his household. What should I do? Would it not be best for me to make a clean breast of it before them all? But alas! I lacked the courage.

The coachman went out, and we were left for five minutes without any servant, and Mr O'Conor the while became more and more savage. I attempted to say a word to Fanny, but failed. My voice stuck in my throat.

'I don't think he has got any others,' said Tizzy – 'at least none others left.'

On the whole I am glad I did not marry into the family, as I could not have endured that girl to stay in my house as a sister-in-law.

'Where the d—— has that other fellow gone to?' said Tom. 'Jack, do go out and see what is the matter. If anybody is drunk send for me.'

'Oh, there is nobody drunk.' said Tizzy.

Jack went out, and the coachman returned; but what was done and said I hardly remember. The whole room seemed to swim round and round, and as far as I can recollect the company sat mute, neither eating nor drinking. Presently Jack returned.

'It's all right,' said he. I always liked Jack. At the present moment he just looked towards me and laughed slightly.

'All right?' said Tom. 'But is the fellow coming?'

'We can do with Richard, I suppose,' said Jack.

'No – I can't do with Richard,' said the father. 'And I will know what it all means. Where is that fellow Larry?'

Larry had been standing just outside the door, and now he entered gently as a mouse. No sound came from his footfall, nor was there in his face that look of pain which it had worn for the last fifteen minutes. But he was not the less abashed, frightened, and unhappy.

'What is all this about, Larry?' said his master, turning to him. 'I insist upon knowing.'

'Och thin, Mr Green, yer honer, I wouldn't be afther telling agin yer honer; indeed I wouldn't thin, av the masther would only let me hould my tongue.' And he looked across at me, deprecating my anger.

'Mr Green!' said Mr O'Conor.

'Yes, yer honer. It's all along of his honer's thick shoes'; and Larry, stepping backwards towards the door, lifted them up from some corner, and coming well forward, exposed them with the soles uppermost to the whole table.

'And that's not all, yer honer; but they've squoze the very soles of me into a jelly.'

There was now a loud laugh, in which Jack and Peter and Fanny and Kate and Tizzy all joined; as too did Mr O'Conor – and I also myself after a while.

'Whose boots are they?' demanded Miss O'Conor senior, with her severest tone and grimmest accent.

''Deed then and the divil may have them for me, miss,' answered Larry. 'They war Mr Green's, but the likes of him won't wear them agin afther the likes of me – barring he wanted them very particular,' added he, remembering his own pumps.

I began muttering something, feeling that the time had come when I must tell the tale. But Jack, with great good nature, took up the story, and told it so well that I hardly suffered in the telling.

'And that's it,' said Tom O'Conor, laughing till I thought he would have fallen from his chair. 'So you've got Larry's shoes on——'

'And very well he fills them,' said Jack.

'And it's his honer that's welcome to 'em,' said Larry, grinning from ear to ear now that he saw that 'the masther' was once more in a good humour.

'I hope they'll be nice shoes for dancing,' said Kate.

'Only there's one down at the heel I know,' said Tizzy.

'The servant's shoes!' This was an exclamation made by the maiden lady, and intended apparently only for her brother's ear. But it was clearly audible by all the party.

'Better that than no dinner,' said Peter.

But what are you to do about the dancing?' said Fanny, with an air of dismay on her face which flattered me with an idea that she did care whether I danced or no.

In the meantime Larry, now as happy as an emperor, was tripping round the room without any shoes to encumber him as he withdrew the plates from the table.

'And it's his honer that's welcome to 'em,' said he again, as he pulled off the tablecloth with a flourish. 'And why wouldn't he, and he able to folly the hounds betther nor any Englishman that iver war in these parts before – anyways so Mick says!'

31

Now Mick was the huntsman, and this little tale of eulogy from Larry went far towards easing my grief. I had ridden well to the hounds that day, and I knew it.

There was nothing more said about the shoes, and I was soon again at my ease, although Miss O'Conor did say something about the impropriety of Larry walking about in his stocking feet. The ladies, however, soon withdrew – to my sorrow, for I was getting on swimmingly with Fanny, and then we gentlemen gathered round the fire and filled our glasses.

In about ten minutes a very light tap was heard, the door was opened to the extent of three inches, and a female voice which I readily recognized called to Jack.

Jack went out, and in a second or two put his head back into the room and called to me: 'Green,' he said, 'just step here a moment, there's a good fellow.' I went out, and there I found Fanny standing with her brother.

'Here are the girls at their wits' ends,' said he, 'about your dancing. So Fanny has put a boy upon one of the horses, and proposes that you should send another line to Mrs Meehan at Ballyglass. It's only ten miles, and he'll be back in two hours.'

I need hardly say that I acted in conformity with this advice. I went into Mr O'Conor's bookroom with Jack and his sister, and there scribbled a note. It was delightful to feel how intimate I was with them, and how anxious they were to make me happy.

'And we won't begin till they come,' said Fanny.

'Oh, Miss O'Conor, pray don't wait,' said I.

'Oh, but we will,' she answered. 'You have your wine to drink, and then there's the tea; and then we'll have a song or two. I'll spin it out; see if I don't.' And so we went to the front door where the boy was already on his horse – her own nag as I afterwards found.

'And Patsey,' said she 'ride for your life; and Patsey, whatever you do, don't come back without Mr Green's pumps – his dancing shoes, you know.'

And in about two hours the pumps did arrive: and I don't think I ever spent a pleasanter evening or got more satisfaction out of a pair of shoes. They had not been two minutes on my feet before Larry was carrying a tray of negus across the room in those which I had worn at dinner.

'The Dillon girls are going to stay here,' said Fanny as I wished her good night at two o'clock. 'And we'll have dancing every evening as long as you remain.'

'But I shall leave tomorrow,' said I.

'Indeed you won't. Papa will take care of that.'

And so he did. 'You had better go over to Ballyglass yourself tomorrow,' said he, 'and collect your own things. There's no knowing else what you may have to borrow off Larry.'

I stayed there three weeks, and in the middle of the third I thought that everything would be arranged between me and Fanny. But the aunt interfered; and in about a twelvemonth after my adventures she consented to make a more fortunate man happy for his life.

When in Rome

PETER USTINOV

AN EXCITING PROPOSITION came my way when I was twenty-eight years old. MGM were going to remake *Quo Vadis*, and I was a candidate for the role of Nero. Arthur Hornblow was to be the producer, and I was tested by John Huston. I threw everything I knew into this test, and to my surprise John Huston did little to restrain me, encouraging me in confidential whispers to be even madder. Apparently the test was a success, but then the huge machine came to a halt, and the project was postponed for a year.

At the end of the year, the producer was Sam Zimbalist and the director Mervyn Leroy. They also approved my test, but warned me in a wire that I might be found to be a little young for the part. I cabled back that if they postponed again I might be too old, since Nero died at thirty-one. A second cable from them read 'Historical Research Has Proved You Correct Stop The Part Is Yours'.

To celebrate I purchased the first new car in my life, a rather ugly post-war Delage convertible in cream with a cherry-red top which it took three men to open and many more to shut, and cherry-red upholstery which indelibly stained the clothing of all who sat on it. I determined to drive round Spain on the way to Rome, where the film was to be shot. I broke down in Granada, Seville, Barcelona, Madrid, Badajoz, Jerez de la Frontera, Lorca, Perpignan, Narbonne, Cannes, San Remo, and at the gates of Rome, where a ball-race broke in a wheel, causing it to overheat. When the car was raised, I saw a stamping on the underside of the chassis dating it October 1938. The ugly body had been added in 1949 to a chassis which had survived the Occupation in some shed, and now it had been sold to a patsy as a brand-new car. I only bought it in order to replace a second-hand one, also built in 1938, which was one of the most agreeable cars I ever owned, and reliable to boot.

Rome was in the throes of Holy Year, and bursting with pilgrims. It was also one of the hottest summers on record. I met Mervyn Leroy for the first time some hours before we began to shoot. He is an affectionate man of less than average height and of slight build. His blue eyes are friendly, although he has a vocational addiction to shouting, which is the right of any army commander, and, I was quick to discover, the production of an American epic is the nearest peacetime equivalent of a military operation, with time as the enemy.

I spoke to him with unaccustomed earnestness about my role, and asked him if he had any observations to make.

'Nero? Son of a bitch,' he declared.

I was inclined to agree with him.

'You know what he did to his mother?' he suddenly said, with decent Jewish concern, as though there was something one ought to do about it.

I replied that, yes, I did know what he did to his mother.

'Son of a bitch,' repeated Mervyn, almost angry.

I nodded my head. So far we saw eye to eye. 'But is there any specific aspect of the man you wish me to bring out?' I asked.

To my surprise, Mervyn replied by doing a tap-dance routine.

I applauded, and he beamed with pleasure.

'I used to be a hoofer,' he said.

I said, truthfully, that I didn't know that.

There was a long pause while I wondered uncomfortably if by some hideous chance he expected Nero to tap-dance.

'Nero,' said Mervyn.

I pricked up my ears.

'The way I see him . . .'

'Yes?'

'He's a guy plays with himself nights.'

At the time I thought it a preposterous assessment, but a little later I was not so sure. It was a profundity at its most workaday level, and it led me to the eventual conviction that no nation can make Roman pictures as well as the Americans.

The Romans were pragmatic, a people of relaxed power with *nouveau-riche* lapses of taste. They too believed in the beneficence of atrium living, in pampering the body with steam and the laying on of heavy hands after the excesses of a four-star cuisine. They too believed in dressing for comfort, and the intrigues in their senate matched anything in Washington, while their total belief in Roman know-how led to a few ugly surprises, as did the total belief in American know-how in Vietnam. They too garnished their official walls with flags and eagles, and eventually the Roman way of life was all-important, being practised even when the later Emperors were of Iberian or Dalmatian origin; it mattered little, what mattered was a family feeling, a *modus vivendi* which was sometimes gracious, sometimes coarse, sometimes civilized and sometimes violent and cruel, and yet, ever, unmistakably, Roman.

The inevitable vulgarities of the script contributed as much to its authenticity as its rare felicities. I felt then as I feel today, in spite of the carping of critical voices, that *Quo Vadis*, good or bad according to taste, was an extraordinarily authentic film, and the nonsense Nero was sometimes made to speak was very much like the nonsense Nero probably did speak.

So gargantuan was the production that I was sent to the Rome Opera House for three singing lessons, in the belief that such a crash course might make of me another Mario Lanza as I sang my lament to the burning city.

I arrived at the Opera one morning in an atmosphere of high tension. Apparently *Samson and Delilah* had just been hissed the night before, and I was taken to be the new Samson from Paris. I pointed out that I would consider the part after I had had my lessons, but not before. It was on this abrasive and highly operatic note that I was ushered into the presence of my professor.

He confessed to me after dismissing a distraught soprano who had just waded through the mad scene from *Lucia di Lammermoor* that in agreeing to teach me how to sing in three lessons, he was motivated by financial considerations. I reassured him that such considerations had not been absent from my mind when accepting to play the part of Nero. We drank a toast to MGM only with our eyes, and he confessed that his task was hopeless. Three years, perhaps, he said, but three lessons...

He sat down disconsolately at a piano which was as out of tune in its way as the late departed soprano had been in hers. It twanged like a guitar on some notes, like a banjo on others, and other yellowed notes produced no sound at all. Almost at once the score, by the Hungarian composer Miklos Rozsa, proved rather too advanced for the professor, who was accustomed to the predictable patterns of Donizetti and Verdi. He berated the music for its inordinate number of flats, and delivered to me the pith of his first year's course in a single lesson.

'Always, as I tell Gobbi, always breathe with the forehead,' he declared.

I wrinkled my brow as though it contained a small pulse. He was enchanted. Never, he informed me, had any pupil been quicker on the uptake.

At the start of the second lesson, he asked me what I remembered of the first lesson.

'Breathe with the — ?' he asked.

'Forehead,' I replied.

'Bravo!' he cried. 'What a memory! Really fantastic.' Now followed the second lesson, containing all I would learn in the second year, in concentrated form. 'As I tell Gobbi, think with the diaphragm,' he said.

I adopted a distinctly constipated look, which seemed to me the faithful outward proof that my diaphragm was wrapped in thought. I set the pulse going in my forehead at the same time.

'My God, it's fantastic, fantastic! One at a time, yes, perhaps, but both together, so soon! Fantastic! What a talent!'

Before the third and final lesson, he decided on the usual refresher.

'Da Capo,' he said. 'Breathe with the — ?'

'Forehead.'
'Bravo! Think with the — ?'
'Diaphragm.'
'Bravissimo!'
And here followed the third and most difficult lesson.
'As I say to Gobbi, always, in all circumstances, sing ... with the *eye!*'
I came away as enriched musically as the professor had been enriched financially, and whereas those who saw the film might not have guessed that I was thinking with my diaphragm or indeed breathing with my forehead, I fear it was painfully obvious that I was singing with my eye.

The heat was absolutely tremendous. Among the senators surrounding me on the hallowed balcony from which we were supposed to watch Rome in flames, there were some eminent English actors, among them Nicholas Hannen and D.A. Clarke-Smith. To add to the heat of the sun, braziers were burning all around us, shedding black ash on our togas, and the lights bored into us from above. A gallant lady harpist from the American Academy in Rome sat, drenched in perspiration, on a podium, waiting to accompany my hand movements on the lyre with her daintier sounds. Mervyn Leroy was shouting orders and counter-orders from a crane, and thin green rivers began snaking their way down my face from my laurel-wreath, which was made of inferior metal, and emanated a horrible ferrous odour. It was utter misery in this creative cauldron, and I feared for the health of the other actors as their nostrils grew black with dust from the braziers, and their lungs began heaving in their boiling chests. A miniature of Rome caught fire to add to the inferno, and a back-projection screen came alive with visual pyrotechnics behind us. At last we were ready to shoot. I recalled the words of my crazed song, 'O Lambent Flames, O Force Divine', and cleared what throat I could still sense.

Just then Mervyn cried, 'Let me down! Let me down, for Christ's sake, will you?'

A sense of exasperated anti-climax set in as Mervyn disappeared from sight. Then the balcony began to shake, indicating someone was scaling it. Mervyn's head appeared over the battlements, cigar gripped between his teeth, his eyes confident and understanding like those of a manager telling a half-dead boxer that he's leading on points, and he summoned me to within confidential distance.

Waving his Havana at the burning city, he said quietly, 'Don't forget, you're responsible for all this.' Mervyn was never a director to leave anything to chance.

The third in the triumvirate of inseparable English actors was Felix Aylmer. They were inseparable only because of *The Times*, and more particularly of its crossword puzzle. Whichever of them was called latest would stop on the way to the studio and buy three copies of the airmail edition. They would sit on the set, their glasses on their noses, and solve its riddles.

It didn't take long to notice a curious atmosphere among them, however. Felix Aylmer and D.A. Clarke-Smith would only communicate with one another through Nicholas Hannen. This fact gave rise to odd dialogue like

CLARKE-SMITH: Revulsion.

AYLMER: Ask him where?

HANNEN: Where?

CLARKE-SMITH: Sixteen across.

AYLMER: Too many letters, tell him.

CLARKE-SMITH: Tell him I already know.

HANNEN: He already knows, he says.

Intrigued by the absurdity of this dialogue, reminiscent of Eugène Ionesco in his English mood, I asked Nicholas Hannen to explain it. He revealed that the two had not spoken since 1924, when Clarke-Smith's wife had left him after a nocturnal argument, and had taken sanctuary at Felix Aylmer's cottage. Hot on her heels, Clarke-Smith banged on Aylmer's door. The two men in pyjamas and dressing-gowns faced each other.

'I have reason to believe my wife is here,' cried Clarke-Smith.

'She's in the spare room, D.A. Let's be reasonable and talk about this in the morning, after a good night's rest.'

Those were the last words they had exchanged until 'Revulsion', 'Ask him where?'

Occasionally they were summoned to work, and they tucked their copies of *The Times* into their togas. Unfortunately D.A. Clarke-Smith was afflicted with a hacking cough, which he successfully suppressed, thereby only making the air-mail edition of *The Times* noisier as it was buffeted against his heaving chest, making a sound of someone stamping on a pile of autumn leaves. Immediately the sound-man looked up at the eaves.

'Goddam birds nesting up there,' he said.

Shooting was frequently held up while technicians attempted to winkle out the imaginary intruders. When nothing was found, they searched for rats, for ticking pipes, for mirages.

I would never give away my friends and their humble enjoyments. After twenty-six years of silence, they deserved a little consideration.

There were, of course, absurdities galore, as there could scarcely fail to be in a production of such magnitude: the fighting bull enclosed in a freight car of the Portuguese State Railways, and lured out into a corral designed for horses by the ten-gallon-hatted experts, against the considered advice of a diminutive Portuguese bullfighter, with the result that at the height of the luncheon break, an angry bull ambled into the

Commissary, having butted his way to an easy freedom. Then there was the animal which Buddy Baer as Ursus was supposed to wrestle, and kill by breaking its neck. Out of prudence, the idea of a bull as specified in the book was rejected, especially after the company's previous experience with this animal. Consequently a chloroformed cow was selected, placed in such a way that the udders were invisible. Unfortunately every time that Buddy Baer twisted its neck, this had the effect of bringing the poor animal to, and every time he stood in triumph with his foot on its carcass, the cow looked up at him and mooed pathetically. And let me not forget Mervyn's inspired instruction to a couple of mountainous wrestlers, one Italian, one Turkish, who were supposed to kill each other with savage grunts and groans for my pleasure as I nibbled at larks and fondled my favourites: 'Action! And make every word count!'

I returned to London brimful of new experiences, feeling that I had widened my horizons irrevocably. In any case, no one who spends close to five months in Rome, that glut of over-ripe peaches in a dish of hills, can ever be quite the same. The emphasis on sin, perhaps inevitable in a place so overtly dedicated to the material majesty of God, and in which the spiritual majesty has to be taken for granted by those less than entirely gullible, gives one a feeling of turpitude and languor. The climate, the sleepy days and wide-awake nights, add to this sentiment of nervous exacerbation and squalid temptation, and one turns away from the city with a kind of weary revulsion, only to be impatient for one's return.

Butch Minds the Baby

DAMON RUNYON

ONE EVENING ALONG ABOUT seven o'clock I am sitting in Mindy's restaurant putting on the gefillte fish, which is a dish I am very fond of, when in come three parties from Brooklyn wearing caps as follows: Harry the Horse, Little Isadore, and Spanish John.

Now these parties are not such parties as I will care to have much truck with, because I often hear rumours about them that are very discreditable, even if the rumours are not true. In fact, I hear that many citizens of Brooklyn will be very glad indeed to see Harry the Horse, Little Isadore and Spanish John move away from there, as they are always doing something that is considered a knock to the community, such as robbing people, or maybe shooting or stabbing them, and throwing pineapples, and carrying on generally.

I am really much surprised to see these parties on Broadway, as it is well known that the Broadway coppers just naturally love to shove such parties around, but there they are in Mindy's, and there I am, so of course I give them a very large hello, as I never wish to seem inhospitable, even to Brooklyn parties. Right away they come over to my table and sit down, and Little Isadore reaches out and spears himself a big hunk of my gefillte fish with his fingers, but I overlook this, as I am using the only knife on the table.

Then they all sit there looking at me without saying anything, and the way they look at me makes me very nervous indeed. Finally I figure that maybe they are a little embarrassed being in a high-class spot such as Mindy's, with legitimate people around and about, so I say to them, very polite:

'It is a nice night.'

'What is nice about it?' asks Harry the Horse, who is a thin man with a sharp face and sharp eyes.

Well, now that it is put up to me in this way, I can see there is nothing so nice about the night, at that, so I try to think of something else jolly to say, while Little Isadore keeps spearing at my gefillte fish with his fingers, and Spanish John nabs one of my potatoes.

'Where does Big Butch live?' Harry the Horse asks.

'Big Butch?' I say, as if I never hear the name before in my life, because in this man's town it is never a good idea to answer any question without thinking it over, as some time you may give the right answer to the wrong

40

guy, or the wrong answer to the right guy. 'Where does Big Butch live?' I
ask them again.

'Yes, where does he live?' Harry the Horse says, very impatient. 'We
wish you to take us to him.'

'Now wait a minute, Harry,' I say, and I am now more nervous than
somewhat. 'I am not sure I remember the exact house Big Butch lives in,
and furthermore I am not sure Big Butch will care to have me bringing
people to see him, especially three at a time, and especially from
Brooklyn. You know Big Butch has a very bad disposition, and there is
no telling what he may say to me if he does not like the idea of me taking
you to him.'

'Everything is very kosher,' Harry the Horse says. 'You need not be
afraid of anything whatever. We have a business proposition for Big
Butch. It means a nice score for him, so you take us to him at once, or the
chances are I will have to put the arm on somebody around here.'

Well, as the only one around there for him to put the arm on at this
time seems to be me, I can see where it will be good policy for me to take
these parties to Big Butch especially as the last of my gefillte fish is just
going down Little Isadore's gullet, and Spanish John is finishing up my
potatoes, and is donking a piece of ryebread in my coffee, so there is
nothing more for me to eat.

So I lead them over into West Forty-ninth Street, near Tenth Avenue,
where Big Butch lives on the ground floor of an old brownstone-front
house, and who is sitting out on the stoop but Big Butch himself. In fact,
everybody in the neighbourhood is sitting out on the front stoops over
there, including women and children, because sitting out on the front
stoops is quite a custom in this section.

Big Butch is peeled down to his undershirt and pants, and he has no
shoes on his feet, as Big Butch is a guy who loves his comfort.
Furthermore, he is smoking a cigar, and laid out on the stoop beside him
on a blanket is a little baby with not much clothes on. This baby seems to
be asleep, and every now and then Big Butch fans it with a folded
newspaper to shoo away the mosquitoes that wish to nibble on the baby.
These mosquitoes come across the river from the Jersey side on hot nights
and they seem to be very fond of babies.

'Hello, Butch,' I say, as we stop in front of the stoop.

'Sh-h-h-h!' Butch says, pointing at the baby, and making more noise
with his shush than an engine blowing off steam. Then he gets up and
tiptoes down to the sidewalk where we are standing, and I am hoping
that Butch feels all right, because when Butch does not feel so good he is
apt to be very short with one and all. He is a guy of maybe six foot two
and a couple of feet wide, and he has big hairy hands and a mean look.

In fact, Big Butch is known all over this man's town as a guy you must
not monkey with in any respect, so it takes plenty of weight off me when I

see that he seems to know the parties from Brooklyn, and nods at them very friendly, especially at Harry the Horse. And right away Harry states a most surprising proposition to Big Butch.

It seems that there is a big coal company which has an office in an old building down in West Eighteenth Street, and in this office is a safe, and in this safe is the company pay roll of twenty thousand dollars cash money. Harry the Horse knows the money is there because a personal friend of his who is the paymaster for the company puts it there late this very afternoon.

It seems that the paymaster enters into a dicker with Harry the Horse and Little Isadore and Spanish John for them to slug him while he is carrying the pay roll from the bank to the office in the afternoon, but something happens that they miss connections on the exact spot, so the paymaster has to carry the sugar on to the office without being slugged, and there it is now in two fat bundles.

Personally it seems to me as I listen to Harry's story that the paymaster must be a very dishonest character to be making deals to hold still while he is being slugged and the company's sugar taken away from him, but of course it is none of my business, so I take no part in the conversation.

Well, it seems that Harry the Horse and Little Isadore and Spanish John wish to get the money out of the safe, but none of them knows anything about opening safes, and while they are standing around in Brooklyn talking over what is to be done in this emergency Harry suddenly remembers that Big Butch is once in the business of opening safes for a living.

In fact, I hear afterwards that Big Butch is considered the best safe-opener east of the Mississippi River in his day, but the law finally takes to sending him to Sing Sing for opening these safes, and after he is in and out of Sing Sing three different times for opening safes Butch gets sick and tired of the place, especially as they pass what is called the Baumes Law in New York, which is a law that says if a guy is sent to Sing Sing four times hand running, he must stay there the rest of his life, without any argument about it.

So Big Butch gives up opening safes for a living, and goes into business in a small way, such as running beer, and handling a little Scotch now and then, and becomes an honest citizen. Furthermore, he marries one of the neighbour's children over on the West Side by the name of Mary Murphy, and I judge the baby on this stoop comes of this marriage between Big Butch and Mary because I can see that it is a very homely baby, indeed. Still, I never see many babies that I consider rose geraniums for looks, anyway.

Well, it finally comes out that the idea of Harry the Horse and Little Isadore and Spanish John is to get Big Butch to open the coal company's safe and take the pay-roll money out, and they are willing to give him fifty per cent of the money for his bother, taking fifty per cent for themselves for finding the plant, and paying all the overhead, such as the paymaster, out of their bit, which strikes me as a pretty fair sort of deal for Big Butch. But Butch only shakes his head.

'It is old-fashioned stuff,' Butch says. 'Nobody opens pete boxes for a living any more. They make the boxes too good, and they are all wired up with alarms and are a lot of trouble generally. I am in a legitimate business now and going along. You boys know I cannot stand another fall, what with being away three times already, and in addition to this I must mind the baby. My old lady goes to Mrs Clancy's wake tonight up in the Bronx, and the chances are she will be there all night, as she is very fond of wakes, so I must mind little John Ignatius Junior.'

'Listen, Butch,' Harry the Horse says, 'this is a very soft pete. It is old-fashioned, and you can open it with a toothpick. There are no wires on it, because they never put more than a dime in it before in years. It just happens they have to put the twenty G's in it tonight because my pal the paymaster makes it a point not to get back from the jug with the scratch in time to pay off today, especially after he sees we miss out on him. It is the softest touch you will ever know, and where can a guy pick up ten G's like this?'

I can see that Big Butch is thinking the ten G's over very seriously, at that, because in these times nobody can afford to pass up ten G's, especially a guy in the beer business which is very, very tough just now. But finally he shakes his head again and says like this:

'No,' he says, 'I must let it go, because I must mind the baby. My old lady is very, very particular about this, and I dast not leave little John Ignatius Junior for a minute. If Mary comes home and finds I am not minding the baby she will put the blast on me plenty. I like to turn a few honest bobs now and then as well as anybody, but,' Butch says, 'John Ignatius Junior comes first with me.'

Then he turns away and goes back to the stoop as much as to say he is through arguing, and sits down beside John Ignatius Junior again just in time to keep a mosquito from carrying off one of John's legs. Anybody can see that Big Butch is very fond of this baby, although personally I will not give you a dime for a dozen babies, male and female.

Well, Harry the Horse and Little Isadore and Spanish John are very much disappointed, and stand around talking among themselves, and paying no attention to me, when all of a sudden Spanish John, who never has much to say up to this time, seems to have a bright idea. He talks to Harry and Isadore, and they get all pleasured up over what he has to say, and finally Harry goes to Big Butch.

'Sh-h-h-h!' Big Butch says, pointing to the baby as Harry opens his mouth.

'Listen, Butch,' Harry says in a whisper, 'we can take the baby with us, and you can mind it and work, too.'

'Why,' Big Butch whispers back, 'this is quite an idea indeed. Let us go into the house and talk things over.'

So he picks up the baby and leads us into his joint, and gets out some pretty fair beer, though it is needled a little, at that, and we sit around the kitchen chewing the fat in whispers. There is a crib in the kitchen, and Butch puts the baby in this crib, and it keeps on snoozing away first rate while we are talking. In fact, it is sleeping so sound that I am commencing to figure that Butch must give it some of the needled beer he is feeding us, because I am feeling a little dopey myself.

Finally Butch says that as long as he can take John Ignatius Junior with him he sees no reason why he shall not go and open the safe for them, only he says he must have five per cent more to put in the baby's bank when he gets back, so as to round himself up with his ever-loving wife in case of a beef from her over keeping the baby out in the night air. Harry the Horse says he considers this extra five per cent a little strong, but Spanish John, who seems to be a very square guy, says that after all it is only fair to cut the baby in if it is to be with them when making the score, and Little Isadore seems to think this is all right, too. So Harry the Horse gives in, and says five per cent it is.

Well, as they do not wish to start out until after midnight, and as there is plenty of time, Big Butch gets out some more needled beer, and then he goes looking for the tools with which he opens safes, and which he says he does not see since the day John Ignatius Junior is born and he gets them out to build the crib.

Now this is a good time for me to bid one and all farewell, and what keeps me there is something I cannot tell you to this day, because personally I never before have any idea of taking part in a safe opening, especially with a baby, as I consider such actions very dishonourable. When I come to think over things afterwards, the only thing I can figure is the needled beer, but I wish to say I am really very much surprised at myself when I find myself in a taxicab along about one o'clock in the morning with these Brooklyn parties and Big Butch and the baby.

Butch has John Ignatius Junior rolled up in a blanket, and John is still pounding his ear. Butch has a satchel of tools, and what looks to me like a big flat book, and just before we leave the house Butch hands me a package and tells me to be very careful with it. He gives Little Isadore a smaller package, which Isadore shoves into his pistol pocket, and when Isadore sits down in the taxi something goes wa-wa, like a sheep, and Big Butch becomes very indignant because it seems Isadore is sitting on John Ignatius Junior's doll, which says 'Mamma' when you squeeze it.

It seems Big Butch figures that John Ignatius Junior may wish something to play with in case he wakes up, and it is a good thing for

Little Isadore that the mamma doll is not squashed so it cannot say 'Mamma' any more, or the chances are Little Isadore will get a good bust in the snoot.

We let the taxicab go a block away from the spot we are headed for in West Eighteenth Street, between Seventh and Eighth Avenues, and walk the rest of the way two by two. I walk with Big Butch carrying my package, and Butch is lugging the baby and his satchel and the flat thing that looks like a book. It is so quiet down in West Eighteenth Street at such an hour that you can hear yourself think, and in fact I hear myself thinking very plain that I am a big sap to be on a job like this, especially with a baby, but I keep going just the same, which shows you what a very big sap I am, indeed.

There are very few people in West Eighteenth Street when we get there, and one of them is a fat guy who is leaning against a building almost in the centre of the block, and who takes a walk for himself as soon as he sees us. It seems that this fat guy is the watchman at the coal company's office and is also a personal friend of Harry the Horse, which is why he takes the walk when he sees us coming.

It is agreed before we leave Big Butch's house that Harry the Horse and Spanish John are to stay outside the place as lookouts, while Big Butch is inside opening the safe, and that Little Isadore is to go with Butch. Nothing whatever is said by anybody about where I am to be at any time, and I can see that, no matter where I am, I will still be an outsider, but, as Butch gives me the package to carry, I figure he wishes me to remain with him.

It is no bother at all getting into the office of the coal company, which is on the ground floor, because it seems the watchman leaves the front door open, this watchman being a most obliging guy, indeed. In fact, he is so obliging that by and by he comes back and lets Harry the Horse and Spanish John tie him up good and tight, and stick a handkerchief in his mouth and chuck him in an areaway next to the office, so nobody will think he has anything to do with opening the safe in case anybody comes around asking.

The office looks out on the street, and the safe that Harry the Horse and Little Isadore and Spanish John wish Big Butch to open is standing up against the rear wall of the office facing the street windows. There is one little electric light burning very dim over the safe so that when anybody walks past the place outside, such as a watchman, they can look in through the window and see the safe at all times, unless they are blind. It is not a tall safe, and it is not a big safe, and I can see Big Butch grin when he sees it, so I figure this safe is not much of a safe, just as Harry the Horse claims.

Well, as soon as Big Butch and the baby and Little Isadore and me get into the office, Big Butch steps over to the safe and unfolds what I think is

the big flat book, and what is it but a sort of screen painted on one side to
look exactly like the front of a safe. Big Butch stands this screen up on the
floor in front of the real safe, leaving plenty of space in between, the idea
being that the screen will keep anyone passing in the street outside from
seeing Butch while he is opening the safe, because when a man is opening
a safe he needs all the privacy he can get.

Big Butch lays John Ignatius Junior down on the floor on the blanket
behind the phony safe front and takes his tools out of the satchel and
starts to work opening the safe, while Little Isadore and me get back in a
corner where it is dark, because there is not room for all of us back of the
screen. However, we can see what Big Butch is doing, and I wish to say
while I never before see a professional safe-opener at work, and never
wish to see another, this Butch handles himself like a real artist.

He starts drilling into the safe around the combination lock, working
very fast and very quiet, when all of a sudden what happens but John
Ignatius Junior sits up on the blanket and lets out a squall. Naturally this
is most disquieting to me, and personally I am in favour of beaning John
Ignatius Junior with something to make him keep still, because I am
nervous enough as it is. But the squalling does not seem to bother Big
Butch. He lays down his tools and picks up John Ignatius Junior and
starts whispering, 'There, there, there, my itty oddleums. Da-dad is
here.'

Well, this sounds very nonsensical to me in such a situation, and it
makes no impression whatever on John Ignatius Junior. He keeps on
squalling, and I judge he is squalling pretty loud because I see Harry the
Horse and Spanish John both walk past the window and look in very
anxious. Big Butch jiggles John Ignatius Junior up and down and keeps
whispering baby talk to him, which sounds very undignified coming from
a high-class safe-opener, and finally Butch whispers to me to hand him
the package I am carrying.

He opens the package, and what is in it but a baby's nursing bottle full
of milk. Moreover, there is a little tin stew pan, and Butch hands the pan
to me and whispers to me to find a water tap somewhere in the joint and
fill the pan with water. So I go stumbling around in the dark in a room
behind the office and bark my shins several times before I find a tap and
fill the pan. I take it back to Big Butch, and he squats there with the baby
on one arm, and gets a tin of what is called canned heat out of the
package, and lights this canned heat with his cigar lighter, and starts
heating the pan of water with the nursing bottle in it.

Big Butch keeps sticking his finger in the pan of water while it is
heating, and by and by he puts the rubber nipple of the nursing bottle in
his mouth and takes a pull at it to see if the milk is warm enough, just like
I see dolls who have babies do. Apparently the milk is okay, as Butch
hands the bottle to John Ignatius Junior, who grabs hold of it with both

hands, and starts sucking on the business end. Naturally he has to stop squalling, and Big Butch goes to work on the safe again, with John Ignatius Junior sitting on the blanket, pulling on the bottle and looking wiser than a treeful of owls.

It seems the safe is either a tougher job than anybody figures, or Big Butch's tools are not so good, what with being old and rusty and used for building baby cribs, because he breaks a couple of drills and works himself up into quite a sweat without getting anywhere. Butch afterwards explains to me that he is one of the first guys in this country to open safes without explosives, but he says to do this work properly you have to know the safes so as to drill to the tumblers of the lock just right, and it seems that this particular safe is a new type to him, even if it is old, and he is out of practice.

Well, in the meantime, John Ignatius Junior finishes his bottle and starts mumbling again, and Big Butch gives him a tool to play with, and finally Butch needs this tool and tries to take it away from John Ignatius Junior, and the baby lets out such a squawk that Butch has to let him keep it until he can sneak it away from him, and this causes more delay.

Finally Big Butch gives up trying to drill the safe open, and he whispers to us that he will have to put a little shot in it to loosen up the lock, which is all right with us, because we are getting tired of hanging around and listening to John Ignatius Junior's glug-glugging. As far as I am personally concerned, I am wishing I am home in bed.

Well, Butch starts pawing through his satchel looking for something and it seems that what he is looking for is a little bottle of some kind of explosive with which to shake the lock on the safe up some, and at first he cannot find this bottle, but finally he discovers that John Ignatius Junior has it and is gnawing at the cork, and Butch has quite a battle making John Ignatius Junior give it up.

Anyway, he fixes the explosive in one of the holes he drills near the combination lock on the safe, and then puts in a fuse, and just before he touches off the fuse Butch picks up John Ignatius Junior and hands him to Little Isadore, and tells us to go into the room behind the office. John Ignatius Junior does not seem to care for Little Isadore, and I do not blame him, at that, because he starts to squirm around quite some in Isadore's arms and lets out a squall, but all of a sudden he becomes very quiet indeed, and, while I am not able to prove it, something tells me that Little Isadore has his hand over John Ignatius Junior's mouth.

Well, Big Butch joins us right away in the back room, and sound comes out of John Ignatius Junior again as Butch takes him from Little Isadore, and I am thinking that it is a good thing for Isadore that the baby cannot tell Big Butch what Isadore does to him.

'I put in just a little bit of a shot,' Big Butch says, 'and it will not make any more noise than snapping your fingers.'

But a second later there is a big whoom from the office, and the whole joint shakes, and John Ignatius laughs right out loud. The chances are he thinks it is the Fourth of July.

'I guess maybe I put in too big a charge,' Big Butch says, and then he rushes into the office with Little Isadore and me after him, and John Ignatius Junior still laughing very heartily for a small baby. The door of the safe is swinging loose, and the whole joint looks somewhat wrecked, but Big Butch loses no time in getting his dukes into the safe and grabbing out two big bundles of cash money, which he sticks inside his shirt.

As we go into the street Harry the Horse and Spanish John come running up much excited, and Harry says to Big Butch like this:

'What are you trying to do,' he says, 'wake up the whole town?'

'Well,' Butch says, 'I guess maybe the charge is too strong, at that, but nobody seems to be coming, so you and Spanish John walk over to Eighth Avenue, and the rest of us will walk to Seventh, and if you go along quiet, like people minding their own business, it will be all right.'

But I judge Little Isadore is tired of John Ignatius Junior's company by this time, because he says he will go with Harry the Horse and Spanish John, and this leaves Big Butch and John Ignatius Junior and me to go the other way. So we start moving, and all of a sudden two cops come tearing around the corner towards which Harry and Isadore and Spanish John are going. The chances are the cops hear the earthquake Big Butch lets off and are coming to investigate.

But the chances are, too, that if Harry the Horse and the other two keep on walking along very quietly like Butch tells them to, the coppers will pass them up entirely, because it is not likely that coppers will figure anybody to be opening safes with explosives in this neighbourhood. But the minute Harry the Horse sees the coppers he loses his nut, and he outs with the old equalizer and starts blasting away, and what does Spanish John do but get his out, too, and open up.

The next thing anybody knows, the two coppers are down on the ground with slugs in them, but other coppers are coming from every which direction, blowing whistles and doing a little blasting themselves, and there is plenty of excitement, especially when the coppers who are not chasing Harry the Horse and Little Isadore and Spanish John start poking around the neighbourhood and find Harry's pal, the watchman, all tied up nice and tight where Harry leaves him, and the watchman explains that some scoundrels blow open the safe he is watching.

All this time Big Butch and me are walking in the other direction toward Seventh Avenue, and Big Butch has John Ignatius in his arms, and John Ignatius is now squalling very loud indeed. The chances are he is still thinking of the big whoom back there which tickles him so and is wishing to hear some more whooms. Anyway, he is beating his own best record for squalling, and as we go walking along Big Butch says to me like this:

'I dast not run,' he says, 'because if any coppers see me running they will start popping at me and maybe hit John Ignatius Junior, and besides running will joggle the milk up in him and make him sick. My old lady always warns me never to joggle John Ignatius Junior when he is full of milk.'

'Well, Butch,' I say, 'there is no milk in me, and I do not care if I am joggled up, so if you do not mind, I will start doing a piece of running at the next corner.'

But just then around the corner of Seventh Avenue towards which we are headed comes two or three coppers with a big fat sergeant with them, and one of the coppers, who is half-out of breath as if he has been doing plenty of sprinting, is explaining to the sergeant that somebody blows a safe down the street and shoots a couple of coppers in the getaway.

And there is Big Butch, with John Ignatius Junior in his arms and twenty G's in his shirt front and a tough record behind him, walking right up to them.

I am feeling very sorry, indeed, for Big Butch, and very sorry for myself, too, and I am saying to myself that if I get out of this I will never associate with anyone but ministers of the gospel as long as I live. I can remember thinking that I am getting a better break than Butch, at that, because I will not have to go to Sing Sing for the rest of my life, like him, and I also remember wondering what they will give John Ignatius Junior, who is still tearing off these squalls, with Big Butch saying, 'There, there, there, Daddy's itty woogleums.' Then I hear one of the coppers say to the fat sergeant:

'We better nail these guys. They may be in on this.'

Well, I can see it is goodbye to Butch and John Ignatius Junior and me, as the fat sergeant steps up to Big Butch, but instead of putting the arm on Butch, the fat sergeant only points at John Ignatius Junior and asks very sympathetic:

'Teeth?'

'No,' Big Butch says. 'Not teeth. Colic. I just get the doctor here out of bed to do something for him, and we are going to a drug store to get some medicine.'

Well, naturally I am very much surprised at this statement, because of course I am not a doctor, and if John Ignatius Junior has colic it serves him right, but I am only hoping they do not ask for my degree, when the fat sergeant says:

'Too bad. I know what it is. I got three of them at home. But,' he says, 'it acts more like it is teeth than colic.'

Then as Big Butch and John Ignatius Junior and me go on about our business I hear the fat sergeant say to the copper, very sarcastic:

'Yea, of course a guy is out blowing safes with a baby in his arms! You will make a great detective, you will!'

I do not see Big Butch for several days after I learn that Harry the Horse and Little Isadore and Spanish John get back to Brooklyn all right, except they are a little nicked up here and there from the slugs the coppers toss at them, while the coppers they clip are not damaged so very much. Furthermore, the chances are I will not see Big Butch for several years, if it is left to me, but he comes looking for me one night, and he seems to be all pleasured up about something.

'Say,' Big Butch says to me, 'you know I never give a copper credit for knowing any too much about anything, but I wish to say this fat sergeant we run into the other night is a very, very smart duck. He is right about it being teeth that is ailing John Ignatius Junior, for what happens yesterday but John cuts his first tooth.'

A Linguistic Experiment

JEROME K. JEROME

The author and his friend Harris decide that they are in need of a change and arrange to accompany their bachelor friend George on a bicycling tour of the Black Forest, leaving behind the cares and comforts of domestic married life. However, before they can set off, some preparation is necessary, including, in George's opinion, the acquisition and 'testing' of a certain phrase-book....

ON MONDAY AFTERNOON Harris came round; he had a cycling paper in his hand.

I said: 'If you take my advice, you will leave it alone.'

Harris said: 'Leave what alone?'

I said: 'That brand-new, patent, revolution in cycling, record-breaking, tomfoolishness, whatever it may be, the advertisement of which you have there in your hand.'

He said: 'Well, I don't know; there will be some steep hills for us to negotiate; I guess we shall want a good brake.'

I said: 'We shall want a brake, I agree; what we shall not want is a mechanical surprise that we don't understand, and that never acts when it is wanted.'

'This thing,' he said, 'acts automatically.'

'You needn't tell me,' I said. 'I know exactly what it will do, by instinct. Going uphill it will jamb the wheel so effectively that we shall have to carry the machine bodily. The air at the top of the hill will do it good, and it will suddenly come right again. Going downhill it will start reflecting what a nuisance it has been. This will lead to remorse, and finally to despair. It will say to itself: "I'm not fit to be a brake. I don't help these fellows; I only hinder them. I'm a curse, that's what I am"; and, without a word of warning, it will "chuck" the whole business. That is what that brake will do. Leave it alone. You are a good fellow,' I continued, 'but you have one fault.'

'What?' he asked indignantly.

'You have too much faith,' I answered. 'If you read an advertisement, you go away and believe it. Every experiment that every fool has thought of in connection with cycling you have tried. Your guardian angel appears to be a capable and conscientious spirit, and hitherto she has seen you through; take my advice and don't try her too far. She must have had a busy time since you started cycling. Don't go on till you make her mad.'

He said: 'If every man talked like that there would be no advancement made in any department of life. If nobody ever tried a new thing the world would come to a standstill. It is by....'

'I know all that can be said on that side of the argument,' I interrupted. 'I agree in trying new experiments up to thirty-five; *after* thirty-five I consider a man is entitled to think of himself. You and I have done our duty in this direction, you especially. You have been blown up by a patent gas lamp....'

He said: 'I really think, you know, that was my fault; I think I must have screwed it up too tight.'

I said: 'I am quite willing to believe that if there was a wrong way of handling the thing that is the way you handle it. You should take that tendency of yours into consideration; it bears upon the argument. Myself, I did not notice what you did; I only know we were riding peacefully and pleasantly along the Whitby Road, discussing the Thirty Years War, when your lamp went off like a pistol shot. The start sent me into the ditch; and your wife's face, when I told her there was nothing the matter and that she was not to worry, because the two men would carry you upstairs, and the doctor would be round in a minute bringing the nurse with him, still lingers in my memory.'

He said: 'I wish you had thought to pick up the lamp. I should like to have found out what was the cause of its going off like that.'

I said: 'There was not time to pick up the lamp. I calculate it would have taken two hours to have collected it. As to its "going off," the mere fact of its being advertised as the safest lamp ever invented would of itself, to anyone but you, have suggested accident. Then there was that electric lamp,' I continued.

'Well, that really did give a fine light,' he replied; 'you said so yourself.'

I said: 'It gave a brilliant light in the King's Road, Brighton, and frightened a horse. The moment we got into the dark beyond Kemp Town it went out, and you were summoned for riding without a light. You may remember that on sunny afternoons you used to ride about with that lamp shining for all it was worth. When lighting-up time came it was naturally tired, and wanted a rest.'

'It was a bit irritating, that lamp,' he murmured; 'I remember it.'

I said: 'It irritated me; it must have been worse for you. Then, there are saddles,' I went on – I wished to get this lesson home to him. 'Can you think of any saddle ever advertised that you have *not* tried?'

He said: 'It has been an idea of mine that the right saddle is to be found.'

I said: 'You give up that idea; this is an imperfect world of joy and sorrow mingled. There may be a better land where bicycle saddles are made out of rainbow, stuffed with cloud; in this world the simplest thing is to get used to something hard. There was that saddle you bought in Birmingham; it was divided in the middle, and looked like a pair of kidneys.'

He said: 'You mean that one constructed on anatomical principles.'

'Very likely,' I replied. 'The box you bought it in had a picture on the cover, representing a sitting skeleton – or rather that part of a skeleton which does sit.'

He said: 'It was quite correct; it showed you the true position of the....'

I said: 'We will not go into details; the picture always seemed to me indelicate.'

He said: 'Medically speaking, it was right.'

'Possibly,' I said, 'for a man who rode in nothing but his bones. I only know that I tried it myself, and that to a man who wore flesh it was agony. Every time you went over a stone or a rut it nipped you; it was like riding on an irritable lobster. You rode that for a month.'

'I thought it only right to give it a fair trial,' he answered.

I said: 'You gave your family a fair trial also; if you will allow me the use of slang. Your wife told me that never in the whole course of your married life had she known you so bad tempered, so unchristian-like, as you were that month. Then you remember that other saddle, the one with the spring under it.'

He said: 'You mean "the Spiral,"'

I said: 'I mean the one that jerked you up and down like a jack-in-the-box; sometimes you came down again in the right place, and sometimes you didn't. I am not referring to these matters merely to recall painful memories, but I want to impress you with the folly of trying experiments at your time of life.'

He said: 'I wish you wouldn't harp so much on my age. A man at thirty-four....'

'A man at what?'

He said: 'If you don't want the thing, don't have it. If your machine runs away with you down a mountain, and you and George get flung through a church roof, don't blame me.'

'I cannot promise for George,' I said; 'a little thing will sometimes irritate him, as you know. If such an accident as you suggest happen, he may be cross, but I will undertake to explain to him that it was not your fault.'

'Is the thing all right?' he asked.

'The tandem,' I replied, 'is well.'

He said: 'Have you overhauled it?'

I said: 'I have not, nor is anyone else going to overhaul it. The thing is now in working order, and it is going to remain in working order till we start.'

I have had experience of this 'overhauling.' There was a man at Folkestone; I used to meet him on the Lees. He proposed one evening we should go for a long bicycle ride together on the following day, and I agreed. I got up early, for me; I made an effort, and was pleased with myself. He came half an hour late: I was waiting for him in the garden. It was a lovely day. He said:

'That's a good-looking machine of yours. How does it run?'

'Oh, like most of them!' I answered; 'easily enough in the morning; goes a little stiffly after lunch.'

He caught hold of it by the front wheel and the fork, and shook it violently.

I said: 'Don't do that; you'll hurt it.'

I did not see why he should shake it; it had not done anything to him. Besides, if it wanted shaking, I was the proper person to shake it. I felt much as I should had he started whacking my dog.

He said: 'This front wheel wobbles.'

I said: 'It doesn't if you don't wobble it.' It didn't wobble, as a matter of fact – nothing worth calling a wobble.

He said: 'This is dangerous; have you got a screw-hammer?'

I ought to have been firm, but I thought that perhaps he really did know something about the business. I went to the tool shed to see what I could find. When I came back he was sitting on the ground with the front wheel between his legs. He was playing with it, twiddling it round between his fingers; the remnant of the machine was lying on the gravel path beside him.

He said: 'Something has happened to this front wheel of yours.'

'It looks like it, doesn't it?' I answered. But he was the sort of man that never understands satire.

He said: 'It looks to me as if the bearings were all wrong.'

I said: 'Don't you trouble about it any more; you will make yourself tired. Let us put it back and get off.'

He said: 'We may as well see what is the matter with it, now it is out.' He talked as though it had dropped out by accident.

Before I could stop him he had unscrewed something somewhere, and out rolled all over the path some dozen or so little balls.

'Catch 'em!' he shouted; 'catch 'em! We mustn't lose any of them.' He was quite excited about them.

We grovelled round for half an hour, and found sixteen. He said he hoped we had got them all, because, if not, it would make a serious difference to the machine. He said there was nothing you should be more careful about in taking a bicycle to pieces than seeing you did not lose any of the balls. He explained that you ought to count them as you took them out, and see that exactly the same number went back in each place. I promised, if ever I took a bicycle to pieces I would remember his advice.

I put the balls for safety in my hat, and I put my hat upon the doorstep. It was not a sensible thing to do, I admit. As a matter of fact, it was a silly thing to do. I am not as a rule addle headed; his influence must have affected me.

He then said that while he was about it he would see to the chain for me, and at once began taking off the gearcase. I did try to persuade him from that. I told him what an experienced friend of mine once said to me solemnly:

'If anything goes wrong with your gearcase, sell the machine and buy a new one; it comes cheaper.'

He said: 'People talk like that who understand nothing about machines. Nothing is easier than taking off a gearcase.'

I had to confess he was right. In less than five minutes he had the gearcase in two pieces, lying on the path, and was grovelling for screws. He said it was always a mystery to him the way screws disappeared.

We were still looking for the screws when Ethelbertha came out. She seemed surprised to find us there; she said she thought we had started hours ago.

He said: 'We shan't be long now. I'm just helping your husband to overhaul this machine of his. It's a good machine; but they all want going over occasionally.'

Ethelbertha said: 'If you want to wash yourselves when you have done you might go into the back kitchen, if you don't mind; the girls have just finished the bedrooms.'

She told me that if she met Kate they would probably go for a sail; but that in any case she would be back to lunch. I would have given a sovereign to be going with her. I was getting heartily sick of standing about watching this fool breaking up my bicycle.

Common sense continued to whisper to me: 'Stop him, before he does any more mischief. You have a right to protect your own property from the ravages of a lunatic. Take him by the scruff of the neck, and kick him out of the gate!'

But I am weak when it comes to hurting other people's feelings, and I let him muddle on.

He gave up looking for the rest of the screws. He said screws had a knack of turning up when you least expected them, and that now he would see to the chain. He tightened it till it would not move; next he loosened it until it was twice as loose as it was before. Then he said we had better think about getting the front wheel back into its place again.

I held the fork open, and he worried with the wheel. At the end of ten minutes I suggested he should hold the forks, and that I should handle the wheel; and we changed places. At the end of his first minute he dropped the machine, and took a short walk round the croquet lawn,

55

with his hands pressed together between his thighs. He explained as he walked that the thing to be careful about was to avoid getting your fingers pinched between the forks and the spokes of the wheel. I replied I was convinced, from my own experience, that there was much truth in what he said. He wrapped himself up in a couple of dusters, and we commenced again. At length we did get the thing into position; and the moment it was in position he burst out laughing.

I said: 'What's the joke?'

He said: 'Well, I am an ass!'

It was the first thing he had said that made me respect him. I asked him what had led him to the discovery.

He said: 'We've forgotten the balls!'

I looked for my hat; it was lying topsyturvy in the middle of the path, and Ethelbertha's favourite hound was swallowing the balls as fast as he could pick them up.

'He will kill himself,' said Ebbson – I have never met him since that day, thank the Lord; but I think his name was Ebbson – 'they are solid steel.'

I said: 'I am not troubling about the dog. He has had a bootlace and a packet of needles already this week. Nature's the best guide; puppies seem to require this kind of stimulant. What I am thinking about is my bicycle.'

He was of a cheerful disposition. He said: 'Well, we must put back all we can find, and trust to providence.'

We found eleven. We fixed six on one side and five on the other, and half an hour later the wheel was in its place again. It need hardly be added that it really did wobble now; a child might have noticed it. Ebbson said it would do for the present. He appeared to be getting a bit tired himself. If I had let him, he would, I believe, at this point have gone home. I was determined now, however, that he should stop and finish; I had abandoned all thoughts of a ride. My pride in the machine he had killed. My only interest lay now in seeing him scratch and bump and pinch himself. I revived his drooping spirits with a glass of beer and some judicious praise. I said:

'Watching you do this is of real use to me. It is not only your skill and dexterity that fascinates me, it is your cheery confidence in yourself, your inexplicable hopefulness, that does me good.'

Thus encouraged, he set to work to refix the gearcase. He stood the bicycle against the house, and worked from the off side. Then he stood it against a tree, and worked from the near side. Then I held it for him, while he lay on the ground with his head between the wheels, and worked at it from below, and dropped oil upon himself. Then he took it away from me, and doubled himself across it like a pack-saddle, till he lost his balance and slid over on to his head. Three times he said:

'Thank heaven, that's right at last!'

And twice he said:

'No, I'm damned if it is after all!'

What he said the third time I try to forget.

Then he lost his temper and tried bullying the thing. The bicycle, I was glad to see, showed spirit; and the subsequent proceedings degenerated into little else than a rough-and-tumble fight between him and the machine. One moment the bicycle would be on the gravel path, and he on top of it; the next, the position would be reversed – he on the gravel path, the bicycle on him. Now he would be standing flushed with victory, the bicycle firmly fixed between his legs. But his triumph would be short-lived. By a sudden, quick movement it would free itself, and, turning upon him, hit him sharply over the head with one of its handles.

At a quarter to one, dirty and dishevelled, cut and bleeding, he said: 'I think that will do'; and rose and wiped his brow.

The bicycle looked as if it also had had enough of it. Which had received most punishment it would have been difficult to say. I took him into the back kitchen, where, so far as was possible without soda and proper tools, he cleaned himself, and sent him home.

The bicycle I put into a cab and took round to the nearest repairing shop. The foreman of the works came up and looked at it.

'What do you want me to do with that?' said he.

'I want you,' I said, 'so far as is possible, to restore it.'

'It's a bit far gone,' said he; 'but I'll do my best.'

He did his best, which came to two pounds ten. But it was never the same machine again; and at the end of the season I left it in an agent's hands to sell. I wished to deceive nobody; I instructed the man to advertise it as a last year's machine. The agent advised me not to mention any date. He said:

'In this business it isn't a question of what is true and what isn't; it's a question of what you can get people to believe. Now, between you and me, it don't look like a last year's machine; so far as looks are concerned, it might be a ten-year-old. We'll say nothing about date; we'll just get what we can.'

I left the matter to him, and he got me five pounds, which he said was more than he had expected.

There are two ways you can get exercise out of a bicycle: you can 'overhaul' it, or you can ride it. On the whole, I am not sure that a man who takes his pleasure overhauling does not have the best of the bargain. He is independent of the weather and the wind; the state of the roads troubles him not. Give him a screw-hammer, a bundle of rags, an oil-can, and something to sit down upon, and he is happy for the day. He has to put up with certain disadvantages, of course; there is no joy without alloy. He himself always looks like a tinker, and his machine always suggests the idea that, having stolen it, he has tried to disguise it; but as he rarely gets beyond the first milestone with it, this, perhaps, does not much matter. The mistake some people make is in thinking they can get both forms of sport out of the same machine. This is impossible; no machine will stand the double strain. You must make up your mind whether you are going to be an 'overhauler' or a rider. Personally, I prefer to ride, therefore I take care to have near me nothing that can tempt me to overhaul. When anything happens to my machine I wheel it to the nearest repairing shop. If I am too far from the town or village to walk, I sit by the roadside and wait till a cart comes along. My chief danger, I always find, is from the wandering overhauler. The sight of a broken-down machine is to the overhauler as a wayside corpse to a crow; he swoops down upon it with a friendly yell of triumph. At first I used to try politeness. I would say:

'It's nothing; don't you trouble. You ride on, and enjoy yourself, I beg it of you as a favour; please go away.'

Experience has taught me, however, that courtesy is of no use in such an extremity. Now I say:

'You go away and leave the thing alone, or I will knock your silly head off.'

And if you look determined, and have a good stout cudgel in your hand, you can generally drive him off.

George came in later in the day. He said:

'Well, do you think everything will be ready?'

I said: 'Everything will be ready by Wednesday, except, perhaps, you and Harris.'

He said: 'Is the tandem all right?'

'The tandem,' I said, 'is well.'

He said: 'You don't think it wants overhauling?'

I replied: 'Age and experience have taught me that there are few matters concerning which a man does well to be positive. Consequently, there remain to me now but a limited number of questions upon which I feel any degree of certainty. Among such still-unshaken beliefs, however, is the conviction that that tandem does not want overhauling. I also feel a presentiment that, provided my life is spared, no human being between now and Wednesday morning is going to overhaul it.'

George said: 'I should not show temper over the matter, if I were you. There will come a day, perhaps not far distant, when that bicycle, with a couple of mountains between it and the nearest repairing shop, will, in spite of your chronic desire for rest, *have* to be overhauled. Then you will clamour for people to tell you where you put the oil-can, and what you have done with the screw-hammer. Then, while you exert yourself holding the thing steady against a tree, you will suggest that somebody else should clean the chain and pump the back wheel.'

I felt there was justice in George's rebuke – also a certain amount of prophetic wisdom. I said:

'Forgive me if I seemed unresponsive. The truth is, Harris was round here this morning. . . .'

George said: 'Say no more; I understand. Besides, what I came to talk to you about was another matter. Look at that.'

He handed me a small book bound in red cloth. It was a guide to English conversation for the use of German travellers. It commenced 'On a Steamboat,' and terminated 'At the Doctor's'; its longest chapter being devoted to conversation in a railway carriage, among, apparently, a compartment load of quarrelsome and ill-mannered lunatics: 'Can you not get farther away from me, sir?' – 'It is impossible, madam; my neighbour, here, is very stout' – 'Shall we not endeavour to arrange our legs?' – 'Please have the goodness to keep your elbows down' – 'Pray do not inconvenience yourself, madam, if my shoulder is of any accommodation to you,' whether intended to be said sarcastically or not, there was nothing to indicate – 'I really must request you to move a little, madam, I can hardly breathe,' the author's idea being, presumably, that by this time the whole party was mixed up together on the floor. The chapter concluded with the phrase: 'Here we are at our destination, God be thanked! (*Gott sei dank!*)' a pious exclamation, which under the circumstances must have taken the form of a chorus.

At the end of the book was an appendix, giving the German traveller hints concerning the preservation of his health and comfort during his sojourn in English towns; chief among such hints being advice to him to always travel with a supply of disinfectant powder, to always lock his bedroom door at night, and to always carefully count his small change.

'It is not a brilliant publication,' I remarked, handing the book back to George; 'it is not a book that personally I would recommend to any German about to visit England; I think it would get him disliked. But I have read books published in London for the use of English travellers abroad every whit as foolish. Some educated idiot, misunderstanding seven languages, would appear to go about writing these books for the misinformation and false guidance of modern Europe.'

'You cannot deny,' said George, 'that these books are in large request. They are bought by the thousand, I know. In every town in Europe there must be people going about talking this sort of thing.'

'Maybe,' I replied; 'but fortunately, nobody understands them. I have noticed, myself, men standing on railway platforms and at street corners reading aloud from such books. Nobody knows what language they are speaking; nobody has the slightest knowledge of what they are saying. This is, perhaps, as well; were they understood they would probably be assaulted.'

George said: 'Maybe you are right; my idea is to see what would happen if they were understood. My proposal is to get to London early on Wednesday morning, and spend an hour or two going about and shopping with the aid of this book. There are one or two little things I want – a hat and a pair of bedroom slippers, among other articles. Our boat does not leave Tilbury till twelve, and that just gives us time. I want to try this sort of talk where I can properly judge of its effect. I want to see how the foreigner feels when he is talked to in this way.'

It struck me as a sporting idea. In my enthusiasm I offered to accompany him, and wait outside the shop. I said I thought that Harris would like to be in it, too – or rather outside.

George said that was not quite his scheme. His proposal was that Harris and I should accompany him into the shop. With Harris, who looks formidable, to support him, and myself at the door to call the police if necessary, he said he was willing to adventure the thing.

We walked round to Harris's, and put the proposal before him. He examined the book, especially the chapters dealing with the purchase of shoes and hats. He said:

'If George talks to any bootmaker or any hatter the things that are put down here, it is not support he will want; it is carrying to the hospital that he will need.'

That made George angry.

'You talk,' said George, 'as though I were a foolhardy boy without any sense. I shall select from the more polite and less irritating speeches; the grosser insults I shall avoid.'

This being clearly understood, Harris gave in his adhesion; and our start was fixed for early Wednesday morning.

George came down on Tuesday evening, and slept at Harris's place. We thought this a better arrangement than his own suggestion, which was that we should call for him on our way and 'pick him up.' Picking George up in the morning means picking him out of bed to begin with, and shaking him awake – in itself an exhausting effort with which to commence the day; helping him find his things and finish his packing; and then waiting for him while he eats his breakfast, a tedious entertainment from the spectator's point of view, full of wearisome repetition.

I knew that if he slept at Beggarbush he would be up in time; I have slept there myself, and I know what happens. About the middle of the night, as you judge, though in reality it may be somewhat later, you are startled out of your first sleep by what sounds like a rush of cavalry along the passage, just outside your door. Your half-awakened intelligence fluctuates between burglars, the Day of Judgment, and a gas explosion. You sit up in bed and listen intently. You are not kept waiting long; the next moment a door is violently slammed, and somebody, or something, is evidently coming downstairs on a tea-tray.

'I told you so,' says a voice outside, and immediately some hard substance, a head one would say from the ring of it, rebounds against the panel of your door.

By this time you are charging madly round the room for your clothes. Nothing is where you put it overnight, the articles most essential have disappeared entirely; and meanwhile the murder, or revolution, or whatever it is, continues unchecked. You pause for a moment, with your head under the wardrobe, where you think you can see your slippers, to listen to a steady, monotonous thumping upon a distant door. The victim, you presume, has taken refuge there; they mean to have him out and finish him. Will you be in time? The knocking ceases, and a voice, sweetly reassuring in its gentle plaintiveness, asks meekly:

'Pa, may I get up?'

You do not hear the other voice, but the responses are:

'No, it was only the bath – no, she ain't really hurt – only wet, you know. Yes, ma, I'll tell 'em what you say. No, it was a pure accident. Yes; good night, papa.'

Then the same voice, exerting itself so as to be heard in a distant part of the house, remarks:

'You've got to come upstairs again. Pa says it isn't time yet to get up.'

You return to bed, and lie listening to somebody being dragged upstairs, evidently against their will. By a thoughtful arrangement the spare rooms at Beggarbush are exactly underneath the nurseries. The same somebody, you conclude, still offering the most creditable opposition, is being put back into bed. You can follow the contest with much exactitude, because every time the body is flung down upon the spring mattress, the bedstead, just above your head, makes a sort of jump; while every time the body succeeds in struggling out again, you are aware by the thud upon the floor. After a time the struggle wanes, or maybe the bed collapses; and you drift back into sleep. But the next moment, or what seems to be the next moment, you again open your eyes under the consciousness of a presence. The door is being held ajar, and four solemn faces, piled one on top of the other, are peering at you, as though you were some natural curiosity kept in this particular room. Seeing you awake, the top face, walking calmly over the other three, comes in and sits on the bed in a friendly attitude.

'Oh!' it says, 'we didn't know you were awake. I've been awake some time.'

'So I gather,' you reply shortly.

'Pa doesn't like us to get up too early,' it continues. 'He says everybody else in the house is liable to be disturbed if we get up. So, of course, we mustn't.'

The tone is that of gentle resignation. It is instinct with the spirit of virtuous pride, arising from the consciousness of self-sacrifice.

'Don't you call this being up?' you suggest.

'Oh no; we're not really up, you know, because we're not properly dressed.' The fact is self-evident. 'Pa's always very tired in the morning,' the voice continues; 'of course, that's because he works hard all day. Are you ever tired in the morning?'

At this point he turns and notices, for the first time, that the three other children have also entered, and are sitting in a semicircle on the floor. From their attitude it is clear they have mistaken the whole thing for one of the slower forms of entertainment, some comic lecture or conjuring exhibition, and are waiting patiently for you to get out of bed and do something. It shocks him, the idea of their being in the guest's bedchamber. He peremptorily orders them out. They do not answer him, they do not argue; in dead silence, and with one accord they fall upon him. All you can see from the bed is a confused tangle of waving arms and legs, suggestive of an intoxicated octopus trying to find bottom. Not a word is spoken; that seems to be the etiquette of the thing. If you are sleeping in your pyjamas, you spring from the bed, and only add to the confusion; if you are wearing a less showy garment, you stop where you are and shout commands, which are utterly unheeded. The simplest plan is to leave it to the eldest boy. He does get them out after a while, and closes the door upon them. It reopens immediately, and one, generally Muriel, is shot back into the room. She enters as from a catapult. She is handicapped by having long hair, which can be used as a convenient handle. Evidently aware of this natural disadvantage, she clutches it herself tightly in one hand, and punches with the other. He opens the door again, and cleverly uses her as a battering-ram against the wall of those without. You can hear the dull crash as her head enters among them, and scatters them. When the victory is complete, he comes back and resumes his seat on the bed. There is no bitterness about him; he has forgotten the whole incident.

'I like the morning,' he says, 'don't you?'

'Some mornings,' you agree, 'are all right; others are not so peaceful.'

He takes no notice of your exception; a far-away look steals over his somewhat ethereal face.

'I should like to die in the morning,' he says; 'everything is so beautiful then.'

'Well,' you answer, 'perhaps you will, if your father ever invites an irritable man to come and sleep here, and doesn't warn him beforehand.'

He descends from his contemplative mood, and becomes himself again.

'It's jolly in the garden,' he suggests; 'you wouldn't like to get up and have a game of cricket, would you?'

It was not the idea with which you went to bed, but now, as things have turned out, it seems as good a plan as lying there hopelessly awake; and you agree.

You learn, later in the day, that the explanation of the proceeding is that you, unable to sleep, woke up early in the morning, and thought you would like a game of cricket. The children, taught to be ever courteous to guests, felt it their duty to humour you. Mrs Harris remarks at breakfast that at least you might have seen to it that the children were properly dressed before you took them out; while Harris points out to you, pathetically, how by your one morning's example and encouragement, you have undone his labour of months.

On this Wednesday morning, George, it seems, clamoured to get up at a quarter past five, and persuaded them to let him teach them cycling tricks round the cucumber frames on Harris's new wheel. Even Mrs Harris, however, did not blame George on this occasion; she felt intuitively the idea would not have been entirely his.

It is not that the Harris children have the faintest notion of avoiding blame at the expense of a friend and comrade. One and all they are honesty itself in accepting responsibility for their own misdeeds. It simply is, that is how the thing presents itself to their understanding. When you explain to them that you had no original intention of getting up at five o'clock in the morning to play cricket on the croquet lawn, or to mimic the history of the early Church by shooting with a crossbow at dolls tied to a tree; that as a matter of fact, left to your own initiative, you would have slept peacefully till roused in Christian fashion with a cup of tea at eight, they are firstly astonished, secondly apologetic, and thirdly sincerely contrite. In the present instance, waiving the purely academic question whether the awakening of George at a little before five was due to natural instinct on his part, or to the accidental passing of a home-made boomerang through his bedroom window, the dear children frankly admitted that the blame for his uprising was their own. As the eldest boy said:

'We ought to have remembered that Uncle George had a long day before him, and we ought to have dissuaded him from getting up. I blame myself entirely.'

But an occasional change of habit does nobody any harm; and besides, as Harris and I agreed, it was good training for George. In the Black Forest we should be up at five every morning; that we had determined on. Indeed, George himself had suggested half past four, but Harris and I had argued that five would be early enough as an average; that would enable us to be on our machines by six, and to break the back of our journey before the heat of the day set in. Occasionally, we might start a little earlier, but not as a habit.

I myself was up that morning at five. This was earlier than I had intended. I had said to myself on going to sleep, 'Six o'clock, sharp!'

There are men I know who can wake themselves at any time to the minute. They say to themselves literally, as they lay their heads upon the pillow, 'Four-thirty,' 'Four-forty-five,' or 'Five-fifteen,' as the case may be; and as the clock strikes they open their eyes. It is very wonderful this; the more one dwells upon it, the greater the mystery grows. Some Ego within us, acting quite independently of our conscious self, must be capable of counting the hours while we sleep. Unaided by clock or sun, or any other medium known to our five senses, it keeps watch through the darkness. At the exact moment it whispers 'Time!' and we awake. The work of an old riverside fellow I once talked with called him to be out of bed each morning half an hour before high tide. He told me that never once had he overslept himself by a minute. Latterly, he never even troubled to work out the tide for himself. He would lie down tired, and sleep a dreamless sleep, and each morning at a different hour this ghostly watchman, true as the tide itself, would silently call him. Did the man's spirit haunt through the darkness the muddy river stairs; or had it knowledge of the ways of Nature? Whatever the process, the man himself was unconscious of it.

In my own case my inward watchman is, perhaps, somewhat out of practice. He does his best; but he is over-anxious; he worries himself, and loses count. I say to him, maybe, 'Five-thirty, please'; and he wakes me with a start at half past two. I look at my watch. He suggests that, perhaps, I forgot to wind it up. I put it to my ear; it is still going. He thinks, maybe, something has happened to it; he is confident himself it is half past five, if not a little later. To satisfy him, I put on a pair of slippers and go downstairs to inspect the dining-room clock. What happens to a man when he wanders about the house in the middle of the night, clad in a dressing-gown and a pair of slippers, there is no need to recount; most men know by experience. Everything – especially everything with a sharp corner – takes a cowardly delight in hitting him. When you are wearing a pair of stout boots, things get out of your way; when you venture among furniture in woolwork slippers and no socks, it comes at you and kicks you. I return to bed bad tempered, and refusing to listen to his further absurd suggestion that all the clocks in the house have entered into a conspiracy against me, take half an hour to get to sleep again. From four to five he wakes me every ten minutes. I wish I had never said a word to him about the thing. At five o'clock he goes to sleep himself, worn out, and leaves it to the girl, who does it half an hour later than usual.

On this particular Wednesday he worried me to such an extent, that I got up at five simply to be rid of him. I did not know what to do with myself. Our train did not leave till eight; all our luggage had been packed and sent on the night before, together with the bicycles, to Fenchurch Street station. I went into my study; I thought I would put in an hour's writing. The early morning, before one has breakfasted, is not, I take it, a good season for literary effort. I wrote three paragraphs of a story, and then read them over to myself. Some unkind things have been said about my work; but nothing has yet been written which would have done justice to those three paragraphs. I threw them into the waste-paper basket, and sat trying to remember what, if any, charitable institutions provided pensions for decayed authors.

To escape from this train of reflection, I put a golf-ball in my pocket, and selecting a driver, strolled out into the paddock. A couple of sheep were browsing there, and they followed and took a keen interest in my practice. The one was a kindly, sympathetic old party. I do not think she understood the game; I think it was my doing this innocent thing so early in the morning that appealed to her. At every stroke I made she bleated:

'Go—o—o—d, go—o—o—d ind—e—e—d!'

She seemed as pleased as if she had done it herself.

As for the other one, she was a cantankerous, disagreeable old thing, as discouraging to me as her friend was helpful.

'Ba—a—a—d, da—a—a—m ba—a—a—d!' was her comment on almost every stroke. As a matter of fact, some were really excellent strokes; but she did it just to be contradictory, and for the sake of irritating. I could see that.

By a most regrettable accident, one of my swiftest balls struck the good sheep on the nose. And at that the bad sheep laughed – laughed distinctly and undoubtedly, a husky, vulgar laugh; and, while her friend stood glued to the ground, too astonished to move, she changed her note for the first time and bleated:

'Go—o—o—d, ve—e—ry go—o—o—d! Be—e—e—est sho—o—o—ot he—e—e's ma—a—a—de!'

I would have given half a crown if it had been she I had hit instead of the other one. It is ever the good and amiable who suffer in this world.

I had wasted more time than I had intended in the paddock, and when Ethelbertha came to tell me it was half past seven, and the breakfast was on the table, I remembered that I had not shaved. It vexes Ethelbertha my shaving quickly. She fears that to outsiders it may suggest a poor-spirited attempt at suicide, and that in consequence it may get about the neighbourhood that we are not happy together. As a further argument, she has also hinted that my appearance is not of the kind that can be trifled with.

On the whole, I was just as glad not to be able to take a long farewell of Ethelbertha; I did not want to risk her breaking down. But I should have liked more opportunity to say a few farewell words of advice to the children, especially as regards my fishing-rod, which they will persist in using for cricket stumps; and I hate having to run for a train. Quarter of a mile from the station I overtook George and Harris; they were also running. In their case – so Harris informed me, jerkily, while we trotted side by side – it was the new kitchen stove that was to blame. This was the first morning they had tried it, and from some cause or other it had blown up the kidneys and scalded the cook. He said he hoped that by the time we returned they would have got more used to it.

We caught the train by the skin of our teeth, as the saying is, and reflecting upon the events of the morning, as we sat gasping in the carriage, there passed vividly before my mind the panorama of my Uncle Podger, as on two hundred and fifty days in the year he would start from Ealing Common by the nine-thirteen train to Moorgate Street.

From my Uncle Podger's house to the railway station was eight minutes' walk. What my uncle always said was:

'Allow yourself a quarter of an hour, and take it easily.'

What he always did was to start five minutes before the time and run. I do not know why, but this was the custom of the suburb. Many stout City gentlemen lived at Ealing in those days – I believe some live there still – and caught early trains to Town. They all started late; they all carried a black bag and a newspaper in one hand, and an umbrella in the other; and for the last quarter of a mile to the station, wet or fine, they all ran.

Folks with nothing else to do, nursemaids chiefly and errand boys, with now and then a perambulating costermonger added, would gather on the common of a fine morning to watch them pass, and cheer the most deserving. It was not a showy spectacle. They did not run well, they did not even run fast; but they were earnest, and they did their best. The exhibition appealed less to one's sense of art than one's natural admiration for conscientious effort.

Occasionally a little harmless betting would take place among the crowd.

'Two to one agin the old gent in the white weskit!'

'Ten to one on old Blowpipes, bar he don't roll over hisself 'fore 'e gets there!'

'Heven money on the Purple Hemperor!' – a nickname bestowed by a youth of entomological tastes upon a certain retired military neighbour of my uncle's – a gentleman of imposing appearance when stationary, but apt to colour highly under exercise.

My uncle and the others would write to the *Ealing Press* complaining bitterly concerning the supineness of the local police; and the editor would add spirited leaders upon the Decay of Courtesy among the Lower Orders, especially throughout the western suburbs. But no good ever resulted.

It was not that my uncle did not rise early enough; it was that troubles came to him at the last moment. The first thing he would do after breakfast would be to lose his newspaper. We always knew when Uncle Podger had lost anything, by the expression of astonished indignation with which, on such occasions, he would regard the world in general. It never occurred to my Uncle Podger to say to himself:

'I am a careless old man. I lose everything: I never know where I have put anything. I am quite incapable of finding it again for myself. In this respect I must be a perfect nuisance to everybody about me. I must set to work and reform myself.'

On the contrary, by some peculiar course of reasoning, he had convinced himself that whenever he lost a thing it was everybody else's fault in the house but his own.

'I had it in my hand here not a minute ago!' he would exclaim.

From his tone you would have thought he was living surrounded by conjurers, who spirited away things from him merely to irritate him.

'Could you have left it in the garden?' my aunt would suggest.

'What should I want to leave it in the garden for? I don't want the paper in the garden; I want the paper in the train with me.'

'You haven't put it in your pocket?'

'God bless the woman! Do you think I should be standing here at five minutes to nine looking for it if I had it in my pocket all the while? *Do* you think I'm a fool?'

Here somebody would explain, 'What's this?' and hand him from somewhere a paper neatly folded.

'I do wish people would leave my things alone,' he would growl, snatching at it savagely.

He would open his bag to put it in, and then glancing at it, he would pause, speechless with sense of injury.

'What's the matter?' aunt would ask.

'The day before yesterday's!' he would answer, too hurt even to shout, throwing the paper down upon the table.

If only sometimes it had been yesterday's it would have been a change. But it was always the day before yesterday's; except on Tuesday; then it would be Saturday's.

We would find it for him eventually; as often as not he was sitting on it. And then he would smile, not genially, but with the weariness that comes to a man who feels that fate has cast his lot among a band of hopeless idiots.

'All the time, right in front of your noses. . .!' He would not finish the sentence; he prided himself on his self-control.

This settled, he would start for the hall, where it was the custom of my Aunt Maria to have the children gathered, ready to say goodbye to him.

My aunt never left the house herself, if only to make a call next door, without taking a tender farewell of every inmate. One never knew, she would say, what might happen.

One of them, of course, was sure to be missing, and the moment this was noticed all the other six, without an instant's hesitation, would scatter with a whoop to find it. Immediately they were gone it would turn up by itself from somewhere quite near, always with the most reasonable explanation for its absence; and would at once start off after the others to explain to them that it was found. In this way, five minutes at least would be taken up in everybody's looking for everybody else, which was just sufficient time to allow my uncle to find his umbrella and lose his hat. Then, at last, the group reassembled in the hall, the drawing-room clock would commence to strike nine. It possessed a cold, penetrating chime that always had the effect of confusing my uncle. In his excitement he would kiss some of the children twice over, pass by others, forget whom he had kissed and whom he hadn't, and have to begin all over again. He used to say he believed they mixed themselves up on purpose, and I am not prepared to maintain that the charge was altogether false. To add to his troubles, one child always had a sticky face and that child would always be the most affectionate.

If things were going too smoothly, the eldest boy would come out with some tale about all the clocks in the house being five minutes slow, and of his having been late for school the previous day in consequence. This would send my uncle rushing impetuously down to the gate, where he would recollect that he had with him neither his bag nor his umbrella. All the children that my aunt could not stop would charge after him, two of them struggling for the umbrella, the others surging round the bag. And when they returned we would discover on the hall table the most important thing of all that he had forgotten, and wondered what he would say about it when he came home.

We arrived at Waterloo a little after nine, and at once proceeded to put George's experiment into operation. Opening the book at the chapter entitled 'At the Cab Rank,' we walked up to a hansom, raised our hats, and wished the driver 'Good morning.'

This man was not to be outdone in politeness by any foreigner, real or imitation. Calling to a friend named 'Charles' to 'hold the steed', he sprang from his box, and returned to us a bow that would have done credit to Mr Turveydrop himself. Speaking apparently in the name of the nation, he welcomed us to England, adding a regret that Her Majesty was not at the moment in London.

We could not reply to him in kind. Nothing of this sort had been anticipated by the book. We called him 'coachman,' at which he again bowed to the pavement, and asked him if he would have the goodness to drive us to the Westminster Bridge Road.

He laid his hand upon his heart, and said the pleasure would be his.

Taking the third sentence in the chapter, George asked him what his fare would be.

The question, as introducing a sordid element into the conversation, seemed to hurt his feelings. He said he never took money from distinguished strangers; he suggested a souvenir – a diamond scarf pin, a gold snuffbox, some little trifle of that sort by which he could remember us.

As a small crowd had collected, and as the joke was drifting rather too far in the cabman's direction, we climbed in without further parley, and were driven away amid cheers. We stopped the cab at a boot shop a little past Astley's Theatre that looked the sort of place we wanted. It was one of those overfed shops that the moment their shutters are taken down in the morning disgorge their goods all round them. Boxes of boots stood piled on the pavement or in the gutter opposite. Boots hung in festoons about its doors and windows. Its sunblind was as some grimy vine, bearing bunches of black and brown boots. Inside, the shop was a bower of boots. The man, when we entered, was busy with a chisel and hammer opening a new crate full of boots.

George raised his hat, and said 'Good morning.'

The man did not even turn round. He struck me from the first as a disagreeable man. He grunted something which might have been 'Good morning,' or might not, and went on with his work.

George said: 'I have been recommended to your shop by my friend, Mr X.'

In response, the man should have said: 'Mr X is a most worthy gentleman; it will give me the greatest pleasure to serve any friend of his.'

What he did say was: 'Don't know him; never heard of him.'

This was disconcerting. The book gave three or four methods of buying boots; George had carefully selected the one centred round 'Mr X,' as being of all the most courtly. You talked a good deal with the shopkeeper about this 'Mr X,' and then, when by this means friendship and understanding had been established, you slid naturally and gracefully into the immediate object, of your coming, namely, your desire for boots, 'cheap and good.' This gross, material man cared, apparently, nothing for the niceties of retail dealing. It was necessary with such a one to come to business with brutal directness. George abandoned 'Mr X,' and turning back to a previous page, took a sentence at random. It was not a happy selection; it was a speech that would have been superfluous made to any bootmaker. Under the present circumstances, threatened and stifled as we were on every side by boots, it possessed the dignity of positive imbecility. It ran: 'One has told me that you have here boots for sale.'

For the first time the man put down his hammer and chisel, and looked at us. He spoke slowly, in a thick and husky voice. He said:

'What d'ye think I keep boots for – to smell 'em?'

He was one of those men that begin quietly and grow more angry as they proceed, their wrongs apparently working within them like yeast.

'What d'ye think I am,' he continued, 'a boot collector? What d'ye think I'm running this shop for – my health? D'ye think I love the boots, and can't bear to part with a pair? D'ye think I hand 'em about here to look at 'em? Ain't there enough of 'em? Where d'ye think you are – in an international exhibition of boots? What d'ye think these boots are – a historical collection? Did you ever hear of a man keeping a boot shop and not selling boots? D'ye think I decorate the shop with 'em to make it look pretty? What d'ye take me for – a prize idiot?'

I have always maintained that these conversation books are never of any real use. What we wanted was some English equivalent for the well-known German idiom: 'Behalten Sie Ihr Haar auf.'

Nothing of the sort was to be found in the book from beginning to end. However, I will do George the credit to admit he chose the very best sentence that was to be found therein and applied it. He said:

'I will come again, when, perhaps, you will have some more boots to show me. Till then, adieu!'

With that we returned to our cab and drove away, leaving the man standing in the centre of his boot-bedecked doorway addressing remarks to us. What he said, I did not hear, but the passersby appeared to find it interesting.

George was for stopping at another boot shop and trying the experiment afresh; he said he really did want a pair of bedroom slippers. But we persuaded him to postpone their purchase until our arrival in some foreign city, where the tradespeople are no doubt more inured to this sort of talk, or else more naturally amiable. On the subject of the hat, however, he was adamant. He maintained that without that he could not travel, and, accordingly, we pulled up at a small shop in the Blackfriars Road.

The proprietor of this shop was a cheery, bright-eyed little man, and he helped us rather than hindered us.

When George asked him in the words of the book: 'Have you any hats?' he did not get angry; he just stopped and thoughtfully scratched his chin.

'Hats,' said he. 'Let me think. Yes' – here a smile of positive pleasure broke over his genial countenance – 'yes, now I come to think of it, I believe I have a hat. But, tell me, why do you ask me?'

George explained to him that he wished to purchase a cap, a travelling cap, but the essence of the transaction was that it was to be a 'good cap.'

The man's face fell.

'Ah,' he remarked, 'there, I am afraid, you have me. Now, if you had wanted a bad cap, not worth the price asked for it; a cap good for nothing but to clean windows with, I could have found you the very thing. But a good cap – no; we don't keep them. But wait a minute,' he continued, on seeing the disappointment that spread over George's expressive countenance, 'don't be in a hurry. I have a cap here' – he went to a drawer and opened it – 'it is not a good cap, but it is not so bad as most of the caps I sell.'

He brought it forward, extended on his palm.

'What do you think of that?' he asked. 'Could you put up with that?'

George fitted it on before the glass, and, choosing another remark from the book, said:

'This hat fits me sufficiently well, but, tell me, do you consider that it becomes me?'

The men stepped back and took a bird's-eye view.

'Candidly,' he replied, 'I can't say that it does.'

He turned from George, and addressed himself to Harris and myself.

'Your friend's beauty,' said he, 'I should describe as elusive. It is there, but you can easily miss it. Now, in that cap, to my mind, you do miss it.'

At that point it occurred to George that he had had sufficient fun with this particular man. He said:

'That is all right. We don't want to lose the train. How much?'

Answered the man: 'The price of that cap, sir, which, in my opinion, is twice as much as it is worth, is four-and-six. Would you like it wrapped up in brown paper, sir, or in white?'

George said he would take it as it was, paid the man four-and-six in silver, and went out. Harris and I followed.

At Fenchurch Street we compromised with our cabman for five shillings. He made us another courtly bow, and begged us to remember him to the Emperor of Austria.

Comparing views in the train, we agreed that we had lost the game by two points to one; and George, who was evidently disappointed, threw the book out of the window.

We found our luggage and the bicycles safe on the boat, and with the tide at twelve dropped down the river.

The Whore of Mensa
WOODY ALLEN

ONE THING ABOUT BEING a private investigator, you've got to learn to go with your hunches. That's why when a quivering pat of butter named Word Babcock walked into my office and laid his cards on the table, I should have trusted the cold chill that shot up my spine.

'Kaiser?' he said. 'Kaiser Lupowitz?'

'That's what it says on my license,' I owned up.

'You've got to help me. I'm being blackmailed. Please!'

He was shaking like the lead singer in a rumba band. I pushed a glass across the desk top and a bottle of rye I keep handy for nonmedicinal purposes. 'Suppose you relax and tell me all about it.'

'You ... you won't tell my wife?'

'Level with me, Word. I can't make any promises.'

He tried pouring a drink, but you could hear the clicking sound across the street, and most of the stuff wound up in his shoes.

'I'm a working guy,' he said. 'Mechanical maintenance. I build and service joy buzzers. You know – those little fun gimmicks that give people a shock when they shake hands?'

'So?'

'A lot of your executives like 'em. Particularly down on Wall Street.'

'Get to the point.'

'I'm on the road a lot. You know how it is – lonely. Oh, not what you're thinking. See, Kaiser, I'm basically an intellectual. Sure, a guy can meet all the bimbos he wants. But the really brainy women – they're not so easy to find on short notice.'

'Keep talking.'

'Well, I heard of this young girl. Eighteen years old. A Vassar student. For a price, she'll come over and discuss any subject – Proust, Yeats, anthropology. Exchange of ideas. You see what I'm driving at?'

'Not exactly.'

'I mean, my wife is great, don't get me wrong. But she won't discuss Pound with me. Or Eliot. I didn't know that when I married her. See, I need a woman who's mentally stimulating, Kaiser. And I'm willing to pay for it. I don't want an involvement – I want a quick intellectual experience, then I want the girl to leave. Christ, Kaiser, I'm a happily married man.'

'How long has this been going on?'

'Six months. Whenever I have that craving, I call Flossie. She's a madam, with a master's in comparative lit. She sends me over an intellectual, see?'

So he was one of those guys whose weakness was really bright women. I felt sorry for the poor sap. I figured there must be a lot of jokers in his position, who were starved for a little intellectual communication with the opposite sex and would pay through the nose for it.

'Now she's threatening to tell my wife,' he said.

'Who is?'

'Flossie. They bugged the motel room. They got tapes of me discussing *The Waste Land* and *Styles of Radical Will*, and, well, really getting into some issues. They want ten grand or they go to Carla. Kaiser, you've got to help me! Carla would die if she knew she didn't turn me on up here.'

The old call-girl racket. I had heard rumors that the boys at headquarters were on to something involving a group of educated women, but so far they were stymied.

'Get Flossie on the phone for me.'

'What?'

'I'll take your case, Word. But I get fifty dollars a day, plus expenses. You'll have to repair a lot of joy buzzers.'

'It won't be ten Gs' worth, I'm sure of that,' he said with a grin, and picked up the phone and dialled a number. I took it from him and winked. I was beginning to like him.

Seconds later, a silky voice answered, and I told her what was on my mind. 'I understand you can help me set up an hour of good chat,' I said.

'Sure, honey. What do you have in mind?'

'I'd like to discuss Melville.'

'*Moby Dick* or the shorter novels?'

'What's the difference?'

'The price. That's all. Symbolism's extra.'

'What'll it run me?'

'Fifty, maybe a hundred for *Moby Dick*. You want a comparative discussion – Melville and Hawthorne? That could be arranged for a hundred.'

'The dough's fine,' I told her and gave her the number of a room at the Plaza.

'You want a blonde or a brunette?'

'Surprise me,' I said, and hung up.

I shaved and grabbed some black coffee while I checked over the Monarch College Outline series. Hardly an hour had passed before there was a knock on my door. I opened it, and standing there was a young redhead who was packed into her slacks like two big scoops of vanilla ice cream.

'Hi, I'm Sherry.'

They really knew how to appeal to your fantasies. Long straight hair, leather bag, silver earrings, no make-up.

'I'm surprised you weren't stopped, walking into the hotel dressed like that,' I said. 'The house dick can usually spot an intellectual.'

'A five-spot cools him.'

'Shall we begin?' I said, motioning her to the couch.

She lit a cigarette and got right to it. 'I think we could start by approaching *Billy Budd* as Melville's justification of the ways of God to man, *n'est-ce pas?*'

'Interestingly, though, not in a Miltonian sense.' I was bluffing. I wanted to see if she'd go for it.

'No. *Paradise Lost* lacked the substructure of pessimism.' She did.

'Right, right. God, you're right,' I murmured.

'I think Melville reaffirmed the virtues of innocence in a naïve yet sophisticated sense – don't you agree?'

I let her go on. She was barely nineteen years old, but already she had developed the hardened facility of the pseudo-intellectual. She rattled off her ideas glibly, but it was all mechanical. Whenever I offered an insight, she faked a response: 'Oh, yes, Kaiser. Yes, baby, that's deep. A platonic comprehension of Christianity – why didn't I see it before?'

We talked for about an hour and then she said she had to go. She stood up and I laid a C-note on her.

'Thanks, honey.'

'There's plenty more where that came from.'

'What are you trying to say?'

I had piqued her curiosity. She sat down again.

'Suppose I wanted to – have a party?' I said.

'Like, what kind of party?'

'Suppose I wanted Noam Chomsky explained to me by two girls?'

'Oh, wow.'

'If you'd rather forget it ...'

'You'd have to speak with Flossie,' she said. 'It'd cost you.'

Now was the time to tighten the screws. I flashed my private-investigator's badge and informed her it was a bust.

'What!'

'I'm fuzz, sugar, and discussing Melville for money is an 802. You can do time.'

'You louse!'

'Better come clean, baby. Unless you want to tell your story down at Alfred Kazin's office, and I don't think he'd be too happy to hear it.'

She began to cry. 'Don't turn me in, Kaiser,' she said. 'I needed the money to complete my master's. I've been turned down for a grant. *Twice*. Oh, Christ.'

It all poured out – the whole story. Central Park West upbringing,

Socialist summer camps, Brandeis. She was every dame you saw waiting in line at the Elgin or the Thalia, or penciling the words 'Yes, very true' into the margin of some book on Kant. Only somewhere along the line she had made a wrong turn.

'I needed cash. A girl friend said she knew a married guy whose wife wasn't very profound. He was into Blake. She couldn't hack it. I said sure, for a price I'd talk Blake with him. I was nervous at first, I faked a lot of it. He didn't care. My friend said there were others. Oh, I've been busted before. I got caught reading *Commentary* in a parked car, and I was once stopped and frisked at Tanglewood. Once more and I'm a three-time loser.'

'Then take me to Flossie.'

She bit her lip and said, 'The Hunter College Book Store is a front.'

'Yes?'

'Like those bookie joints that have barbershops outside for show. You'll see.'

I made a quick call to headquarters and then said to her, 'Okay, sugar. You're off the hook. But don't leave town.'

She tilted her face up toward mine gratefully. 'I can get you photographs of Dwight Macdonald reading,' she said.

'Some other time.'

I walked into the Hunter College Book Store. The salesman, a young man with sensitive eyes, came up to me. 'Can I help you?' he said.

'I'm looking for a special edition of *Advertisements for Myself*. I understand the author had several thousand gold-leaf copies printed up for friends.'

'I'll have to check,' he said. 'We have a WATS line to Mailer's house.'

I fixed him with a look. 'Sherry sent me,' I said.

'Oh, in that case, go on back,' he said. He pressed a button. A wall of books opened, and I walked like a lamb into that bustling pleasure palace known as Flossie's.

Red flocked wallpaper and a Victorian décor set the tone. Pale, nervous girls with black-rimmed glasses and blunt-cut hair lolled around on sofas, riffling Penguin Classics provocatively. A blonde with a big smile winked at me, nodded toward a room upstairs, and said, 'Wallace Stevens, eh?' But it wasn't just intellectual experiences – they were peddling emotional ones, too. For fifty bucks, I learned, you could 'relate without getting close.' For a hundred, a girl would lend you her Bartók records, have dinner, and then let you watch while she had an anxiety attack. For one-fifty, you could listen to FM radio with twins. For three bills, you got the works: A thin Jewish brunette would pretend to pick you up at the Museum of Modern Art, let you read her master's, get you involved in a screaming quarrel at Elaine's over Freud's conception of women, and then fake a suicide of your choosing – the perfect evening, for some guys. Nice racket. Great town, New York.

'Like what you see?' a voice said behind me. I turned and suddenly found myself standing face to face with the business end of a .38. I'm a guy with a strong stomach, but this time it did a back flip. It was Flossie, all right. The voice was the same, but Flossie was a man. His face was hidden by a mask.

'You'll never believe this,' he said, 'but I don't even have a college degree. I was thrown out for low grades.'

'Is that why you wear that mask?'

'I devised a complicated scheme to take over *The New York Review of Books*, but it meant I had to pass for Lionel Trilling. I went to Mexico for an operation. There's a doctor in Juarez who gives people Trilling's features – for a price. Something went wrong. I came out looking like Auden, with Mary McCarthy's voice. That's when I started working the other side of the law.'

Quickly, before he could tighten his finger on the trigger, I went into action. Heaving forward, I snapped my elbow across his jaw and grabbed the gun as he fell back. He hit the ground like a ton of bricks. He was still whimpering when the police showed up.

'Nice work, Kaiser,' Sergeant Holmes said. 'When we're through with this guy, the FBI wants to have a talk with him. A little matter involving some gamblers and an annotated copy of Dante's *Inferno*. Take him away, boys.'

Later that night, I looked up an old account of mine named Gloria. She was blond. She had graduated *cum laude*. The difference was she majored in physical education. It felt good.

Introduction to Cold Comfort

STELLA GIBBONS

After the death of her parents, level-headed and practical young Flora Poste finds herself, in spite of an extensive (and expensive) education, completely unequipped to earn her own living. Ever decisive, Flora determines to throw herself on the mercy of her cousins the Starkadders of Cold Comfort Farm on the edge of the Sussex downs. On her arrival, she is horrified at the chaotic state of the farm and knuckles down at once to the business of 'civilizing' her wild and doom-laden cousins. After a first day spent in almost total isolation, Flora is just beginning to realize the full extent of the task before her....

FLORA'S SPIRITS WERE usually equable, but by lunchtime the next day the combined forces of the unceasing rain, the distressing manner in which the farmhouse and its attendant buildings seemed sinking into decay before her eyes, and the appearance and characters of her relatives, had produced in her a feeling of gloom which was as unusual as it was disagreeable.

'This will not do,' she thought, as she looked out on the soaking countryside from her bedroom window, whence she had retreated to arrange some buds and branches which she had picked on her morning walk. 'I am probably hungry; lunch will restore my spirits.'

And yet, on second thoughts, it seemed probable that lunch cooked by a Starkadder and partaken of in solitude would only make her worse.

She had managed yesterday's meals successfully. Judith had provided a cutlet and some junket for her at one o'clock, served beside a smoky fire, in a little parlour with faded green wallpaper, next door to the dairy. Here, too, Flora had partaken of tea and supper. These two meals were served by Mrs Beetle – an agreeable surprise. It appeared that Mrs Beetle came in to the farm and did her daughter's work on those occasions when Meriam was being confined. Flora's arrival had coincided with one of these times, which, as we know, were frequent. Mrs Beetle also came in each day to prepare Aunt Ada Doom's meals.

So Flora had thus far escaped meeting Seth and Reuben or any of the other male Starkadders. Judith, Adam, Mrs Beetle, and an occasional glimpse of Elfine represented her whole knowledge of the inhabitants and servants of the farm.

But she was not satisfied. She wished to meet her young cousins, her Aunt Ada Doom, and Amos. How could she tidy up affairs at Cold Comfort if she did not meet any of the Starkadders? And yet she shrank from boldly entering the kitchen where the family sat at the manger, and introducing herself. Such a move would lower her dignity, and, hence, her future power. It was all very difficult. Perhaps Judith did not actively intend to keep Flora from meeting the rest of the family, but she had so far achieved just this result.

But today, Flora had decided, she would meet her cousins, Seth and Reuben. She thought that teatime would present a good opportunity on which to carry out her intention. If the Starkadders did not partake of tea (and it was probable that they did not) she would prepare it herself, and tell the Starkadders that she intended with their nominal permission to do so every afternoon during her visit.

But this point could be considered later. At the moment, she was going down into Howling to see if there was a pub in which she could lunch. In any other household such a proceeding would be enough to terminate her stay. Here, they probably would not even notice her absence.

At one o'clock, therefore, Flora was in the saloon bar of the Condemn'd Man, the only public-house in Howling, asking Mrs Murther the landlady if she 'did' lunches?

A smile indicated a shuddering thankfulness, as of one who peers into a pit into which others have fallen while she has escaped, passed over the face of Mrs Murther, as she replied that she did not.

'At least, only for two days in August, and not always then,' she added, gladly.

'Couldn't you pretend it is August now?' demanded Flora, who was ravenous.

'No,' replied Mrs Murther, simply.

'Well, if I buy a steak at the butcher's, will you cook it for me?'

Mrs Murther unexpectedly said that she would; and added even more surprisingly that Flora could have some of what they was having themselves, an offer which Flora a little rashly accepted.

What they was having themselves proved to be apple tart and vegetables, so Flora did quite well. She obtained her steak after some little delay with the butcher, who thought she was mad; and it seemed to her that a surprisingly short time elapsed between the purchasing of the steak and her sitting down before it, browned and savoury, in the parlour of the Condemn'd Man.

Nor did the hovering presence of Mrs Murther cast an atmosphere sufficiently dismal to spoil her appetite. Mrs Murther seemed resigned, rather than despairing. Her face and manner suggested the Cockney phrase dear and familiar to Flora in London: 'Oh, well, mustn't grumble', though Flora knew better than to expect to hear it in

Howling, where everybody felt that they must grumble, and all the time at that.

'Now I must be off and see to my other gentleman's dinner,' said Mrs Murther, having hovered long enough to see that Flora had all the salt and pepper, bread, forks, and the rest of it that she wanted.

'Have you another gentleman?' asked Flora.

'Yes. Stayin' here. A book-writer,' rejoined Mary Murther.

'He would be,' muttered Flora. 'What's his name?' (for she wondered if she knew him).

'Mybug,' was the improbable answer.

Flora simply did not believe this, but she was too busy eating to start a long and exhausting argument. She decided that Mr Mybug must be a genius. A person who was merely talented would have weakly changed his name by deed-poll.

What a bore it was, she though. Had she not enough to do at Cold Comfort without there being a genius named Mybug staying a mile away from the farm who would probably fall in love with her? For she knew from experience that intellectuals and geniuses seldom fell for females of their own kidney, who had gone all queer about the shoes and coiffure, but concentrated upon reserved but normal and properly dressed persons like herself, who were both repelled and alarmed (not to say bored) by the purposeful advances of the said geniuses and intellectuals.

'Well – what kind of books does he write?' she asked.

'He's doin' one now about another young fellow who wrote books, and then his sisters pretended *they* wrote them, and then they all died of consumption, poor young mommets.'

'Ha! A life of Branwell Brontë,' thought Flora. 'I might have known it. There has been increasing discontent among the male intellectuals for some time at the thought that a woman wrote *Wuthering Heights*. I thought one of them would produce something of this kind, sooner or later. Well, I must just avoid him, that's all.'

And she fell to finishing her apple tart a little more quickly than was comfortable, for she was nervous lest Mr Mybug should come in, and fall in love with her.

'Don't you 'urry yourself; 'e's never in afore half past two,' soothed Mrs Murther, reading her thoughts with disconcerting readiness. 'He's up on the Downs in all weathers, and a nice old lot of mud 'e brings into the 'ouse too. Was everything all right? That'll be one and sixpence, please.'

Flora felt better on her return walk to the farm. She decided that she would spend the afternoon arranging her books.

There were sounds of life in the yard as she crossed it. Buckets clattered in the cowshed, and the hoarse bellow of the bull came from his dark shed. ('I don't believe he's ever let out into the fields when the sun's shining,' through Flora, and made a note to see about him, as well as about the Starkadders.) Belligerent noises came from the henhouse, but nobody was to be seen.

At four o'clock she came downstairs to look for some tea. She did not bother to glance into her little parlour to see if her own tea were on the table. She went straight into the kitchen.

Of course, there were no preparations for tea in the kitchen; she realized, as soon as she saw the ashy fire and the crumbs and fragments of carrot left on the table from dinner, that it was rather optimistic of her to have expected any.

But she was not daunted. She filled the kettle, put some wood on the fire and set the kettle on it, flicked the reminders of dinner off the table with Adam's drying-up towel (which she held in the tongs), and set out a ring of cups and saucers about the dinted pewter teapot. She found a loaf and some butter, but no jam, of course, or anything effeminate of that sort.

Just as the kettle boiled and she darted forward to rescue it, a shadow darkened the door and there stood Reuben, looking at Flora's gallant preparations with an expression of stricken amazement mingled with fury.

'Hullo,' said Flora, getting her blow in first. 'I feel sure you must be Reuben. I'm Flora Poste, your cousin, you know. How do you do? I'm so glad to see somebody has come in for some tea. Do sit down. Do you take milk? (No sugar . . . of course . . . or do you? I do, but most of my friends don't.)'

***The man's big body, etched menacingly against the bleak light that stabbed in from the low windows, did not move. His thoughts swirled like a beck in spate behind the sodden grey furrows of his face. A woman . . . Blast! Blast! Come to wrest away from him the land whose love fermented in his veins, like slow yeast. She-woman. Young, soft-coloured, insolent. His gaze was suddenly edged by a fleshy taint. Break her. Break. Keep and hold and hold fast the land. The land, the iron furrows of frosted earth under the rainlust, the fecund spears of rain, the swelling, slow burst of seed-sheaths, the slow smell of cows and cry of cows, the trampling bride-path of the bull in his hour. All his, his . . .

'Will you have some bread and butter?' asked Flora, handing him a cup of tea. 'Oh, never mind your boots. Adam can sweep the mud up afterwards. Do come in.'

Defeated, Reuben came in.

He stood at the table facing Flora and blowing heavily on his tea and staring at her. Flora did not mind. It was quite interesting: like having tea with a rhinoceros. Besides, she was rather sorry for him. Amongst all the Starkadders, he looked as though he got the least kick out of life. After all, most of the family got a kick out of something. Amos got one from religion, Judith got one out of Seth, Adam got his from cowdling the dumb beasts, and Elfine got hers from dancing about on the Downs in a fog in a peculiar green dress, while Seth got his from mollocking. But Reuben just didn't seem to get a kick out of anything.

'Is it too hot?' she asked, and handed him the milk, with a smile.

The opaque curve purred softly down into the teak depths of the cup. He went on blowing it, and staring at her. Flora wanted to set him at ease (if he had an ease?), so she composedly went on with her tea, wishing there were some cucumber sandwiches.

After a silence which lasted seven minutes by a covert glance at Flora's watch, a series of visible tremors which passed across the expanse of Reuben's face, and a series of low, preparatory noises which proceeded from his throat, persuaded her that he was about to speak to her. Cautious as a cameraman engaged in shooting a family of fourteen lions, Flora made no sign.

Her control was rewarded. After another minute Reuben brought forth the following sentence:

'I ha' scranleted two hundred furrows come five o'clock down i' the bute.'

It was a difficult remark, Flora felt, to which to reply. Was it a complaint? If so, one might say, 'My dear, how too sickening for you!' But then, it might be a boast, in which case the correct reply would be, 'Attaboy!' or more simply, 'Come, that's capital.' Weakly she fell back on the comparatively safe remark:

'Did you?' in a bright, interested voice.

She saw at once that she had said the wrong thing. Reuben's eyebrows came down and his jaw came out. Horrors! He thought she was doubting his word!

'Aye, I did, tu. Two hundred. Two hundred from Ticklepenny's Corner down to Nettle Flitch. Aye, wi'out hand to aid me. Could you ha' done that?'

'No, indeed,' replied Flora, heartily, and her guardian angel (who must, she afterwards decided, have been doing a spot of overtime) impelled her to add: 'But then, you see, I shouldn't want to.'

This seemingly innocent confession had a surprising effect on Reuben. He banged down his cup and thrust his face forward, peering intently into hers.

'Wouldn't you, then? Ah, but you'd pay a hired man good money to do it for you, I'll lay – wastin' the farm's takin's.'

Flora was now beginning to see what was the matter. He thought she had designs on the farm!

'Indeed I wouldn't,' she retorted promptly. 'I wouldn't care if Ticklepenny's Corner wasn't scranleted at all. I don't want to have anything to do with Nettle Flitch. I'd let' – she smiled pleasantly up to

Reuben – 'I'd let you do it all instead.'

But this effort went sour on her, to her dismay.

'Let!' shouted Reuben, thumping the table. 'Let! A mirksy, capsy word to use to a man as has nursed a farm like a sick mommet – and a man as knows every inch of soil and patch o' sukebind i' the place. Let . . . aye, a fine word —'

'I really think we had better get this straight,' interrupted Flora. 'It will make things so much easier. I don't want the farm. Really, I don't. In fact' – she hesitated whether she should tell him that it seemed incredible to her that anyone could possibly want it, but decided that this would be rude as well as unkind – 'well, such an idea never came into my head. I know nothing about farming, and I don't want to. I would much rather leave it to people who do know everything about it, like you. Why, just think what a mess I should make of the sukebind harvest and everything. You must see that I am the last person in the world who would be any use at scranleting. I am sure you will believe me.'

A second series of tremors, of a slightly more complicated type than the first, passed across Reuben's face. He seemed about to speak, but in the end he did not. He slapped down his cup, gave a last stare at Flora, and stumped out of the kitchen.

This was an unsatisfactory end to the interview, which had begun well; but she was not disturbed. It was obvious that, even if he did not believe her, he wanted to; and that was half the battle. He had even been on the verge of believing her when she made that lucky remark about not wanting to scranlet; and only his natural boorishness and his suspicious nature had prevented him. The next time she assured him that she was not after Cold Comfort Farm, Reuben would be convinced that she spoke the truth.

The fire was now burning brightly. Flora lit a candle, which she had brought down from her bedroom, and took up some sewing with which to beguile the time until supper in her own room. She was making a petticoat and decorating it with drawn threadwork.

A little later, as she sat peacefully sewing, Adam came in from the yard. He wore, as a protection from the rain, a hat which had lost – in who knows what dim hintermath of time – the usual attributes of shape, colour, and size, and those more subtle race-memory associations which identify hats as hats, and now resembled some obscure natural growth, some moss or sponge or fungus, which had attached itself to a host.

He was carrying between finger and thumb a bunch of thorn twigs, which Flora presumed that he had just picked from one of the trees in the yard; and he held them ostentatiously in front of him, like a torch.

He glanced spitefully at Flora from under the brim of the hat as he crossed the kitchen, but said nothing to her. As he placed the twigs carefully on a shelf above the sink, he glanced round at her, but she went on sewing, and said never a word. So after rearranging the twigs once or twice, and coughing, he muttered:

'Aye, them'll last me till Michaelmas to cletter the dishes wi' – there's nothing like a thorn twig for cletterin' dishes. Aye, a rope's as good as a halter to a willin' horse. Curses, like rookses, flies home to rest in bosomses and barnses.'

It was clear that he had not forgotten Flora's advice about using a little mop to clean the dishes. As he shuffled away, she thought that she must remember to buy one for him the next time she went into Howling.

Flora had scarcely time to get over this before there sounded a step in the yard outside, and there entered a young man who could only be Seth.

Flora looked up with a cool smile.

'How do you do? Are you Seth? I'm your cousin, Flora Poste. I'm afraid you're too late for any tea ... unless you would like to make some fresh for yourself.'

He came over to her with the lounging grace of a panther, and leaned against the mantelpiece. Flora saw at once that he was not the kind that could be fobbed off with offers of tea. She was for it.

'What's that you're making?' he asked. Flora knew that he hoped it was a pair of knickers. She composedly shook out the folds of the petticoat and replied that it was an afternoon teacloth.

'Aye ... woman's nonsense,' said Seth, softly. (Flora wondered why he had seen fit to drop his voice by half an octave.) 'Women are all alike – ay fussin' over their fal-lals and bedazin' a man's eyes, when all they really want is man's blood and his heart out of his body and his soul and his pride ...'

'Really?' said Flora, looking in her workbox for her scissors.

'Aye.' His deep voice had jarring notes which were curiously blended into an animal harmony like the natural cries of stoat or weasel. 'That's all women want – a man's life. Then when they've got him bound up in their fal-lals and bedazin' ways and their softness, and he can't move because of the longin' for them as cries in his man's blood – do you know what they do then?'

'I'm afraid not,' said Flora. 'Would you mind passing me that reel of cotton on the mantelpiece, just by your ear? Thank you so much.' Seth passed it mechanically, and continued.

'They eat him, same as a hen-spider eats a cock-spider. That's what women do – if a man lets 'em.'

'Indeed,' commented Flora.

'Aye – but I said "if" a man lets 'em. Now I – I don't let no women eat me. I eats them instead.'

Flora thought an appreciative silence was the best policy to pursue at this point. She found it difficult, indeed, to reply to him in words, since his conversation, in which she had participated before (at parties in

Bloomsbury as well as in drawing-rooms in Cheltenham), was, after all, mainly a kind of jockeying for place, a shifting about of the pieces on the board before the real game began. And if, in her case, one of the players was merely a little bored by it all and was wondering whether she would be able to brew some hot milk before she went to bed that night, there was not much point in playing.

True, in Cheltenham and in Bloomsbury gentlemen did not say in so many words that they ate women in self-defence, but there was no doubt that that was what they meant.

'That shocks you, eh?' said Seth, misinterpreting her silence.

'Yes, I think it's dreadful,' replied Flora, good-naturedly meeting him halfway.

He laughed. It was a cruel sound like the sputter of the stoat as it sinks its feet into the neck of a rabbit.

'Dreadful ... aye! You're all alike. You're just the same as the rest, for all your London ways. Mealy-mouthed as a schoolkid. I'll lay you don't understand half of what I've been saying, do you? ... Liddle innercent.'

'I am afraid I wasn't listening to all of it,' she replied, 'but I am sure it was very interesting. You must tell me all about your work some time ... What do you do, now, on the evenings when you aren't – er – eating people?'

'I goes over to Beershorn,' replied Seth, rather sulkily. The dark flame of his male pride was a little suspicious of having its leg pulled.

'To play darts?' Flora knew her A.P.H.

'Noa ... me play that kid's game with a lot of old men? That's a good 'un, that is. No. I goes to the talkies.'

And something in the inflection which Seth gave to the last word of his speech, the lingering, wistful, almost cooing note which invaded his curiously animal voice, caused Flora to put down her sewing in her lap and to glance up at him. Her gaze rested thoughtfully upon his irregular but handsome features.

'The talkies, do you? Do you like them?'

'Better nor anything in the whoal world,' he said, fiercely. 'Better nor my mother nor this farm nor Violet down at the Vicarage, nor anything.'

'Indeed,' mused his cousin, still eyeing his face thoughtfully. 'That's interesting. Very interesting indeed.'

'I've got seventy-four photographs o' Lotta Funchal,' confided Seth, becoming in his discussions of his passion like those monkeys which are described as 'almost human.' 'Aye, an' forty o' Jenny Carrol, and fifty-five o' Laura Vallee, and twenty o' Carline Heavytree, and fifteen of Sigrid Maelstrom. Aye, an' ten o' Panella Baxter. Signed ones.'

Flora nodded, displaying courteous interest, but showing nothing of the plan which had suddenly occurred to her; and Seth, after a suspicious glance at her, suddenly decided that he had been betrayed into talking to a woman about something else than love, and was angry.

So, muttering that he was going off to Beershorn to see 'Sweet Sinners' (he was evidently inflamed by this discussion of his passion), he took himself off.

The rest of the evening passed quietly. Flora supped off an omelette and some coffee, which she prepared in her own sitting-room. After supper she finished the design upon the breast of her petticoat, read a chapter of *Macaria, or Altars of Sacrifice*, and went to bed at ten o'clock.

All this was pleasant enough. And while she was undressing, she reflected that her campaign for the tidying up of Cold Comfort was progressing quite well, when she thought that she had only been there two days. She had made overtures to Reuben. She had instructed Meriam, the hired girl, in the precautionary arts, and she had gotten her bedroom curtains washed (they hung full and crimson in the candle-light). She had discovered the nature of Seth's *grande passion*, and it was not Women, but the Talkies. She had had a plan for making the most of Seth, but she could think that out in detail later. She blew out the candle.

But (she thought, settling her cool forehead against the cold pillow) this habit of passing her evenings in peaceful solitude in her own sitting-room must not make her forget her plan of campaign. It was clear that she must take some of her meals with the Starkadders, and learn to know them.

She sighed: and fell asleep.

How I Killed a Bear

CHARLES DUDLEY WARNER

SO MANY CONFLICTING accounts have appeared about my casual encounter with an Adirondack bear last summer, that in justice to the public, to myself and to the bear, it is necessary to make a plain statement of the facts. Besides, it is so seldom I have occasion to kill a bear, that the celebration of the exploit may be excused.

The encounter was unpremeditated on both sides. I was not hunting for a bear, and I have no reason to suppose that a bear was looking for me. The fact is, that we were both out blackberrying and met by chance – the usual way. There is among the Adirondack visitors always a great deal of conversation about bears - a general expression of the wish to see one in the woods, and much speculation as to how a person would act if he or she chanced to meet one. But bears are scarce and timid, and appear only to a favored few.

It was a warm day in August, just the sort of a day when an adventure of any kind seemed impossible. But it occurred to the housekeepers at our cottage – there were four of them – to send me to the clearing, on the mountain back of the house, to pick blackberries. It was, rather, a series of small clearings, running up into the forest, much overgrown with bushes and briers, and not unromantic. Cows pastured there, penetrating through the leafy passages from one opening to another, and browsing among the bushes. I was kindly furnished with a six-quart pail, and told not to be gone long.

Not from any predatory instinct, but to save appearances, I took a gun. It adds to the manly aspect of a person with a tin pail if he also carries a gun. It was possible I might start up a partridge; though how I was to hit him, if he started up instead of standing still, puzzled me. Many people use a shotgun for partridges. I prefer the rifle: it makes a clean job of death, and does not prematurely stuff the bird with globules of lead. The rifle was a Sharps, carrying a ball cartridge (ten to the pound) – an excellent weapon belonging to a friend of mine, who had intended, for a good many years back, to kill a deer with it. He could hit a tree with it – if the wind did not blow, and the atmosphere was just right, and the tree was not too far off – nearly every time. Of course, the tree must have some size. Needless to say that I was at that time no sportsman. Years ago I killed a robin under the most humiliating circumstances. The bird was in a low cherrytree. I loaded a big shotgun pretty full, crept up under the

86

tree, rested the gun on the fence, with the muzzle more than ten feet from the bird, shut both eyes and pulled the trigger. When I got up to see what had happened, the robin was scattered about under the tree in more than a thousand pieces, no one of which was big enough to enable a naturalist to decide from it to what species it belonged. This disgusted me with the life of a sportsman. I mention the incident to show, that although I went blackberrying armed, there was not much inequality between me and the bear.

In this blackberry patch bears had been seen. The summer before, our colored cook, accompanied by a little girl of the vicinage, was picking berries there one day, when a bear came out of the woods and walked toward them. The girl took to her heels, and escaped. Aunt Chloe was paralyzed with terror. Instead of attempting to run, she sat down on the ground where she was standing, and began to weep and scream, giving herself up for lost. The bear was bewildered by this conduct. He approached and looked at her; he walked around and surveyed her. Probably he had never seen a colored person before, and did not know whether she would agree with him: at any rate, after watching her a few moments, he turned about and went into the forest. This is an authentic instance of the delicate consideration of a bear, and is much more remarkable than the forbearance towards the African slave of the well-known lion, because the bear had no thorn in his foot.

When I had climbed the hill, I set up my rifle against a tree, and began picking berries, lured on from bush to bush by the black gleam of fruit (that always promises more in the distance than it realizes when you reach it); penetrating farther and farther, through leaf-shaded cowpaths flecked with sunlight, into clearing after clearing. I could hear on all sides the tinkle of bells, the cracking of sticks, and the stamping of cattle that were taking refuge in the thicket from the flies. Occasionally, as I broke through a covert, I encountered a meek cow, who stared at me stupidly for a second, and then shambled off into the brush. I became accustomed to this dumb society, and picked on in silence, attributing all the woodnoises to the cattle, thinking nothing of any real bear. In point of fact, however, I was thinking all the time of a nice romantic bear, and, as I picked, was composing a story about a generous she-bear who had lost her cub, and who seized a small girl in this very wood, carried her tenderly off to a cave, and brought her up on bear's milk and honey. When the girl got big enough to run away, moved by her inherited instincts, she escaped, and came into the valley to her father's house (this part of the story was to be worked out, so that the child would know her father by some family resemblance, and have some language in which to address him), and told him where the bear lived. The father took his gun, and, guided by the unfeeling daughter, went into the woods and shot the bear, who never made any resistance, and only, when dying, turned

87

reproachful eyes upon her murderer. The moral of the tale was to be, kindness to animals.

I was in the midst of this tale, when I happened to look some rods away to the other edge of the clearing, and there was a bear! He was standing on his hindlegs, and doing just what I was doing – picking blackberries. With one paw he bent down the bush, while with the other he clawed the berries into his mouth – green ones and all. To say that I was astonished is inside the mark. I suddenly discovered that I didn't want to see a bear, after all. At about the same moment the bear saw me, stopped eating berries, and regarded me with a glad surprise. It is all very well to imagine what you would do under such circumstances. Probably you wouldn't do it: I didn't. The bear dropped down on his forefeet, and came slowly towards me. Climbing a tree was of no use, with so good a climber in the rear. If I started to run, I had no doubt the bear would give chase; and although a bear cannot run down hill as fast as he can run uphill, yet I felt that he could get over this rough, brush-tangled ground faster than I could.

The bear was aproaching. It suddenly occurred to me how I could divert his mind until I could fall back upon my military base. My pail was nearly full of excellent berries – much better than the bear could pick himself. I put the pail on the ground, and slowly backed away from it, keeping my eye, as beast tamers do, on the bear. The ruse succeeded.

The bear came up to the berries, and stopped. Not accustomed to eat out of a pail, he tipped it over, and nosed about in the fruit, 'gorming' (if there is such a word) it down, mixed with leaves and dirt, like a pig. The bear is a worse feeder than the pig. Whenever he disturbs a maple-sugar camp in the spring, he always upsets the buckets of syrup, and tramples round in the sticky sweets, wasting more than he eats. The bear's manners are thoroughly disagreeable.

As soon as my enemy's head was down, I started and ran. Somewhat out of breath, and shaky, I reached my faithful rifle. It was not a moment too soon. I heard the bear crashing through the brush after me. Enraged at my duplicity, he was now coming on with blood in his eye. I felt that the time of one of us was probably short. The rapidity of thought at such moments of peril is well known. I thought an octavo volume, had it illustrated and published, sold fifty thousand copies, and went to Europe on the proceeds, while the bear was loping across the clearing. As I was cocking the gun, I made a hasty and unsatisfactory review of my whole life. I noted that, even in such a compulsory review, it is almost impossible to think of any good thing you have done. The sins come out uncommonly strong. I recollected a newspaper subscription I had delayed paying years and years ago, until both editor and newspaper were dead, and which now never could be paid to all eternity.

The bear was coming on.

I tried to remember what I had read about encounters with bears. I couldn't recall an instance in which a man had run away from a bear in the woods and escaped, although I recalled plenty where the bear had run from the man and got off. I tried to think what is the best way to kill a bear with a gun, when you are not near enough to club him with the stock. My first thought was to fire at his head; to plant the ball between his eyes: but this is a dangerous experiment. The bear's brain is very small; and, unless you hit that, the bear does not mind a bullet in his head; that is, not at the time. I remembered that the instant death of the bear would follow a bullet planted just back of his foreleg, and sent into his heart. This spot is also difficult to reach, unless the bear stands off, side towards you, like a target. I finally determined to fire at him generally.

The bear was coming on.

The contest seemed to me very different from anything at Creedmoor. I had carefully read the reports of the shooting there; but it was not easy to apply the experience I had thus acquired. I hesitated whether I had better fire lying on my stomach; or lying on my back, and resting the gun on my toes. But in neither position, I reflected, could I see the bear until he was upon me. The range was too short; and the bear wouldn't wait for me to examine the thermometer, and note the direction of the wind. Trial of the Creedmore method, therefore, had to be abandoned; and I bitterly regretted that I had not read more accounts of offhand shooting.

For the bear was coming on.

I tried to fix my last thoughts upon my family. As my family is small, this was not difficult. Dread of displeasing my wife, or hurting her feelings, was uppermost in my mind. What would be her anxiety as hour after hour passed on, and I did not return! What would the rest of the household think as the afternoon passed, and no blackberries came! What would be my wife's mortification when the news was brought that her husband had been eaten by a bear! I cannot imagine anything more ignominious than to have a husband eaten by a bear. And this was not my only anxiety. The mind at such times is not under control. With the gravest fears the most whimsical ideas will occur. I looked beyond the mourning friends, and thought what kind of an epitaph they would be compelled to put upon the stone. Something like this:

HERE LIE THE REMAINS

OF

———— ————

EATEN BY A BEAR

Aug. 20, 1877.

It is a very unheroic and even disagreeable epitaph. That 'eaten by a bear' is intolerable. It is grotesque. And then I thought what an inadequate language the English is for compact expression. It would not answer to put upon the stone simply 'eaten,' for that is indefinite, and requires explanation: it might mean eaten by a cannibal. This difficulty could not occur in the German, where *essen* signifies the act of feeding by a man, and *fressen* by a beast. How simple the thing would be in German! –

HIER LIEGT

HOCHWOHLGEBOREN

HERR ———— ————,

GEFRESSEN

Aug. 20, 1877.

That explains itself. The well-born one was eaten by a beast, and presumably by a bear – an animal that has a bad reputation since the days of Elisha.

The bear was coming on; he had, in fact, come on. I judged that he could see the whites of my eyes. All my subsequent reflections were confused. I raised the gun, covered the bear's breast with the sight, and let drive. Then I turned, and ran like a deer. I did not hear the bear pursuing. I looked back. The bear had stopped. He was lying down. I then remembered that the best thing to do after having fired your gun is to reload it. I slipped in a charge, keeping my eyes on the bear. He never stirred. I walked back suspiciously. There was a quiver in the hindlegs, but no other motion. Still, he might be shamming: bears often sham. To make sure, I approached, and put a ball into his head. He didn't mind it now; he minded nothing. Death had come to him with a merciful suddenness. He was calm in death. In order that he might remain so, I blew his brains out, and then started for home. I had killed a bear!

Notwithstanding my excitement, I managed to saunter into the house with an unconcerned air. There was a chorus of voices:

'Where are your blackberries?'

'Why were you gone so long?'

'Where's your pail?'

'I left the pail.'

'Left the pail? What for?'

'A bear wanted it.'

'Oh, nonsense!'

'Well, the last I saw of it a bear had it.'

'Oh, come! You didn't really see a bear?'

'Yes, but I did really see a real bear.'

'Did he run?'

'Yes; he ran after me.'

'I don't believe a word of it! What did you do?'

'Oh! nothing particular – except kill the bear.'

Cries of 'Gammon!' 'Don't believe it!' 'Where's the bear?'

'If you want to see the bear, you must go up into the woods. I couldn't bring him down alone.'

Having satisfied the household that something extraordinary had occurred, and excited the posthumous fear of some of them for my own safety, I went down into the valley to get help. The great bear-hunter, who keeps one of the summer boarding-houses, received my story with a smile of incredulity; and the incredulity spread to the other inhabitants and to the boarders, as soon as the story was known. However, as I insisted in all soberness, and offered to lead them to the bear, a party of forty or fifty people at last started off with me to bring the bear in. Nobody believed there was any bear in the case; but everybody who could get a gun carried one; and we went into the woods, armed with guns, pistols, pitchforks and sticks, against all contingencies or surprises – a crowd made up mostly of scoffers and jeerers.

'But when I led the way to the fatal spot, and pointed out the bear, lying peacefully wrapped in his own skin, something like terror seized the boarders, and genuine excitement the natives. It was a no-mistake bear, by George! and the hero of the fight – well, I will not insist upon that. But what a procession that was, carrying the bear home! and what a congregation was speedily gathered in the valley to see the bear! Our best preacher up there never drew anything like it on Sunday.

And I must say that my particular friends, who were sportsmen, behaved very well on the whole. They didn't deny that it was a bear, although they said it was small for a bear. Mr Deane, who is equally good with a rifle and a rod, admitted that it was a very fair shot. He is probably the best salmonfisher in the United States, and he is an equally good hunter. I suppose there is no person in America who is more desirous to kill a moose than he. But he needlessly remarked, after he had examined the wound in the bear, that he had seen that kind of a shot made by a cow's horn.

This sort of talk affected me not. When I went to sleep that night, my last delicious thought was, 'I've killed a bear!'

A Day in the Life of a Milligan

SPIKE MILLIGAN

In the heart of the rural Irish border country a reluctant labourer sets forth at the beginning of another working day....

THE DAN MILLIGAN CYCLED tremendously towards the Church of St Theresa of the Little Flowers. Since leaving the area known as his wife he had brightened up a little. 'Man alive! The *size* of her though, she's a danger to shipping, I mean, every time I put me key in the front door I'll wonder what I'm lettin' meself in for.' Away down a lumpy road he pedalled, his right trouser leg being substantially chewed to pulp in the chain. His voice was raised in that high nasal Irish tenor, known and hated the world over.

'Ohhhhhhhhhhhhhhh IIIIIIIIIIIIIII
    Once knew a judy in Dubleen Town
    Her eyes were blue and her hair was brown,
    One night on the grass I got her down
    And I...'

The rest of the words were lost to view as he turned a bend in the road. Farther along, from an overhanging branch, a pure-blooded Irish cow watched the Milligan approach. It also watched him hit the pothole, leave the bike, strike the ground, clutch the shin, scream the agony, swear the word. 'Caw!' said the crow. 'Balls!' said the Milligan. Peering intently from behind the wall was something that Milligan could only hope was a face. The fact that it was hanging from a hat gave credulity to his belief.

'Are you all right, Milligan?' said the face in the hat.

'Oh ho!' Milligan's voice showed recognition. 'It's Murphy. Tell me, why are you wearing dat terrible lookin' trilby?'

'We sold der hat stand, an' dere's no place ter hang it.' Murphy's face was a replica of the King Edwards he grew. He did in fact look like King Edward the Seventh. He also resembled King Edward the Third, Fifth and Second, making a grand total of King Edward the Seventeenth. He had a mobile face, that is, he always took it with him. His nose was what the French call retroussé, or as we say, like a pig; his nostrils were so acutely angled, in stormy weather the rain got in and forced him indoors.

His eyebrows grew from his head like Giant Coypu rats, but dear friends, when you and I talk of eyebrows, we know not what eyebrows be until we come face to face with the *Murphy's* eyebrows! The man's head was a veritable plague of eyebrows, black, grey, brown and red they grew, thick as thieves. They covered two-thirds of his skull, both his temples and the entire bridge of his nose. In dry weather they bristled from his head like the spears of an avenging army and careless flies were impaled by the score. In winter they glistened with hoar-frost and steamed by the fire. When wet they hung down over his eyes and he was put to shaking himself like a Cocker Spaniel before he could proceed. For all their size dose eyebrows were as mobile as piglets, and in moments of acute agitation had been seen as far south as his chin. At the first sight of Milligan they had wagged up and down, agitati ma non troppo. As he spoke they both began to revolve round his head at speed.

'I heeerd a crash,' said Murphy. 'I examined meself, and I knew it wasn't me.'

'It was me,' said Milligan. 'I felled off me bi-cycle. Tank heaven the ground broke me fall.'

'Oh yes, it's very handy like dat,' said Murphy, settling his arms along the wall.

'Oh dear, dear!' said Milligan, getting to his feet. 'I've scratched all the paint off the toe of me boot.'

'Is dat right den, you paint yer boots?'

'True, it's the most economical way. Sometimes I paints 'em brown, when I had enough o' dat I paints 'em black again. Dat way people tink you got more than one pair, see? Once when I played the cricket I painted 'em white, you should try dat.'

'Oh no,' said Murphy solemnly. 'Oh no, I don't like inteferring wid nature. Der natural colour of boots is black as God ordained, any udder colour and a man is askin' fer trouble.'

'Oh, and what I may ask is wrong wid brown boots?'

'How do I know? I never had a pair.'

'Take my tip, Murphy, you got to move wid der times man. The rich people in Dublin are all wearin' the brown boots; when scientists spend a lifetime inventin' a thing like the brown boots, we should take advantage of the fact.'

'No, thank you,' said Murphy's eyebrows, 'I'll stick along wid the inventor of the black boots. After all they don't show the dirt.'

'Dat's my argument, black don't show the dirt, brown ones don't show the mud and a good pair of green boots won't show the grass.'

'By Gor', you got something dere,' said the Murphy. 'But wait, when you was wearing dem white boots, what didn't dey show?'

'They didn't show me feet,' said Milligan, throwing himself on to the bike and crashing down on the other side.

'Caw!' said the crow.

'BALLS!' said Milligan. 'I'll be on me way.' He remounted and pedalled off.

'No, stay and have a little more chat,' called Murphy across the widening gap. 'Parts round here are lonely and sparse populated.'

'Well it's not for the want of you tryin',' came the fading reply.

The day brewed hotter now, it was coming noon. The hedgerows hummed with small things that buzzed and bumbled in the near heat. From the cool woods came a babel of chirruping birds. The greenacious daisy-spattled fields spread out before Milligan, the bayonets of grass shining bravely in the sun, above him the sky was an exaltation of larks. Slowfully Milligan pedalled on his way. Great billy bollers of perspiration were running down his knees knose and kneck, the torrents ran down his shins into his boots where they escaped through the lace holes as steam. 'Now,' thought the Milligan, 'why are me legs goin' round and round? eh? I don't tink it's me doin' it, in fact, if I had me way dey wouldn't be doin' it at all. But dere dey are goin' round and round; what den was der drivin' force behind dose legs? Me wife! *That's* what's drivin' 'em round and round, dat's the truth, dese legs are terrified of me wife, terrified of bein' kicked in the soles of the feet again.' It was a disgrace how a fine mind like his should be taken along by a pair of terrified legs. If only his mind had a pair of legs of its own they'd be back at the cottage being bronzed in the Celtic sun.

The Milligan had suffered from his legs terribly. During the war in Italy. While his mind was full of great heroisms under shell fire, his legs were carrying the idea, at speed, in the opposite direction. The Battery Major had not understood.

'Gunner Milligan? You have been acting like a coward.'

'No sir, not true. I'm a hero wid coward's legs, I'm a hero from the waist up.'

'Silence! Why did you leave your post?'

'It had woodworm in it, sir, the roof of the trench was falling in.'

'Silence! You acted like a coward!'

'I wasn't acting sir!'

'I could have you shot!'

'Shot?' Why didn't they shoot me in peacetime? I was still the same coward.'

'Men like you are a waste of time in war. Understand?'

'Oh? Well den! Men like *you* are a waste of time in peace.'

'Silence when you speak to an officer,' shouted the Sgt Major at Milligan's neck.

All his arguments were of no avail in the face of military authority. He was court martialled, surrounded by clanking top brass who were not cowards and therefore biased.

'I may be a coward, I'm not denying dat sir,' Milligan told the prosecution. 'But you can't really *blame* me for being a coward. If I am, then you might as well hold me responsible for the shape of me nose, the colour of me hair and the size of me feet.'

'Gunner Milligan,' Captain Martin stroked a cavalry moustache on an infantry face. 'Gunner Milligan,' he said. 'Your personal evaluations of cowardice do not concern the court. To refresh your memory I will read the precise military definition of the word.'

He took a book of King's Regulations, opened a marked page and read 'Cowardice'. Here he paused and gave Milligan a look.

He continued: 'Defection in the face of the enemy. Running away.'

'I was not running away sir, I was retreating.'

'The whole of your Regiment were advancing, and you decided to retreat?'

'Isn't dat what you calls personal initiative?'

'Your action might have caused your comrades to panic and retreat.'

'Oh, I see! One man retreating is called running away, but a whole Regiment running away is called a retreat? I demand to be tried by cowards!'

A light, commissioned-ranks-only laugh passed around the court. But this was no laughing matter. These lunatics could have him shot.

'Have you anything further to add?' asked Captain Martin.

'Yes,' said Milligan. 'Plenty. For one ting I had no desire to partake in dis war. I was dragged in. I warned the Medical Officer, I told him I was a coward, and he marked me A.1. for Active Service. I gave everyone fair warning! I told me Battery Major before it started, I even wrote to Field Marshal Montgomery. Yes, I warned everybody, and now you're all acting surprised?'

Even as Milligan spoke his mind, three non-cowardly judges made a mental note of Guilty.

'Is that all?' queried Martin with all the assurance of a conviction. Milligan nodded. What was the use? After all, if Albert Einstein stood for a thousand years in front of fifty monkeys explaining the theory of relativity, at the end, they'd still be just monkeys.

Anyhow it was all over now, but he still had these cowardly legs which, he observed, were still going round and round. 'Oh dear, dis weather, I niver knowed it so hot.' It felt as though he could have grabbed a handful of air and squeezed the sweat out of it. 'I wonder,' he mused, 'how long can I go on losin' me body fluids at dis rate before I'm struck down with the dehydration? Ha ha! The answer to me problems,' he said, gleefully drawing level with the front door of the 'Holy Drunkard' pub.

'Hello! Hi-lee, Ho-la, Hup-la!' he shouted through the letter box.

Upstairs, a window flew up like a gun port, and a pig-of-a-face stuck itself out.

'What do you want, Milligan?' said the pig-of-a-face. Milligan doffed his cap.

'Ah, Missis O'Toole, you're looking more lovely dan ever. Is there any chance of a cool libation for a tirsty traveller?'

'Piss off!' said the lovely Mrs O'Toole.

'Oh what a witty tongue you have today,' said Milligan, gallant in defeat. Well, he thought, you can fool some of the people all the time and all the people some of the time, which is just long enough to be President of the United States, and on that useless profundity, Milligan himself pedalled on, himself, himself.

'Caw!' said a crow.

'Balls!' said Milligan.

Father Patrick Rudden paused as he trod the gravel path of the church drive. He ran his 'kerchief round the inside of his holy clerical collar. Then he walked slowly to the grave of the late Miss Griselda Strains and pontifically lowered his ecclesiastical rump on to the worn slab, muttering a silent apology to the departed lady, but reflecting, it wouldn't be the first time she'd had a man on top of her, least of all one who apologized as he did. He was a tall handsome man touching fifty, but didn't appear to be speeding. His stiff white hair was yellowed with frequent applications of anointment oil. The width of neck and shoulder suggested a rugby player, the broken nose confirmed it. Which shows how wrong you can be as he never played the game in his life. The clock in the church tower said 4.32, as it had done for three hundred years. It was right once a day and that was better than no clock at all. How old the church was no-one knew. It was, like Mary Brannigan's black baby, a mystery. Written records went back to 1530. The only *real* clue was the discovery of a dead skeleton under the ante-chapel. Archaeologists from Dublin had got wind of it and come racing up in a lorry filled with little digging men, instruments and sandwiches.

'It's the bones of an Ionian monk,' said one grey professor. For weeks they took photos of the dear monk. They measured his skull, his shins, his dear elbows; they took scrapings from his pelvis, they took a plaster cast of the dear fellow's teeth, they dusted him with resin and preserving powders and finally the professors had all agreed, the Monk was one thousand five hundred years old. 'Which accounts for him being dead,' said the priest, and that was that.

Money! That was the trouble. Money! The parish was spiritually solvent but financially bankrupt. Money! The Lord will provide, but to date he was behind with his payments. Money! Father Rudden had tried everything to raise funds, he even went to the bank. 'Don't be a fool, Father!' said the manager, 'Put that gun down.' Money! There was the occasion he'd promised to make fire to fall from heaven. The church had been packed. At the psychological moment the priest had mounted the pulpit and called loudly 'I command fire to fall from heaven!' A painful silence followed. The priest seemed uneasy. He repeated his invocation much louder, 'I COMMAND FIRE TO FALL FROM HEAVEN!' The sibilant voice of the verger came wafting hysterically from the loft. 'Just a minute, Father, the cat's pissed on the matches!'

It had been a black day for the church. Money! That was the trouble. His own shoes were so worn he knew every pebble in the church drive by touch. He poked a little gold nut of cheap tobacco into his pipe. As he drew smoke he looked at the honeyed stone of St Theresa, the church he had pastored for thirty years. A pair of nesting doves flew from the ivy on the tower. It was pretty quiet around here. There had been a little excitement during the insurgence; the Sinn Fein had held all their meetings in the bell tower and in consequence were all stone deaf. The priest didn't like bloodshed, after all we only have a limited amount, but what was he to do?

Freedom! The word had been burning through the land for nearly four hundred years. The Irish had won battles for everyone but themselves; now the fever of liberty was at the high peak of delirium, common men were incensed by injustice; now the talk was over and the guns were speaking. Father Rudden had thrown in his lot with 'the lads' and had harboured gunmen on the run. They had won but alas, even then, Ulster had come out against the union. For months since the armistice, dozens of little semi-important men with theodolites and creased trousers, were running in all directions in a frenzy of mensuration, threats and rock-throwing, all trying to agree the new border.

The sound of a male bicycle frame drew the priest's attention. There coming up the drive was the worst Catholic since Genghis Khan.

'Ah, top of the morning to yez, Father,' Milligan said dismounting.

'Well, well, Dan Milligan.' There was surprise and pleasure in the priest's voice. 'Tell me, Dan, what are you doing so far from your dear bed?'

'I'm feeling much better, Father.'

'Oh? You been ill then?'

'No, but I'm feeling much better now dan I felt before.'

There was a short pause, then a longer one, but so close were they together, you couldn't tell the difference.

'It's unexpectedly hot fer dis time of the year, Father.'

'Very hot, Milligan. Almost hot enough to burn a man's conscience, eh?'

'Ha ha, yes, Father,' he laughed weakly, his eyes two revelations of guilt.

'When did you last come to church, Milligan?'

'Oh, er, I forget – but I got it on me Baptismal certificate.'

The priest gave Milligan a long meaning stare which Milligan did not know the meaning of. Then the Milligan, still holding his bike, sat down next to the priest. 'By Gor Father, wot you tink of dis weather?'

Oh, it's hot all right,' said Father Rudden relighting his pipe. Producing a small clay decoy pipe, Milligan started to pat his empty pockets. 'Here,' said the priest, throwing him his tobacco pouch.

'Oh tank you Father, an unexpected little treat.'

Together the two men sat in silence; sometimes they stood in silence which after all is sitting in silence only higher up. An occasional signal of smoke escaped from the bowl and scurried towards heaven. 'Now Milligan,' the priest eventually said, 'what is the purpose of this visit?' Milligan knew that this was, as the Spaniards say, 'El Momento de la Verdad', mind you, he didn't think it in Spanish, but if he had, that's what it would have looked like.

'Well Father,' he began, puffing to a match, 'well, I – "puff-puff-puff" – I come to see – "puff-puff" – if dis grass cuttin' – job – "puff-puff" – is still goin'.'

The inquiry shook the priest into stunned silence. In that brief moment the Milligan leaped on to his bike with a 'Ah well, so the job's gone, good-bye.' The priest recovered quickly, restraining Milligan by the seat of the trousers.

'Oh, steady Father,' gasped Milligan, 'dem's more then me trousers yer clutchin'.'

'Sorry, Milligan,' said the priest, releasing his grip. 'We celibates are inclined to forget them parts.' 'Well you can forget mine fer a start,' thought Milligan. Why in God's name did men have to have such tender genitals. He had asked his grandfather that question. 'Don't worry 'bout yer old genitals lad,' said the old man, 'they'll stand up fer themselves.'

What about that terrible, terrible evening so long ago? Dan Milligan was seventeen, he had arrived for his first date with Mary Nolan. Her father had ushered him into the parlour with a forked vermin stick. Alone in the room with him was Mary's youngest brother, a little toddler of four. The little fellow carried in his hand such an innocent thing as a clay lion, but this, plus momentum, and brought unexpectedly into violent contact with Milligan's testicles, caused him to writhe and scream with pain; at which moment the radiant Mary chose to enter the room. To be caught clutching himself so was too much for the sensitive Dan. With only the whites of his eyes showing, he disguised his convulsions as a macabre Highland fling. Cross-eyed, bent double and screaming 'Och aye!' he danced from the room and she never saw him again. For many years after, young Dan Milligan wore an outsized cricketer's protective cup; during the mixed bathing season, many ladies made his acquaintance, only to be disappointed later.

'Yes, there's plenty of work to be done, Dan,' the priest was saying. He led Milligan to the gardener's hut. A small wood plank shed tucked in a cluster of cool elms. 'Michael Collins himself hid in here from the Tans,' said the priest proudly as he opened the door.

'Did he ever cut the grass?'

'No, but once, when the English was after him he set fire to it. What a blaze! Twenty courtin' couples nearly burnt to death! Them's the tools.' The priest pointed to four sentinel scythes standing in the corner like steel flamingoes.

'Ooh!' Milligan backed away. 'They look awful heavy, Father. Would you like ter lift one to see if me fears are well founded?'

'Saints alive, Milligan, there's no weight in 'em at all, man,' said the priest, lifting one and making long sweeping strokes. 'See? No weight in 'em at all,' he repeated, holding his groin for suspected rupture. He stood at the door and pointed out. 'You can start against that wall there and work inwards. If only I was younger.'

So saying the priest made off up the path. As he did, Milligan thought he heard suppressed laughter coming from the holy man. Carefully Milligan folded his jacket and cap and placed them on the roots of a flowering oak. He turned and faced the ocean of tall waving grass. His unshaven face took on that worried look of responsibility. Spitting in his hands he took hold of the instrument. Placing his feet apart he threw the scythe behind him, then, with a cry of 'Hi ayeee! Hoo! Hup-la!' he let go with a mighteous low curling chop; it started way behind him but, never a man of foresight, so great was the initial momentum, by the time the scythe had travelled ninety degrees it was beyond his control. All he could do was hang on; the great blade flashed past his white terrified face disappearing behind his back, taking both of his arms out of sight and sockets, at the same time corkscrewing his legs which gave off an agonized crackling sound from his knees. For a brief poetic moment he stayed twisted and poised, then fell sideways like a felled ox. 'Must be nearly lunch time,' he thought as he hit the ground. The Lord said: 'Six days shalt thou labour and on the seventh thou shalt rest.' He hadn't reckoned wid the unions. Forty-eight hours a week shalt thou labour and on the seventh thou shalt get double time. Ha. It was more profitable to be in the unions.

As Milligan laboured unevenly through the afternoon, long overgrown tombstones came to light,

R.I.P.
Tom Conlon O'Rourke.
Not Dead, just Sleeping.

'He's not kiddin' anyone but himself,' Milligan chuckled irreverently. What was all dis dyin' about, anyhow? It was a strange and mysterious thing, no matter how you looked at it. 'I wonder what heaven is really like? Must be pretty crowded by now, it's been goin' a long time.' Did they have good lunches? Pity dere was so little information. Now, if there was more brochures on the place, more people might be interested in going dere. *Dat's* what the church needed, a good Public Relations man. 'Come to heaven where it's real cool.' 'Come to heaven and enjoy the rest.' 'Come to heaven where old friends meet, book now to avoid disappointment!' Little catch phrases like dat would do the place a power of good. Mind you, dere were other questions, like did people come back to earth after they die, like them Buddhists say.

In dat religion you got to come back as an animal. Mmm, a cat! Dat's the best animal to come back as, sleep all day, independent, ha! that was the life, stretched out in front of a fire, but no, Oh hell, they might give me that terrible cat operation, no no I forgot about that. Come to think of it, who the hell wants to come back again anyhow? Now, honest, how many people in life have had a good enough time to come back? Of course if you could come back as a woman you could see the other side of life? By gor, dat would be an experience, suppose you wakes up one morning and finds you're a woman? What would he do? Go for a walk and see what happens. Oh yes, all this dyin' was a funny business, still, it was better to believe in God than not. You certainly couldn't believe in men. Bernard Shaw said 'Every man over forty is a scoundrel', ha ha ha, Milligan laughed aloud, 'Every one round dese parts is a scoundrel at sixteen!' Bernard Shaw, dere was a great man, the Irish Noel Coward. A tiny insect with wings hovered stock still in front of Milligan's face. 'I wonder if he's tryin' to hypnotize me,' he thought, waving the creature away.

The sun bled its scarlet way to the horizon and the skies nodded into evening. The birds flew to their secret somewheres, and bats grew restless at the coming of night. Milligan puzzled at the church clock. 4.32? Good heavens, it gets dark early round here.

'How are you getting on then, Dan?'

At the sound of the priest's voice, Milligan put on a brief energetic display of hoeing. The priest blew his nose. 'Farnnn – farnnnnnnnn,' it went, in a deep melodious E♭. 'I think you've done enough for today, it's nearly seven.'

'Seven?' Milligan cursed in his head. 'Trust me to work to a bloody stopped clock!'

'You mustn't kill yerself, Milligan.'

'I'm in the right place if I do.'

They both laughed.

A cool breeze blew in from the Atlantic, fetching the smell of airborne waves. The first ectoplasms of evening mist were forming over the river. Here and there fishes mouthed an O at the still surface. The Angelus rang out its iron prayer. Murphy, out in his fields, dropped his hoe and joined hands in prayer. 'The Angel of the Lord declared unto Mary.'

The near Godless Milligan trundled his bike towards the Holy Drinker.

'IIIIIII

       Once knew a Judy in Dubleen town
       Her eyes were blue and her hair was brown
       One night on the grass I got her downnnn
       and the...'

The rest of the words were lost to view as the song turned a bend* in the road.

'I wonder if I'll see him again,' pondered Father Rudden. For that reason he had refrained from paying Milligan by the day.

*This was a different bend to the previous one. S.M.

Adventures of a YMCA Lad

H.L. MENCKEN

WHEN I REACH THE SHADES at last it will no doubt astonish Satan to discover, on thumbing my *dossier*, that I was once a member of the YMCA. Yet a fact is a fact. What is more remarkable, I was not recruited by a missionary to the heathen, but joined at the suggestion of my father, who enjoyed and deserved the name of an infidel. I was then a little beyond fourteen years old, and a new neighborhood branch of the Y, housed in a nobby pressed-brick building, had just been opened in West Baltimore, only a few blocks from our home in Hollins street. The whole upper floor was given over to a gymnasium, and it was this bait, I gathered, that fetched my father, for I was already a bookworm and beginning to be a bit round-shouldered, and he often exhorted me to throw back my shoulders and stick out my chest.

Apparently he was convinced that exercise on the wooden horse and flying rings would cure my scholarly stoop, and make a kind of grenadier of me. If so, he was in error, for I remain more or less Bible-backed to this day, and am often mistaken for a Talmudist. All that the YMCA's horse and rings really accomplished was to fill me with an ineradicable distaste, not only for Christian endeavor in all its forms, but also for every variety of callisthenics, so that I still begrudge the trifling exertion needed to climb in and out of a bathtub, and hate all sports as rabidly as a person who likes sports hates common sense. If I had my way no man guilty of golf would be eligible to any office of trust or profit under the United States, and all female athletes would be shipped to the white-slave corrals of the Argentine.

Indeed, I disliked that gymnasium so earnestly that I never got beyond its baby-class, which was devoted to teaching freshmen how to hang their clothes in the lockers, get into their work-suits, and run round the track. I was in those days a fast runner and could do the 100 yards, with a fair wind, in something better than fourteen seconds, but how anyone could run on a quadrangular track with sides no more than fifty feet long was quite beyond me. The first time I tried it I slipped and slid at all four corners, and the second time I came down with a thump that somehow contrived to skin both my shins. The man in charge of the establishment – the boys all called him Professor – thereupon put me to the punching-bag, but at my fourth or fifth wallop it struck back, and I was floored again. After that I tried all the other insane apparatus in the place, including the horizontal bars, but I always got into trouble very quickly, and never made enough progress to hurt myself seriously, which might have been some comfort, at least on the psychological side. There were other boys who fell from the highest trapezes, and had to be sent home in hacks, and yet others who broke their arms or legs and were heroic figures about the building for months afterward, but the best I ever managed was a bloody nose, and that was caused, not by my own enterprise, but by another boy falling on me from somewhere near the roof. If he had landed six inches farther inshore he might have fractured my skull or broken my neck, but all he achieved was to scrape my nose. It hurt a-plenty, I can tell you, and it hurt still worse when the Professor doused it with arnica, and splashed a couple of drops into each of my eyes.

Looking back over the years, I see that that ghastly gymnasium, if I had continued to frequent it, might have given me an inferiority complex, and bred me up a foe of privilege. I was saved, fortunately, by a congenital complacency that has been a godsend to me, more than once, in other and graver situations. Within a few weeks I was classifying all the boys in the place in the inverse order of their diligence and prowess, and that classification, as I have intimated, I adhere to at the present moment. The youngsters who could leap from bar to bar without slipping and were facile on the trapeze I equated with simians of the genus *Hylobates*, and convinced myself that I was surprised when they showed a capacity for articulate speech. As for the weight-lifters, chinners, somersaulters, leapers and other such virtuosi of straited muscle, I dismissed them as *Anthropoidea* far inferior, in all situations calling for taste or judgment, to schoolteachers or mules. .

I should add that my low view of these prizemen was unaccompanied by personal venom; on the contrary, I got on with them very well, and even had a kind of liking for some of them – that is, in their private capacities. Very few, I discovered, were professing Christians, though the YMCA, in those days even more than now, was a furnace of Protestant divinity. They swore when they stubbed their toes, and the older of them entertained us youngsters in the locker-room with their adventures in amour. The chief free-and-easy trysting-place in West Baltimore, at the time, was a Baptist church specializing in what was called 'young people's work.' It put on gaudy entertainments, predominantly secular in character, on Sunday nights, and scores of the poor working girls of the section dropped in to help with the singing and lasso beaux. I gathered from the locker-room talk that some of those beaux demanded dreadful prices for their consent to the lassoing. Whether this boasting was true or not I did not know, for I never attended the Sabbath evening orgies myself, but at all events it showed that those who did so were of an antinomian tendency, and far from ideal YMCA fodder. When the secretaries came to the gymnasium to drum up customers for prayer-meetings downstairs the Lotharios always sounded razzberries and cleared out.

On one point all hands were agreed, and that was on the point that the Professor was what, in those days, was called a pain in the neck. When he mounted a bench and yelled 'Fellows!' my own blood always ran cold, and his subsequent remarks gave me a touch of homicidal mania. Not until many years afterward, when a certain eminent political in Washington took to radio crooning, did I ever hear a more offensive voice. There were tones in it like the sound of molasses dripping from a barrel. It was not at all effeminate, but simply saccharine. Had I been older in worldly wisdom it would have suggested to me a suburban curate gargling over the carcass of a usurer who had just left the parish its richest and stupidest widow. As I was, an innocent boy, I could only compare it to the official chirping of a Sunday-school superintendent. What the Professor had to say was usually sensible enough, and I don't recall him ever mentioning either Heaven or Hell; it was simply his tone and manner that offended me. He is now dead, I take it, for many years, and I only hope that he has had good luck *post mortem*, but while he lived his harangues to his students gave me a great deal of unnecessary pain, and definitely slanted my mind against the YMCA. Even when, many years later, I discovered as a newspaper correspondent that the Berlin outpost thereof, under the name of the *christliche Verein junger Männer*, was so enlightened that it served beer in its lamissary, I declined to change my attitude.

But I was driven out of the YMCA at last, not by the Professor nor even by his pupils in the odoriferous gymnasium – what a foul smell, indeed, a gymnasium has! how it suggests a mixture of Salvation Army, elephant house, and county jail! – but by a young member who, so far as I observed, never entered the Professor's domain at all. He was a pimply, officious fellow of seventeen or eighteen, and to me, of course, he seemed virtually a grown man. The scene of his operations was the reading-room, whither I often resorted in self-defense when the Professor let go with 'Fellows!' and began one of his hortations. It was quiet there, and though most of the literature on tap was pietistic I enjoyed going through it, for my long interest in the sacred sciences had already begun. One evening, while engaged upon a pamphlet detailing devices for catching boys and girls who knocked down part of their Sunday-school money, I became aware of the pimply one, and presently saw him go to a bookcase and select a book. Dropping into a chair, he turned its pages feverishly, and presently he found what he seemed to be looking for, and cleared his throat to attact attention. The four or five of us at the long table all looked up.

'See here, fellows,' he began – again that ghastly 'fellows!' – 'let me have your ears for just a moment. Here is a book' – holding it up – 'that is worth all the other books ever written by mortal man. There is nothing like it on earth except the One Book that our Heavenly Father Himself gave us. It is pure gold, pure meat. There is not a wasted word in it. Every syllable is a perfect gem. For example, listen to this —'

What it was he read I don't recall precisely, but I remember that it was some thumping and appalling platitude or other – something on the order of 'Honesty is the best policy,' 'A guilty conscience needs no accuser,' or 'It is never too late to mend.' I guessed at first that he was trying to be ironical, but it quickly appeared that he was quite serious, and before his audience managed to escape he had read forty or fifty such specimens of otiose rubbish, and following nearly every one of them he indulged himself in a little homily, pointing up its loveliness and rubbing in its lesson. The poor ass, it appeared, was actually enchanted, and wanted to spread his joy. It was easy to recognize in him the anti-social animus of a born evangelist, but there was also something else – a kind of voluptuous delight in the shabby and preposterous, a perverted aesthetic-ism like that of a latter-day movie or radio fan, a wild will to roll in and snuffle balderdash as a cat rolls in and snuffles catnip. I was, as I have said, less than fifteen years old, but I had already got an overdose of such blah in the McGuffey Readers and penmanship copybooks of the time, so I withdrew as quickly as possible, unhappily aware that even the Professor was easier to take than this jitney Dwight L. Moody. I got home all tuckered out, and told my father (who was sitting up reading for the tenth or twentieth time a newspaper account of the hanging of two labor leaders) that the YMCA fell a good deal short of what it was cracked up to be.

He bade me go back the next evening and try again, and I did so in filial duty. Indeed, I did so a dozen or more nights running, omitting Sundays, when the place was given over to spiritual exercises exclusively. But each and every night that imbecile was in the reading-room, and each and every night he read from that revolting book to all within ear-shot. I gathered gradually that it was having a great run in devotional circles, and was, in fact, a sort of moral best-seller. The author, it appeared, was a Methodist bishop, and a great hand at inculcating righteousness. He not only knew by heart all the immemorial platitudes, stretching back to the days of Gog and Magog; he had also invented many more or less new ones, and it was these novelties that especially aroused the enthusiasm of his disciple. I wish I could recall some of them, but my memory has always had a humane faculty for obliterating the intolerable, and so I can't. But you may take my word for it that nothing in the subsequent writings of Dr Orison Swett Marden or Dr Frank Crane was worse.

In a little while my deliverance was at hand, for though my father had shown only irritation when I described to him the pulpit manner of the Professor, he was immediately sympathetic when I told him about the bishop's book, and the papuliferous exegete's laboring of it. 'You had better quit,' he said, 'before you hit him with a spittoon, or go crazy. There ought to be a law against such roosters.' *Rooster* was then his counter-word, and might signify anything from the most high-toned and elegant Shriner, bank cashier or bartender to the most scurvy and abandoned Socialist. This time he used it in its most opprobrious sense, and so my career in the YMCA came to an end. I carried away from it, not only an indelible distrust of every sort of athlete, but also a loathing of Methodist bishops, and it was many years afterward before I could bring myself to admit any such right rev. father in God to my friendship. I have since learned that some of them are very pleasant and amusing fellows, despite their professional enmity to the human race, but the one who wrote that book was certainly nothing of the sort. If, at his decease, he escaped Hell, then moral theology is as full of false alarms as secular law.

The House of Fahy

E.Œ. SOMERVILLE & MARTIN ROSS

NOTHING COULD SHAKE the conviction of Maria that she was by nature and by practice a house dog. Every one of Shreelane's many doors had, at one time or another, slammed upon her expulsion, and each one of them had seen her stealthy, irrepressible return to the sphere that she felt herself so eminently qualified to grace. For her the bone, thriftily interred by Tim Connor's terrier, was a mere diversion; even the fruitage of the ·ash-pit had little charm for an accomplished *habitué* of the kitchen. She knew to a nicety which of the doors could be burst open by assault, at which it was necessary to whine sycophantically; and the clinical thermometer alone could furnish a parallel for her perception of mood in those in authority. In the case of Mrs Cadogan she knew that there were seasons when instant and complete self-effacement was the only course to pursue; therefore when, on a certain morning in July, on my way through the downstairs regions to my office, I saw her approach the kitchen door with her usual circumspection, and, on hearing her name enunciated indignantly by my cook, withdraw swiftly to a city of refuge at the back of the hay-rick, I drew my own conclusions.

Had she remained, as I did, she would have heard the disclosure of a crime that lay more heavily on her digestion than her conscience.

'I can't put a thing out o' me hand but he's watching me to whip it away!' declaimed Mrs Cadogan, with all the disregard of her kind for the accident of sex in the brute creation. ''Twas only last night I was back in the scullery when I heard Bridget let a screech, and there was me brave dog up on the table eating the roast beef that was after coming out from the dinner!'

'Brute!' interjected Philippa, with what I well knew to be a simulated wrath.

'And I had planned that bit of beef for the luncheon,' continued Mrs Cadogan in impassioned lamentation, 'the way we wouldn't have to inthrude on the cold turkey! Sure he has it that dhragged, that all we can do with it now is run it through the mincing machine for the Major's sandwiches.'

At this appetizing suggestion I thought fit to intervene in the deliberations.

'One thing,' I said to Philippa afterwards, as I wrapped up a bottle of Yanatas in a Cardigan jacket and rammed it into an already apoplectic

Gladstone bag, 'that I do draw the line at, is taking that dog with us. The whole business is black enough as it is.'

'Dear,' said my wife, looking at me with almost clairvoyant abstraction, 'I could manage a second evening dress if you didn't mind putting my tea-jacket in your portmanteau.'

Little, thank Heaven! as I know about yachting, I knew enough to make pertinent remarks on the incongruity of an ancient sixty-ton hireling and a fleet of smart evening dresses; but none the less I left a pair of indispensable boots behind, and the tea-jacket went into my portmanteau.

It is doing no more than the barest justice to the officers of the Royal Navy to say that, so far as I know them, they cherish no mistaken enthusiasm for a home on the rolling deep when a home anywhere else presents itself. Bernard Shute had unfortunately proved an exception to this rule. During the winter, the invitation to go for a cruise in the yacht that was in process of building for him hung over me like a cloud; a timely strike in the builder's yard brought a respite, and, in fact, placed the completion of the yacht at so safe a distance that I was betrayed into specious regrets, echoed with an atrocious sincerity by Philippa. Into a life pastorally compounded of Petty Sessions and lawn tennis parties, retribution fell when it was least expected. Bernard Shute hired a yacht in Queenstown, and one short week afterwards the worst had happened, and we were packing our things for a cruise in her, the only alleviation being the knowledge that, whether by sea or land, I was bound to return to my work in four days.

We left Shreelane at twelve o'clock, a specially depressing hour for a start, when breakfast has died in you, and lunch is still remote. My last act before mounting the dogcart was to put her collar and chain on Maria and immure her in the potato-house, whence, as we drove down the avenue, her wails rent the heart of Philippa and rejoiced mine. It was a very hot day, with a cloudless sky; the dust lay thick on the white road, and on us also, as, during two baking hours, we drove up and down the long hills and remembered things that had been left behind, and grew hungry enough to eat sandwiches that tasted suspiciously of roast beef.

The yacht was moored in Clountiss Harbour; we drove through the village street, a narrow and unlovely thoroughfare, studded with public-houses, swarming with children and poultry, down through an ever-growing smell of fish, to the quay.

Thence we first viewed our fate, a dingy-looking schooner, and the hope I had secretly been nourishing that there was not wind enough for her to start, was dispelled by the sight of her topsail going up. More than ever at that radiant moment – as the reflection of the white sail quivered on the tranquil blue, and the still water flattered all it reproduced, like a fashionable photographer – did I agree with George Herbert's advice,

'Praise the sea, but stay on shore.'

'We must hail her, I suppose,' I said drearily. I assailed the *Eileen Oge*, such being her inappropriate name, with desolate cries, but achieved no immediate result beyond the assembling of some village children round us and our luggage.

'Mr Shute and the two ladies was after screeching here for the boat awhile ago,' volunteered a horrid little girl, whom I had already twice frustrated in the attempt to seat an infant relative on our bundle of rugs. 'Timsy Hallahane says 'twould be as good for them to stay ashore, for there isn't as much wind outside as 'd out a candle.'

With this encouraging statement the little girl devoted herself to the alternate consumption of gooseberries and cockles.

All things come to those who wait, and to us arrived at length the gig of the *Eileen Oge*, and such, by this time, were the temperature and the smells of the quay that I actually welcomed the moment that found us leaving it for the yacht.

'Now, Sinclair, aren't you glad we came?' remarked Philippa, as the clear green water deepened under us, and a light briny air came coolly round us with the motion of the boat.

As she spoke, there was an outburst of screams from the children on the quay, followed by a heavy splash.

'Oh stop!' cried Philippa in an agony; 'one of them has fallen in! I can see its poor little brown head!'

''Tis a dog, ma'am,' said briefly the man who was rowing stroke.

'One might have wished it had been that little girl,' said I, as I steered to the best of my ability for the yacht.

We had traversed another twenty yards or so, when Philippa, in a voice, in which horror and triumph were strangely blended, exclaimed, 'She's following us!'

'Who? The little girl?' I asked callously,

'No,' returned Philippa; 'worse!'

I looked round, not without a prevision of what I was to see, and beheld the faithful Maria swimming steadily after us, with her brown muzzle thrust out in front of her, ripping through the reflections like a plough.

'Go home!' I roared, standing up and gesticulating in fury that I well knew to be impotent. 'Go home, you brute!'

Maria redoubled her efforts, and Philippa murmured uncontrollably: 'Well, she *is* a dear!'

Had I had a sword in my hand I should undoubtedly have slain Philippa; but before I could express my sentiments in any way, a violent shock flung me endways on top of the man who was pulling stroke. Thanks to Maria, we had reached our destination all unawares; the two men, respectfully awaiting my instructions, had rowed on with disciplined steadiness, and, as a result, we had rammed the *Eileen Oge* amidships, with a vigour that brought Mr Shute tumbling up the companion to see what had happened.

'Oh, it's you, is it?' he said, with his mouth full. 'Come in; don't knock! Delighted to see you, Mrs Yeates; don't apologize. There's nothing like a hired ship after all – it's quite jolly to see the splinters fly – shows you're getting your money's worth. Hullo! who's this?'

This was Maria, feigning exhaustion, and noisily treading water at the boat's side.

'What, poor old Maria? Wanted to send her ashore, did he? Heartless ruffian!'

Thus was Maria installed on board the *Eileen Oge*, and the element of fatality had already begun to work.

There was just enough wind to take us out of Clountiss harbour, and with the last of the outrunning tide we crept away to the west. The party on board consisted of our host's sister, Miss Cecilia Shute, Miss Sally Knox, and ourselves; we sat about in conventional attitudes in deck chairs and on adamantine deck bosses, and I talked to Miss Shute with feverish brilliancy, and wished the patience-cards were not in the cabin; I knew the supreme importance of keeping one's mind occupied, but I dared not face the cabin. There was a long, almost imperceptible swell, with little queer seabirds that I have never seen before – and trust I never shall again – dotted about on its glassy slopes. The coast-line looked low and grey and dull, as, I think, coast-lines always do when viewed from the deep. The breeze that Bernard had promised us we should find outside was barely enough to keep us moving. The burning sun of four o'clock focused its heat on the deck; Bernard stood up among us, engaged in what he was pleased to call 'handling the stick,' and beamed almost as offensively as the sun.

'Oh, we're slipping along,' he said, his odiously healthy face glowing like copper against the blazing blue sky. 'You're going a great deal faster than you think, and the men say we'll pick up a breeze once we're round the Mizen.'

I made no reply; I was not feeling ill, merely thoroughly disinclined for conversation. Miss Sally smiled wanly, and closing her eyes, laid her head on Philippa's knee. Instructed by a dread freemasonry, I knew that for her the moment had come when she could no longer bear to see the rail rise slowly above the horizon, and with an equal rhythmic slowness sink below it. Maria moved restlessly to and fro, panting and yawning, and occasionally rearing herself on her hind legs against the side, and staring forth with wild eyes at the headachy sliding of the swell. Perhaps she was meditating suicide; if so I sympathized with her, and since she was obviously going to be sick I trusted that she would bring off the suicide with as little delay as possible. Philippa and Miss Shute sat in unaffected serenity in deck chairs, and stitched at white things – tea cloths for the *Eileen Oge*, I believe, things in themselves a mockery – and talked untiringly, with that singular indifference to their marine surroundings that I have often observed in ladies who are not seasick. It always stirs me afresh to wonder why they have not remained ashore: nevertheless, I prefer their tranquil and total lack of interest in seafaring matters to the blatant Vikingism of the average male who is similarly placed.

Somehow, I knew not how, we crawled onwards, and by about five o'clock we had rounded the Mizen, a gaunt spike of a headland that starts up like a boar's tusk above the ragged lip of the Irish coast, and the *Eileen Oge* was beginning to swing and wallop in the long sluggish rollers that the American liners know and despise. I was very far from despising them. Down in the west, resting on the sea's rim, a purple bank of clouds lay awaiting the descent of the sun, as seductively and as malevolently as a damp bed at a hotel awaits a traveller.

The end, so far as I was concerned, came at teatime. The meal had been prepared in the saloon, and thither it became incumbent on me to accompany my hostess and my wife. Miss Sally, long past speech, opened, at the suggestion of tea, one eye, and disclosed a look of horror. As I tottered down the companion I respected her good sense. The *Eileen Oge* had been built early in the sixties, and headroom was not her strong point; neither, apparently, was ventilation. I began by dashing my forehead against the frame of the cabin door, and then, shattered morally and physically, entered into the atmosphere of the pit. After which things, and the sight of a plate of rich cake, I retired in good order to my cabin, and began upon the Yanatas.

I pass over some painful intermediate details and resume at the moment when Bernard Shute woke me from a drugged slumber to announce that dinner was over.

'It's been raining pretty hard,' he said, swaying easily with the swing of the yacht; 'but we've got a clinking breeze, and we ought to make Lurriga Harbour tonight. There's a good anchorage there, the men say. They're rather a lot of swabs, but they know this coast, and I don't. I took 'em over with the ship all standing.

'Where are we now?' I asked, something heartened by the blessed word 'anchorage.'

'You're running up Sheepskin Bay – it's a thundering big bay; Lurriga's up at the far end of it, and the night's as black as the inside of a cow. Dig out and get something to eat, and come on deck – What! no dinner?' – I had spoken morosely, with closed eyes – 'Oh, rot! you're on an even keel now. I promised Mrs Yeates I'd make you dig out. You're as bad as a soldier officer that we were ferrying to Malta one time in the old *Tamar*. He got one leg out of his berth when we were going down the

Channel, and he was too sick to pull it in again till we got to Gib!'

I compromised on a drink and some biscuits. The ship was certainly steadier, and I felt sufficiently restored to climb weakly on deck. It was by this time past ten o'clock, and heavy clouds blotted out the last of the afterglow, and smothered the stars at their birth. A wet warm wind was lashing the *Eileen Oge* up a wide estuary; the waves were hunting her, hissing under her stern, racing up to her, crested with the white glow of phosphorus, as she fled before them. I dimly discerned in the greyness the more solid greyness of the shore. The mainsail loomed out into the darkness, nearly at right angles to the yacht, with the boom creaking as the following wind gave us an additional shove. I know nothing of yacht sailing, but I can appreciate the grand fact that in running before a wind the boom is removed from its usual sphere of devastation.

I sat down beside a bundle of rugs that I had discovered to be my wife, and thought of my whitewashed office at Shreelane and its bare but stationary floor, with a yearning that was little short of passion. Miss Sally had long since succumbed; Miss Shute was tired, and had turned in soon after dinner.

'I suppose she's overdone by the delirious gaiety of the afternoon,' said I acridly, in reply to this information.

Philippa cautiously poked her head from the rugs, like a tortoise from under its shell, to see that Bernard, who was standing near the steersman, was out of hearing.

'In all your life, Sinclair,' she said impressively, 'you never knew such a time as Cecilia and I have had down there! We've had to wash *everything* in the cabins, and remake the beds, and *hurl* the sheets away – they were covered with black fingermarks – and while we were doing that, in came the creature that calls himself the steward, to ask if he might get something of his that he had left in Miss Shute's 'birthplace'! and he rooted out from under Cecilia's mattress a pair of socks and half a loaf of bread!'

'Consolation to Miss Shute to know her berth has been well aired,' I said, with the nearest approach to enjoyment I had known since I came on board; 'and has Sally made any equally interesting discoveries?'

'She said she didn't care what her bed was like; she just dropped into it. I must say I am sorry for her,' went on Philippa; 'she hated coming. Her mother made her accept.'

'I wonder if Lady Knox will make her accept *him*!' I said. 'How often has Sally refused him, does any one know?'

'Oh, about once a week,' replied Philippa; 'just the way I kept on refusing you, you know!'

Something cold and wet was thrust into my hand, and the aroma of damp dog arose upon the night air; Maria had issued from some lair at the sound of our voices, and was now, with palsied tremblings, slowly trying to drag herself on to my lap.

'Poor thing, she's been so dreadfully ill,' said Philippa. 'Don't send her away, Sinclair. Mr Shute found her lying on his berth not able to move; didn't you, Mr Shute?'

'She found out that she was able to move,' said Bernard, who had crossed to our side of the deck; 'it was somehow borne in upon her when I got at her with a boot-tree. I wouldn't advise you to keep her in your lap, Yeates. She stole half a ham after dinner, and she might take a notion to make the only reparation in her power.'

I stood up and stretched myself stiffly. The wind was freshening, and though the growing smoothness of the water told that we were making shelter of some kind, for all that I could see of land we might as well have been in mid-ocean. The heaving lift of the deck under my feet, and the lurching swing when a stronger gust filled the ghostly sails, were more disquieting to me in suggestion than in reality, and, to my surprise, I found something almost enjoyable in rushing through darkness at the pace at which we were going.

'We're a small bit short of the mouth of Lurriga Harbour yet, sir,' said the man who was steering, in reply to a question from Bernard. 'I can see the shore well enough; sure I know every yard of wather in the bay —'

As he spoke he sat down abruptly and violently; so did Bernard, so did I. The bundle that contained Philippa collapsed upon Maria.

'Main sheet!' bellowed Bernard, on his feet in an instant, as the boom swung in and out again with a terrific jerk. 'We're ashore!'

In response to this order three men in succession fell over me while I was still struggling on the deck, and something that was either Philippa's elbow, or the acutest angle of Maria's skull, hit me in the face. As I found my feet the cabin skylight was suddenly illuminated by a wavering glare. I got across the slanting deck somehow, through the confusion of shouting men and the flapping thunder of the sails, and saw through the skylight a gush of flame rising from a pool of fire around an overturned lamp on the swing-table. I avalanched down the companion and was squandered like an avalanche on the floor at the foot of it. Even as I fell, McCarthy the steward dragged the strip of carpet from the cabin floor and threw it on the blaze; I found myself, in some unexplained way, snatching a railway rug from Miss Shute and applying it to the same purpose, and in half a dozen seconds we had smothered the flame and were left in total darkness. The most striking feature of the situation was the immovability of the yacht.

'Great Ned!' said McCarthy, invoking I know not what heathen deity, 'is it on the bottom of the say we are? Well, whether or no, thank God we have the fire quinched!'

We were not, so far, at the bottom of the sea, but during the next few minutes the chances seemed in favour of our getting there. The yacht had run her bows upon a sunken ridge of rock, and after a period of feminine indecision as to whether she were going to slide off again, or roll over into deep water, she elected to stay where she was, and the gig was lowered with all speed, in order to tow her off before the tide left her.

My recollection of this interval is but hazy, but I can certify that in ten minutes I had swept together an assortment of necessaries and knotted them into my counterpane, had broken the string of my eye-glass, and lost my silver match-box; had found Philippa's curling-tongs and put them in my pocket; had carted all the luggage on deck; had then applied myself to the manly duty of reassuring the ladies, and had found Miss Shute merely bored, Philippa enthusiastically anxious to be allowed to help to pull the gig, and Miss Sally radiantly restored to health and spirits by the cessation of movement and the probability of an early escape from the yacht.

The rain had, with its usual opportunities, begun again; we stood in it under umbrellas, and watched the gig jumping on its tow-rope like a dog on a string, as its crew plied the labouring oar in futile endeavour to move the *Eileen Oge*. We had run on the rock at half-tide, and the increasing slant of the deck as the tide fell brought home to us the pleasing probability that at low water – viz. about 2 a.m. – we should roll off the rock and go to the bottom. Had Bernard Shute wished to show himself in the most advantageous light to Miss Sally he could scarely have bettered the situation. I looked on in helpless respect while he whom I had known as the scourge of the hunting field, the terror of the shooting party, rose to the top of a difficult position and kept there, and my respect was, if possible, increased by the presence of mind with which he availed himself of all critical moments to place a protecting arm round Miss Knox.

By about 1 a.m. the two gaffs with which Bernard had contrived to shore up the slowly heeling yacht began to show signs of yielding, and, in approved shipwreck fashion, we took to the boats, the yacht's crew in the gig remaining in attendance on what seemed likely to be the last moments of the *Eileen Oge*, while we, in the dinghy, sought for the harbour. Owing to the tilt of the yacht's deck, and the roughness of the broken water round her, getting into the boat was no mean feat of gymnastics. Miss Sally did it like a bird, alighting in the inevitable arms of Bernard; Miss Shute followed very badly, but, by innate force of character, successfully; Philippa, who was enjoying every moment of her shipwreck, came last, launching herself into the dinghy with my silver shoe-horn clutched in one hand, and in the other the tea-basket. I heard the hollow clank of its tin cups as she sprang, and appreciated the heroism with which Bernard received one of its corners in his waist. How or when Maria left the yacht I know not, but when I applied myself to the bow oar I led off with three crabs, owing to the devotion with which she thrust her head into my lap.

I am no judge of these matters, but in my opinion we ought to have been swamped several times during that row. There was nothing but the phosphorus of breaking waves to tell us where the rocks were, and nothing to show where the harbour was except a solitary light, a masthead light, as we supposed. The skipper had assured us that we could not go wrong if we kept 'a westerly course with a little northing in it'; but it seemed simpler to steer for the light, and we did so. The dinghy climbed along over the waves with an agility that was safer than it felt; the rain fell without haste and without rest, the oars were as inflexible as crowbars, and somewhat resembled them in shape and weight; nevertheless, it was Elysium when compared with the afternoon leisure of the deck of the *Eileen Oge*.

At last we came, unexplainably, into smooth water, and it was at about this time that we were first aware that the darkness was less dense than it had been, and that the rain had ceased. By imperceptible degrees a greyness touched the back of the waves, more a dreariness than a dawn, but more welcome than thousands of gold and silver. I looked over my shoulder and discerned vague bulky things ahead; as I did so, my oar was suddenly wrapped in seaweed. We crept on; Maria stood up with her paws on the gunwale, and whined in high agitation. The dark objects ahead resolved themselves into rocks, and without more ado Maria pitched herself into the water. In half a minute we heard her shaking herself on shore. We slid on; the water swelled under the dinghy, and lifted her keel on to grating gravel.

'We couldn't have done it better if we'd been the Hydrographer Royal,' said Bernard, wading knee-deep in a light wash of foam, with the painter in his hand; 'but all the same, that masthead light is someone's bedroom candle!'

We landed hauled up the boat, and then feebly sat down on our belongings to review the situation, and Maria came and shook herself over each of us in turn. We had run into a little cove, guided by the philanthropic beam of a candle in the upper window of a house about a hundred yards away. The candle still burned on, and the anaemic daylight exhibited to us our surroundings, and we debated as to whether we could at 2.45 a.m. present ourselves as objects of compassion to the owner of the candle. I need hardly say that it was the ladies who decided on making the attempt, having, like most of their sex, a courage incomparably superior to ours in such matters; Bernard and I had not a grain of genuine compunction in our souls, but we failed in nerve.

We trailed up from the cove, laden with emigrants' bundles, stumbling on wet rocks in the half-light, and succeeded in making our way to the house.

It was a small two-storeyed building, of that hideous breed of architecture usually dedicated to the rectories of the Irish Church; we felt that there was something friendly in the presence of a pair of carpet slippers in the porch, but there was a hint of exclusiveness in the fact that there was no knocker and that the bell was broken. The light still burned in the upper window, and with a faltering hand I flung gravel at the glass. This summons was appallingly responded to by a shriek; there was a flutter of white at the panes, and the candle was extinguished.

'Come away!' exclaimed Miss Shute, 'it's a lunatic asylum!'

We stood our ground, however, and presently heard a footstep within, a blind was poked aside in another window, and we were inspected by an unseen inmate; then someone came downstairs, and the hall door was opened by a small man with a bald head and a long sandy beard. He was attired in a brief dressing-gown, and on his shoulder sat, like an angry ghost, a large white cockatoo. Its crest was up on end, its beak was a good two inches long and curved like a Malay kris; its claws gripped the little man's shoulder. Maria uttered in the background a low and thunderous growl.

'Don't take any notice of the bird, please,' said the little man nervously, seeing our united gaze fixed upon this apparition; 'he's extremely fierce if annoyed.'

The majority of our party here melted away to either side of the hall door, and I was left to do the explaining. The tale of our misfortunes had its due effect, and we were ushered into a small drawing-room, our host holding open the door for us, like a nightmare footman with bare shins, a gnome-like bald head, and an unclean spirit swaying on his shoulder. He opened the shutters, and we sat decorously round the room, as at an afternoon party, while the situation was further expounded on both sides. Our entertainer, indeed favoured us with the leading items of his family history, amongst them the facts that he was a Dr Fahy from Cork, who had taken somebody's rectory for the summer, and had been prevailed on by some of his patients to permit them to join him as paying guests.

'I said it was a lunatic asylum,' murmured Miss Shute to me.

'In point of fact,' went on our host, 'there isn't an empty room in the house, which is why I can only offer your party the use of this room and the kitchen fire, which I make a point of keeping burning all night.'

He leaned back complacently in his chair, and crossed his legs; then, obviously remembering his costume, sat bolt upright again. We owed the guiding beams of the candle to the owner of the cockatoo, an old Mrs Buck, who was, we gathered, the most paying of all the patients, and also obviously, the one most feared and cherished by Dr Fahy. 'She has a candle burning all night for the bird, and her door open to let him walk about the house when he likes,' said Dr Fahy; 'indeed, I may say her passion for him amounts to dementia. He's very fond of me, and Mrs Fahy's always telling me I should be thankful, as whatever he did we'd be bound to put up with it!'

Dr Fahy had evidently a turn for conversation that was unaffected by circumstance; the first beams of the early sun were lighting up the rep chair covers before the door closed upon his brown dressing-gown, and upon the stately white back of the cockatoo, and the demoniac possession of laughter that had wrought in us during the interview burst forth unchecked. It was most painful and exhausting, as much laughter always is; but by far the most serious part of it was that Miss Sally, who was sitting in the window, somehow drove her elbow through a pane of glass, and Bernard, in pulling down the blind to conceal the damage, tore it off the roller.

There followed on this catastrophe a period during which reason tottered and Maria barked furiously. Philippa was the first to pull herself together, and to suggest an adjournment to the kitchen fire that, in honour of the paying guests, was never quenched, and, respecting the repose of the household, we proceeded thither with a stealth that convinced Maria we were engaged in a rat hunt. The boots of paying guests littered the floor, the debris of their last repast covered the table; a cat in some unseen fastness crooned a war song to Maria, who feigned unconsciousness and fell to scientific research in the scullery.

We roasted our boots at the range, and Bernard, with all a sailor's gift for exploration and theft, prowled in noisome purlieus and emerged with a jug of milk and a lump of salt butter. No one who has not been a burglar can at all realize what it was to roam through Dr Fahy's basement storey, with the rookery of paying guests asleep above, and to feel that, so far, we had repaid his confidence by breaking a pane of glass and a blind, and putting the scullery tap out of order. I have always maintained that there was something wrong with it before I touched it, but the fact remains that when I had filled Philippa's kettle, no human power could prevail upon it to stop flowing. For all I know to the contrary it is running still.

It was in the course of our furtive return to the drawing-room that we were again confronted by Mrs Buck's cockatoo. It was standing in malign meditation on the stairs, and on seeing us it rose, without a word of warning, upon the wing, and with a long screech flung itself at Miss Sally's golden-red head, which a ray of sunlight had chanced to illumine. There was a moment of stampede, as the selected victim, pursued by the cockatoo, fled into the drawing-room; two chairs were upset (one, I think, broken), Miss Sally enveloped herself in a window curtain, Philippa and Miss Shute effaced themselves beneath a table; the cockatoo, foiled of its prey, skimmed, still screeching, round the ceiling. It was Bernard who, with a well-directed sofa-cushion, drove the enemy from the room. There was only a chink of the door open, but the cockatoo turned on his side as he flew, and swung through it like a woodcock.

We slammed the door behind him, and at the same instant there came a thumping on the floor overhead, muffled, yet peremptory.

'That's Mrs Buck!' said Miss Shute, crawling from under the table; 'the room over this is the one that had the candle in it.'

We sat for a time in awful stillness, but nothing further happened, save a distant shriek overhead, that told the cockatoo had sought and found sanctuary in his owner's room. We had tea *sotto voce*, and then, one by one, despite the amazing discomfort of the drawing-room chairs, we dozed off to sleep.

It was at about five o'clock that I woke with a stiff neck and an uneasy remembrance that I had last seen Maria in the kitchen. The others, looking, each of them, about twenty years older than their age, slept in various attitudes of exhaustion. Bernard opened his eyes as I stole forth to look for Maria, but none of the ladies awoke. I went down the evil-smelling passage that led to the kitchen stairs, and, there on a mat, regarding me with intelligent affection, was Maria; but what – oh, what was the white thing that lay between her forepaws?

The situation was too serious to be coped with alone. I fled noiselessly back to the drawing-room and put my head in; Bernard's eyes – blessed be the light sleep of sailors! – opened again, and there was that in mine that summoned him forth. (Blessed also be the light step of sailors!)

We took the corpse from Maria, witholding perforce the language and the slaughtering that our hearts ached to bestow. For a minute or two our eyes communed.

'I'll get the kitchen shovel,' breathed Bernard, 'you open the hall door!'

A moment later we passed like spirits into the open air, and on into a little garden at the end of the house. Maria followed us, licking her lips. There were beds of nasturtiums, and of purple stocks, and of marigolds. We chose a bed of stocks, a plump bed, that looked like easy digging. The windows were all tightly shut and shuttered, and I took the cockatoo from under my coat and hid it, temporarily, behind a box border. Bernard had brought a shovel and a coal scoop. We dug like badgers. At eighteen inches we got down into shale and stones, and the coal scoop struck work.

'Never mind,' said Bernard; 'we'll plant the stocks on top of him.' It was a lovely morning, with a new-born blue sky and a light northerly breeze. As we returned to the house, we looked across the wavelets of the little cove and saw, above the rocky point round which we had groped last night, a triangular white patch moving slowly along.

'The tide's lifted her!' said Bernard, standing stock-still. He looked at Mrs Buck's window and at me. 'Yeates!' he whispered, 'let's quit!'

It was now barely six o'clock, and not a soul was stirring. We woke the ladies and convinced them of the high importance of catching the tide. Bernard left a note on the hall table for Dr Fahy, a beautiful note of leavetaking and gratitude, and apology for the broken window (for which he begged to enclose half a crown). No allusion was made to the other casualties. As we neared the strand he found an occasion to say to me:

'I put in a postscript that I thought it best to mention that I had seen the cockatoo in the garden, and hoped it would get back all right. That's quite true, you know! But look here, whatever you do, you must keep it all dark from the ladies —'

At this juncture Maria overtook us with the cockatoo in her mouth.

'Not a Porterhouse Man'

TOM SHARPE

*During the first days of his time as research graduate at Porterhouse
College, Cambridge, young Zipser finds himself confused and bewildered,
first by the weird anachronisms of the system and then, increasingly, by his
own wildly irrational obsession with a college charwoman....*

ZIPSER WALKED DOWN Free School Lane past the black clunch walls of
Corpus. The talk on 'Population Control in the Indian Subcontinent' had
gone on longer than he had expected, partly due to the enthusiasm of the
speaker and partly to the intractable nature of the problem itself. Zipser
had not been sure which had been worse, the delivery, if that was an
appropriate word to use about a speech that concerned itself with
abortion, or the enthusiastic advocacy of vasectomy which had prolonged
the talk beyond its expected limits. The speaker, a woman doctor with
the United Nations Infant Prevention Unit in Madras, who seemed to
regard infant mortality as a positive blessing, had disparaged the coil as
useless, the pill as expensive, female sterilization as complicated, had
described vasectomy so seductively that Zipser had found himself
crossing and recrossing his legs and wishing to hell that he hadn't come.
Even now as he walked back to Porterhouse through the snow-covered
streets he was filled with foreboding and a tendency to waddle. Still, even
if the world seemed doomed to starvation, he had had to get out of
Porterhouse for the evening. As the only research graduate in the College
he found himself isolated. Below him the undergraduates pursued a wild
promiscuity which he envied but dared not emulate, and above him the
Fellows found compensation for their impotence in gluttony. Besides he
was not a Porterhouse man, as the Dean had pointed out when he had
been accepted. 'You'll have to live in College to get the spirit of the
place,' he had said, and while in other colleges research graduates lived
in cheap and comfortable digs, Zipser found himself occupying an
exceedingly expensive suite of rooms in Bull Tower and forced to follow
the regime of an undergraduate. For one thing he had to be in by twelve
or face the wrath of Skullion and the indelicate enquiries next morning of
the Dean. The whole system was anachronistic and Zipser wished he had
been accepted by one of the other colleges. Skullion's attitude he found
particularly unpleasant. The Porter seemed to regard him as an
interloper, and lavished a wealth of invective on him normally reserved

for tradesmen. Zipser's attempts to mollify him by explaining that Durham was a university and that there had been a Durham College in Oxford in 1380 had failed hopelessly. If anything, the mention of Oxford had increased Skullion's antipathy.

'This is a gentleman's college,' he had said, and Zipser, who didn't claim to be even a putative gentleman, had been a marked man ever since. Skullion had it in for him.

As he crossed Market Hill he glanced at the Guildhall clock. It was twelve thirty-five. The main gate would be shut and Skullion in bed. Zipser slackened his pace. There was no point in hurrying now. He might just as well stay out all night now. He certainly wasn't going to knock Skullion up and get cursed for his pains. It wouldn't have been the first time he had wandered about Cambridge all night. Of course there was Mrs Biggs the bedder to be taken care of. She came to wake him every morning and was supposed to report him if his bed hadn't been slept in but Mrs Biggs was accommodating. 'A pound in the purse is worth a flea in the ear,' she had explained after his first stint of night wandering, and Zipser had paid up cheerfully. Mrs Biggs was all right. He was fond of her. There was something almost human about her in spite of her size.

Zipser shivered. It was partly the cold and partly the thought of Mrs Biggs. The snow was falling heavily now and it was obvious he couldn't stay out all night in this weather. It was equally clear that he wasn't going to wake Skullion. He would have to climb in. It was an undignified thing for a graduate to do but there was no alternative. He crossed Trinity Street and went past Caius. At the bottom he turned right and came to the back gate in the lane. Above him the iron spikes on top of the wall looked more threatening than ever. Still, he couldn't stay out. He would probably freeze to death if he did. He found a bicycle in front of Trinity Hall and dragged it up the lane and put it against the wall. Then he climbed up until he could grasp the spikes with his hands. He paused for a moment and then with a final kick he was up with one knee on the wall and his foot under the spikes. He eased himself up and swung the other leg over, found a foothold and jumped. He landed softly in the flowerbed and scrambled to his feet. He was just moving off down the path under the beech-trees when something moved in the shadow and a hand fell on his shoulder. Zipser reacted instinctively. With a wild flurry he struck out at his attacker and the next moment a bowler hat was in mid-air and Zipser himself, ignoring the College rules which decreed that only Fellows could walk on the lawns, was racing across the grass towards New Court. Behind him on the gravel path Skullion lay breathing heavily. Zipser glanced over his shoulder as he dashed through the gate into the Court and saw his dark shape on the ground. Then he was in O staircase and climbing the stairs to his rooms. He shut the door and stood in the darkness panting. It must have been Skullion. The bowler hat told him that. He had assaulted a College porter, bashed his face and chopped him down. He went to the window and peered out and it was then that he realized what a fool he had been. His footsteps in the snow would give him away. Skullion would follow them to the Bull Tower. But there was no sign of the Porter. Perhaps he was still lying out there unconscious. Perhaps he had knocked him out. Zipser shuddered at this fresh indication of his irrational nature, and its terrible consequences for mankind. Sex and violence, the speaker had said, were the twin poles of the world's lifeless future, and Zipser could see now what she had meant.

Anyway, he could not leave Skullion lying out there to freeze to death even if going down to help him meant that he would be sent down from the University for 'assaulting a college porter', his thesis on the Pumpernickel as A Factor in the Politics of 16th-Century Westphalia uncompleted. He went to the door and walked slowly downstairs.

Skullion got to his feet and picked up his bowler, brushed the snow off it and put it on. His waistcoat and jacket were covered with patches of snow and he brushed them down with his hands. His right eye was swelling. Young bastard had caught him a real shiner. 'Getting too old for this job,' he muttered, muddled feelings of anger and respect competing in his mind. 'But I can still catch him.' He followed the footsteps across the lawn and down the path to the gate into New Court. His eye had swollen now so that he could hardly see out of it, but Skullion wasn't thinking about his eye. He wasn't thinking about catching the culprit. He was thinking back to the days of his youth. 'Fair's fair. If you can't catch 'em, you can't report 'em,' old Fuller, the Head Porter at Porterhouse had said to him when he first came to the College and what was true then was true now. He turned left at the gate and went down the Cloister to the Lodge and went through to his bedroom. 'A real shiner,' he said examining the swollen eye in the mirror behind the door. It could do with a bit of beefsteak. He'd get some from the College kitchen in the morning. He took off his jacket and was unbuttoning his waistcoat when the door of the Lodge opened. Skullion buttoned his waistcoat again and put on his jacket and went out into the office.

Zipser stood in the doorway of O staircase and watched Skullion cross the Court to the Cloisters. Well, at least he wasn't lying out in the snow. Still he couldn't go back to his room without doing something. He had better go down and see if he was all right. He walked across the Court and into the Lodge. It was empty and he was about to turn away and go back to his room when the door at the back opened and Skullion appeared. His right eye was black and swollen and his face, old and veined, had a deformed lop-sided look about it.

'Well?' Skullion asked out of the side of his mouth. One eye peered angrily at Zipser.

'I just came to say I'm sorry,' Zipser said awkwardly.

'Sorry?' Skullion asked as if he didn't understand.

'Sorry about hitting you.'

'What makes you think you hit me?' The lop-sided face glared at him. Zipser scratched his forehead.

'Well, anyway I'm sorry. I thought I had better see if you were all right.'

'You thought I was going to report you, didn't you?' Skullion asked contemptuously. 'Well, I'm not. You got away.'

Zipser shook his head.

'It wasn't that. I thought you might be ... well ... hurt.'

Skullion smiled grimly.

'Hurt? Me hurt? What's a little hurt matter?' He turned and went back into the bedroom and shut the door. Zipser went out into the Court. He didn't understand. You knocked an old man down and he didn't mind. It wasn't logical. It was all so bloody irrational. He walked back to his room and went to bed.

Zipser overslept. His exertions, both mental and physical, had left him exhausted. By the time he woke, Mrs Biggs was already busy in his outer room, moving furniture and dusting. Zipser lay in bed listening to her. Like something out of Happy Families, he thought. Mrs Biggs the Bedder. Skullion the Head Porter. The Dean. The Senior Tutor. Relics of some ancient childish game. Everything about Porterhouse was like that. Masters and Servants.

Lying there listening to the ponderous animality of Mrs Biggs' movements, Zipser considered the curious turn of events that had forced him into the role of a master while Mrs Biggs maintained an aggressive servility quite out of keeping with her personality and formidable physique. He found the relationship peculiar, and further complicated by the sinister attractions she held for him. It must be that in her fullness Mrs Biggs retained a natural warmth which in its contrast to the artificiality of all else in Cambridge made its appeal. Certainly nothing else could explain it. Taken in her particulars, and Zipser couldn't think of any other way of taking her, the bedder was quite remarkably without attractions. It wasn't simply the size of her appendages that was astonishing but the sheer power. Mrs Biggs' walk was a thing of menacing maternity, while her face retained a youthfulness quite out of keeping with her volume. Only her voice declared her wholly ordinary. That and her conversation, which hovered tenuously close to the obscene and managed to combine servility with familiarity in a manner he found

unanswerable. He got out of bed and began to dress. It was one of the
ironies of life, he thought, that in a college that prided itself on its
adherence to the values of the past, Mrs Biggs' manifest attractions
should go unrecognized. In paleolithic times she would have been a
princess and he was just wondering at what particular moment of history
the Mrs Biggses had ceased to represent all that was finest and fairest in
womanhood when she knocked on the door.

'Mr Zipser, are you decent?' she called.

'Hang on. I'm coming,' Zipser called back.

'I shouldn't be at all surprised,' Mrs Biggs muttered audibly. Zipser
opened the door.

'I haven't got all day,' Mrs Biggs said brushing past him provocatively.

'I'm sorry to have kept you,' said Zipser sarcastically.

'Kept me indeed. Listen to who's talking. And what makes you think
I'd mind being kept?'

Zipser blushed. 'That's hardly what I meant,' he said hotly.

'Very complimentary I'm sure,' said Mrs Biggs, regarding him with
arch disapproval. 'Got out of bed the wrong side this morning, did we?'

Zipser noted the plural with a delicious shudder and lowered his eyes.
Mrs Biggs' boots, porcinely tight, entranced him.

'Mr Skullion's got a black eye this morning,' the bedder continued. 'A
right purler. Not before time either. I says to him, "Somebody's been
taking a poke at you." You know what he says?' Zipser shook his head.
'He says, "I'll thank you to keep your comments to yourself, Mrs Biggs."
That's what he says. Silly old fool. Don't know which century he's living
in.' She went into the other room and Zipser followed her. He put a kettle
on to make coffee while Mrs Biggs bustled about picking things up and
putting them down again in a manner which suggested that a great deal
of work was being done but which merely helped to emphasize her
feelings. All the time she rattled on with her daily dose of inconsequential
information while Zipser dodged about the room like a toreador trying to
avoid a talkative bull. Each time she brushed past him he was aware of
an animal magnetism that overrode considerations of taste and that
aesthetic sensibility his education was supposed to have given him.
Finally he stood in the corner, hardly able to contain himself, and
watched her figure as it walloped about the room. Her words lost all
meaning, became mere soothing sounds, waves of accompaniment to the
surge of her thighs and the great rollers of her buttocks dimpled and
shimmering beneath her skirt. 'Well I says, "You know what you can
do. . . ."' Mrs Biggs' voice echoed Zipser's terrible thought. She bent over
to plug in the vacuum-cleaner and her breasts plunged in her blouse and
undulated with a force of attraction Zipser found almost irresistible. He
felt himself moved out of his corner like a boxer urged forward by

unnatural passion for an enormous opponent. Words crowded into his mouth. Unwanted words. Unspeakable words.

'I want you,' he said and was saved the final embarrassment by the vacuum-cleaner which roared into life.

'What's that you said?' Mrs Biggs shouted above the din. She was holding the suction pipe against a cushion on the armchair. Zipser turned purple.

'Nothing,' he bawled, and fell back into his corner.

'Bag's full,' said Mrs Biggs, and switched the machine off.

In the silence that followed Zipser leant against the wall, appalled at his terrible avowal. He was about to make a dash for the door when Mrs Biggs bent over and undid the clips on the back of the vacuum-cleaner. Zipser stared at the backs of her knees. The boots, the creases, the swell of her thighs, the edge of her stockings, the crescent. . . .

'Bag's full,' Mrs Biggs said again. 'You can't get any suction when the bag's full.'

She straightened up holding the bag grey and swollen . . . Zipser shut his eyes. Mrs Biggs emptied the bag into the wastepaper basket. A cloud of grey dust billowed up into the room.

'Are you feeling all right, dearie?' she asked, peering at him with motherly concern. Zipser opened his eyes and stared into her face.

'I'm all right,' he managed to mutter trying to take his eyes off her lips. Mrs Biggs' lipstick gleamed thickly. 'I didn't sleep well. That's all.'

'Too much work and not enough play makes Jack a dull boy,' said Mrs Biggs holding the bag limply. To Zipser the thing had an erotic appeal he dared not analyse. 'Now you just sit down and I'll make you some coffee and you'll feel better.' Mrs Biggs' hand grasped his arm and guided him to a chair. Zipser slumped into it and stared at the vacuum-cleaner while Mrs Biggs, bending once again and even more revealingly now that Zipser was sitting down and closer to her, inserted the bag into the back of the machine and switched it on. A terrible roar, and the bag was sucked into the interior with a force which corresponded entirely to Zipser's feelings. Mrs Biggs straightened up and went through to the gyp room to make coffee while Zipser shifted feebly in the chair. He couldn't imagine what was happening to him. It was all too awful. He had to get away. He couldn't go on sitting there while she was in the room. He'd do something terrible. He couldn't control himself. He'd say something. He was about to get up and sneak out when Mrs Biggs came back with two cups of coffee.

'You do look funny,' she said, putting a cup into his hand. 'You ought to go and see a doctor. You might be going down with something.'

'Yes,' said Zipser obediently. Mrs Biggs sat down opposite him and sipped her coffee. Zipser tried to keep his eyes off her legs and found himself gazing at her breasts.

'Do you often get taken queer?' Mrs Biggs inquired.

'Queer?' said Zipser, shaken from his reverie by the accusation. 'Certainly not.'

'I was only asking,' said Mrs Biggs. She took a mouthful of coffee with a schlurp that was distinctly suggestive. 'I had a young man once,' she continued, 'just like you. Got took queer every now and then. Used to throw himself about and wriggle something frightful. Took me all my time to hold him down, it did.'

Zipser stared at her frenziedly. The notion of being held down while wriggling by Mrs Biggs was more than he could bear. With a sudden lurch that spilt his coffee Zipser hurled himself out of the chair and dashed from the room. He rushed downstairs and out into the safety of the open air. 'I've got to do something. I can't control myself. First Skullion and now Mrs Biggs.' He walked hurriedly out of Porterhouse and through Clare towards the University Library.

Alone in Zipser's room, Mrs Biggs switched on the vacuum-cleaner and poked the handle round the room. As she worked she sang to herself loudly, 'Love me tender, love me true.' Her voice, raucously off key, was drowned by the roar of the Electrolux.

Zipser sat on the third floor of the north wing of the University Library trying to bring his mind to bear on The Influence of Pumpernickel on the Politics of 16th-Century Osnabruck but without success. He no longer cared that it had been known as *bonum paniculum* and his interest in Westphalian local politics had waned. The problem of his feelings for Mrs Biggs was more immediate.

He had spent an hour in the stacks browsing feverishly through textbooks of clinical psychology in search of a medical explanation of the symptoms of irrational violence and irrepressible sexuality which had manifested themselves in his recent behaviour. From what he read it had begun to look as if he were suffering from a multitude of different diseases. On the one hand his reaction to Skullion suggested paranoia, 'violent behaviour as a result of delusions of persecution', while the erotic compulsion of his feelings for Mrs Biggs was even more alarming and seemed to indicate schizophrenia with sadomasochistic tendencies. The combination of the two diseases, paranoid schizophrenia, was apparently the worst possible form of insanity and quite incurable. Zipser sat staring out of the windows at the trees in the garden beyond the footpath and contemplated a lifetime of madness. He couldn't imagine what had suddenly occasioned the outbreak. The textbooks implied that heredity had a lot to do with it, but apart from an uncle who had a passion for concrete dwarves in his front garden and who his mother had said was a bit touched in the head, he couldn't think of anyone in the family who was actually and certifiably insane.

The explanation had to lie elsewhere. His feelings for the bedder deviated from every known norm. So for that matter did Mrs Biggs. She bulged where she should have dimpled and bounced when she should have been still. She was gross, vulgar, garrulous and, Zipser had no doubt in his mind, thoroughly insanitary. To find himself irresistibly attacted to her was the worst thing he could think of. It was perfectly all right to be queer. It was positively fashionable. To have constant and insistent sexual desires for French au pair girls, Swedish language students, girls in Boots, even undergraduates at Girton, was normality itself, but Mrs Biggs came into the category of the unmentionable. And the knowledge that but for the fortuitous intervention of the vacuum-cleaner he would have revealed his true feelings for her threw him into a panic. He left his table and went downstairs and walked back into town.

As he reached Great St Mary's the clock was striking twelve. Zipser stopped and studied the posters on the railings outside the church which announced forthcoming sermons.

CHRIST AND THE GAY CHRISTIAN. Rev. F. Leaney.

HAS SALT LOST ITS SAVOUR? Anglican attitudes to disarmament. Rev. B. Tomkins.

JOB, A MESSAGE FOR THE THIRD WORLD. Right Reverend Sutty, Bishop of Bombay.

JESUS JOKES. Fred Henry by permission of ITA & the management of the Palace Theatre, Scunthorpe.

BOMBS AWAY. A Christian's attitude to Skyjacking by Flight Lieutenant Jack Piggett, BOAC.

Zipser stared at the University Sermons with a sudden sense of loss. What had happened to the old Church, the Church of his childhood, the friendly Vicar and the helping hand? Not that Zipser had ever been to church, but he had seen them on television and had been comforted by the knowledge that they were still there in *Songs of Praise* and *Saints Alive* and *All Gas and Gaiters*. But now when he needed help there was only this pale parody of the daily paper with its mishmash of politics and sensationalism. Not a word about evil and how to cope with it. Zipser felt betrayed. He went back into Porterhouse in search of help. He'd go and see the Senior Tutor. There was just time before lunch. Zipser climbed the stairs to the Tutor's rooms and knocked on the door.

Zipser's interview with the Senior Tutor had left him with a sense of embarrassment that had unnerved him completely. His attempt to explain the nature of his compulsion had been fraught with difficulties. The Senior Tutor kept poking his little finger in his ear and wriggling it around and examining the end of it when he took it out while Zipser talked, as if he held some waxy deposit responsible for the flow of obscene

127

information that was reaching his brain. When he finally accepted that his ears were not betraying him and that Zipser was in fact confessing to being attracted by his bedder, he had muttered something to the effect that the Chaplain would expect him for tea that afternoon and that, failing that, a good psychiatrist might help. Zipser had left miserably and had spent the early part of the afternoon in his room trying to concentrate on his thesis without success. The image of Mrs Biggs, a cross between a cherubim in menopause and a booted succubus, kept intruding. Zipser turned for escape to a book of photographs of starving children in Nagaland but in spite of this mental flagellation Mrs Biggs prevailed. He tried Hermitsch on *Fall Out & the Andaman Islanders* and even *Sterilization, Vasectomy and Abortion* by Allard, but these holy writs all failed against the pervasive fantasy of the bedder. It was as if his social conscience, his concern for the plight of humanity at large, the universal and collective pity he felt for all mankind, had been breached in some unspeakably personal way by the inveterate triviality and egoism of Mrs Biggs. Zipser, whose life had been filled with a truly impersonal charity – he had spent holidays from school working for SOBB, the Save Our Black Brothers campaign – and whose third worldliness was impeccable, found himself suddenly the victim of a sexual idiosyncrasy which made a mockery of his universalism. In desperation he turned to *Syphilis, the Scourge of Colonialism*, and stared with horror at the pictures. In the past it had worked like a charm to quell incipient sexual desires while satisfying his craving for evidence of natural justice. The notion of the Conquistadores dying of the disease after raping South American Indians no longer had its old appeal now that Zipser himself was in the grip of a compulsive urge to rape Mrs Biggs. By the time it came for him to go to the Chaplain's rooms for tea, Zipser had exhausted the resources of his theology. So too, it seemed, had the Chaplain.

'Ah my boy,' the Chaplain boomed as Zipser negotiated the bric-a-brac that filled the Chaplin's sitting-room. 'So good of you to come. Do make yourself comfortable.' Zipser nudged past a gramophone with a papiermâché horn, circumvented a brass-topped table with fretsawed legs, squeezed beneath the fronds of a castor-oil plant and finally sat down on a chair by the fire. The Chaplain scuttled backwards and forwards between his bathroom and the teatable muttering loudly to himself a liturgy of things to fetch. 'Teapot hot. Spoons. Milk jug. You do take milk?' 'Yes, thank you,' said Zipser. 'Good. Good. So many people take lemon, don't they? One always forgets these things. Tea-cosy. Sugar basin.' Zipser looked round the room for some indication of the Chaplain's interests but the welter of conflicting objects, like the addition of random numbers to a code, made interpretation impossible. Apart from senility the furnishings had so little in common that they seemed to indicate a wholly catholic taste.

'Crumpets,' said the Chaplain scurrying out of the bathroom. 'Just the thing. You toast them.' He speared a crumpet on the end of a toasting-fork and thrust the fork into Zipser's hand. Zipser poked the crumpet at the fire tentatively and felt once again that dissociation from reality that seemed so much a part of life in Cambridge. It was as if everyone in the College sought to parody himself, as if a parody of a parody could become itself a new reality. Behind him the Chaplain stumbled over a footrest and deposited a jar of honey with a boom on the brass-topped table. Zipser removed the crumpet, blackened on one side and ice cold on the other, and put it on a plate. He toasted another while the Chaplain tried to spread butter on the one he had half done. By the time they had finished Zipser's face was burning from the fire and his hands were sticky with a mixture of melted butter and honey. The Chaplain sat back in his chair and filled his pipe from a tobacco jar with the Porterhouse crest on it.

'Do help yourself, my dear boy,' said the Chaplain, pushing the jar towards him.

'I don't smoke.'

The Chaplain shook his head sadly. 'Everyone should smoke a pipe,' he said. 'Calms the nerves. Puts things in perspective. Couldn't do without mine.' He leant back, puffing vigorously. Zipser stared at him through a haze of smoke.

'Now then where were we?' he asked. Zipser tried to think. 'Ah yes, your little problem, that's right,' said the Chaplain finally. 'I knew there was something.'

Zipser stared into the fire resentfully.

'The Senior Tutor said something about it. I didn't gather very much but then I seldom do. Deafness, you know.'

Zipser nodded sympathetically.

'The affliction of the elderly. That and rheumatism. It's the damp, you know. Comes up from the river. Very unhealthy living so close to the Fens.' His pipe percolated gently. In the comparative silence Zipser tried to think what to say. The Chaplain's age and his evident physical disabilities made it difficult for Zipser to conceive that he could begin to understand the problem of Mrs Biggs.

'I really think there's been a misunderstanding,' he began hesitantly and stopped. It was evident from the look on the Chaplain's face that there was no understanding at all.

'You'll have to speak up,' the Chaplain boomed. 'I'm really quite deaf.'

'I can see that,' Zipser said. The Chaplain beamed at him.

'Don't hesitate to tell me,' he said. 'Nothing you say can shock me.'

'I'm not surprised,' Zipser said.

The Chaplain's smile remained insistently benevolent. 'I know what we'll do,' he said, hopping to his feet and reaching behind his chair. 'It's something I use for confession sometimes.' He emerged holding a loudhailer and handed it to Zipser. 'Press the trigger when you're going to speak.'

Zipser held the thing up to his mouth and stared at the Chaplain over the rim. 'I really don't think this is going to help,' he said finally. His words reverberated through the room and set the teapot rattling on the brass table.

'Of course it is,' shouted the Chaplain, 'I can hear perfectly.'

'I didn't mean that,' Zipser said desperately. The fronds of the castor-oil plant quivered ponderously. 'I meant I don't think it's going to help to talk about. . . .' He left the dilemma of Mrs Biggs unspoken.

The Chaplain smiled in absolution and puffed his pipe vigorously. 'Many of the young men who come to see me,' he said, invisible in a cloud of smoke, 'suffer from feelings of guilt about masturbation.'

Zipser stared frantically at the smoke screen. 'Masturbation? Who said anything about masturbation?' he bawled into the loudhailer. It was apparent someone had. His words, hideously amplified, billowed forth from the room and across the Court outside. Several undergraduates by the fountain turned and stared up at the Chaplain's windows. Deafened by his own vociferousness, Zipser sat sweating with embarrassment.

'I understood from the Senior Tutor that you wanted to see me about a sexual problem,' the Chaplain shouted.

Zipser lowered the loudhailer. The thing clearly had disadvantages.

'I can assure you I don't masturbate,' he said.

The Chaplain looked at him incomprehendingly. 'You press the trigger when you want to speak,' he explained. Zipser nodded dumbly. The knowledge that to communicate with the Chaplain at all he had to announce his feelings for Mrs Biggs to the world at large presented him with a terrible dilemma made no less intolerable by the Chaplain's shouted replies.

'It often helps to get these things into the open,' the Chaplain assured him. Zipser had his doubts about that. Admissions of the sort he had to make broadcast through a loudhailer were not likely to be of any help at all. He might just as well go and propose to the wretched woman straightaway and be done with it. He sat with lowered head while the Chaplain boomed on.

'Don't forget that anything you tell me will be heard in the strictest confidence,' he shouted. 'You need have no fears that it will go any further.'

'Oh sure,' Zipser muttered. Outside in the Quad a small crowd of undergraduates had gathered by the fountain to listen.

Half an hour later Zipser left the room, his demoralization quite complete. At least he could congratulate himself that he had revealed nothing of his true feelings and the Chaplain's kindly probings, his tentative questions, had elicited no response. Zipser had sat silently through a sexual catechism only bothering to shake his head when the Chaplain broached particularly obscene topics. In the end he had listened to a lyrical description of the advantages of au pair girls. It was obvious that the Chaplain regarded foreign girls as outside the sexual canons of the Church.

'So much less danger of a permanently unhappy involvement,' he had shouted, 'and after all I often think that's what they come here for. Ships that pass in the night and not on one's own doorstep you know.' He paused and smiled at Zipser salaciously. 'We all have to sow our wild oats at some time or other and it's much better to do it abroad. I've often thought that's what Rupert Brooke had in mind in that line of his about some corner of a foreign field. Mind you, one can hardly say that he was particularly healthy, come to think of it, but there we are. That's my advice to you, dear boy. Find a nice Swedish girl, I'm told they're very good, and have a ball. I believe that's the modern idiom. Yes, Swedes or French, depending on your taste. Spaniards are a bit difficult, I'm told, and then again they tend to be rather hairy. Still, buggers can't be choosers as dear old Sir Winston said at the queer's wedding. Ha, ha.'

Zipser staggered from the room. He knew now what muscular Christianity meant. He went down the dark staircase and was about to go out into the Court when he saw the group standing by the fountain. Zipser turned and fled up the stairs and locked himself in the lavatory on the top landing. He was still there an hour later when First Hall began.

Getting a Glass of Water

FREDERICK W. COZZENS

ONE EVENING MRS S. had retired, and I was busy writing, when it struck me a glass of ice-water would be palatable. So I took the candle and a pitcher, and went down to the pump. Our pump is in the kitchen. A country pump in the kitchen is more convenient; but a well with buckets is certainly most picturesque. Unfortunately, our well-water has not been sweet since it was cleaned out. First I had to open a bolted door that lets you into the basement hall, and then I went to the kitchen door, which proved to be locked. Then I remembered that our girl always carried the key to bed with her, and slept with it under her pillow. Then I retraced my steps, bolted the basement door, and went up in the dining-room. As is always the case, I found, when I could not get any water, I was thirstier than I supposed I was. Then I thought I would wake our girl up. Then I concluded not to do it. Then I thought of the well, but I gave that up on account of its flavor. Then I opened the closet doors; there was no water there; and then I thought of the dumbwaiter! The novelty of the idea made me smile; I took out two of the movable shelves, stood the pitcher on the bottom of the dumbwaiter, got in myself with the lamp; let myself down, until I suppose I was within a foot of the floor below, and then let go!

We came down so suddenly, that I was shot out of the apparatus as if it had been a catapult; it broke the pitcher, extinguished the lamp, and landed me in the middle of the kitchen at midnight, with no fire, and the air not much above the zero point. The truth is, I had miscalculated the distance of the descent – instead of falling one foot, I had fallen five. My first impulse was, to ascend by the way I came down, but I found that impracticable. Then I tried the kitchen door; it was locked. I tried to force it open; it was made of two-inch stuff, and held its own. Then I hoisted a window, and there were the rigid iron bars. If ever I felt angry at anybody it was at myself, for putting up those bars to please Mrs Sparrowgrass. I put them up, not to keep people in, but to keep people out.

I laid my cheek against the ice-cold barriers and looked out at the sky; not a star was visible; it was as black as ink overhead. Then I thought of Baron Trenck, and the prisoner of Chillon. Then I made a noise! I shouted until I was hoarse, and ruined our preserving-kettle with the poker. That brought our dogs out in full bark, and between us we made night hideous. Then I thought I heard a voice, and listened   it was Mrs Sparrowgrass calling to me from the top of the staircase. I tried to make her hear me, but the infernal dogs united with howl and growl and bark, so as to drown my voice, which is naturally plaintive and tender. Besides, there were two bolted doors and double deafened floors between us; how could she recognize my voice, even if she did hear it? Mrs Sparrowgrass called once or twice, and then got frightened; the next thing I heard was a sound as if the roof had fallen in, by which I understood that Mrs Sparrowgrass was springing the rattle! That called out our neighbor, already wide awake; he came to the rescue with a bull-terrier, a Newfoundland pup, a lantern and a revolver. The moment he saw me at the window, he shot at me, but fortunately just missed me. I threw myself under the kitchen table and ventured to expostulate with him, but he would not listen to reason. In the excitement I had forgotten his name, and that made matters worse. It was not until he had roused up everybody around, broken in the basement door with an axe, gotten into the kitchen with his cursed savage dogs and shooting-iron, and seized me by the collar, that he recognized me – and then, he wanted me to explain it! But what kind of an explanation could I make to him? I told him he would have to wait until my mind was composed, and then I would let him understand the whole matter fully. But he never would have had the particulars from me, for I do not approve of neighbors that shoot at you, break in your door, and treat you, in your own house, as if you were a jailbird. He knows all about it, however – somebody has told him – *somebody* tells everybody everything in our village.

The Wrong Boot

EVELYN WAUGH

Lord Copper, aristocratic owner of The Daily Beast *newspaper, has
been advised of an impending political crisis in the African state of
Ishmaelia. At a fashionable lunch party to which the noble lord is invited
the name of John Boot is much bandied about as being a writer of
distinction, admired by the PM himself. Why not send this distinguished
figure as special* Beast *correspondent to the beleaguered country? Unfortunately, Lord Copper is a little vague and, by the evening of the same day,
every detail except the surname Boot has eluded him. An extraordinary case
of mistaken identity ensues....*

THAT EVENING, MR SALTER, foreign editor of *The Beast*, was summoned to
dinner at his chief's country seat at East Finchley. It was a highly
unwelcome invitation; Mr Salter normally worked at the office until nine
o'clock. That evening he had planned a holiday at the opera; he and his
wife had been looking forward to it with keen enjoyment for some weeks.
As he drove out to Lord Copper's frightful mansion he thought sadly of
those carefree days when he had edited the Woman's Page, or, better
still, when he had chosen the jokes for one of Lord Copper's comic
weeklies. It was the policy of the Megalopolitan to keep the staff alert by
constant changes of occupation. Mr Salter's ultimate ambition was to
take charge of the Competitions. Meanwhile he was Foreign Editor and
found it a dog's life.

The two men dined alone. They ate parsley soup, whiting, roast veal,
cabinet pudding; they drank whisky and soda. Lord Copper explained
Nazism, Fascism and Communism; later, in his ghastly library, he
outlined the situation in the Far East. '*The Beast* stands for strong
mutually antagonistic governments everywhere,' he said. 'Self-sufficiency
at home, self-assertion abroad.'

Mr Salter's side of the conversation was limited to expressions of
assent. When Lord Copper was right he said, 'Definitely, Lord Copper;'
when he was wrong, 'Up to a point.'

'Let me see, what's the name of the place I mean? Capital of Japan?
Yokohama, isn't it?'

'Up to a point, Lord Copper.'

'And Hong Kong belongs to us, doesn't it?'

'Definitely, Lord Copper.'

After a time: 'Then there's this civil war in Ishmaelia. I propose to feature it. Who did you think of sending?'

'Well, Lord Copper, the choice seems between sending a staff reporter who will get the news but whose name the public doesn't know, or to get someone from outside with a name as a military expert. You see, since we lost Hitchcock...'

'Yes, yes. He was our only man with a European reputation. *I know.* Zinc will be sending him. *I know.* But he was wrong about the battle of Hastings. It *was* 1066. I looked it up. I won't employ a man who isn't big enough to admit when he's wrong.'

'We might share one of the Americans?'

'No, I tell you who I want; Boot.'

'Boot?'

'Yes, Boot. He's a young man whose work I'm very much interested in. He has the most remarkable style and he's been in Patagonia and the Prime Minister keeps his books by his bed. Do *you* read him?'

'Up to a point, Lord Copper.'

'Well, get on to him tomorrow. Have him up to see you. Be cordial. Take him out to dinner. Get him at any price. Well, at any reasonable price,' he added, for there had lately been a painful occurrence when instructions of this kind, given in an expansive mood, had been too literally observed and a trick cyclist who had momentarily attracted Lord Copper's attention had been engaged to edit the Sports Page on a five years' contract at five thousand a year.

Mr Salter went to work at midday. He found the Managing Editor cast in gloom.

'It's a terrible paper this morning,' he said. 'We paid Professor Jellaby thirty guineas for the feature article and there's not a word in it one can understand. Beaten by *The Brute* in every edition on the Zoo Mercy Slaying story. And *look at the Sports Page.*'

Together, in shame, the two men read the trick cyclist's Sports Page.

'Who's Boot?' asked Mr Salter at last.

'I know the name,' said the Managing Editor.

'The chief wants to send him to Ishmaelia. He's the Prime Minister's favourite writer.'

'Not the chap I was thinking of,' said the Managing Editor.

'Well, I've got to find him.' He listlessly turned the pages of the morning paper. 'Boot,' he said. 'Boot, Boot. Boot. Why! *Boot* – here he is. Why didn't the chief say he was a staff man?'

At the back of the paper, ignominiously sandwiched between Pip and Pop, the Bedtime Pets, and the recipe for a dish named 'Waffle Scramble', lay the bi-weekly half-column devoted to Nature:

LUSH PLACES, edited by William Boot, Countryman.

'Do you suppose that's the right one?'

'Sure of it. The Prime Minister is nuts on rural England.'

'He's supposed to have a particularly high-class style: *"Feather-footed through the plashy fen passes the questing vole"* ... would that be it?'

'Yes,' said the Managing Editor. 'That must be good style. At least it doesn't sound like anything else to me. I know the name well now you mention it. Never seen the chap. I don't think he's ever been to London. Sends his stuff in by post. All written out in pen and ink.'

'I've got to ask him to dinner.'

'Give him cider.'

'Is that what countrymen like?'

'Yes, cider and tinned salmon is the staple diet of the agricultural classes.'

'I'll send him a telegram. Funny the chief wanting to send him to Ishmaelia.'

'Change and decay in all around I see,' sang Uncle Theodore, gazing out of the morning-room window.

Thus, with startling loudness, he was accustomed to relieve his infrequent fits of depression; but decay, rather than change, was characteristic of the immediate prospect.

The immense trees which encircled Boot Magna Hall, shaded its drives and rides, and stood (tastefully disposed and the whim of some forgotten, provincial predecessor of Repton), singly and in groups about the park, had suffered, some from ivy, some from lightning, some from the various malignant disorders that vegetation is heir to, but all principally from old age. Some were supported with trusses and crutches of iron, some were filled with cement; some, even now, in June, could show only a handful of green leaves at their extremities. Sap ran thin and slow; a gusty night always brought down a litter of dead timber.

The lake was moved by strange tides. Sometimes, as at the present moment, it sank to a single, opaque pool in a wilderness of mud and rushes; sometimes it rose and inundated five acres of pasture. There had once been an old man in one of the lodges who understood the workings of the water system; there were sluice gates hidden among the reeds, and manholes, dotted about in places known only to him, furnished with taps and cocks; that man had been able to control an ornamental cascade and draw a lofty jet of water from the mouth of the dolphin on the South terrace. But he had been in his grave fifteen years and the secret had died with him.

The house was large but by no means too large for the Boot family, which at this time numbered eight. There were in the direct line: William who owned the house and estate, William's sister Priscilla who claimed to own the horses, William's widowed mother who owned the contents of the house and exercised ill-defined rights over the flower garden, and William's widowed grandmother who was said to own 'the money'. No one knew how much she possessed; she had been bedridden as long as William's memory went back. It was from her that such large cheques issued as were from time to time necessary for balancing the estate accounts and paying for Uncle Theodore's occasional, disastrous visits to London. Uncle Theodore, the oldest of the male collaterals, was by far the gayest. Uncle Roderick was in many ways the least eccentric. He had managed the estates and household throughout William's minority and continued to do so with a small but regular deficit which was made up annually by one of grandmamma's cheques. The widowed Lady Trilby was William's Great-Aunt Anne, his father's elder sister; she owned the motor car, a vehicle adapted to her own requirements; it had a horn which could be worked from the back seat; her weekly journey to church resounded through the village like the Coming of the Lord. Uncle Bernard devoted himself to a life of scholarship but had received little general recognition, for his researches, though profound, were narrow, being connected solely with his own pedigree. He had traced William's descent through three different lines from Ethelred the Unready and only lack of funds fortunately prevented him from prosecuting a claim to the abeyant barony of de Butte.

All the Boots, in one way or another, had about a hundred a year each as pocket money. It was therefore convenient for them to live together at Boot Magna where wages and household expenses were counted in with Uncle Roderick's annual deficit. The richest member of the household, in ready cash, was Nannie Bloggs, who had been bedridden for the last thirty years; she kept her savings in a red flannel bag under the bolster. Uncle Theodore made attempts on them from time to time, but she was a sharp old girl and, since she combined a longstanding aversion to Uncle Theodore with a preternatural aptitude for bringing off showy doubles during the flat racing season, her hoard continued to grow. The Bible and the Turf Guide were her only reading. She got great delight from telling each member of the family, severally and secretly, that he or she was her heir.

In other rooms about the house reposed: Nannie Price, ten years the junior of Nannie Bloggs, and bedridden from about the same age. She gave her wages to Chinese Missions and had little influence in the house; Sister Watts, old Mrs Boot's first nurse, and Sister Sampson, her second: Miss Scope, Aunt Anne's governess, veteran invalid of some years seniority in bed to old Mrs Boot herself: and Bentinck the butler: James, the first footman, had been confined to his room for some time, but he was able on warm days to sit in an armchair at the window. Nurse Granger was still on her feet, but as her duties included the charge of all eight sick rooms, it was thought she would not long survive. Ten servants waited upon the household and upon one another, but in a desultory fashion, for they could spare very little time from the five meat meals which tradition daily allowed them. In the circumstances the Boots did not entertain and were indulgently spoken of in the district as being 'poor as church mice.'

The fashionable John Courteney Boot was a remote cousin, or, as Uncle Bernard preferred, the member of a cadet branch. William had never met him; he had met very few people indeed. It was not true to say, as the Managing Editor of *The Beast* had said, that he had never been to London, but his visits had been infrequent enough for each to be distinct and perennially horrifying in his memory.

'Change and decay in all around I see,' sang Uncle Theodore. It was his habit to sing the same line over and over again. He was waiting for the morning papers. So were William and Uncle Roderick. They were brought by the butcher, often blotched with red, any time between eleven and midday, and then, if not intercepted, disappeared among the sick rooms to return at teatime hopelessly mutilated, for both Bentinck and old Mrs Boot kept scrapbooks, and Sister Sampson had the habit of cutting out coupons and losing them in the bedclothes. This morning they were late. It was a matter of great anxiety to William.

He had never been to the Megalopolitan offices or met anyone connected with *The Beast*. His job as author of *Lush Places* had been passed on to him by the widow on the death of its previous holder, the Rector of Boot Magna. He had carefully modelled his style on the late Rector's, at first painfully, now almost without effort. The work was of the utmost importance to him: he was paid a guinea a time and it gave him the best possible excuse for remaining uninterruptedly in the country.

And now it was in danger. On the previous Thursday a very dreadful thing had happened. Drawing on the observations of a lifetime and after due cross-examination of the head keeper and half an hour with the encyclopaedia, William had composed a lyrical but wholly accurate account of the badger; one of his more finished essays. Priscilla in a playful mood had found the manuscript and altered it, substituting for 'badger' throughout 'the great crested grebe'. It was not until Saturday morning when, in this form, it appeared in *The Beast*, that William was aware of the outrage.

His mail had been prodigious; some correspondents were sceptical, others derisive; one lady wrote to ask whether she read him aright in thinking he condoned the practice of baiting these rare and beautiful birds with terriers and deliberately destroying their earthy homes; how could this be tolerated in the so-called twentieth century? A major in Wales challenged him categorically to produce a single authenticated case of a great crested grebe attacking young rabbits. It had been exceedingly painful. All through the weekend William had awaited his dismissal, but Monday and Tuesday passed without a word from *The Beast*. He composed and despatched a light dissertation on water voles and expected the worst. Perhaps the powers at *The Beast* were too much enraged even to send back his manuscript; when Wednesday's paper came he would find another tenant of *Lush Places*. It came. He hunted frantically for his half column. It was there, a green oasis between Waffle Scramble and the Bedtime Pets. *'Feather-footed through the plashy fen passes the questing vole . . .'* It was all right. By some miracle Saturday's shame had been covered.

His uncles peevishly claimed the paper; he surrendered it readily. He stood at the french window blinking at the summer landscape; the horses at grass beyond the ha-ha skipped and frolicked.

'Confound the thing,' said Uncle Rockerick behind him. 'Can't find the cricket anywhere. Whole page seems to be given up to some damn-fool cycling championship at Cricklewood Stadium.'

William did not care. In the fullness of his gratitude he resolved to give rodents a miss that Saturday (though he was particularly attached to them) and write instead of wild flowers and birdsong. He might even risk something out of the poets.

> *'Nay not so much as out of bed?*
> *When all the birds have Matins said,'*

he sang, in his heart, to the recumbent figures above him. And then, wheezing heavily, with crumbs on his mouth, ponderously straddling across the morning-room, came Troutbeck, the aged boy, bearing a telegram. Curiosity and resentment contended for mastery in Troutbeck's demeanour; curiosity because telegrams were of rare occurrence at Boot Magna; resentment at the interruption of his 'elevenses' – a lavish and ruminative feast which occupied the servants' hall from ten-thirty until noon.

William's face quickly reassured him that he had not been called from the table on any frivolous pretext. 'Bad news,' he was able to report. 'Shocking bad news for Master William.'

'It couldn't hardly be a death,' said the third housemaid. 'All the family's here.'

'Whatever it was we shall soon know,' said Troutbeck. 'It struck Master William all of a heap. Might I thank you to pass the chutney.'

Bad news indeed! Oblivious to the sunshine and the grazing horses and the stertorous breathing of his Uncle Theodore, William re-read the frightful doom that had fallen on him.

REQUEST YOUR IMMEDIATE PRESENCE HERE URGENT LORD COPPERS PERSONAL DESIRE SALTER BEAST.

'Nothing serious, I hope!' said Uncle Theodore, to whom telegrams, in the past, had from time to time brought news as disquieting as to any man living.

'Yes,' said William, 'I have been called to London.'

'Have you, my boy? That's interesting. I was thinking of running up for a night myself . . .'

But Uncle Theodore was speaking to the air. William was already at work, setting into motion the elaborate household machinery which would, too soon, effect his departure.

After an early luncheon, William went to say goodbye to his grand-mother. She looked at him with doleful, mad eyes. 'Going to London, eh? Well, I hardly suppose I shall be alive when you return. Wrap up warm, dear.' It was eternal winter in Mrs Boot's sunny bedroom.

All the family who had the use of their legs attended on the steps to see William off; Priscilla bathed in tears of penitence. Nannie Bloggs sent him down three golden sovereigns. Aunt Anne's motor car was there to take him away. At the last moment Uncle Theodore attempted to get in at the offside, but was detected and deterred. 'Just wanted to see a chap in Jermyn Street about some business,' he said wistfully.

It was always a solemn thing for a Boot to go to London; solemn as a funeral for William on this afternoon. Once or twice on the way to the station, once or twice as the train stopped on the route to Paddington, William was tempted to give up the expedition in despair. Why should he commit himself to this abominable city merely to be railed at and, for all he knew of Lord Copper's temperament, physically assaulted? But sterner counsels prevailed. He might bluff it out. Lord Copper was a townsman, a provincial townsman at that, and certainly did not know the difference between a badger and a great crested grebe. It was William's word against a few cantankerous correspondents, and people who wrote to the newspapers were proverbially unbalanced. By the time he reached Westbury he had sketched out a little scene for himself, in which he stood resolutely in the board room defying the doctrinaire zoology of Fleet Street; every inch a Boot, thrice descended from Ethrelred the Unready; rightful 15th Baron de Butte, haughty as a chieftain, honest as a peasant. 'Lord Copper,' he was saying, 'no man shall call me a liar unchastised. The great crested grebe *does* hibernate.'

He went to the dining-car and ordered some whisky. The steward said, 'We're serving teas. Whisky after Reading.' After Reading he tried again. 'We're serving dinners. I'll bring you one to your carriage.' When it came, William spilled it down his tie. He gave the steward one of Nannie Bloggs' sovereigns in mistake for a shilling. It was contemptuously refused and everyone in the carriage stared at him. A man in a bowler hat said, 'May I look? Don't often see one of them nowadays. Tell you what I'll do, I'll toss you for it. Call.'

William said, 'Heads.'

'Tails it is,' said the man in the bowler hat, putting it in his waistcoat pocket. He then went on reading his paper and everyone stared harder at William. His spirits began to sink; the mood of defiance passed. It was always the way; the moment he left the confines of Boot Magna he found himself in a foreign and hostile world. There was a train back at ten o'clock that night. Wild horses would not keep him from it. He would see Lord Copper, explain the situation fully and frankly, throw himself upon his mercy and, successful or defeated, catch the train at ten. By Reading he had worked out this new and humble policy. He would tell Lord Copper about Priscilla's tears; great men were proverbially vulnerable to appeals of that kind. The man opposite him looked over the top of his paper. 'Got any more quids?'

'No,' said William.

'Pity.'

At seven he reached Paddington and the atrocious city was all around him.

The Megalopolitan building, numbers 700–853 Fleet Street, was disconcerting. At first William thought that the taxi driver, spotting a bumpkin, had driven him to the wrong address.

His acquaintance with offices was very small. At the time of his coming of age he had spent several mornings with the family solicitor in King's Bench Walk. At home he knew the local Estate Agents and Auctioneers, the Bank and the Town Hall. He had once seen in Taunton a barely intelligible film about newspaper life in New York where neurotic men in shirt sleeves and eyeshades had rushed from telephone to tape machines, insulting and betraying one another in surroundings of unredeemed squalor. From these memories he had a confused expectation that was rudely shocked by the Byzantine vestibule and Sassanian lounge of Copper House. He thought at first that he must have arrived at some new and less exclusive rival of the RAC. Six lifts seemed to be in perpetual motion; with dazzling frequency their doors flew open to reveal now left, now right, now two or three at a time, like driven game, a series of girls in Caucasian uniform. 'Going up,' they cried in Punch-and-Judy accents and, before anyone could enter, snapped their doors and disappeared from view. A hundred or so men and women of all ranks and ages passed before William's eyes. The sole stationary objects were a chryselephantine effigy of Lord Copper in coronation robes, rising above the throng, on a polygonal malachite pedestal, and a concierge, also more than life size, who sat in a plate-glass enclosure, like a fish in an aquarium, and gazed at the agitated multitude with fishy, supercilious eyes. Under his immediate care were a dozen page boys in skyblue uniforms, who between errands pinched one another furtively on a long bench. Medals of more battles than were ever fought by human arms or on earthly fields glittered on the porter's chest. William discovered a small vent in his tank and addressed him diffidently. 'Is his Lordship at home?'

'We have sixteen peers on the staff. Which was you referring to?'

'I wish to see Lord Copper.'

'Ho! Cyril, show this gentleman to a chair and give him a form.'

A minute blue figure led William to a desk and gave him a piece of paper. William filled it in. *'Mr Boot wishes to see Lord Copper. Subject: great crested grebes.'*

Cyril took the paper to the concierge, who read it, looked searchingly at William and mouthed, 'Fetch the gentleman.'

William was led forward.

'You wish to see Lord Copper?'

'Yes, please.'

'Ho! no you don't. Not about great crested grebes.'

'And badgers too,' said William. 'It is rather a long story.'

'I'll be bound it is. Tell you what, you go across the street and tell it to Lord Zinc at *The Daily Brute* office. That'll do just as well, now won't it?'

'I've got an appointment,' said William, and produced his telegram.

The concierge read it thoughtfully, held it up to the light, and said 'Ah!'; read it again and said: 'What you want to see is Mr Salter. Cyril, give the gentleman another form.

Five minutes later William found himself in the office of the foreign editor.

It was an encounter of great embarrassment for both of them. For William it was the hour of retribution; he advanced, heavy with guilt, to meet whatever doom had been decreed for him. Mr Salter had the more active part. He was under orders to be cordial and spring Lord Copper's proposal on the poor hick when he had won his confidence by light conversation and heavy hospitality.

His knowledge of rural life was meagre. He had been born in West Kensington and educated at a large London day-school. When not engaged in one or other capacity in the vast Megalopolitan organization he led a life of blameless domesticity in Welwyn Garden City. His annual holiday was, more often than not, spent at home; once or twice when Mrs Salter complained of being run down, they had visited prosperous resorts on the East Coast. 'The country,' for him, meant what you saw in the train between Liverpool Street and Frinton. If a psychoanalyst, testing his associations, had suddenly said to Mr Salter the word 'farm', the surprising response would have been 'Bang', for he had once been blown up and buried while sheltering in a farm in Flanders. It was his single intimate association with the soil. It had left him with the obstinate though admittedly irrational belief that agriculture was something alien and highly dangerous. Normal life, as he saw it, consisted in regular journeys by electric train, monthly cheques, communal amusements and a cosy horizon of slates and chimneys; there was something unEnglish and not quite right about 'the country', with its solitude and self-sufficiency, its bloody recreations, its darkness and silence and sudden, inexplicable noises; the kind of place where you never knew from one minute to the next that you might not be tossed by a bull or pitchforked by a yokel or rolled over and broken up by a pack of hounds.

He had been round the office canvassing opinions about the subjects of conversation proper to countrymen. 'Mangelwurzels are a safe topic,' he had been told, 'only you mustn't call them that. It's a subject on which farmers are very touchy. Call them roots ...'

He greeted William with cordiality. 'Ah, Boot, how are you? Don't think I've had the pleasure before. Know your work well of course. Sit down. Have a cigarette or' – had he made a floater? – 'or do your prefer your churchwarden?'

William took a cigarette. He and Mr Salter sat opposite one another. Between them, on the desk, lay an open atlas in which Mr Salter had been vainly trying to find Reykjavik.

There was a pause, during which Mr Salter planned a frank and disarming opening. 'How are your roots, Boot?' It came out wrong.

'How are your boots, root?' he asked.

William, glumly awaiting some fulminating rebuke, started and said, 'I beg your pardon?'

'I mean brute,' said Mr Salter.

William gave it up. Mr Salter gave it up. They sat staring at one another, fascinated, hopeless. Then:

'How's hunting?' asked Mr Salter, trying a new line. 'Foxes pretty plentiful?'

'Well, we stop in the summer, you know.'

'Do you? Everyone away, I suppose?'

Another pause: 'Lot of foot and mouth, I expect,' said Mr Salter hopefully.

'None, I'm thankful to say.'

'Oh!'

Their eyes fell. They both looked at the atlas before them.

'You don't happen to know where Reykjavik is?'

'No.'

'Pity. I hoped you might. No one in the office does.'

'Was that what you wanted to see me about?'

'Oh, no, not at all! Quite the contrary.'

Another pause.

William saw what was up. This decent little man had been deputed to sack him and could not get it out. He came to the rescue. 'I expect you want to talk about the great crested grebe.'

'Good God, no,' said Mr Salter, with instinctive horror, adding politely, 'At least not unless *you* do.'

'No, not at all,' said William, 'I thought *you* might want to.'

'Not at all,' said Mr Salter.

'That's all right, then.'

'Yes, that's all right ...' Desperately: 'I say, how about some zider?'

'Zider?'

'Yes. I expect you feel like a drop of zider about this time, don't you? We'll go out and have some.'

The journalists in the film had been addicted to straight rye. Silent but wondering, William followed the foreign editor. They shared the lift with a very extraordinary man, bald, young, fleshless as a mummy, dressed in brown and white checks, smoking a cheroot. 'He does the Sports Page now,' said Mr Salter apologetically, when he was out of hearing.

In the public house at the corner, where *The Beast* reporters congregated, the barmaid took their order with surprise. 'Cider? I'll see.' Then she produced two bottles of sweet and fizzy liquid. William and Mr Salter sipped suspiciously.

'Not quite what you're used to down on the farm, I'm afraid.'

'Well, to tell you the truth, I don't often drink it. We give it to the haymakers, of course, and I sometimes have some of theirs.' Then, fearing that this might sound snobbish, he added, 'My Uncle Bernard drinks it for his rheumatism.'

'You're sure you wouldn't sooner have something else?'

'No.'

'You mean you wouldn't?'

'I mean I would.'

'Really?'

'Really; much sooner.'

'Good for you, Garge,' said Mr Salter, and from that moment a new, more human note was apparent in their relationship; conversation was still far from easy, but they had this bond in common, that neither of them liked cider.

Mr Salter clung to it strenuously. 'Interesting you don't like cider,' he said. 'Neither do I.'

'No,' said William. 'I never have since I was sick as a small boy, in the hay field.'

'It upsets me inside.'

'Exactly.'

'Now whisky never did anyone any harm.'

'No.'

Interest seemed to flag. Mr Salter tried once more. 'Make much parsnip wine down your way?'

'Not much ...' It was clearly his turn now. He sipped and thought and finally said: 'Pretty busy at the office, I expect?'

'Yes, very.'

'Tell me – I've often wondered – do you keep a machine of your own or send out to the printers?'

'We have machines of our own.'

'Do you? They must work jolly fast.'

'Yes.'

'I mean, you have to get it written and printed and corrected and everything all on the same day, otherwise the news would become stale. People would have heard it on the wireless, I mean.'

'Yes.'

'D'you do much of the printing yourself?'

'No. You see, I'm the foreign editor.'

'I suppose that's why you wanted to find Reykjavik.'

'Yes.'

'Jolly difficult knowing where all these places are.'

'Yes.'

'So many of them, I mean.'

'Yes.'

'Never been abroad myself.'

This seemed too good an opening to be missed. 'Would you like to go to Ishmaelia?'

'No.'

'Not at all?'

'Not at all. For one thing I couldn't afford the fare.'

'Oh, we would pay the fare,' said Mr Salter, laughing indulgently.

So that was it. Transportation. The sense of persecution which had haunted William for the last three hours took palpable and grotesque shape before him. It was too much. Conscious of a just cause and a free soul he rose and defied the nightmare. 'Really,' he said, in ringing tones, 'I call that a bit thick. I admit I slipped up on the great crested grebe, slipped up badly. As it happened, it was not my fault. I came here prepared to explain, apologize and, if need be, make reparation. You refused to listen to me. "Good God, no", you said, when I offered to explain. And now you calmly propose to ship me out of the country because of a trifling and, in my opinion, justifiable error. Who does Lord Copper think he is? The mind boggles at the vanity of the man. If he chooses to forget my eighteen months' devoted and unremitting labour in his service, he is, I admit, entitled to dismiss me ...'

'Boot, Boot, old man,' cried Mr Salter, 'you've got this all wrong. With the possible exception of the Prime Minister, you have no more ardent admirer than Lord Copper. He wants you to *work* for him in Ishmaelia.'

'Would he pay my fare back?'

'Yes, of course.'

'Oh, that's rather different.... Even so it seems a silly sort of scheme. I mean, how will it look in *Lush Places* when I start writing about sandstorms and lions and whatever they have in Ishmaelia? Not *lush*, I mean.'

'Let me tell you about it at dinner.'

They took a taxicab down Fleet Street and the Strand to the grill room where *The Beast* staff always entertained when they were doing so at the paper's expense.

'Do you *really* want tinned salmon?'

'No.'

'Sure?'

'Quite sure.'

Mr Salter regarded his guest with renewed approval and handed him the menu.

The esteem William had won by his distaste for cider and tinned salmon survived the ordering of dinner. William did not, as had seemed only too likely, demand pickled walnuts and Cornish pasties; nor did he, like the Budapest correspondent whom Mr Salter had last entertained in his room, draw attention to himself by calling for exotic Magyar dishes and, on finding no one qualified to make them, insist on preparing for himself, with chafing dish and spirit lamp, before a congregation of puzzled waiters, a nauseous sauce of sweet peppers, honey and almonds. He ordered a mixed grill, and, while he was eating, Mr Salter attempted, artfully, to kindle his enthusiasm for the new project.

'See that man there, that's Pappenhacker.'

William looked, and saw.

'Yes?'

'The cleverest man in Fleet Street.'

William looked again. Pappenhacker was young and swarthy, with great horn goggles and a receding, stubbly chin. He was having an altercation with some waiters.

'Yes?'

'He's going to Ishmaelia for the *Daily Twopence*.'

'He seems to be in a very bad temper.'

'Not really. He's always like that to waiters. Most of the staff of the *Twopence* are – they're University men, you see. Pappenhacker's very clever, of course, but he gets rather unpopular.'

'He looks as if he were going to hit them.'

'Yes, he does sometimes. Quite a lot of restaurants won't have him in. You see, you'll meet a lot of interesting people when you go to Ishmaelia.'

'Mightn't it be rather dangerous?'

Mr Salter smiled; to him, it was as though an Arctic explorer had expressed a fear that the weather might turn cold. 'Nothing to what you are used to in the country,' he said. 'You'll be surprised to find how far the war correspondents keep from the fighting. Why Hitchcock reported the whole Abyssinia campaign from Asmara and gave us some of the most colourful, eyewitness stuff we ever printed. In any case your life will be insured by the paper for five thousand pounds. No, no, Boot, I don't think you need worry about risk.'

'And you'd go on paying me my wages?'

'Certainly.'

'*And* my fare there *and* back, *and* my expenses?'

'Yes.'

William thought the matter over carefully. At length he said: 'No.'

'No?'

'No. It's very kind of you, but I think I would sooner not go. I don't like the idea at all.' He looked at his watch. 'I must be going to Paddington soon to catch my train.'

'Listen,' said Mr Salter. 'I don't think you have fully understood the situation. Lord Copper is particularly interested in your work and, to be frank, he insists on your going. We are willing to pay a very fair salary. Fifty pounds a month was the sum suggested.'

'*Fifty pounds a month!*' said William goggling.

'A week,' said Mr Salter hastily.

'Gosh,' said William.

'And think what you can make on your expenses,' urged Mr Salter. 'At least another twenty. I happened to see Hitchcock's expense sheet when he was working for us in Shanghai. He charged three hundred pounds for camels alone.'

'But I don't think I shall know what to do with a camel.'

Mr Salter saw he was not making his point clear. 'Take a single example,' he said. 'Supposing you want to have dinner. Well, you go to a restaurant and do yourself proud, best of everything. Bill perhaps may be two pounds. Well, you put down five pounds for entertainment on your expenses. You've had a slap-up dinner, you're three pounds to the good, and everyone is satisfied.'

'But you see I don't like restaurants and no one pays for dinner at home, anyway. The servants just bring it in.'

'Or supposing you want to send flowers to your girl. You just go to a shop, send a great spray of orchids and put them down as "Information".'

'But I haven't got a girl and there are heaps of flowers at home.' He looked at his watch again. 'Well, I'm afraid I must be going. You see, I have a day-return ticket. I tell you what I'll do. I'll consult my family and let you know in a week or two.'

'Lord Copper wants you to leave tomorrow.'

'Oh, I couldn't do that, anyway, you know. I haven't packed or anything. And I daresay I should need some new clothes. Oh, no, that's out of the question.'

'We might offer a larger salary.'

'Oh, no, thank you. It isn't that. It's just that I don't want to go.'

'Is there *nothing* you want?'

'D'you know, I don't believe there is. Except to keep my job in *Lush Places* and go on living at home.'

It was a familiar cry; during his fifteen years of service with the Megalopolitan Company Mr Salter had heard it upon the lips of countless distressed colleagues; upon his own. In a moment of compassion he remembered the morning when he had been called from his desk in *Clean Fun*, never to return to it. The post had been his delight and pride; one for which he believed he had a particular aptitude. . . . First he would open the morning mail and sort the jokes sent him by the private contributors (one man sent him thirty or forty a week) into those that were familiar, those that were indecent, and those that deserved the half-crown postal order payable upon publication. Then he would spend an hour or two with the bound *Punches* noting whatever seemed topical. Then the ingenious game began of fitting these legends to the funny illustrations previously chosen for him by the Art Editor. Serene and delicate sunrise on a day of tempest! From this task of ordered discrimination he had been thrown into the ruthless cut-throat, rough and tumble of *The Beast* Woman's Page. From there, crushed and bedraggled, he had been tossed into the editorial chair of the Imperial and Foreign News. . . . His heart bled for William, but he was true to the austere traditions of his service. He made the reply that had silenced so many resentful novices in the past.

'Oh, but Lord Copper expects his staff to work wherever the best interests of the paper call them. I don't think he would employ anyone of whose loyalty he was doubtful, *in any capacity*.'

'You mean if I don't go to Ishmaelia I get the sack?'

'Yes,' said Mr Salter. 'In so many words that is exactly what I – what Lord Copper means. . . . Won't you have a glass of port before we return to the office?'

The Adventures of a Christmas Turkey

MARK LEMON

SOME FEW YEARS AGO I met with a great sorrow, and as the hunting season was at an end, and I could not resort to my usual remedy for vexation, I turned sulky, and went alone to an out of the way seaside place on the coast of Sussex. It was a small shipbuilding town, and one fine July afternoon I was lying on the beach listening idly to the hammers and mallets of the shipwrights 'closing rivets up' or caulking the sides of some stormworn collier. The noise of a wandering circus band occasionally mingled with the sounds of industry, but all were sufficiently distant to make the quiet murmuring of the sea more distinct and soothing. Between me and the town were oysterbeds, fed by one or two creeks which were filled and emptied by the tides, and a tract of coarse brown grass which had grown up between the shingle long deserted by the sea. I had stolen away, as I have said, from a great grief, and sat looking upon the deep green waters, ever upheaving and falling as from the action of some mighty heart, that, like my own, was full to silence. I had strange dreams that day, lying lonely on the beach – dreams of other dreams which had made up much of my life which had passed, and, perhaps, of the life which is left to me. After a time some schoolboys came shouting and laughing across the brown grass to the seaside, and soon made playfellows of the waves, as though the restless waters had never wrecked mighty ships and drowned hosts of men, or torn down rocks, and cliffs, and solid masonry. The play ended, I was again alone, looking upon the sea, recalling the time when I had had such sport, and wondering if any of that merry group would ever sit, as I then sat, thankful for the silence and the solitude of the quiet shore. The solitude and silence were thus disturbed:

'If ever I catch you near those oysterbeds again, I'll rope's end you till you're as blue-lined as a sailor's shirt.'

The speaker was evidently in earnest, and close behind me. He was a fiery-faced, white-headed old gentleman, of a nautical build, and the boy he held by the collar, and whom he was thus addressing, was seaborn also, as his suit of tar and canvas certified.

'I wasn't anigh 'em!' cried the boy. 'I see another boy mucking [loitering] about there, but it wasn't me. You let me goa!' And the lad struggled like a dogfish.

'I know that it was you,' said Captain Crump (I afterwards learned the speaker's name); 'and those periwinkles I found you boiling in your mother's teakettle came out of my beds, I've no doubt.'

'They wasn't my winkles,' replied the boy: 'I never eats them; they always terrifies [annoys] me so when I does. You let me goa, or I'll kick your bad leg, I will.'

Captain Crump gave his captive another hearty shake and a tap on the head with his walking-cane (the boy's skull must have been as strong as a cocoanut shell not to have cracked with the blow), receiving a sharp kick in exchange, and the belligerents parted company.

The boy put a few yards between himself and the enemy, wiped his streaming eyes with the back of his hand, and, mounting a pile of shingle, bawled out:

'Captain Crump! Hallo, Captain Crump! how did you like your Christmas turkee?'

There was nothing particularly uncivil in the inquiry that I could discover, but it hit Captain Crump in a tender part, and set him gesticulating like an insane windmill – if you will allow me such a figure of speech.

That the Captain was mentally expressing a great deal no one could doubt who saw his distended eyes and cheeks, the latter being as red as his nose in its normal state, and nothing incombustible could be redder than that useful and prominent feature of Captain Crump's physiognomy. There is nothing new or remarkable in a red nose, I am aware. In fact, to mention such a distinction is commonplace; but Captain Crump, owner of the oyster and periwinkle beds, was a commonplace character, and he had a red nose.

The boy scampered away over the brown grass like a human plover (the *oyster-catcher*, perhaps), occasionally pausing to utter his cry of 'Christmas turkee!' until he could no longer be heard, but only seen, evidently screaming in defiance of Captain Crump.

I do not know what there was in my appearance to justify the confidence, but the irritated gentleman stopped at the place where I was lying, and without any preface began the explanation of his late extraordinary display of temper and annoyance; and, to my surprise, I confess, I learned that the oysters and periwinkles had nothing to do with the matter.

I was glad to leave my own sad thoughts for a while, and therefore encouraged my new acquaintance to be communicative; and what he told me as we walked over the brown grass to Littletown, and what I gathered from the landlady of the Ship Torbay in the course of the ensuing evening, I will tell to you if you will listen to me.

On the extreme right of Littletown, looking towards the sea, stands a neat one-storied cottage, distinguished by a high flagstaff, from which, on high days and holidays, floats the union jack or the Maltese cross, and on other days a man-o'-war's whip flouts any breeze that may be stirring. On one side of a neatly-kept garden, ornamented here and there with flint boulders and bordered with large shingle, is a wire inclosure containing a number of hencoops, formerly belonging to an Indiaman wrecked upon the coast in the year 18—. A variety of poultry strut, scratch, and peck away their lives within, being carefully, tenderly, and daily fed by Mrs Crump, the kindly, good-natured spouse of Captain Crump, who is the proprietor of the aforesaid cottage, flagpost, flags, garden, boulders, shingle, hencoops, and poultry. An old ship's gun formerly stood at the foot of the flagpost; but, being discharged on some occasion of public rejoicing, it proved to have been cracked, and burst into a hundred pieces, fortunately doing no other damage than destroying all the front windows of Crump's Cottage, and throwing Mrs Crump's pet parrot into a fit of convulsions. The bird moulted, in consequence, all but its head feathers, and looked very like a late Vice-Chancellor in his bathing-dress and with his wig on.

On the extreme left of Littletown stood another villa of more urban pretensions, 'verandahed, and stuccoed, and cockneyfied,' according to Captain Crump, but made 'snug and comfortable,' according to the opinion of its owners, Mr and Mrs Macgrey; and I have no doubt but their estimate was the just one. Mr Alexander Macgrey had made his own way in the world. From carrying a pedlar's pack, he had secured a small competency in a City warehouse, and, having no children to keep him in harness to the end of his days, had wisely written the word 'Content' at the bottom of his last year's balance-sheet and come to settle at his wife's birthplace, Littletown. Captain William Crump was also a Littletownian, and, as a matter of course, had known Mrs Macgrey when they were boy and girl together; but for some unguessed-at reason, Captain Crump resisted all approaches to intimacy on the part of the Macgreys – almost treating the gentleman with open rudeness. The ladies were more amiable, and never failed to recognize each other at church, or in the very small marketplace, which boasted of one butcher's stall and a greengrocer's barrow, and now and then ventured to give each other the state of the weather when they passed in the street. The gentlemen bowed, sometimes; although one would have supposed that, being so nearly on an equality in point of station and education, they would have been glad of each other's society, as Littletown was only inhabited by boatbuilders, shipchandlers, and their like.

Except John Bishopp, general shopkeeper, who added the cultivation of a few acres of land to the vending of the multifarious articles of his commercial establishment; he lived midway between the Crumps and the Macgreys and made his money out of both. John Bishopp was a jolly sort of man that everybody liked, and, as his business took him about the country a good deal, the management of the shop was principally left to Mrs Bishopp, who was a good woman enough, as times go, although a bit of a shrew. John kept her in pretty fair order, and when he stayed rather later than he ought to have done over his pipe and alepot, he received (what he called) 'his supper of carp-pie' with good humour, but always expected to hear no more of his delinquencies in the morning. A very wise regulation that of John Bishopp, and young couples would do well to adopt it. What say you, dear grandmamma, who have had some patching and botching of the matrimonial yoke to do in your time?

Captain William Crump was, as you may have imagined, a Captain by courtesy only. He had amassed money in many ways during some thirty years' service in the merchant navy, and had retired to Littletown to spend the evening of his busy life. He had rather a warm temper, which he kept well supplied with fuel in the form of three-quarter grog, although he never drank to excess, if you accepted his own notion of temperance. He had many odd opinions, whims, and prejudices, but was not a bad fellow, take him for all in all. One of his whims led to the incidents of this story, and with that we have, therefore, only to do at present. It was this: Having found it impossible to procure in Littletown a turkey for his Christmas dinner, 18—, he had determined before the next coming of that festive season to rear one for his own consumption, and had therefore added to Mrs Crump's ornithological collection a fine young bird to be reared, fattened, and sacrificed at the Christmastide ensuing. It wrung the tender soul of Mrs Crump to know that the pretty creature she tended daily, and which came at last to feed from her hand like her other favourites, was doomed to a culinary end; but her duty as a wife overcame her feelings as a philanthropist, and she saw with a melancholy pleasure the satisfactory progress of the condemned. One November night, however, by some unknown and undiscovered means the thriving bird broke its leg, and so serious was the fracture that amputation became necessary, to the great grief of Mrs Crump and the exceeding wrath of her irritable husband. The turkey soon suffered in flesh from the absence of its lost member, and would probably have been unworthy of its high destiny had not Captain Crump – handy as most sailors are – made it a wooden leg, which was so cleverly contrived that motion again became easy, and plumpness was restored long before the day of execution, which had been fixed for December the 22nd. On the morning of that day Mrs Crump shut herself up in the bedroom, whilst Captain Crump and his man Jabez proceeded to execution in the stable, and it was some satisfaction to the sensitive lady to know that the victim made a most exemplary end, and died weighing 14 lb. 6 oz. As the Captain kept no quadruped except a cat, the turkey was suspended to the hook which usually supports the stable-lantern, and Crump and Jabez were both engaged in silent contemplation of the noble bird, when a gipsy-looking man approached, laden with branches of holly and mistletoe for sale. Now, one of Captain Crump's prejudices was a thorough hatred of the whole Bohemian race, declaring them to be, without exception, rogues and vagabonds of the worst kind; and it is believed he would have willingly subscribed to have chartered the *Great Eastern* and freighted her with all the tribes of Cooper, Lee, and Bonnys, provided the owners would have undertaken to have scuttled the Leviathan in the deepest depths of the Atlantic.

'Buy any holly and mistletoe?' asked the gipsy, 'capital lot here, your honour, cheap.'

'No!' roared Crump from the stable, whilst Jabez winked at the man and motioned him to be gone.

'Holly werry scarce, your honour,' continued the gipsy, 'and mistletoe hard to be got. Brought this ten mile, or more. You shall have it cheap.'

'No!' again shouted Crump. 'Do you think I'll encourage such scamps as you in destroying honest gentlemen's plantations in the dead of the night? No, you vagabond!'

'Easy, mister!' said the gipsy. 'I've travelled this country these thirty years, and I couldn't do that if I stole holly or anything else. I bought it at C—— in open market, and ain't ashamed who sees me selling it.'

Captain Crump's rejoinder contained several adjectives of an exceptional character, and cannot be recorded in these pages.

The gipsy had been used to hard words all his life; so, gathering up the holly and mistletoe which he had spread out for Captain Crump's inspection, said, mildly enough, 'No harm done, master, as I see. A poor chap must try to turn an honest penny or starve, which you don't seem likely to do this Christmas. That's an uncommon fine turkey!'

'What's that to you, you ——' etc., etc., replied Crump.

'Oh, nothing; I'm sure of that. It's long afore you'd ask me to take my Christmas dinner at your expense,' said the gipsy, leaning against the stable-door. 'But it is an uncommon fine turkey, I'll pound it, whoever has the luck to eat it.'

Now Captain Crump, like many seagoing people, had a strong dash of the superstitious in his composition, and he felt an unpleasant sensation as the gipsy spoke, although the words were simple enough. Before he could make any reply the man had said, 'Good day, master,' and walked away towards Littletown.

In a few minutes the gipsy was forgotten, and Mrs Crump and the maidservant were summoned to inspect and admire their future Christmas dinner; and it was a sad evidence of the selfishness of human nature when Mrs Crump forgot all the past and asked, without a tremor in her voice, 'whether it was to be boiled or roasted?'

Jabez did not sleep on the premises, and he was allowed to go home earlier than usual in order that he might ascertain who in Littletown were likely to have sausages, and to bespeak the quantity requisite for the proper adornment of the sacrifice. He had been gone some time, and the evening was closing in, when Captain Crump proceeded to shut the stable-door, and discovered to his annoyance that Jabez had taken the key with him. The ears of Jabez must have burned finely if warm words spoken behind his back could have quickened their circulation. Not that there was any real cause for anger, as Mrs Crump had a duplicate key to the lock, and all was made secure for the night. 'Fast bind, fast find,' said the Captain, as he heard the bolt shoot home. And with that satisfactory conclusion he went to bed as the kitchen clock struck ten.

He awoke in the morning and found that adages are not always to be relied on, for the stable-door was still locked, but the turkey was gone; and Jabez vowed he had not seen the key since the day before.

Of course everyone suspects that the gipsy took away the key and then stole the turkey. It might have been so, for he was hiding something under some litter in an old hovel a good mile or more away from Littletown about twelve o'clock that very night.

Another of Captain Crump's prejudices was an objection to being laughed at, and he dreaded his loss becoming known to anyone – the Macgreys in particular – and therefore he all but swore the family to silence. Moreover, Crump had gone about the world with his eyes open, and he wisely concluded that if his lost dinner was to be cooked in Littletown he should smell it out the sooner by allowing the marauder to become bold from a false feeling of security. So Captain Crump and Jabez prowled about Littletown with still tongues, but with most observant eyes and noses.

December the twenty-third, and John Bishopp was tucking himself up snugly in his chaise-cart before his own shop-door preparatory to starting for C——, where he had business. It was a fresh frosty morning, with a briskish wind blowing about the curls and cap border of Mrs Bishopp, who stood in the doorway to see all right and to give her husband a few words of advice at parting.

'Now, don't you be late, John,' said Mrs Bishopp, 'Recollect tomorrow's Christmas Eve, and there's more than I can do, mind that.'

'All right, my dear,' replied John Bishopp.

'Mind it is all right,' said his wife; 'and don't you get keeping Christmas before it comes. I haven't forgot ——'

Nor had John, evidently, for, with a wink and smile, he drove off at once, not thinking it necessary to wait for any more of Mrs Bishopp's reminiscences.

Before that good helpmate could make up her mind to go indoors and cease looking after her husband, the gipsy had approached her with his Christmas ware.

'Buy a little holly, ma'am?' said the man; 'berries uncommon scarce this Christmas.'

'No. Go along, my man,' answered Mrs Bishopp. 'I have no money to spare for such nonsense.'

'I'll sell it you cheap, missus,' continued the man, 'and a bunch of mistletoe as well, though I don't think you need wait for that to have your share of the kissing.'

'What do you mean by that, you impudent fellow?' said Mrs Bishopp; 'a dirty tramp like you talking in that way to me! If I could see the police I'd give you in charge, I would,' and the insulted lady retired into her citadel and closed her castle-gate with a bang.

The gipsy scratched his head as though surprised at the reception of his compliment, and then muttered to himself,

'I should like to take the starch out of you, my lady; and if I only knew how, I'd do it. Why, she bristled up like a hotchy-witchy!* She'd make a first-rate romany† for the fiery old seacock at the flagpost yonder.' And then bawling, 'Any holly? Buy any holly or mistletoe?' at last found a customer in Mrs Macgrey, who always gave Christmas a welcome after the manner of her ancestors.

The gipsy made so good a bargain that, as the December day closed in, he was found, clean shaven and tidily dressed, seated in the taproom of the Fox Inn, not far from the old hovel he had visited the night before. He was well known in those parts as a tinker, hawker, and higgler, and was a welcome visitor at most of the publics, as he could sing a score of songs, play on a tin whistle, and do many hankypanky tricks with cards, to the wonder and amusement of the rustic frequenters of such places. He was a merry fellow always, and, though no one would have cared to stand bail for his honesty, none could prove him to have been dishonest. Ah! I know what you are about to say. What was he hiding in the old hovel? It is thought to be cant nowadays to say that such a man as the gipsy, was as honest, according to his lights, as many a well-to-do gentleman who never had the one-thousandth part of the temptations to go wrong that our poor Bohemian has had crossing his path since he was old enough to beg a penny by the roadside. Hunger, cold, hard words, and hard thoughts of him have invited him at times to evil; and now and then he had listened to the tempter and gone a mile or two on the broad way that leads to perdition. And the recording angel has had, haply, to write down many kindly actions of the gipsy's life and many a wrong resisted; so let us not sit in judgment upon him.

Still, you ask, and rightly, what did he hide in the old hovel?

Why, Captain Crump's Christmas turkey, to be sure, prompted thereto by an irresistible desire to revenge himself on the fiery old

* Hedgehog.   † Wife or companion.

skipper. And there the gipsy was at the Fox Inn, waiting until the young moon should have made her short journey in the heavens, to recover the hidden turkey and replace it in Captain Crump's stable before the morning. It was a foolish and dangerous jest, and might have stopped the gipsy's rambles for many a long month.

Two jolly-faced men in a chaise-cart are approaching the Fox Inn. Both speak somewhat thickly, and roll against each other now and then, or sway about with the motion of the cart. The driver is John Bishopp, and the other the host of the Fox Inn, whom John picked up in the morning on his way to C——, John had been repelling his friend's repeated invitation to alight when they should get to the Fox, and his resistance had been growing weaker and weaker ever since the bright windows of the inn had shown themselves, contrasting their ruddy glow with the cold grey of the winter's night. As John pulled up at the door, the last hearty chorus to one of the gipsy's songs came pealing from within, and drove away all the little good resolution remaining in the Littletown trader. The ostler was roused up, the horse led into an adjoining shed, and ordered 'a bit of wet hay and a horsecloth,' as Mr Bishopp would stay only five mintues. When the ostler was again roused up from his sleep in the shed, beside the horse and the chaise-cart, he could have sworn he had been dozing an hour.

John Bishopp and his friend, mine host of the Fox, were soon at their ease in the little bar-parlour, toasting each other a 'Merry Christmas' in some steaming mixture, and listening to

THE TINKER'S SONG

'Tis I am the tinker, Joe,
And where is there one like me,
If your saucepans are only so, so,
And your kettles won't boil for tea?
In my tent there is never a table,
Our furniture's rather queer,
But I eats of the best when I'm able,
Or puts up with bacon and beer!
    Oh, there's nothing like tinkering!

I envy no king or churchwarden
As spouts at the parish boards,
And I'm sure I'd not give a farden
To sit in the House of Lords!
Though my tent has got many a flaw,
Where the wind when it likes may pass,
In the winter I sleep upon straw,
And in summer I sleeps on the grass.
    Oh, there's nothing like tinkering!

The two cronies would have sat out the night had not the mistress of the inn stopped the supplies and sent out the gipsy to order Mr Bishopp's horse. A quarter of an hour passed before the chaise came to the door, the ostler having been very hard to wake, at least so said the gipsy. The parting between John Bishopp and his crony was somewhat tedious and tautological, and the combined efforts of the ostler, the host, and the gipsy were required to place John comfortably in his chaise-cart. Once up, he was 'all right,' and as the horse had travelled the same road a hundred times before there was no doubt of a safe journey to John Bishopp.

Leaving the topers at the Fox to finish their orgy and go home as they list, we will stop at John Bishopp's shop, as the boy is putting up the shutters and the master has driven to the door. The 'carp-pie' would be very hot and highly seasoned that night, for it was too evident to Mrs Bishopp how her husband had been employing the later hours of the day. John contented himself by standing, or rather wobbling, at the head of the horse, and merely remarking, 'Whoa!' at certain intervals, whilst Mrs Bishopp, her assistant, and the maid unloaded the cart, placing the various packages on the counter.

'Now, Mr Bishopp, let Tom take the horse to the stable, if you please; and if you are able to walk come into the shop, and don't let the neighbours see the state you're in. Now, Mr Bishopp.' And the angry woman's voice might have been heard all over Littletown and miles out at sea.

John, with much 'backing and filling,' managed to make the doorway, and then, with great judgment, brought up alongside the counter, and made himself fast with his hands, whilst Mrs Bishopp overhauled the cargo and required John to check it.

'Six pounds of black tea,' said Mrs Bishopp.

'Ri-i-ght,' replied John.

'Twelve pounds of candles.'

'Ri-i-ght, my dear.'

'A gross of lucifers.'

'Cor-rect, 'Lizabeth.'

'Two sides of bacon.'

'Streaky — ri-i-ght.'

'Four Dutch cheeses.'

'Four's the lot.'

'And a turkey,' said Mrs Bishopp, adding, 'whatever you bought that for I *don't* know.'

Nor John either. 'A tur-ur-key?' he asked, opening both his eyes until they seemed like the two lenses of an opera-glass. 'I haven't bought a turkey, Mrs B-ishopp.'

'You don't know what you *have* bought, it strikes me,' said the justly-angered wife. 'Here's a turkey sure enough, and, as I live, it's got a wooden leg.'

John tried to obtain a nearer view of the bird, but, lurching (to preserve our nautical metaphors) a good deal in the endeavour, put his larboard fin into the treacle-jar which had been left on the counter. Tom, the shop lad, and Susan, the maid, were quite justified in laughing aloud, although it made Mrs Bishopp more angry.

John could not bring his confused mind to recognize this turkey. He tried to recall the day's proceedings, the persons he had met, and the subjects of his conversation, and he always stopped at the second glass 'hot without sugar' in the little bar-parlour of the Fox Inn.

The mystery is soon explained. When the gipsy heard that Mr Bishopp had arrived at the Fox, and was disposed to remain there, certain collections of Mrs Bishopp's hard words came back to him, and the spirit of mischief whispered in his ear to send Captain Crump's turkey as a present to his enemy, nothing doubting but Fortune would manufacture some small tribulation out of it, and so revenge him for the morning's indignity.

It was with this intent that the gipsy had offered his services to call the ostler, but before arousing the sleeper the turkey was taken from the old hovel and deposited in John Bishopp's cart. Consequently the morning brought no clearer knowledge to John Bishopp as to his possession of the wooden-legged stranger, and he was half inclined to drive to the Fox and make some inquiries, but his own fear of ridicule and Mrs Bishopp forbade it.

Mrs Macgrey, we have seen, was an observer of old Christmas customs, and in the course of making her preparation for the next day, called at the multifarious establishment of John Bishopp, little thinking that she should there find hanging at the back of the shop one of the desires of her hospitable heart – a Christmas turkey.

'What a beauty! What a weight! What a rarity in Littletown! Was it very dear?'

Now, Mrs Bishopp, as soon as she awoke that morning, had questioned John upon the purchase of the turkey, but, as I have said, he could remember nothing about it. John's money was right enough, except a shilling or so; still, he might have bought it on credit, and a demand for payment would certainly arrive from some quarter or the other. The careful tradeswoman, therefore, made sure of a market, and Mrs Macgrey went home the happy possessor (as she believed) of the only turkey in Littletown.

For two days Crump Cottage had been anything but an Agapemone. Captain Crump kept his anger at his loss bottled up when abroad, but drew the cork the moment he arrived at home. Jabez generally received the first bumper of wrath, and the remainder was very fairly distributed between Mrs Crump and the maidservant. Not the least tidings had reached Crump of his lost dinner, and tomorrow was Christmas Day. So incensed and so incoherent was he at last, that he threatened to hang Jabez up as a stable lantern and put Mrs Crump in a hencoop. Jabez liked his place and liked his old master also, despite his fiery temper, and so he made no remonstrance, but walked down quietly to Littletown, determined to make some private inquiries. It so chanced that John Bishopp was the first person Jabez met, and, as John stood very high in his opinion, Jabez resolved to confide the secret to him. As he unbosomed himself John Bishopp changed red and purple (being the only colours he was capable of displaying), and, as he said to his wife, 'felt as though one was pouring cold water down his back,' which was not a pleasant sensation on a frosty December day. John wisely kept silent, however, as visions of the magistrate's bench and the county gaol presented themselves. He, John Bishopp, was, without doubt, a receiver of stolen goods, and how to account for the possession he knew not! So, promising Jabez not to mention what he had told him, except to his wife, and faithfully intending to keep his word, for his own sake, John Bishopp hurried home as fast as he could.

Mrs Bishopp was somewhat startled at her husband's haggard appearance, but consoled herself with the hope that it was the proper consequence of yesterday's irregularity. She was not left long in doubt; for John beckoned her into their little parlour and closed the door when she had entered.

'Elizabeth,' said John, in a hoarse whisper, 'where's that turkey?'

'Sold to Mrs Macgrey, I'm thankful to say,' replied the wife. John fairly reeled at the intelligence, and sat down flop in the old leather chair by the fire.

It was some time before he could repeat, in answer to his wife's inquiries, the story he had heard from Jabez, and its effect was nearly as terrible upon the wife as upon the husband.

'Oh, John, John, this comes of your love of drinking! Stolen? And from Captain Crump! Our good name's gone for ever': and Mrs Bishopp, believing what she said, set up a tremendous bellowing. The sight of his wife's sorrow roused up John.

'No, my dear, not so bad as that. It's an awkward job, for certain, but our character's too good to be hurt by it. At worst it will only be a row with old Crump, should he ever hear the truth on't.'

John Bishopp, why not have gone, like a man, and told the tale to Captain Crump, and not allowed him to learn the truth from his stable-door?

Yes, from his stable-door; for on opening it on December the 24th he found on the inside what follows, written in chalk:

if you wants to no ware your turke is arsk missus bishup.

159

Captain Crump nearly committed apoplexy, so irate was he on reading the above, for it was now evident that someone had access to his stable whenever he pleased, and might, for aught that he knew to the contrary, pay nocturnal visits to his larder and wine-cellar. However, when he had cooled down a little, he determined to take the door's advice, and, as he did want to know where his turkey was, he would ask Mrs Bishopp – and he did.

Mrs Bishopp was only a woman, and an ignorant one into the bargain. She had therefore that disregard for the truth which usually distinguishes such persons when they are in a position of difficulty, and resolutely resolved to screen herself and her husband the moment she saw Captain Crump enter the shop, guessing his errand.

'Mrs Bishopp,' said Crump emphatically, and without pausing to sit down, 'have you a turkey?'

'A turkey! Captain Crump?' replied Mrs Bishopp, smiling. 'La, bless you sir, turkeys ain't for people in our state of life.'

'No, I know that,' said Crump; 'but I've lost one that I've been rearing these ten months, and some —— has stolen it.'

'Not me, I beg to say, Captain Crump,' observed Mrs Bishopp, with a toss of her head.

'I don't say you have,' answered Crump; 'but some one chalked on my stable-door: "If you want to know where your turkey is, ask Mrs Bishopp!"'

'And now you have done so, and got your answer, Captain Crump, perhaps you'll inquire elsewhere,' said Mrs Bishopp, affecting to be hurt and indignant; and, as Crump had no further evidence to offer, he was about to depart, when a servant-girl opened the door and said, without entering the shop:

'Did you know our turkey's got a wooden leg?'

Captain Crump had always been a man of action and decision, and he proved eminently so on the present occasion; for, before Mrs Bishopp could utter a word in reply, Crump had fixed the maidservant's head between the shop-door and the post, and was furiously demanding who she was, where she came from, and whence she had got a turkey. The cries of the girl were the only answers to his inquiries; and, Mrs Bishopp having succeeded in releasing the unfortunate domestic, the affrighted creature ran with all speed to her master's house, followed at a much diminished rate by Captain Crump.

Could he believe his eyes! Yes, she enters the house of the man he dislikes most in Littletown, if not in the universe. If that turkey is his turkey, what a Christmas dinner of revenge he will have! Thirty years – well, presently.

Captain Crump hastened home, and informed his wife of the discovery he had made, put on his best coat, and posted off, despite the earnest remonstrances of Mrs Crump, to the police-office, and there obtained the assistance of the stolid young man who paraded the streets of Littletown as guardian of the peace.

Captain Crump knocked at Mr Macgrey's with an emphasis that declared him to be master of the situation; and the consternation of the maid may be imagined when, on opening the door, she discovered her assailant of the morning, and instantly rushed into the back garden. Captain Crump and the officer did not stand for the ceremony of an introduction, but proceeded at once to the kitchen, and there, sure enough, was the abducted turkey, partly plucked of its feathers, but retaining still its wooden leg.

The stupid policeman, acting under the directions of the captain, seized the bird, and then entered the parlour where Mr and Mrs Macgrey were seated, perfectly unconscious of their perilous position.

Captain Crump's lips quivered, and his ruby nose glowed like a hot coal, as he delivered himself as follows: 'Officer, the turkey which you hold in your hands is my property. You know where you found it; and I give that man into custody as a thief or a receiver.'

The effect of this speech may be imagined. Mr Macgrey, ordinarily a peaceful man, was for knocking the speaker down with the poker; but his wife's better discretion interposed and she attempted to account for their possession of the turkey.

Captain Crump was obduracy itself. He would hear of no explanation from anyone, and kept iterating, each time with increasing energy, 'Officer, do your duty!' And there is little doubt but that the stupid policeman would have dragged off Mr Macgrey had not Mrs Crump arrived at the scene of action, and, by a counter command, delayed that unpleasant operation.

Captain Crump was not the man to be mollified by uxorial intervention; and the stupid policeman stood like the traditional donkey between two bundles of hay, not knowing whom to obey. At last Mrs Macgrey said, in her softest tones:

'William! William Crump!'

Crump started as though a voice from the spirit-world had spoken.

'William!' repeated Mrs Macgrey, 'is there to be no forgiveness between us? I know the cause of this violence, and am ashamed of you, William.'

Mrs Crump began to bridle a little at this.

'Thirty years ago, when we were almost boy and girl in this place, we thought we were in love with each other.'

Mrs Crump gave a short angry cough.

'In that time, when we walked hand-in-hand on yonder seashore, the moon and the sea the only witnesses to the loving words then spoken ——'

Mrs Crump said, 'Well, I'm sure!' and Mr Macgrey blew his nose pettishly.

'At that time, William, could we have believed that you would seek to bring sorrow and disgrace to me – me, your once loved Mary?'

The stupid policeman being ordered out of the room by general consent walked, from force of habit, straight to the kitchen.

'Answer me, William. Is all forgotten? Can you do this cruel thing?' said Mrs Macgrey, laying her hand gracefully on Crump's shoulder.

Crump tried to reply, but found he had a great ball in his throat, and so he could only point at Mr Macgrey and then at the fourth finger of his own left hand.

'True, I have married another; so have you,' said Mrs Macgrey.

'Well, I'm glad you've remembered that at last,' said Mrs Crump, fairly nettled. 'I thought such a trifling circumstance had escaped your recollection.'

'So did I,' grunted Macgrey.

'Are you all angry with me?' asked the candid Mrs Macgrey, quite theatrically. 'Had I married him, Mrs Crump, you would not have been the happy woman I know you to be – and deserve to be.'

'Alexander,' she paused until Mr Macgrey raised his eyes from the carpet at which he had been intently gazing, 'did I not give you the preference – if that was a gift worth having?'

'William, William Crump, I gave you the chance of marrying a worthier woman than myself. Take her to your heart and own I speak the truth.'

Crump had nothing for it but to open his arms and press his lawful wife to his full-frilled bosom.

Alexander Macgrey accepted a similar invitation from his Mary, silently wishing, however, that this *confessio amoris* had not been necessary.

As a matter of course, the two ladies next embraced each other, and the two gentlemen, for the first time in their lives, shook hands, vowing a lifelong friendship; and it was arranged that the turkey, which had so nearly brought discord among them, should furnish forth their Christmas dinner. The story of the turkey oozed out by degrees, and the gipsy has not been seen in Littletown for some time, whilst John Bishopp is reported to have turned his fright to such good account that he has never been more than properly jolly ever since. The only ill consequence that has remained is, the opportunity afforded to a few of the worst boys in Littletown to tease Captain Crump by impertinent inquiries about his last Christmas dinner.

The Stalled Ox

SAKI

THEOPHIL ESHLEY WAS an artist by profession, a cattle painter by force of environment. It is not to be supposed that he lived on a ranch or a dairy farm, in an atmosphere pervaded with horn and hoof, milking-stool, and branding-iron. His home was in a park-like, villa-dotted district that only just escaped the reproach of being suburban. On one side of his garden there abutted a small, picturesque meadow, in which an enterprising neighbour pastured some small picturesque cows of the Channel Island persuasion. At noonday in summertime the cows stood knee-deep in tall meadow-grass under the shade of a group of walnut trees, with the sunlight falling in dappled patches on their mouse-sleek coats. Eshley had conceived and executed a dainty picture of two reposeful milch-cows in a setting of walnut tree and meadow-grass and filtered sunbeam, and the Royal Academy had duly exposed the same on the walls of its Summer Exhibition. The Royal Academy encourages orderly, methodical habits in its children. Eshley had painted a successful and acceptable picture of cattle drowsing picturesquely under walnut trees, and as he had begun, so, of necessity, he went on. His 'Noontide Peace,' a study of two dun cows under a walnut tree, was followed by 'A Midday Sanctuary,' a study of a walnut tree, with two dun cows under it. In due succession there came 'Where the Gadflies Cease from Troubling,' 'The Haven of the Herd,' and 'A Dream in Dairyland,' studies of walnut trees and dun cows. His two attempts to break away from his own tradition were signal failures: 'Turtle Doves Alarmed by Sparrow-hawk' and 'Wolves on the Roman Campagna' came back to his studio in the guise of abominable heresies, and Eshley climbed back into grace and the public gaze with 'A Shaded Nook Where Drowsy Milkers Dream.'

On a fine afternoon in late autumn he was putting some finishing touches to a study of meadow weeds when his neighbour, Adela Pingsford, assailed the outer door of his studio with loud peremptory knockings.'

'There is an ox in my garden,' she announced, in explanation of the tempestuous intrusion.

'An ox,' said Eshley blankly, and rather fatuously; 'what kind of ox?'

'Oh, I don't known what kind,' snapped the lady. 'A common or garden ox, to use the slang expression. It is the garden part of it that I object to. My garden has just been put straight for the winter, and an ox roaming about in it won't improve matters. Besides, there are the chrysanthemums just coming into flower,'

'How did it get into the garden?' asked Eshley.

'I imagine it came in by the gate,' said the lady impatiently; 'it couldn't have cimbed the walls, and I don't suppose any one dropped it from an aeroplane as a Bovril advertisement. The immediately important question is not how it got in, but how to get it out.'

'Won't it go?' said Eshley.

'If it was anxious to go,' said Adela Pingsford rather angrily, 'I should not have come here to chat with you about it. I'm practically all alone; the housemaid is having her afternoon out and the cook is lying down with an attack of neuralgia. Anything that I may have learned at school or in after life about how to remove a large ox from a small garden seems to have escaped from my memory now. All I could think of was that you were a near neighbour and a cattle painter, presumably more or less familiar with the subjects that you painted, and that you might be of some slight assistance. Possibly I was mistaken.'

'I paint dairy cows, certainly,' admitted Eshley, 'but I cannot claim to have had any experience in rounding up stray oxen. I've seen it done on a cinema film, of course, but there were always horses and lots of other accessories; besides, one never knows how much of those pictures are faked.'

Adela Pingsford said nothing, but led the way to her garden. It was normally a fair-sized garden, but it looked small in comparison with the ox, a huge mottled brute, dull red about the head and shoulders, passing to dirty white on the flanks and hindquarters, with shaggy ears and large bloodshot eyes. It bore about as much resemblance to the dainty paddock heifers that Eshley was accustomed to paint as the chief of a Kurdish nomad clan would to a Japanese tea-shop girl. Eshley stood very near the gate while he studied the animal's appearance and demeanour. Adela Pingsford continued to say nothing.

'It's eating a chrysanthemum,' said Eshley at last, when the silence had become unbearable.

'How observant you are,' said Adela bitterly. 'You seem to notice everything. As a matter of fact, it has got six chrysanthemums in its mouth at the present moment.'

The necessity for doing something was becoming imperative. Eshley took a step or two in the direction of the animal, clapped his hands, and made noises of the 'Hish' and 'Shoo' variety. If the ox heard them it gave no outward indication of the fact.

'If any hens should ever stray into my garden,' said Adela, 'I should certainly send for you to frighten them out. You "shoo" beautifully. Meanwhile, do you mind trying to drive that ox away? That is a *Mademoiselle Louise Bichot* that he's begun on now,' she added in icy calm, as a glowing orange head was crushed into the huge munching mouth.

'Since you have been so frank about the variety of the chrysanthemum,' said Eshley, 'I don't mind telling you that this is an Ayrshire ox.'

The icy calm broke down; Adela Pingsford used language that sent the artist instinctively a few feet nearer to the ox. He picked up a peastick and flung it with some determination against the animal's mottled flanks. The operation of mashing *Mademoiselle Louise Bichot* into a petal salad was suspended for a long moment, while the ox gazed with concentrated inquiry at the stick-thrower. Adela gazed with equal concentration and more obvious hostility at the same focus. As the beast neither lowered its head nor stamped its feet Eshley ventured on another javelin exercise with another peastick. The ox seemed to realize at once that it was to go; it gave a hurried final pluck at the bed where the chrysanthemums had been, and strode swiftly up the garden. Eshley ran to head it towards the gate, but only succeeded in quickening its pace from a walk to a lumbering trot. With an air of inquiry, but with no real hesitation, it crossed the tiny strip of turf that the charitable called the croquet lawn, and pushed its way through the open French window into the morning-room. Some chrysanthemums and other autumn herbage stood about the room in vases, and the animal resumed its browsing operations; all the same, Eshley fancied that the beginnings of a hunted look had come into its eyes, a look that counselled respect. He discontinued his attempt to interfere with its choice of surroundings.

'Mr Eshley,' said Adela in a shaking voice, 'I asked you to drive that beast out of my garden, but I did not ask you to drive it into my house. If I must have it anywhere on the premises, I prefer the garden to the morning-room.'

'Cattle drives are not in my line,' said Eshley; 'if I remember, I told you so at the outset.'

'I quite agree,' retorted the lady, 'painting pretty pictures of pretty little cows is what you're suited for. Perhaps you'd like to do a nice sketch of that ox making itself at home in my morning-room?'

This time it seemed as if the worm had turned; Eshley began striding away.

'Where are you going?' screamed Adela.

'To fetch implements,' was the answer.

'Implements? I won't have you use a lasso. The room will be wrecked if there's a struggle.'

But the artist marched out of the garden. In a couple of minutes he returned, laden with easel, sketching-stool, and painting materials.

'Do you mean to say that you're going to sit quietly down and paint that brute while it's destroying my morning-room? gasped Adela.

'It was your suggestion,' said Eshley, setting his canvas in position.

'I forbid it; I absolutely forbid it!' stormed Adela.

'I don't see what standing you have in the matter,' said the artist; 'you can hardly pretend that it's your ox, even by adoption.'

'You seem to forget that it's in my morning-room, eating my flowers,' came the raging retort.

'You seem to forget that the cook has neuralgia,' said Eshley; 'she may be just dozing off into a merciful sleep and your outcry will waken her. Consideration for others should be the guiding principle of people in our station of life.'

'The man is mad!' exclaimed Adela tragically. A moment later it was Adela herself who appeared to go mad. The ox had finished the vase-flowers and the cover of *Israel Kalisch*, and appeared to be thinking of leaving its rather restricted quarters. Eshley noticed its restlessness and promptly flung it some bunches of Virginia creeper leaves as an inducement to continue the sitting.

'I forget how the proverb runs,' he observed; 'something about "better a dinner of herbs than a stalled ox where hate is." We seem to have all the ingredients for the proverb ready to hand.'

'I shall go to the Public Library and get them to telephone for the police,' announced Adela, and, raging audibly, she departed.

Some minutes later the ox, awakened probably to the suspicion that oil cake and chopped mangold was waiting for it in some appointed byre, stepped with much precaution out of the morning-room, stared with grave inquiry at the no longer obtrusive and peastick-throwing human, and then lumbered heavily but swiftly out of the garden. Eshley packed up his tools and followed the animal's example and 'Larkdene' was left to neuralgia and the cook.

The episode was the turning-point in Eshley's artistic career. His remarkable picture, 'Ox in a Morning-room, Late Autumn,' was one of the sensations and successes of the next Paris Salon, and when it was subsequently exhibited at Munich it was bought by the Bavarian Government, in the teeth of the spirited bidding of three meat-extract firms. From that moment his success was continuous and assured, and the Royal Academy was thankful, two years later, to give a conspicuous position on its walls to his large canvas 'Barbary Apes Wrecking a Boudoir.'

Eshley presented Adela Pingsford with a new copy of *Israel Kalisch*, and a couple of finely flowering plants of *Madame André Blusset*, but nothing in the nature of a real reconciliation has taken place between them.

Darrowby Show

JAMES HERRIOT

During the early days of his veterinary practice in the Yorkshire village of Darrowby James Herriot was prepared to undertake with equanimity any task delegated to him by his senior partner, Siegfried Farnon. Caution was learnt only through bitter experience....

'HOW WOULD YOU LIKE TO officiate at Darrowby Show James?' Siegfried threw the letter he had been reading on to the desk and turned to me.

'I don't mind, but I thought you always did it.'

'I do, but it says in that letter that they've changed the date this year and it happens I'm going to be away that weekend.'

'Oh well, fine. What do I have to do?'

Siegfried ran his eye down his list of calls. 'It's a sinecure, really. More a pleasant day out than anything else. You have to measure the ponies and be on call in case any animals are injured. That's about all. Oh and they want you to judge the Family Pets.'

'Family Pets?'

'Yes, they run a proper dog show but they have an expert judge for that. This is just a bit of fun – all kinds of pets. You've got to find a first, second and third.'

'Right,' I said. 'I think I should just about be able to manage that.'

'Splendid.' Siegfried tipped up the envelope in which the letter had come. 'Here are your car park and luncheon tickets for self and friend if you want to take somebody with you. Also your vet's badge. OK?'

The Saturday of the show brought the kind of weather that must have had the organizers purring with pleasure; a sky of wide, unsullied blue, hardly a whiff of wind and the kind of torrid, brazen sunshine you don't often find in North Yorkshire.

As I drove down towards the show ground I felt I was looking at a living breathing piece of old England; the group of tents and marquees vivid against the green of the riverside field, the women and children in their bright summer dresses, the cattle with their smocked attendants, a line of massive Shire horses parading in the ring.

I parked the car and made for the stewards' tent with its flag hanging limply from the mast. Tristan parted from me there. With the impecunious student's unerring eye for a little free food and entertainment he had

167

taken up my spare tickets. He headed purposefully for the beer tent as I went in to report to the show secretary.

Leaving my measuring stick there I looked around for a while.

A country show is a lot of different things to a lot of different people. Riding horses of all kinds from small ponies to hunters were being galloped up and down and in one ring the judges hovered around a group of mares and their beautiful little foals.

In a corner four men armed with buckets and brushes were washing and grooming a row of young bulls with great concentration, twiddling and crimping the fuzz over the rumps like society hairdressers.

Wandering through the marquees I examined the bewildering variety of produce from stalks of rhubarb to bunches of onions, the flower displays, embroidery, jams, cakes, pies. And the children's section; a painting of 'The Beach at Scarborough' by Annie Heseltine, aged nine; rows of wobbling copperplate handwriting – 'A thing of beauty is a joy for ever', Bernard Peacock, aged twelve.

Drawn by the occasional gusts of melody I strolled across the grass to where the Darrowby and Houlton Silver Band was rendering *Poet and Peasant*. The bandsmen were of all ages from seventies down to one or two boys of about fourteen and most of them had doffed their uniform tunics as they sweated in the hot sun. Pint pots reposed under many of the chairs and the musicians refreshed themselves frequently with leisurely swigs.

I was particularly fascinated by the conductor, a tiny frail man who looked about eighty. He alone had retained his full uniform, cap and all, and he stood apparently motionless in front of the crescent of bandsmen, chin sunk on chest, arms hanging limply by his sides. It wasn't until I came right up to him that I realized his fingers were twitching in time with the music and that he was, in fact, conducting. And the more I watched him the more fitting it seemed that he should do it like that. The Yorkshireman's loathing of exhibitionism or indeed any outward show of emotion made it unthinkable that he should throw his arms about in the orthodox manner; no doubt he had spent weary hours rehearsing and coaching his players but here, when the results of his labours were displayed to the public he wasn't going to swank about it. Even the almost imperceptible twitching of the finger-ends had something guilty about it as if the old man felt he was being caught out in something shameful.

But my attention was jerked away as a group of people walked across on the far side of the band. It was Helen with Richard Edmundson and behind them Mr Alderson and Richard's father deep in conversation. The young man walked very close to Helen, his shining, plastered-down fair hair hovering possessively over her dark head, his face animated as he talked and laughed.

There were no clouds in the sky but it was as if a dark hand had reached across and smudged away the brightness of the sunshine. I turned quickly and went in search of Tristan.

I soon picked out my colleague as I hurried into the marquee with 'Refreshments' over the entrance. He was leaning with an elbow on the makeshift counter of boards and trestles chatting contentedly with a knot of cloth-capped locals, a Woodbine in one hand, a pint glass in the other. There was a general air of earthy bonhomie. Drinking of a more decorous kind would be taking place at the president's bar behind the stewards' headquarters with pink gins or sherry as the main tipple but here it was beer, bottled and draught, and the stout ladies behind the counter were working with the fierce concentration of people who knew they were in for a hard day.

'Yes, I saw her,' Tristan said when I gave him my news. 'In fact there she is now.' He nodded in the direction of the family group as they strolled past the entrance. 'I've had my eye on them for some time – I don't miss much from in here you know, Jim.'

'Ah well.' I accepted a half of bitter from him. 'It all looks pretty cosy. The two dads like blood brothers and Helen hanging on to that bloke's arm.'

Tristan squinted over the top of his pint at the scene outside and shook his head. 'Not exactly. He's hanging on to HER arm.' He looked at me judicially. 'There's a difference, you know.'

'I don't suppose it makes much difference to me either way,' I grunted.

'Well don't look so bloody mournful.' He took an effortless swallow which lowered the level in his glass by about six inches. 'What do you expect an attractive girl to do? Sit at home waiting for you to call? If you've been pounding on her door every night you haven't told me about it.'

'It's all right you talking. I think old man Alderson would set his dogs on me if I showed up there. I know he doesn't like me hanging around Helen and on top of that I've got the feeling he thinks I killed his cow on my last visit.'

'And did you?'

'No, I didn't. But I walked up to a living animal, gave it an injection and it promptly died, so I can't blame him.'

I took a sip at my beer and watched the Alderson party who had changed direction and were heading away from our retreat. Helen was wearing a pale blue dress and I was thinking how well the colour went with the deep brown of her hair and how I liked the way she walked with her legs swinging easily and her shoulders high and straight when the loudspeaker boomed across the show ground.

'Will Mr Herriot, Veterinary Surgeon, please report to the stewards immediately.'

It made me jump but at the same time I felt a quick stab of pride. It was the first time I had heard myself and my profession publicly proclaimed. I turned to Tristan. He was supposed to be seeing practice and this could be something interesting. But he was immersed in a story which he was trying to tell to a little stocky man with a fat, shiny face, and he was having difficulty because the little man, determined to get his full measure of enjoyment, kept throwing himself into helpless convulsions at the end of every sentence, and the finish was a long way away. Tristan took his stories very seriously; I decided not to interrupt him.

A glow of importance filled me as I hurried over the grass, my official badge with 'Veterinary Surgeon' in gold letters dangling from my lapel. A steward met me on the way.

'It's one of the cattle. Had an accident, I think.' He pointed to a row of pens along the edge of the field.

A curious crowd had collected around my patient which had been entered in the in-calf heifers class. The owner a stranger from outside the Darrowby practice came up to me, his face glum.

'She tripped coming off the cattle wagon and went 'ead first into the wall. Knocked one of 'er horns clean off.'

The heifer, a bonny little light roan, was a pathetic sight. She had been washed, combed, powdered and primped for the big day and there she was with one horn dangling drunkenly down the side of her face and an ornamental fountain of bright arterial blood climbing gracefully in three jets from the broken surface high into the air.

I opened my bag. I had brought a selection of the things I might need and I fished out some artery forceps and suture material. The rational way to stop haemorrhage of this type is to grasp the bleeding vessel and ligate it, but it wasn't always as easy as that. Especially when the patient won't cooperate.

The broken horn was connected to the head only by a band of skin and I quickly snipped it away with scissors; then, with the farmer holding the heifer's nose I began to probe with my forceps for the severed vessels. In the bright sunshine it was surprisingly difficult to see the spurting blood and as the little animal threw her head about I repeatedly felt the warm spray across my face and heard it spatter on my collar.

It was when I was beginning to lose heart with my ineffectual groping that I looked up and saw Helen and her boyfriend watching me from the crowd. Young Edmundson looked mildly amused as he watched my unavailing efforts but Helen smiled encouragingly as she caught my eye. I did my best to smile back at her through my bloody mask but I don't suppose it showed.

I gave it up when the heifer gave a particularly brisk toss which sent my forceps flying on to the grass. I did what I should probably have done at the beginning – clapped a pad of cotton wool and antiseptic powder on to the stump and secured it with a figure of eight bandage round the other horn.

'That's it, then,' I said to the farmer as I tried to blink the blood out of my eyes. 'The bleeding's stopped, anyway. I'd advise you to have her properly dehorned soon or she's going to look a bit odd.'

Just then Tristan appeared from among the spectators.

'What's got you out of the beer tent?' I inquired with a touch of bitterness.

'It's lunch time, old lad,' Tristan replied equably. 'But we'll have to get you cleaned up a bit first. I can't be seen with you in that condition. Hang on, I'll get a bucket of water.'

The show luncheon was so excellent that it greatly restored me. Although it was taken in a marquee the committee men's wives had somehow managed to conjure up a memorable cold spread. There was fresh salmon and home fed ham and slices of prime beef with mixed salads and apple pie and the big brimming jugs of cream you only see at farming functions. One of the ladies was a noted cheese maker and we finished with some delicious goat cheese and coffee. The liquid side was catered for too with a bottle of Magnet Pale Ale and a glass at every place.

I didn't have the pleasure of Tristan's company at lunch because he had strategically placed himself well down the table between two strict Methodists so that his intake of Magnet was trebled.

I had hardly emerged into the sunshine when a man touched me on the shoulder.

'One of the dog show judges wants you to examine a dog. He doesn't like the look of it.'

He led me to where a thin man of about forty with a small dark moustache was standing by his car. He held a wire-haired fox terrier on a leash and he met me with an ingratiating smile.

'There's nothing whatever the matter with my dog,' he declared, 'but the chap in there seems very fussy.'

I looked down at the terrier. 'I see he has some matter in the corner of his eyes.'

The man shook his head vigorously. 'Oh no, that's not matter. I've been using some white powder on him and a bit's got into his eyes, that's all.'

'Hmm, well let's see what his temperature says, shall we?'

The little animal stood uncomplaining as I inserted the thermometer. When I took the reading my eyebrows went up.

'It's a hundred and four. I'm afraid he's not fit to go into the show.'

'Wait a minute.' The man thrust out his jaw. 'You're talking like that chap in there. I've come a long way to show this dog and I'm going to show him.'

'I'm sorry but you can't show him with a temperature of a hundred and four.'

'But he's had a car journey. That could put up his temperature.'

I shook my head. 'Not as high as that it couldn't. Anyway he looks sick to me. Do you see how he's half closing his eyes as though he's frightened of the light? It's possible he could have distemper.'

'What? That's rubbish and you know it. He's never been fitter!' The man's mouth trembled with anger.

I looked down at the little dog. He was crouching on the grass miserably. Occasionally he shivered, he had a definite photophobia and there was that creamy blob of pus in the corner of each eye. 'Has he been inoculated against distemper?'

'Well no, he hasn't but why do you keep on about it?'

'Because I think he's got it now and for his sake and for the sake of the other dogs here you ought to take him straight home and see your own vet.'

He glared at me. 'So you won't let me take him into the show tent?'

'That's right. I'm very sorry, but it's out of the question.' I turned and walked away.

I had gone only a few yards when the loudspeaker boomed again.

'Will Mr Herriot please go to the measuring stand where the ponies are ready for him.'

I collected my stick and trotted over to a corner of the field where a group of ponies had assembled; Welsh, Dales, Exmoor, Dartmoor – all kinds of breeds were represented.

For the uninitiated, horses are measured in hands which consist of four inches and a graduated stick is used with a cross piece and a spirit level which rests on the withers, the highest point of the shoulders. I had done a fair bit of it in individual animals but this was the first time I had done the job at a show. With my stick at the ready I stood by the two wide boards which had been placed on the turf to give the animals a reasonably level standing surface.

A smiling young woman led the first pony, a smart chestnut, on to the boards.

'Which class?' I asked.

'Thirteen hands.'

I tried the stick on him. He was well under.

'Fine, next please.'

A few more came through without incident then there was a lull before the next group came up. The ponies were arriving on the field all the time in their boxes and being led over to me, some by their young riders, others by the parents. It looked as though I could be here quite a long time.

During one of the lulls a little man who had been standing near me spoke up.

'No trouble yet?' he asked.

'No, everything's in order,' I replied.

He nodded expressionlessly and as I took a closer look at him his slight body, dark, leathery features and high shoulders seemed to give him the appearance of a little brown gnome. At the same time there was something undeniably horsy about him.

'You'll 'ave some awkward 'uns,' he grunted. 'And they allus say the same thing. They allus tell you the vet at some other show passed their pony.' His swarthy cheeks crinkled in a wry smile.

'Is that so?'

'Aye, you'll see.'

Another candidate, led by a beautiful blonde, was led on to the platform. She gave me the full blast of two big greenish eyes and flashed a mouthful of sparkling teeth at me.

'Twelve two,' she murmured seductively.

I tried the stick on the pony and worked it around, but try as I might I couldn't get it down to that.

'I'm afraid he's a bit big,' I said.

The blonde's smile vanished. 'Have you allowed half an inch for his shoes?'

'I have indeed, but you can see for yourself, he's well over.'

'But he passed the vet without any trouble at Hickley.' She snapped and out of the corner of my eye I saw the gnome nodding sagely.

'I can't help that,' I said. 'I'm afraid you'll have to put him into the next class.'

For a moment two green pebbles from the cold sea bed fixed me with a frigid glare then the blonde was gone taking her pony with her.

Next, a little bay animal was led on to the stand by a hard faced gentleman in a check suit and I must say I was baffled by its behaviour. Whenever the stick touched the withers it sank at the knees so that I couldn't be sure whether I was getting the right reading or not. Finally I gave up and passed him through.

The gnome coughed. 'I know that feller.'

'You do?'

'Aye, he's pricked the pony's withers with a pin so many times that it drops down whenever you try to measure 'im.'

'Never!'

'Sure as I'm standing here.'

I was staggered, but the arrival of another batch took up my attention for a few minutes. Some I passed, others I had to banish to another class and the owners took it in different ways – some philosophically, a few with obvious annoyance. One or two of the ponies just didn't like the look of the stick at all and I had to dance around them as they backed away and reared.

The last pony in this group was a nice grey led by a bouncy man wearing a great big matey smile.

'How are you, all right?' he inquired courteously. 'This 'un's thirteen two.'

The animal went under the stick without trouble but after he had trotted away the gnome spoke up again.

'I know that feller, too.'

'Really?'

'Not 'alf. Weighs down 'is ponies before they're measured. That grey's been standing in 'is box for the last hour with a twelve stone sack of corn on 'is back. Knocks an inch off.'

'Good God! Are you sure?'

'Don't worry, I've seen 'im at it.'

My mind was beginning to reel just a little. Was the man making it all up or were there really these malign forces at work behind all this innocent fun?

'That same feller,' continued the gnome. 'I've seen 'im bring a pony to a show and get half an inch knocked off for shoes when it never 'ad no shoes on.'

I wished he'd stop. And just then there was an interruption. It was the man with the moustache. He sidled up to me and whispered confidentially in my ear.

'Now I've just been thinking. My dog must have got over his journey by now and I expect his temperature will be normal. I wonder if you'd just try him again. I've still got time to show him.'

I turned wearily. 'Honestly, it'll be a waste of time. I've told you, he's ill.'

'Please! Just as a favour.' He had a desperate look and a fanatical light flickered in his eye.

'All right.' I went over to the car with him and produced my thermometer. The temperature was still a hundred and four.

'Now I wish you'd take this poor little dog home,' I said. 'He shouldn't be here.'

For a moment I thought the man was going to strike me. 'There's nothing wrong with him!' he hissed, his whole face working with emotion.

'I'm sorry,' I said, and went back to the measuring stand.

A boy of about fifteen was waiting for me with his pony. It was supposed to be in the thirteen two class but was nearly one and a half inches over.

'Much too big, I'm afraid,' I said. 'He can't go in that class.'

The boy didn't anwer. He put his hand inside his jacket and produced a sheet of paper. 'This is a veterinary certificate to say he's under thirteen two.'

'No good, I'm sorry,' I replied. 'The stewards have told me not to accept any certificates. I've turned down two others today. Everything has to go under the stick. It's a pity, but there it is.'

His manner changed abruptly. 'But you've GOT to accept it!' he shouted in my face. 'There doesn't have to be any measurements when you have a certificate.'

'You'd better see the stewards. Those are my instructions.'

'I'll see my father about this, that's what!' he shouted and led the animal away.

Father was quickly on the scene. Big, fat, prosperous-looking, confident. He obviously wasn't going to stand any nonsense from me.

'Now look here, I don't know what this is all about but you have no option in this matter. You have to accept the certificate.'

'I don't, I assure you,' I answered. 'And anyway, it's not as though your pony was slightly over the mark. He's miles over – nowhere near the height.'

Father flushed dark red. 'Well let me tell you he was passed through by the vet at. . . .'

'I know, I know,' I said, and I heard the gnome give a short laugh. 'But he's not going through here.'

There was a brief silence then both father and son began to scream at me. And as they continued to hurl abuse I felt a hand on my arm. It was the man with the moustache again.

'I'm going to ask you just once more to take my dog's temperature,' he whispered with a ghastly attempt at a smile. 'I'm sure he'll be all right this time. Will you try him again?'

I'd had enough. 'No, I bloody well won't!' I barked. 'Will you kindly stop bothering me and take that poor animal home.'

It's funny how the most unlikely things motivate certain people. It didn't seem a life and death matter whether a dog got into a show or not but it was to the man with the moustache. He started to rave at me.

'You don't know your job, that's the trouble with you! I've come all this way and you've played a dirty trick on me. I've got a friend who's a vet, a proper vet, and I'm going to tell him about you, yes I am. I'm going to tell him about you!'

At the same time the father and son were still in full cry, snarling and mouthing at me and I became suddenly aware that I was in the centre of a hostile circle. The blonde was there too, and some of the others whose ponies I had outed and they were all staring at me belligerently, making angry gestures.

I felt very much alone because the gnome, who had seemed an ally, was nowhere to be seen. I was disappointed in the gnome; he was a big talker but had vanished at the first whiff of danger. As I surveyed the threatening crowd I moved my measuring stick round in front of me; it wasn't much of a weapon but it might serve to fend them off if they rushed me.

And just at that moment, as the unkind words were thick upon the air, I saw Helen and Richard Edmundson on the fringe of the circle, taking it all in. I wasn't worried about him but again it struck me as strange that it should be my destiny always to be looking a bit of a clown when Helen was around.

Anyway, the measuring was over and I felt in need of sustenance. I retreated and went to find Tristan.

The atmosphere in the beer tent was just what I needed. The hot weather had made the place even more popular than usual and it was crowded; many of the inhabitants had been there since early morning and the air was thick with earthy witticisms, immoderate laughter, cries of joy; and the nice thing was that nobody in there cared a damn about the heights of ponies or the temperatures of dogs.

I had to fight my way through the crush to reach Tristan who was leaning across the counter in earnest conversation with a comely young barmaid. The other serving ladies were middle-aged but his practised eye had picked this one out; glossy red hair, a puckish face and an inviting smile. I had been hoping for a soothing chat with him but he was unable to give me his undivided attention, so after juggling with a glass among the throng for a few minutes I left.

Out on the field the sun still blazed, the scent of the trampled grass rose into the warm air, the band was playing a selection from *Rose Marie* and peace began to steal into my soul. Maybe I could begin to enjoy the show now the pinpricks were over; there was only the Family Pets to judge and I was looking forward to that.

For about an hour I wandered among the pens of mountainous pigs and haughty sheep; the rows of Shorthorn cows with their classical wedge-shaped grace, their level udders and dainty feet.

I watched in fascination a contest which was new to me; shirt-sleeved young men sticking a fork into a straw bale and hurling it high over a bar with a jerk of their thick brown arms.

Old Steve Bramley, a local farmer, was judging the heavy horses and I envied him his massive authority as he stumped, bowler-hatted and glowering around each animal, leaning occasionally on his stick as he took stock of the points. I couldn't imagine anyone daring to argue with him.

It was late in the afternoon when the loudspeaker called me to my final duty. The Family Pets contestants were arranged on wooden chairs drawn up in a wide circle on the turf. They were mainly children but behind them an interested ring of parents and friends watched me warily as I arrived.

The fashion for exotic pets was still in its infancy but I experienced a mild shock of surprise when I saw the variety of creatures on show. I suppose I must have had a vague mental picture of a few dogs and cats but I walked round the circle in growing bewilderment looking down at rabbits – innumerable rabbits of all sizes and colours – guinea pigs, white mice, several budgerigars, two tortoises, a canary, a kitten, a parrot, a mynah bird, a box of puppies, a few dogs and cats and a goldfish in a bowl. The smaller pets rested on their owners' knees, the others squatted on the ground.

How, I asked myself was I going to come to a decision here? How did you choose between a parrot and a puppy, a budgie and a bulldog, a mouse and a mynah? Then as I circled it came to me; it couldn't be done. The only way was to question the children in charge and find which ones looked after their pets best, which of them knew most about their feeding and general husbandry. I rubbed my hands together and repressed a chuckle of satisfaction; I had something to work on now.

I don't like to boast but I think I can say in all honesty that I carried out an exhaustive scientific survey of that varied group. From the outset I adopted an attitude of cold detachment, mercilessly banishing any ideas of personal preference. If I had been pleasing only myself I would have given first prize to a gleaming black Labrador sitting by a chair with massive composure and offering me a gracious paw every time I came near. And my second would have been a benevolent tabby – I have always had a thing about tabby cats – which rubbed its cheek against my hand as I talked to its owner. The pups, crawling over each other and grunting obesely, would probably have come third. But I put away these unworthy thoughts and pursued my chosen course.

I was distracted to some extent by the parrot which kept saying 'Hellow' in a voice of devastating refinement like a butler answering a telephone and the mynah which repeatedly adjured me to 'Shut door as you go out,' in a booming Yorkshire baritone.

The only adult in the ring was a bosomy lady with glacial pop eyes and a white poodle on her knee. As I approached she gave me a challenging stare as though defying me to place her pet anywhere but first.

'Hello, little chap,' I said, extending my hand. The poodle responded by drawing its lips soundlessly back from its teeth and giving me much the same kind of look as its owner. I withdrew my hand hastily.

'Oh you needn't be afraid of him,' the lady said frigidly. 'He won't hurt you.'

I gave a light laugh. 'I'm sure he won't.' I held out my hand again. 'You're a nice little dog, aren't you?' Once more the poodle bared his teeth and when I persevered by trying to stroke his ears he snapped noiselessly, his teeth clicking together an inch from my fingers.

'He doesn't like you, I can see that. Do you, darling?' The lady put her cheek against the dog's head and stared at me distastefully as though she knew just how he felt.

'Shut door as you go out,' commanded the mynah gruffly from somewhere behind me.

I gave the lady my questionnaire and moved on.

And among the throng there was one who stood out; the little boy with the goldfish. In reply to my promptings he discoursed knowledgeably about his fish, its feeding, life history and habits. He even had a fair idea of the common diseases. The bowl, too, was beautifully clean and the water fresh; I was impressed.

When I had completed the circuit I swept the ring for the last time with a probing eye. Yes, there was no doubt about it; I had the three prize winners fixed in my mind beyond any question and in an order based on strictly scientific selection. I stepped out into the middle.

'Ladies and gentlemen,' I said, scanning the company with an affable smile.

'Hellow,' responded the parrot fruitily.

I ignored him and continued. 'These are the successful entrants. First, number six, the goldfish. Second, number fifteen, the guinea pig. And third, number ten, the white kitten.'

I half expected a little ripple of applause but there was none. In fact my announcement was greeted by a tight-lipped silence. I had noticed an immediate change in the atmosphere when I mentioned the goldfish. It was striking – a sudden cold wave which swept away the expectant smiles and replaced them with discontented muttering.

I had done something wrong, but what? I looked around helplessly as the hum of voices increased. 'What do you think of that, then?' 'Not fair, is it?' 'Wouldn't have thought it of him?' 'All them lovely rabbits and he hardly looked at them.'

I couldn't make it out, but my job was done, anyway. I pushed between the chairs and escaped to the open field.

'Shut door as you go out,' the mynah requested in deepest bass as I departed.

I sought out Tristan again. The atmosphere in the beer tent had changed, too. The drinkers were long since past their peak and the hilarious babel which had met me on my last visit had died to an exhausted murmur. There was a general air of satiation. Tristan, pint in hand, was being addressed with great solemnity by a man in a flat cap and braces. The man swayed slightly as he grasped Tristan's free hand and gazed into his eyes. Occasionally he patted him on the shoulder with the utmost affection. Obviously my colleague had been forging deep and lasting friendships in here while I was making enemies outside.

I sidled up to him and spoke into his ear. 'Ready to go soon, Triss?'

He turned slowly and looked at me. 'No, old lad,' he said, articulating carefully. 'I'm afraid I shan't be coming with you. They're having a dance here on the showfield later and Doreen has consented to accompany me.' He cast a loving glance across the counter at the redhead who crinkled her nose at him.

I was about to leave when a snatch of conversation from behind made me pause.

'A bloody goldfish!' a voice was saying disgustedly.

'Aye, it's a rum 'un, George,' a second voice replied.

There was a slurping sound of beer being downed.

'But tha knows, Fred,' the first voice said. 'That vet feller had to do it. Didn't 'ave no choice. He couldn't pass over t'squire's son.'

'Reckon you're right, but it's a bugger when you get graft and corruption in t'Family Pets.'

A heavy sigh, then 'It's the way things are nowadays, Fred, Everything's hulterior.'

'You're right there, George. It's hulterior, that's what it is.'

I fought down a rising panic. The Pelhams had been Lords of the Manor of Darrowby for generations and the present squire was Major Pelham. I knew him as a friendly farmer client, but that was all. I'd never heard of his son.

I clutched at Tristan's arm. 'Who is that little boy over there?'

Tristan peered out glassily across the sward. 'The one with the goldfish bowl, you mean?'

'That's right.'

'It's young Nigel Pelham, the squire's son.'

'Oh Gawd,' I moaned. 'But I've never seen him before. Where's he been?'

'Boarding school down south, I believe. On holiday just now.'

I stared at the boy again. Tousled fair hair, grey open-necked shirt, sunburned legs. Just like all the others.

George was at it again. 'Lovely dogs and cats there was, but squire's lad won it with a bloody goldfish.'

'Well, let's be right,' his companion put in. 'If that lad 'ad brought along a bloody stuffed monkey he'd still 'ave got fust prize with it.'

'No doubt about it, Fred. T'other kids might as well 'ave stopped at 'ome.'

'Aye, it's not like it used to be, George. Nobody does owt for nowt these days.

'True, Fred, very true.' There was a gloomy silence punctuated by noisy gulpings. Then, in weary tones: 'Well you and me can't alter it. It's the kind of world we're living in today.'

I reeled out into the fresh air and the sunshine. Looking round at the tranquil scene, the long stretch of grass, the loop of pebbly river with the green hills rising behind, I had a sense of unreality. Was there any part of this peaceful cameo of rural England without its sinister undertones? As if by instinct I made my way into the long marquee which housed the produce section. Surely among those quiet rows of vegetables I would find repose.

The place was almost empty but as I made my way down the long lines of tables I came upon the solitary figure of old John William Enderby who had a little grocer's shop in the town.

'Well how are things?' I inquired.

'Nobbut middlin' lad,' the old man replied morosely.

'Why, what's wrong?'

'Well, ah got a second with me broad beans but only a highly commended for me shallots. Look at 'em.'

I looked. 'Yes, they're beautiful shallots, Mr Enderby.'

'Aye, they are, and nobbut a highly commended. It's a insult, that's what it is a insult.'

'But Mr Enderby . . . highly commended . . . I mean, that's pretty good isn't it?'

'No it isn't, it's a insult!'

'Oh bad luck.'

John William stared at me wide-eyed for a moment. 'It's not bad luck lad, it's nowt but a twist.'

'Oh surely not!'

'Ah'm tellin' you. Jim Houlston got first with 'is shallots and judge is his wife's cousin.'

'Never!'

'It's true,' grunted John William, nodding solemnly. 'It's nowt but a twist.'

'Well I've never heard of such a thing!'

'You don't know what goes on, young man. Ah wasn't even placed with me taties. Frank Thompson got first wi' that lot.' He pointed to a tray of noble tubers.

I studied them. 'I must admit they look splendid potatoes.'

'Aye, they are, but Frank pinched 'em'.

'What?'

'Aye, they took first prize at Brisby show last Thursday and Frank pinched 'em off t'stand.'

I clutched at the nearby table. The foundations of my world were crumbling. 'That can't be true, Mr Enderby.'

'Ah'm not jokin' nor jestin',' declared John William. 'Them's self and same taties, ah'd know them anywhere. It's nowt but a . . . .'

I could take no more. I fled.

Outside the evening sunshine was still warm and the whole field was awash with the soft light which, in the Dales, seems to stream down in a golden flood from the high tops. But it was as if the forces of darkness were pressing on me; all I wanted was to get home.

I hurried to the stewards' tent and collected my measuring stick, running a gauntlet of hostile stares from the pony people I had outed earlier in the day. They were still waving their certificates and arguing.

On my way to the car I had to pass several of the ladies who had watched me judge the pets and though they didn't exactly draw their skirts aside they managed to convey their message. Among the rows of vehicles I spotted the man with the moustache. He still hadn't taken his terrier away and his eyes, full of wounded resentment, followed my every step.

I was opening my door when Helen and her party, also apparently on the way home, passed about fifty yards away. Helen waved. I waved back, and Richard Edmundson gave me a nod before helping her into the front seat of a gleaming, silver Daimler. The two fathers got into the back.

As I settled into the seat of my Austin, braced my feet against the broken floor boards and squinted through the cracked windscreen I prayed that just this once the thing would go on the starter. Holding my breath I pulled at the knob but the engine gave a couple of lazy turns then fell silent.

Fishing the starting handle from under the seat I crept out and inserted it in its hole under the radiator; and as I began the old familiar winding the silver monster purred contemptuously past me and away.

Dropping into the driver's seat again I caught sight of my face in the mirror and could see the streaks and flecks of blood still caked on my cheek and around the roots of my hair. Tristan hadn't done a very good job with his bucket of cold water.

I looked back at the emptying field and at the Daimler disappearing round a distant bend. It seemed to me that in more ways than one the show was over.

The Phantom Elopement

CHARLES DICKENS

Mr Pickwick, chairman and founder of that noble association, the Pickwick Club, is determined to bring to justice the egregious trickster and dissembler Mr Alfred Jingle. Leaving his fellow Pickwickians and new-found friends from Westgate House at Dingley Dell, their benevolent leader and his faithful servant, Sam Weller, follow the villain to the Angel Hotel at Bury St Edmunds. But Mr Jingle has another nasty surprise in store for Mr P....

THERE IS NO MONTH IN the whole year, in which nature wears a more beautiful appearance than in the month of August. Spring has many beauties, and May is a fresh and blooming month, but the charms of this time of year are enhanced by their contrast with the winter season. August has no such advantage. It comes when we remember nothing but clear skies, green fields and sweet-smelling flowers – when the recollection of snow, and ice, and bleak winds, has faded from our minds as completely as they have disappeared from the earth, – and yet what a pleasant time it is! Orchards and corn-fields ring with the hum of labour; trees bend beneath the thick clusters of rich fruit which bow their branches to the ground; and the corn, piled in graceful sheaves, or waving in every light breath that sweeps above it, as if it wooed the sickle, tinges the landscape with a golden hue. A mellow softness appears to hang over the whole earth; the influence of the season seems to extend itself to the very waggon, whose slow motion across the well-reaped field, is perceptible only to the eye, but strikes with no harsh sound upon the ear.

As the coach rolls swiftly past the fields and orchards which skirt the road, groups of women and children, piling the fruit in sieves, or gathering the scattered ears of corn, pause for an instant from their labour, and shading the sun-burnt face with a still browner hand, gaze upon the passengers with curious eyes, while some stout urchin, too small to work, but too mischievous to be left at home, scrambles over the side of the basket in which he has been deposited for security, and kicks and screams with delight. The reaper stops in his work, and stands with folded arms, looking at the vehicle as it whirls past; and the rough cart-horses bestow a sleepy glance upon the smart coach team, which says, as plainly as a horse's glance can, 'It's all very fine to look at, but slow going, over a heavy field, is better than warm work like that, upon a dusty road, after all.' You cast a look behind you, as you turn a corner of the road. The women and children have resumed their labour: the reaper once more stoops to his work: the cart-horses have moved on: and all are again in motion.

The influence of a scene like this, was not lost upon the well-regulated mind of Mr Pickwick. Intent upon the resolution he had formed, of exposing the real character of the nefarious Jingle, in any quarter in which he might be pursuing his fraudulent designs, he sat at first taciturn and contemplative, brooding over the means by which his purpose could be best attained. By degrees his attention grew more and more attracted by the objects around him; and at last he derived as much enjoyment from the ride, as if it had been undertaken for the pleasantest reason in the world.

'Delightful prospect, Sam,' said Mr Pickwick.

'Beats the chimley pots, sir,' replied Mr Weller, touching his hat.

'I suppose you have hardly seen anything but chimney-pots and bricks and mortar all your life, Sam,' said Mr Pickwick, smiling.

'I worn't always a boots, sir,' said Mr Weller, with a shake of the head. 'I wos a vagginer's boy, once.'

'When was that?' inquired Mr Pickwick.

'When I wos first pitched neck and crop into the world, to play at leapfrog with its troubles,' replied Sam. 'I wos a carrier's boy at startin': then a vagginer's, then a helper, then a boots. Now I'm a gen'l'm'n's servant. I shall be a gen'l'm'n myself one of these days, perhaps, with a pipe in my mouth, and a summerhouse in the back garden. Who knows? *I* shouldn't be surprised, for one.'

'You are quite a philosopher, Sam,' said Mr Pickwick.

'It runs in the family, I b'lieve, sir,' replied Mr Weller. 'My father's wery much in that line, now. If my mother-in-law blows him up, he whistles. She flies in a passion, and breaks his pipe; he steps out, and gets another. Then she screams wery loud, and falls into 'sterics: and he smokes wery comfortably 'till she comes to agin. That's philosophy, sir, an't it?'

'A very good substitute for it, at all events,' replied Mr Pickwick, laughing. 'It must have been of great service to you, in the course of your rambling life, Sam.'

'Service, sir,' exclaimed Sam. 'You may say that. Arter I run away from the carrier, and afore I took up with the vagginer, I had unfurnished lodgin's for a fortnight.'

'Unfurnished lodgings?' said Mr Pickwick.

'Yes – the dry arches of Waterloo Bridge. Fine sleeping-place – within ten minutes' walk of all the public offices – only if there is any objection to it, it is that the sitivation's *rayther* too airy. I see some queer sights there.'

'Ah, I suppose you did,' said Mr Pickwick, with an air of considerable interest.

'Sights, sir,' resumed Mr Weller, 'as 'ud penetrate your benevolent heart, and come out on the other side. You don't see the reg'lar wagrants there; trust 'em, they knows better than that. Young beggars, male and female, as hasn't made a rise in their profession, takes up their quarters there sometimes; but it's generally the worn-out, starving, houseless creeturs as rolls themselves in the dark corners o' them lonesome places – poor creeturs as an't up to the twopenny rope.'

'And, pray, Sam, what is the twopenny rope?' inquired Mr Pickwick.

'The twopenny rope, sir,' replied Mr Weller, 'is just a cheap lodgin' house, where the beds is twopence a night.'

'What do they call a bed a rope for?' said Mr Pickwick.

'Bless your innocence, sir, that a'nt it,' replied Sam. 'Wen the lady and gen'l'm'n as keeps the Hot-el first begun business they used to make the beds on the floor; but this wouldn't do at no price, 'cos instead o' taking a moderate twopenn'orth o' sleep, the lodgers used to lie there half the day. So now they has two ropes, 'bout six foot apart, and three from the floor, which goes right down the room; and the beds are made of slips of coarse sacking, stretched across 'em.'

'Well,' said Mr Pickwick.

'Well,' said Mr Weller, 'the adwantage o' the plan's hobvious. At six o'clock every mornin' they lets go the ropes at one end, and down falls all the lodgers. 'Consequence is, that being thoroughly waked, they get up wery quietly, and walk away! Beg your pardon, sir,' said Sam, suddenly breaking off in his loquacious discourse. 'Is this Bury St Edmunds?'

'It is,' replied Mr Pickwick.

The coach rattled through the well-paved streets of a handsome little town, of thriving and cleanly appearance, and stopped before a large inn situated in a wide open street, nearly facing the old abbey.

'And this,' said Mr Pickwick, looking up, 'is the Angel! We alight here, Sam. But some caution is necessary. Order a private room, and do not mention my name. You understand.'

'Right as a trivet, sir,' replied Mr Weller, with a wink of intelligence; and having dragged Mr Pickwick's portmanteau from the hind boot, into which it had been hastily thrown when they joined the coach at Eatanswill, Mr Weller disappeared on his errand. A private room was speedily engaged; and into it Mr Pickwick was ushered without delay.

'Now, Sam,' said Mr Pickwick, 'the first thing to be done is to —'

'Order dinner, sir,' interposed Mr Weller. 'It's wery late, sir.'

'Ah, so it is,' said Mr Pickwick, looking at his watch. 'You are right, Sam.'

'And if I might adwise, sir,' added Mr Weller, 'I'd just have a good night's rest arterwards, and not begin inquiring arter this here deep 'un 'till the mornin'. There's nothin' so refreshin' as sleep, sir, as the servant-girl said afore she drank the egg-cupful o' laudanum.'

'I think you are right, Sam,' said Mr Pickwick. 'But I must first ascertain that he is in the house, and not likely to go away.'

'Leave that to me, sir,' said Sam. 'Let me order you a snug little dinner, and make any inquiries below while it's a getting ready; I could worm ev'ry secret out o' the boots' heart, in five minutes, sir.'

'Do so,' said Mr Pickwick: and Mr Weller at once retired.

In half an hour, Mr Pickwick was seated at a very satisfactory dinner; and in three-quarters Mr Weller returned with the intelligence that Mr Charles Fitz-Marshall had ordered his private room to be retained for him, until further notice. He was going to spend the evening at some private house in the neighbourhood, had ordered the boots to sit up until his return, and had taken his servant with him.

'Now, sir,' argued Mr Weller, when he had concluded his report, 'if I can get a talk with this here servant in the mornin', he'll tell me all his master's concerns.'

'How do you know that?' interposed Mr Pickwick.

'Bless your heart, sir, servants always do,' replied Mr Weller.

'Oh, ah, I forgot that,' said Mr Pickwick. 'Well.'

'Then you can arrange what's best to be done, sir, and we can act according.'

As it appeared that this was the best arrangement that could be made, it was finally agreed upon. Mr Weller, by his master's permission, retired to spend the evening in his own way; and was shortly afterwards elected, by the unanimous voice of the assembled company, into the tap-room chair, in which honourable post he acquitted himself so much to the satisfaction of the gentlemen-frequenters, that their roars of laughter and approbation penetrated to Mr Pickwick's bedroom, and shortened the term of his natural rest by at least three hours.

Early on the ensuing morning, Mr Weller was dispelling all the feverish remains of the previous evening's conviviality, through the instrumentality of a halfpenny shower-bath (having induced a young gentleman attached to the stable-department, by the offer of that coin, to pump over his head and face, until he was perfectly restored), when he was attracted by the appearance of a young fellow in mulberry-coloured livery, who was sitting on a bench in the yard, reading what appeared to be a hymn book, with an air of deep abstraction, but who occasionally stole a glance at the individual under the pump, as if he took some interest in his proceedings, nevertheless.

'You're a rum 'un to look at, you are!' thought Mr Weller, the first time his eyes encountered the glance of the stranger in the mulberry suit: who had a large, sallow, ugly face, very sunken eyes, and a gigantic head, from which depended a quantity of lank black hair. 'You're a rum 'un!'

thought Mr Weller; and thinking this, he went on washing himself, and thought no more about him.

Still the man kept glancing from his hymn book to Sam, and from Sam to his hymn book, as if he wanted to open a conversation. So at last, Sam, by way of giving him an opportunity, said with a familiar nod —

'How are you, governor?'

'I am happy to say, I am pretty well, sir,' said the man, speaking with great deliberation, and closing the book. 'I hope you are the same, sir?'

'Why if I felt less like a walking brandy-bottle, I shouldn't be quite so staggery this mornin',' replied Sam. 'Are you stoppin' in this house, old 'un?'

The mulberry man replied in the affirmative.

'How was it, you worn't one of us, last night?' inquired Sam, scrubbing his face with the towel. 'You seem one of the jolly sort – looks as conwivial as a live trout in a lime basket,' added Mr Weller, in an under tone.

'I was out last night, with my master,' replied the stranger.

'What's his name?' inquired Mr Weller, colouring up very red with sudden excitement, and the friction of the towel combined.

'Fitz-Marshall,' said the mulberry man.

'Give us your hand,' said Mr Weller, advancing: 'I should like to know you. I like your appearance, old fellow.'

'Well, that is very strange,' said the mulberry man, with great simplicity of manner. 'I like yours so much, that I wanted to speak to you, from the very first moment I saw you under the pump.'

'Did you though?'

'Upon my word. Now, isn't that curious?'

'Wery sing'ler,' said Sam, inwardly congratulating himself upon the softness of the stranger. 'What's your name, my patriarch?'

'Job.'

'And a wery good name it is – only one I know, that ain't got a nickname to it. What's the other name?'

'Trotter,' said the stranger. 'What is yours?'

Sam bore in mind his master's caution, and replied.

'My name's Walker; my master's name's Wilkins. Will you take a drop o' somethin' this mornin', Mr Trotter?'

Mr Trotter acquiesced in this agreeable proposal: and having deposited his book in his coat-pocket, accompanied Mr Weller to the tap, where they were soon occupied in discussing an exhilarating compound, formed by mixing together, in a pewter vessel, certain quantities of British Hollands, and the fragrant essence of the clove.

'And what sort of a place have you got?' inquired Sam, as he filled his companion's glass, for the second time.

'Bad,' said Job, smacking his lips, 'very bad.'

'You don't mean that?' said Sam.

'I do, indeed. Worse than that, my master's going to be married.'

'No.'

'Yes; and worse than that, too, he's going to run away with an immense rich heiress, from boarding-school.'

'What a dragon!' said Sam, refilling his companion's glass. 'It's some boarding-school in this town, I suppose, a'nt it?'

Now, although this question was put in the most careless tone imaginable, Mr Job Trotter plainly showed by gestures, that he perceived his new friend's anxiety to draw forth an answer to it. He emptied his glass, looked mysteriously at his companion, winked both of his small eyes, one after the other, and finally made a motion with his arm, as if he were working an imaginary pump-handle: thereby intimating that he (Mr Trotter) considered himself as undergoing the process of being pumped, by Mr Samuel Weller.

'No, no,' said Mr Trotter, in conclusion, 'that's not to be told to everybody. That is a secret – a great secret, Mr Walker.'

As the mulberry man said this, he turned his glass upside down, as a means of reminding his companion that he had nothing left wherewith to slake his thirst. Sam observed the hint; and feeling the delicate manner in which it was conveyed, ordered the pewter vessel to be refilled, whereat the small eyes of the mulberry man glistened.

'And so it's a secret?' said Sam.

'I should rather suspect it was,' said the mulberry man, sipping his liquor, with a complacent face.

'I suppose your mas'r 's wery rich?' said Sam.

Mr Trotter smiled, and holding his glass in his left hand, gave four distinct slaps on the pocket of his mulberry indescribables with his right, as to intimate that his master might have done the same without alarming anybody much by the chinking of coin.

'Ah,' said Sam, 'that's the game, is it?'

The mulberry man nodded significantly.

'Well, and don't you think, old feller,' remonstrated Mr Weller, 'that if you let your master take in this here young lady, you're a precious rascal?'

'I know that,' said Job Trotter, turning upon his companion a countenance of deep contrition, and groaning slightly. 'I know that, and that's what it is that preys upon my mind. But what am I to do?'

'Do!' said Sam; 'di-wulge to the missis, and give up your master.'

'Who'd believe me?' replied Job Trotter. 'The young lady's considered the very picture of innocence and discretion. She'd deny it, and so would my master. Who'd believe me? I should lose my place, and get indicted for a conspiracy, or some such thing; that's all I should take by my motion.'

'There's somethin' in that,' said Sam, ruminating; 'there's somethin' in that.'

'If I knew any respectable gentleman who would take the matter up,' continued Mr Trotter, 'I might have some hope of preventing the elopement; but there's the same difficulty, Mr Walker, just the same. I know no gentleman in this strange place, and ten to one if I did, whether he would believe my story.'

'Come this way,' said Sam, suddenly jumping up, and grasping the mulberry man by the arm. 'My mas'r 's the man you want, I see.' And after a slight resistance on the part of Job Trotter, Sam led his newly-found friend to the apartment of Mr Pickwick, to whom he presented him, together with a brief summary of the dialogue we have just repeated.

'I am very sorry to betray my master, sir,' said Job Trotter, applying to his eyes a pink checked pocket handkerchief about six inches square.

'The feeling does you a great deal of honour,' replied Mr Pickwick; 'but it is your duty, nevertheless.'

'I know it is my duty, sir,' replied Job, with great emotion. 'We should all try to discharge our duty, sir, and I humbly endeavour to discharge mine, sir; but it is a hard trial to betray a master, sir, whose clothes you wear, and whose bread you eat, even though he is a scoundrel, sir.'

'You are a very good fellow,' said Mr Pickwick, much affected, 'an honest fellow.'

'Come, come,' interposed Sam, who had witnessed Mr Trotter's tears with considerable impatience, 'blow this here watercart bis'ness. It won't do no good, this won't.'

'Sam,' said Mr Pickwick, reproachfully, 'I am sorry to find that you have so little respect for this young man's feelings.'

'His feelins is all wery well, sir,' replied Mr Weller; 'and as they're so wery fine, and it's a pity he should lose 'em, I think he'd better keep 'em in his own buzzum, than let 'em ewaporate in hot water, 'specially as they do no good. Tears never yet wound up a clock, or worked a steam ingen'. The next time you go out to a smoking party, young fellow, fill your pipe with that 'ere reflection; and for the present just put that bit of pink gingham into your pocket. 'T'an't so handsome that you need keep waving it about, as if you was a tightrope dancer.'

'My man is in the right,' said Mr Pickwick, accosting Job, 'although his mode of expressing his opinion is somewhat homely, and occasionally incomprehensible.'

'He is, sir, very right,' said Mr Trotter, 'and I will give way no longer.'

'Very well,' said Mr Pickwick. 'Now, where is this boarding-school?'

'It is a large, old, red-brick house, just outside the town, sir,' replied Job Trotter.

'And when,' said Mr Pickwick, 'when is this villainous design to be carried into execution – when is this elopement to take place?'

'Tonight, sir,' replied Job.

'Tonight!' exclaimed Mr Pickwick.

'This very night, sir,' replied Job Trotter. 'That is what alarms me so much.'

'Instant measures must be taken,' said Mr Pickwick. 'I will see the lady who keeps the establishment immediately.'

'I beg your pardon, sir,' said Job, 'but that course of proceeding will never do.'

'Why not?' inquired Mr Pickwick.

'My master, sir, is a very artful man.'

'I know he is,' said Mr Pickwick.

'And he has so wound himself round the old lady's heart, sir,' resumed Job, 'that she would believe nothing to his prejudice, if you went down on your bare knees, and swore it; especially as you have no proof but the word of a servant, who, for anything she knows (and my master would be sure to say so), was discharged for some fault, and does this in revenge.'

'What had better be done, then?' said Mr Pickwick.

'Nothing but taking him in the very fact of eloping, will convince the old lady, sir,' replied Job.

'All them old cats *will* run their heads agin mile-stones,' observed Mr Weller in a parenthesis.

'But this taking him in the very act of elopement, would be a very difficult thing to accomplish, I fear,' said Mr Pickwick.

'I don't know, sir,' said Mr Trotter, after a few moments' reflection. 'I think it might be very easily done.'

'How?' was Mr Pickwick's inquiry.

'Why,' replied Mr Trotter, 'my master and I, being in the confidence of the two servants, will be secreted in the kitchen at ten o'clock. When the family have retired to rest, we shall come out of the kitchen, and the young lady out of her bedroom. A post-chaise will be waiting, and away we go.'

'Well?' said Mr Pickwick.

'Well, sir, I have been thinking that if you were in waiting in the garden behind, alone —'

'Alone,' said Mr Pickwick. 'Why alone?'

'I thought it very natural,' replied Job, 'that the old lady wouldn't like such an unpleasant discovery to be made before more persons than can possibly be helped. The young lady too, sir – consider her feelings.'

'You are very right,' said Mr Pickwick. 'The consideration evinces your delicacy of feeling. Go on; you are very right.'

'Well, sir, I have been thinking that if you were waiting in the back garden alone, and I was to let you in, at the door which opens into it, from the end of the passage, at exactly half-past eleven o'clock, you would be just in the very moment of time to assist me in frustrating the designs of this bad man, by whom I have been unfortunately ensnared.'

Here Mr Trotter sighed deeply.

'Don't distress yourself on that account,' said Mr Pickwick, 'if he had one grain of the delicacy of feeling which distinguishes you, humble as your station is, I should have some hopes of him.'

Job Trotter bowed low; and in spite of Mr Weller's previous remonstrance, the tears again rose to his eyes.

'I never see such a feller,' said Sam. 'Blessed if I don't think he's got a main in his head as is always turned on.'

'Sam,' said Mr Pickwick, with great severity. 'Hold your tongue.'

'Werry well, sir,' replied Mr Weller.

'I don't like this plan,' said Mr Pickwick, after deep meditation. 'Why cannot I communicate with the young lady's friends?'

'Because they live one hundred miles from here, sir,' responded Job Trotter.

'That's a clincher,' said Mr Weller, aside.

'Then this garden,' resumed Mr Pickwick. 'How am I to get into it?'

'The wall is very low, sir, and your servant will give you a leg up.'

'My servant will give me a leg up,' repeated Mr Pickwick, mechanically. 'You will be sure to be near this door that you speak of?'

'You cannot mistake it, sir; it's the only one that opens into the garden. Tap at it when you hear the clock strike, and I will open it instantly.'

'I don't like the plan,' said Mr Pickwick; 'but as I see no other, and as the happiness of this young lady's whole life is at stake, I adopt it. I shall be sure to be there.'

Thus, for the second time, did Mr Pickwick's innate good-feeling involve him in an enterprise from which he would most willingly have stood aloof.

'What is the name of the house?' inquired Mr Pickwick.

'Westgate House, sir. You turn a little to the right when you get to the end of the town; it stands by itself, some little distance off the high road, with the name on a brass plate on the gate.'

'I know it,' said Mr Pickwick. 'I observed it once before, when I was in this town. You may depend upon me.'

'Mr Trotter made another bow, and turned to depart, when Mr Pickwick thrust a guinea into his hand.

'You're a fine fellow,' said Mr Pickwick, 'and I admire your goodness of heart. No thanks. Remember – eleven o'clock.'

'There is no fear of my forgetting it, sir,' replied Job Trotter. With these words he left the room, followed by Sam.

'I say,' said the latter, 'not a bad notion that 'ere crying. I'd cry like a rainwater spout in a shower on such good terms. How do you do it?'

'It comes from the heart, Mr Walker,' replied Job, solemnly. 'Good morning, sir.'

'You're a soft customer, you are; – we've got it all out o' you, any how,' thought Mr Weller, as Job walked away.

We cannot state the precise nature of the thoughts which passed through Mr Trotter's mind, because we don't know what they were.

The day wore on, evening came, and a little before ten o'clock Sam Weller reported that Mr Jingle and Job had gone out together, that their luggage was packed up, and that they had ordered a chaise. The plot was evidently in execution, as Mr Trotter had foretold.

Halfpast ten o'clock arrived, and it was time for Mr Pickwick to issue forth on his delicate errand. Resisting Sam's tender of his great coat, in order that he might have no incumbrance in scaling the wall, he set forth, followed by his attendant.

There was a bright moon, but it was behind the clouds. It was a fine dry night, but it was most uncommonly dark. Paths, hedges, fields, houses, and trees, were enveloped in one deep shade. The atmosphere was hot and sultry, the summer lightning quivered faintly on the verge of the horizon, and was the only sight that varied the dull gloom in which everything was wrapped – sound there was none, except the distant barking of some restless house-dog.

They found the house, read the brass-plate, walked round the wall, and stopped at that portion of it which divided them from the bottom of the garden.

'You will return to the inn, Sam, when you have assisted me over,' said Mr Pickwick.

'Very well, sir.'

'And you will sit up, 'till I return.'

'Cert'nly, sir.'

'Take hold of my leg; and, when I say "Over", raise me gently.'

'All right, sir.'

Having settled these preliminaries, Mr Pickwick grasped the top of the wall, and gave the word 'Over,' which was very literally obeyed. Whether his body partook in some degree of the elasticity of his mind, or whether Mr Weller's notions of a gentle push were of a somewhat rougher description than Mr Pickwick's, the immediate effect of his assistance was to jerk that immortal gentleman completely over the wall on to the bed beneath, where, after crushing three gooseberry bushes and a rose-tree, he finally alighted at full length.

'You ha'n't hurt yourself, I hope, sir?' said Sam, in a loud whisper, as soon as he had recovered from the surprise consequent upon the mysterious disappearance of his master.

'I have not hurt *myself*, Sam, certainly,' replied Mr Pickwick, from the other side of the wall, 'but I rather think that *you* have hurt me.'

'I hope not, sir,' said Sam.

'Never mind,' said Mr Pickwick, rising, 'it's nothing but a few scratches. Go away, or we shall be overheard.'

'Goodbye, sir.'

'Goodbye.'

With stealthy steps Sam Weller departed, leaving Mr Pickwick alone in the garden.

Lights occasionally appeared in the different windows of the house, or glanced from the staircases, as if the inmates were retiring to rest. Not caring to go too near the door, until the appointed time, Mr Pickwick crouched into an angle of the wall, and awaited its arrival.

It was a situation which might well have depressed the spirits of many a man. Mr Pickwick, however, felt neither depression nor misgiving. He knew that his purpose was in the main a good one, and he placed implicit reliance on the highminded Job. It was dull, certainly; not to say, dreary; but a contemplative man can always employ himself in meditation. Mr Pickwick had meditated himself into a doze, when he was roused by the chimes of the neighbouring church ringing out the hour – half-past eleven.

'That is the time,' thought Mr Pickwick, getting cautiously on his feet. He looked up at the house. The lights had disappeared, and the shutters were closed – all in bed, no doubt. He walked on tiptoe to the door, and gave a gentle tap. Two or three minutes passing without any reply, he gave another tap rather louder, and then another rather louder than that.

At length the sound of feet was audible upon the stairs, and then the light of a candle shone through the keyhole of the door. There was a good deal of unchaining and unbolting, and the door was slowly opened.

Now the door opened outwards: and as the door opened wider and wider, Mr Pickwick receded behind it, more and more. What was his astonishment when he just peeped out, by way of caution, to see the servant who had opened it was – not Job Trotter, but a servant-girl with a candle in her hand! Mr Pickwick drew in his head again, with the swiftness displayed by that admirable melodramatic performer, Punch, when he lies in wait for the flat-headed comedian with the tin box of music.

'It must have been the cat, Sarah,' said the girl, addressing herself to some one in the house. 'Puss, puss, puss, – tit, tit, tit.'

But no animal being decoyed by these blandishments, the girl slowly closed the door, and refastened it; leaving Mr Pickwick drawn up straight against the wall.

'This is very curious,' thought Mr Pickwick. 'They are sitting up beyond their usual hour, I suppose. Extremely unfortunate, that they should have chosen this night, of all others, for such a purpose – exceedingly.' And with these thoughts, Mr Pickwick cautiously retired to the angle of the wall in which he had been before ensconced; waiting until such time as he might deem it safe to repeat the signal.

He had not been here five minutes, when a vivid flash of lightning was followed by a loud peal of thunder that crashed and rolled away in the distance with a terrific noise – then came another flash of lightning, brighter than the other, and a second peal of thunder louder than the first; and then down came the rain, with a force and fury that swept everything before it.

Mr Pickwick was perfectly aware that a tree is a very dangerous neighbour in a thunderstorm. He had a tree on his right, a tree on his left, a third before him, and a fourth behind. If he remained where he was, he might fall the victim of an accident; if he showed himself in the centre of the garden, he might be consigned to a constable; – once or twice he tried to scale the wall, but having no other legs this time, than those with which Nature had furnished him, the only effect of his struggles was to inflict a variety of very unpleasant gratings on his knees and shins, and to throw him into a state of the most profuse perspiration.

'What a dreadful situation,' said Mr Pickwick, pausing to wipe his brow after this exercise. He looked up at the house – all was dark. They must be gone to bed now. He would try the signal again.

He walked on tiptoe across the moist gravel, and tapped at the door. He held his breath, and listened at the keyhole. No reply: very odd. Another knock. He listened again. There was a low whispering inside, and then a voice cried —

'Who's there?'

'That's not Job,' thought Mr Pickwick, hastily drawing himself straight up against the wall again. 'It's a woman.'

He had scarcely had time to form this conclusion, when a window above stairs was thrown up, and three or four female voices repeated the query – 'Who's there?'

Mr Pickwick dared not move hand or foot. It was clear that the whole establishment was roused. He made up his mind to remain where he was, until the alarm had subsided: and then by a supernatural effort, to get over the wall, or perish in the attempt.

Like all Mr Pickwick's determinations, this was the best that could be made under the circumstances; but, unfortunately, it was founded upon the assumption that they would not venture to open the door again. What was his discomfiture, when he heard the chain and bolts withdrawn, and saw the door slowly opening, wider and wider! He retreated into the corner, step by step; but do what he would, the interposition of his own person, prevented its being opened to its utmost width.

'Who's there?' screamed a numerous chorus of treble voices from the staircase inside, consisting of the spinster lady of the establishment, three teachers, five female servants, and thirty boarders, all half-dressed, and in a forest of curl-papers.

Of course Mr Pickwick didn't say who *was* there; and then the burden of the chorus changed into – 'Lor' I am so frightened.'

'Cook,' said the lady abbess, who took care to be on the top stair, the very last of the group – 'Cook, why don't you go a little way into the garden?'

'Please, ma'am, I don't like,' responded the cook.

'Lor', what a stupid thing that cook is!' said the thirty boarders.

'Cook,' said the lady abbess, with great dignity; 'don't answer me, if you please. I insist upon your looking into the garden immediately.'

Here the cook began to cry, and the housemaid said it was 'a shame!' for which partisanship she received a month's warning on the spot.

'Do you hear, cook?' said the lady abbess, stamping her foot impatiently.

'Don't you hear your missus, cook?' said the three teachers.

'What an impudent thing, that cook is!' said the thirty boarders.

The unfortunate cook, thus strongly urged, advanced a step or two, and holding her candle just where it prevented her from seeing anything at all, declared there was nothing there, and it must have been the wind. the door was just going to be closed in consequence, when an inquisitive boarder, who had been peeping between the hinges, set up a fearful screaming, which called back the cook and the housemaid, and all the more adventurous, in no time.

'What is the matter with Miss Smithers?' said the lady abbess, as the aforesaid Miss Smithers proceeded to go into hysterics of four young lady power.

'Lor', Miss Smithers dear,' said the other nine-and-twenty boarders.

'Oh, the man – the man – behind the door!' screamed Miss Smithers.

The lady abbess no sooner heard this appalling cry, than she retreated to her own bedroom, double-locked the door, and fainted away comfortably. The boarders, and the teachers, and the servants, fell back upon the stairs, and upon each other; and never was such a screaming, and fainting, and struggling, beheld. In the midst of the tumult Mr Pickwick emerged from his concealment, and presented himself among them.

'Ladies – dear ladies,' said Mr Pickwick.

'Oh, he says we're dear,' cried the oldest and ugliest teacher. 'Oh, the wretch!'

'Ladies,' roared Mr Pickwick, rendered desperate by the danger of his situation. 'Hear me. I am no robber. I want the lady of the house.'

'Oh, what a ferocious monster!' screamed another teacher. 'He wants Miss Tomkins.'

Here there was a general scream.

'Ring the alarm bell, somebody!' cried a dozen voices.

'Don't – don't,' shouted Mr Pickwick. 'Look at me. Do I look like a robber? My dear ladies – you may bind me hand and leg, or lock me up in a closet, if you like. Only hear what I have got to say – only hear me.'

'How did you come in our garden?' faltered the housemaid.

'Call the lady of the house, and I'll tell her everything – everything:'

said Mr Pickwick, exerting his lungs to the utmost pitch. 'Call her – only be quiet, and call her, and you shall hear everything.'

It might have been Mr Pickwick's appearance, or it might have been his manner, or it might have been the temptation – irresistible to a female mind – of hearing something at present enveloped in mystery, that reduced the more reasonable portion of the establishment (some four individuals) to a state of comparative quiet. By them it was proposed, as a test of Mr Pickwick's sincerity, that he should immediately submit to personal restraint; and that gentleman having consented to hold a conference with Miss Tomkins, from the interior of a closet in which the day boarders hung their bonnets and sandwich-bags, he at once stepped into it of his own accord, and was securely locked in. This revived the others; and Miss Tomkins having been brought to, and brought down, the conference began.

'What did you do in my garden, Man?' said Miss Tomkins, in a faint voice.

'I came to warn you, that one of your young ladies was going to elope tonight,' replied Mr Pickwick, from the interior of the closet.

'Elope!' exclaimed Miss Tomkins, the three teachers, the thirty boarders, and the five servants. 'Who with?'

'Your friend, Mr Charles Fitz-Marshall.'

'*My* friend! I don't know any such person.'

'Well; Mr Jingle, then.'

'I never heard the name in my life.'

'Then, I have been deceived, and deluded,' said Mr Pickwick. 'I have been the victim of a conspiracy – a foul and base conspiracy. Send to the Angel, my dear ma'am, if you don't believe me. Send to the Angel for Mr Pickwick's manservant, I implore you, ma'am.'

'He must be respectable – he keeps a manservant,' said Miss Tomkins to the writing and ciphering governess.

'It's my opinion, Miss Tomkins,' said the writing and ciphering governess, 'that his manservant keeps him. *I* think he's a madman, Miss Tomkins, and the other's his keeper.'

'I think you are very right, Miss Gwynn,' responded Miss Tomkins. 'Let two of the servants repair to the Angel, and let the others remain here, to protect us.'

So two of the servants were despatched to the Angel in search of Mr Samuel Weller: and the remaining three stopped behind to protect Miss Tomkins, and the three teachers, and the thirty boarders. And Mr Pickwick sat down in the closet, beneath a grove of sandwich-bags, and awaited the return of the messengers, with all the philosophy and fortitude he could summon to his aid.

An hour and a half elapsed before they came back, and when they did come, Mr Pickwick recognized, in addition to the voice of Mr Samuel

Weller, two other voices, the tones of which struck familiarly on his ear; but whose they were, he could not for the life of him call to mind.

A very brief conversation ensued. The door was unlocked. Mr Pickwick stepped out of the closet, and found himself in the presence of the whole establishment of Westgate House, Mr Samuel Weller, and – old Wardle, and his destined son-in-law, Mr Trundle!

'My dear friend,' said Mr Pickwick, running forward and grasping Mr Wardle's hand, 'my dear friend, pray, for Heaven's sake, explain to this lady the unfortunate and dreadful situation in which I am placed. You must have heard it from my servant; say, at all events, my dear fellow, that I am neither a robber nor a madman.'

'I have said so, my dear friend. I have said so already,' replied Mr Wardle, shaking the right hand of his friend, while Mr Trundle shook the left.

'And whoever says, or has said, he is,' interposed Mr Weller, stepping forwad, 'says that which is not the truth, but so far from it, on the contrary, quite the rewerse. And if there's any number o' men on these here premises as has said so, I shall be wery happy to give 'em all a wery convincing proof o' their being mistaken, in this here wery room, if these wery respectable ladies'll have the goodness to retire, and order 'em up, one at a time.' Having delivered this defiance with great volubility, Mr Weller struck his open palm emphatically with his clenched fist, and winked pleasantly on Miss Tomkins: the intensity of whose horror at his supposing it within the bounds of possibility that there could be any men on the premises of Westgate House Establishment for Young Ladies, it is impossible to describe.

Mr Pickwick's explanation having already been partially made, was soon concluded. But neither in the course of his walk home with his friends, nor afterwards when seated before a blazing fire at the supper he so much needed, could a single observation be drawn from him. He seemed bewildered and amazed. Once, and only once, he turned round to Mr Wardle, and said

'How did you come here?'

'Trundle and I came down here, for some good shooting on the first,' replied Wardle. 'We arrived tonight, and were astonished to hear from your servant that you were here too. But I am glad you are,' said the old fellow, slapping him on the back. 'I am glad you are. We shall have a jovial party on the first, and we'll give Winkle another chance – eh, old boy?'

Mr Pickwick made no reply; he did not even ask after his friends at Dingley Dell, and shortly afterwards retired for the night, desiring Sam to fetch his candle when he rung.

The bell did ring in due course, and Mr Weller presented himself.

'Sam,' said Mr Pickwick, looking out from under the bedclothes.

'Sir,' said Mr Weller.

Mr Pickwick paused, and Mr Weller snuffed the candle.

'Sam,' said Mr Pickwick again, as if with a desperate effort.

'Sir,' said Mr Weller, once more.

'Where is that Trotter?'

'Job, sir?'

'Yes.'

'Gone, sir.'

'With his master, I suppose?'

'Friend or master, or whatever he is, he's gone with him,' replied Mr Weller. 'There's a pair on 'em, sir.'

'Jingle suspected my design, and set that fellow on you, with this story, I suppose?' said Mr Pickwick, half choking.

'Just that, sir,' replied Mr Weller.

'It was all false, of course?'

'All, sir,' replied Mr Weller. 'Reg'lr do, sir; artful dodge.'

'I don't think he'll escape us quite so easily the next time, Sam?' said Mr Pickwick.

'I don't think he will, sir.'

'Whenever I meet that Jingle again, wherever it is,' said Mr Pickwick, raising himself in bed, and indenting his pillow with a tremendous blow, 'I'll inflict personal chastisement on him, in addition to the exposure he so richly merits. I will, or my name is not Pickwick.'

'And wenever I catches hold o' that there melan-cholly chap with the black hair,' said Sam, 'if I don't bring some real water into his eyes, for once in a way, my name a'nt Weller. Goodnight, sir!'

The Waltz
DOROTHY PARKER

WHY, *thank you so much. I'd adore to.*

I don't want to dance with him. I don't want to dance with anybody. And even if I did, it wouldn't be him. He'd be well down among the last ten. I've seen the way he dances; it looks like something you do on Saint Walpurgis Night. Just think, not a quarter of an hour ago, here I was sitting, feeling so sorry for the poor girl he was dancing with. And now *I'm* going to be the poor girl. Well, well. Isn't it a small world?

And a peach of a world, too. A true little corker. Its events are so fascinatingly unpredictable, are not they? Here I was, minding my own business, not doing a stitch of harm to any living soul. And then he comes into my life, all smiles and city manners, to sue me for the favour of one memorable mazurka. Why, he scarcely knows my name, let alone what it stands for. It stands for Despair, Bewilderment, Futility, Degradation, and Premeditated Murder, but little does he wot. I don't wot his name, either; I haven't any idea what it is. Jukes, would be my guess from the look in his eyes. How do you do, Mr Jukes? And how is that dear little brother of yours, with the two heads?

Ah, now why did he have to come around me, with his low requests? Why can't he let me lead my own life? I ask so little – just to be left alone in my quiet corner of the table, to do my evening brooding over all my sorrows. And he must come, with his bows and his scrapes and his may-I-have-this-ones. And I had to go and tell him that I'd adore to dance with him. I cannot understand why I wasn't struck right down dead. Yes, and being struck dead would look like a day in the country, compared to struggling out a dance with this boy. But what could I do? Everyone else at the table had got up to dance, except him and me. There was I, trapped. Trapped like a trap in a trap.

What can you say, when a man asks you to dance with him? I most certainly will *not* dance with you, I'll see you in hell first. Why, thank you, I'd like to awfully, but I'm having labour pains. Oh, yes, *do* let's dance together – it's so nice to meet a man who isn't a scaredy-cat about catching my beri-beri. No. There was nothing for me to do, but say I'd adore to. Well, we might as well get it over with. All right, Cannonball, let's run out on the field. You won the toss; you can lead.

Why, I think it's more of a waltz, really. Isn't it? We might just listen to the music a second. Shall we? Oh, yes, it's a waltz. Mind? Why, I'm simply thrilled. I'd love to waltz with you.

I'd love to waltz with you. I'd love to waltz with you. I'd love to have my tonsils out, I'd love to be in a midnight fire at sea. Well, it's too late now. We're getting under way. *Oh.* Oh, dear. Oh, dear, dear, dear. Oh, this is even worse than I thought it would be. I suppose that's the one dependable law of life – everything is always worse than you thought it was going to be. Oh, if I had any real grasp of what this dance would be like, I'd have held out for sitting it out. Well, it will probably amount to the same thing in the end. We'll be sitting it out on the floor in a minute, if he keeps this up.

I'm so glad I brought it to his attention that this is a waltz they're playing. Heaven knows what might have happened, if he had thought it was something fast; we'd have blown the sides right out of the building. Why does he always want to be somewhere that he isn't? Why can't we stay in one place just long enough to get acclimated? It's this constant rush, rush, rush, that's the curse of American life. That's the reason that we're all of us so – *Ow!* For God's sake, don't *kick*, you idiot; this is only second down. Oh, my shin. My poor, poor shin, that I've had ever since I was a little girl!

Oh, no, no, no. Goodness, no. It didn't hurt the least little bit. And anyway it was my fault. Really it was. Truly. Well, you're just being sweet, to say that. It really was all my fault.

I wonder what I'd better do – kill him this instant, with my naked hands, or wait and let him drop in his traces. Maybe it's best not to make a scene. I guess I'll just lie low, and watch the pace get him. He can't keep this up indefinitely – he's only flesh and blood. Die he must, and die he shall, for what he did to me. I don't want to be of the over-sensitive type, but you can't tell me that kick was unpremeditated. Freud says there are no accidents. I've led no cloistered life, I've known dancing partners who have spoiled my slippers and torn my dress; but when it comes to kicking, I am Outraged Womanhood. When you kick me in the shin, *smile*.

Maybe he didn't do it maliciously. Maybe it's just his way of showing his high spirits. I suppose I ought to be glad that one of us is having such a good time. I suppose I ought to think myself lucky if he brings me back alive. Maybe it's captious to demand of a practically strange man that he leave your shins as he found them. After all, the poor boy's doing the best he can. Probably he grew up in the hill country, and never had no larnin'. I bet they had to throw him on his back to get shoes on him.

Yes, it's lovely, isn't it? It's simply lovely. It's the loveliest waltz. Isn't it? Oh, I think it's lovely, too.

Why, I'm getting positively drawn to the Triple Threat here. He's my hero. He has the heart of a lion, and the sinews of a buffalo. Look at him – never a thought of the consequences, never afraid of his face, hurling himself into every scrimmage, eyes shining, cheeks ablaze. And shall it be said that I hung back? No, a thousand times no. What's it to me if I have to spend the next couple of years in a plaster cast? Come on, Butch, right through them! Who wants to live for ever?

Oh. Oh, dear. Oh, he's all right, thank goodness. For a while I thought they'd have to carry him off the field. Ah, I couldn't bear to have anything happen to him. I love him. I love him better than anybody in the world. Look at the spirit he gets into a dreary, commonplace waltz; how effete the other dancers seem, beside him. He is youth and vigour and courage, he is strength and gaiety and – *Ow!* Get off my instep, you hulking peasant! What do you think I am anyway – a gangplank? *Ow!*

No, of course it didn't hurt. Why, it didn't a bit. Honestly. And it was all my fault. You see, that little step of yours – well, it's perfectly lovely, but it's just a tiny bit tricky to follow at first. Oh, did you work it up yourself? You really did? Well aren't you amazing! Oh, now I think I've got it. Oh, I think it's lovely. I was watching you do it when you were dancing before. It's awfully effective when you look at it.

It's awfully effective when you look at it. I bet I'm awfully effective when you look at me. My hair is hanging along my cheeks, my skirt is swaddling about me, I can feel the cold damp of my brow. I must look like something out of the 'Fall of the House of Usher'. This sort of thing takes a fearful toll of a woman my age. And he worked up his little step himself, he with his degenerate cunning. And it was just a tiny bit tricky at first, but now I think I've got it. Two stumbles, slip, and a twenty-yard dash; yes. I've got it. I've got several other things, too, including a split shin and a bitter heart. I hate this creature I'm chained to. I hated him the moment I saw his leering, bestial face. And here I've been locked in his noxious embrace for the thirty-five years this waltz has lasted. Is that orchestra never going to stop playing? Or must this obscene travesty of a dance go on until hell burns out?

Oh, they're going to play another encore. Oh, goody. Oh, that's lovely. Tired? I should say I'm not tired. I'd like to go on like this forever.

I should say I'm not tired. I'm dead, that's all I am. Dead, and in what a cause! And the music is never going to stop playing, and we're going on like this, Double-Time Charlie and I, throughout eternity. I suppose I won't care any more, after the first hundred thousand years. I suppose nothing will matter then, not heat nor pain nor broken heart nor cruel, aching weariness. Well. It can't come too soon for me.

I wonder why I didn't tell him I was tired. I wonder why I didn't suggest going back to the table. I could have said let's just listen to the music. Yes, and if he would, that would be the first bit of attention he has given it all evening. George Jean Nathan said that the lovely rhythms of the waltz should be listened to in stillness and not be accompanied by strange gyrations of the human body. I think that's what he said. I think it was George Jean Nathan. Anyhow, whatever he said and whoever he was and whatever he's doing now, he's better off than I am. That's safe. Anybody who isn't waltzing with this Mrs O'Leary's cow I've got here is having a good time.

Still if we were back at the table, I'd probably have to talk to him. Look at him – what could you say to a thing like that! Did you go to the circus this year, what's your favourite kind of ice-cream, how do you spell cat? I guess I'm as well off here. As well off as if I were in a cement mixer in full action.

I'm past all feeling now. The only way I can tell when he steps on me is that I can hear the splintering of bones. And all the events of my life are passing before my eyes. There was the time I was in a hurricane in the West Indies, there was the day I got my head cut open in the taxi smash, there was the night the drunken lady threw a bronze ashtray at her own true love and got me instead, there was that summer that the sailboat kept capsizing. Ah, what an easy, peaceful time was mine, until I fell in with Swifty, here. I didn't know what trouble was, before I got drawn into this *danse macabre*. I think my mind is beginning to wander. It almost seems to me as if the orchestra were stopping. It couldn't be, of course; it could never, never be. And yet in my ears there is a silence like the sound of angel voices....

Oh, they've stopped, the mean things. They're not going to play any more. Oh, darn. Oh, do you think they would? Do you really think so, if you gave them twenty dollars? Oh, that would be lovely. And look, do tell them to play this same thing. I'd simply adore to go on waltzing.

A Visit to Grandpa's

DYLAN THOMAS

IN THE MIDDLE OF THE night I woke from a dream full of whips and lariats as long as serpents, and runaway coaches on mountain passes, and wide, windy gallops over cactus fields, and I heard the man in the next room crying, 'Gee-up!' and 'Whoa!' and trotting his tongue on the roof of his mouth.

It was the first time I had stayed in grandpa's house. The floorboards had squeaked like mice as I climbed into bed, and the mice between the walls had creaked like wood as though another visitor was walking on them. It was a mild summer night, but curtains had flapped and branches beaten against the window. I had pulled the sheets over my head, and soon was roaring and riding in a book.

'Whoa there, my beauties!' cried grandpa. His voice sounded very young and loud, and his tongue had powerful hooves, and he made his bedroom into a great meadow. I thought I would see if he was ill, or had set his bedclothes on fire, for my mother had said that he lit his pipe under the blankets, and had warned me to run to his help if I smelt smoke in the night. I went on tiptoe through the darkness to his bedroom door, brushing against the furniture and upsetting a candlestick with a thump. When I saw there was a light in the room I felt frightened, and as I opened the door I heard grandpa shout, 'Gee-up!' as loudly as a bull with a megaphone.

He was sitting straight up in bed and rocking from side to side as though the bed were on a rough road; the knotted edges of the counterpane were his reins; his invisible horse stood in a shadow beyond the bedside candle. Over a white flannel nightshirt he was wearing a red waistcoat with walnut-sized brass buttons. The over-filled bowl of his pipe smouldered among his whiskers like a little, burning hayrick on a stick. At the sight of me, his hands dropped from the reins and lay blue and quiet, the bed stopped still on a level road, he muffled his tongue into silence, and the horses drew softly up.

'Is there anything the matter, grandpa?' I asked, though the clothes were not on fire. His face in the candlelight looked like a ragged quilt pinned upright on the black air and patched all over with goat-beards.

He stared at me mildly. Then he blew down his pipe, scattering the sparks and making a high, wet dog-whistle of the stem, and shouted: 'Ask no questions.'

After a pause, he said slyly: 'Do you ever have nightmares, boy?'

I said: 'No.'

'Oh, yes, you do,' he said.

I said I was woken by a voice that was shouting to horses.

'What did I tell you?' he said. 'You eat too much. Who ever heard of horses in a bedroom?'

He fumbled under his pillow, brought out a small tinkling bag, and carefully untied its strings. He put a sovereign in my hand, and said: 'Buy a cake.' I thanked him and wished him goodnight.

As I closed my bedroom door, I heard his voice crying loudly and gaily, 'Gee-up! gee-up!' and the rocking of the travelling bed.

In the morning I woke from a dream of fiery horses on a plain that was littered with furniture, and of large, cloudy men who rode six horses at a time and whipped them with burning bed-clothes. Grandpa was at breakfast, dressed in deep black. After breakfast he said, 'There was a terrible loud wind last night,' and sat in his armchair by the hearth to make clay balls for the fire. Later in the morning he took me for a walk, through Johnstown village and into the fields on the Llanstephan road.

A man with a whippet said, 'There's a nice morning, Mr Thomas,' and when he had gone, leanly as his dog, into the short-treed green wood he should not have entered because of the notices, grandpa said: 'There, do you hear what he called you? Mister!'

We passed by small cottages, and all the men who leant on the gates congratulated grandpa on the fine morning. We passed through the wood full of pigeons, and their wings broke the branches as they rushed to the tops of the trees. Among the soft, contented voices and the loud, timid flying, grandpa, said, like a man calling across a field: 'If you heard those old birds in the night, you'd wake me up and say there were horses in the trees.'

We walked back slowly, for he was tired, and the lean man stalked out of the forbidden wood with a rabbit held as gently over his arm as a girl's arm in a warm sleeve.

On the last day but one of my visit I was taken to Llanstephan in a governess car, pulled by a short, weak pony. Grandpa might have been driving a bison, so tightly he held the reins, so ferociously cracked the long whip, so blasphemously shouted warnings to boys who played in the road, so stoutly stood with his gaitered legs apart and cursed the demon strength and wilfulness of his tottering pony.

'Look out, boy!' he cried when we came to each corner, and pulled and tugged and jerked and sweated and waved his whip like a rubber sword. And when the pony had crept miserably round each corner, grandpa turned to me with a sighing smile: 'We weathered that one, boy.'

When we came to Llanstephan village at the top of the hill, he left the cart by the 'Edwinsford Arms' and patted the pony's muzzle and gave it sugar, saying: 'You're a weak little pony, Jim, to pull big men like us.'

He had strong beer and I had lemonade, and he paid Mrs Edwinsford with a sovereign out of the tinkling bag; she inquired after his health, and he said that Llangadock was better for the tubes. We went to look at the churchyard and the sea, and sat in the wood called the Sticks, and stood on the concert platform in the middle of the wood where visitors sang on midsummer nights and, year by year, the innocent of the village was elected mayor. Grandpa paused at the churchyard and pointed over the iron gate at the angelic headstones and the poor wooden crosses. 'There's no sense in lying there,' he said.

We journeyed back furiously: Jim was a bison again.

I woke late on my last morning, out of dreams where the Llanstephan sea carried bright sailing boats as long as liners; and heavenly choirs in the Sticks, dressed in bards' robes and brass-buttoned waistcoats, sang in a strange Welsh to the departing sailors. Grandpa was not at breakfast; he rose early. I walked in the fields with a new sling, and shot at the Towy gulls and the rooks in the parsonage trees. A warm wind blew from the summer points of the weather; a morning mist climbed from the ground and floated among the trees and hid the noisy birds; in the mist and the wind my pebbles flew lightly up like hailstones in a world on its head. The morning passed without a bird falling.

I broke my sling and returned for the midday meal through the parson's orchard. Once, grandpa told me, the parson had bought three ducks at Carmarthen Fair and made a pond for them in the centre of the garden, but they waddled to the gutter under the crumbling doorsteps of the house, and swam and quacked there. When I reached the end of the orchard path, I looked through a hole in the hedge and saw that the parson had made a tunnel through the rockery that was between the gutter and the pond and had set up a notice in plain writing: 'This way to the pond.'

The ducks were still swimming under the steps.

Grandpa was not in the cottage. I went into the garden, but grandpa was not staring at the fruit trees. I called across to a man who leant on a spade in the field beyond the garden hedge: 'Have you seen my grandpa this morning?'

He did not stop digging, and answered over his shoulder: 'I seen him in his fancy waistcoat.'

Griff, the barber, lived in the next cottage. I called to him through the open door: 'Mr Griff, have you seen my grandpa?'

The barber came out in his shirtsleeves.

I said: 'He's wearing his best waistcoat.' I did not know if it was important, but grandpa wore his waistcoat only in the night.

'Has grandpa been to Llanstephan?' asked Mr Griff anxiously.

'He went there yesterday in a little trap,' I said.

He hurried indoors and I heard him talking in Welsh, he came out again with his white coat on, and he carried a striped and coloured walking-stick. He strode down the village street and I ran by his side.

When we stopped at the tailor's shop, he cried out, 'Dan!' and Dan tailor stepped from his window where he sat like an Indian priest but wearing a derby hat. 'Dai Thomas has got his waistcoat on,' said Mr Griff, 'and he's been to Llanstephan.'

As Dan tailor searched for his overcoat, Mr Griff was striding on. 'Will Evans,' he called outside the carpenter's shop, 'Dai Thomas has been to Llanstephan, and he's got his waistcoat on.'

'I'll tell Morgan now,' said the carpenter's wife out of the hammering, sawing darkness of the shop.

We called at the butcher's shop and Mr Price's house, and Mr Griff repeated his message like a town crier.

We gathered together in Johnstown square. Dan tailor had his bicycle, Mr Price his pony trap. Mr Griff, the butcher, Morgan carpenter, and I climbed into the shaking trap, and we trotted off towards Carmarthen town. The tailor led the way, ringing his bell as though there were a fire or a robbery, and an old woman by the gate of a cottage at the end of the street ran inside like a pelted hen. Another woman waved a bright handkerchief.

'Where are we going?' I asked.

Grandpa's neighbours were as solemn as old men with black hats and jackets on the outskirts of a fair. Mr Griff shook his head and mourned: 'I didn't expect this again from Dai Thomas.'

'Not after last time,' said Mr Price sadly.

We trotted on, we crept up Constitution Hill, we rattled down into Lammas Street, and the tailor still rang his bell and a dog ran, squealing, in front of his wheels. As we clip-clopped over the cobbles that led down to the Towy bridge, I remembered grandpa's nightly noisy journeys that rocked the bed and shook the walls, and I saw his gay waistcoat in a vision and his patchwork head tufted and smiling in the candlelight. The tailor before us turned round on his saddle, his bicycle wobbled and skidded. 'I see Dai Thomas!' he cried.

The trap rattled on to the bridge, and I saw grandpa there: the buttons of his waistcoat shone in the sun, he wore his tight, black Sunday trousers and a tall, dusty hat I had seen in a cupboard in the attic, and he carried an ancient bag. He bowed to us. 'Good morning, Mr Price,' he said, 'and Mr Griff and Mr Morgan and Mr Evans.' To me he said: 'Good morning, boy.'

Mr Griff pointed his coloured stick at him.

'And what do you think you are doing on Carmarthen bridge in the middle of the afternoon', he said sternly, 'with your best waistcoat and your old hat?'

Grandpa did not answer, but inclined his face to the river wind, so that his beard was set dancing and wagging as though he talked, and watched the coracle men move, like turtles, on the shore.

Mr Griff raised his stunted barber's pole. 'And where do you think you are going', he said, 'with your old black bag?'

Grandpa said: 'I am going to Llangadock to be buried.' And he watched the coracle shells slip into the water lightly, and the gulls complain over the fish-filled water as bitterly as Mr Price complained:

'But you aren't dead yet, Dai Thomas.'

For a moment grandpa reflected, then: 'There's no sense in lying dead in Llanstephan,' he said. 'The ground is comfy in Llangadock; you can twitch your legs without putting them in the sea.'

His neighbours moved close to him. They said: 'You aren't dead, Mr Thomas.'

'How can you be buried, then?'

'Nobody's going to bury you in Llanstephan.'

'Come on home, Mr Thomas.'

'There's strong beer for tea.'

'And cake.'

But grandpa stood firmly on the bridge, and clutched his bag to his side, and stared at the flowing river and the sky, like a prophet who has no doubt.

The Hand that Riles the World

O. HENRY

'MANY OF OUR GREAT MEN,' said I (apropos of many things), 'have declared that they owe their success to the aid and encouragement of some brilliant woman.'

'1 know,' said Jeff Peters. 'I've read in history and mythology about Joan of Arc and Mme Yale and Mrs Caudle and Eve and other noted females of the past. But, in my opinion, the woman of today is of little use in politics or business. What's she best in, anyway? – men make the best cooks, milliners, nurses, housekeepers, stenographers, clerks, hairdressers and launderers. About the only job left that a woman can beat a man in is female impersonator in vaudeville.'

'I would have thought,' said I, 'that occasionally, anyhow, you would have found the wit and intuition of woman invaluable to you in your lines of – er – business.'

'Now, wouldn't you,' said Jeff, with an emphatic nod – 'wouldn't you have imagined that? But a woman is an absolutely unreliable partner in any straight swindle. She's liable to turn honest on you when you are depending upon her the most. I tried 'em once.

'Bill Humble, an old friend of mine in the Territories, conceived the illusion that he wanted to be appointed United States Marshal. At that time me and Andy was doing a square, legitimate business of selling walking-canes. If you unscrewed the head of one and turned it up to your mouth a half-pint of good rye whisky would go trickling down your throat to reward you for your act of intelligence. The deputies was annoying me and Andy some, and when Bill spoke to me about his officious aspirations, I saw how the appointment as Marshal might help along the firm of Peters & Tucker.

'"Jeff," says Bill to me, "you are a man of learning and education, besides having knowledge and information concerning not only rudiments but facts and attainments.

'"I do so," says I, "and I have never regretted it. I am not one," says I, "who would cheapen education by making it free. Tell me," says I, "which is of the most value to mankind, literature or horse-racing?"

'"Why – er – playing the po—— I mean, of course, the poets and the great writers have got the call, of course," says Bill.

'"Exactly," says I. "Then why do the master minds of finance and philanthropy," says I, "charge us $2 to get into a race-track and let us into a library free? Is that distilling into the masses," says I, "a correct estimate of the relative value of the two means of self-culture and disorder?"

'"You are arguing outside of my faculties of sense and rhetoric," says Bill. "What I wanted you to do is to go to Washington and dig out this appointment for me. I haven't no ideas of cultivation and intrigue. I'm a plain citizen and I need the job. I've killed seven men," says Bill; "I've got nine children; I've been a good Republican ever since the first of May; I can't read nor write, and I see no reason why I ain't illegible for the office. And I think your partner, Mr Tucker," goes on Bill, "is also a man of sufficient ingratiation and connected system of mental delinquency to assist you in securing the appointment. I will give you preliminary," says Bill, "$1,000 for drinks, bribes and car-fares in Washington. If you land the job I will pay you $1,000 more, cash down, and guarantee you impunity in bootlegging whisky for twelve months. Are you patriotic to the West enough to help me put this thing through the Whitewashed Wigwam of the Great Father of the most eastern flag station of the Pennsylvania Railroad?" says Bill.

'Well, I talked to Andy about it, and he liked the idea immense. Andy was a man of an involved nature. He was never content to plod along, as I was, selling to the peasantry some little tool like a combination steak beater, shoe horn, marcel waver, monkey-wrench, nail file, potato masher and Multum in Parvo tuning-fork. Andy had the artistic temper, which is not to be judged as a preacher's or a moral man's is by purely commercial deflections. So we accepted Bill's offer, and strikes out for Washington.

'Says I to Andy, when we got located at a hotel on South Dakota Avenue, GSSW, "now, Andy, for the first time in our lives we've got to do a real dishonest act. Lobbying is something we've never been used to; but we've got to scandalize ourselves for Bill Humble's sake. In a straight and legitimate business," says I, "we could afford to introduce a little foul play and chicanery, but in a disorderly and heinous piece of malpractice like this it seems to me that the straightforward and above board way is the best. I propose," says, I, "that we hand over $500 of this money to the chairman of the national campaign committee, get a receipt, lay the receipt on the President's desk and tell him about Bill. The President is a man who would appreciate a candidate who went about getting office that way instead of pulling wires."

'Andy agreed with me, but after we talked the scheme over with the hotel clerk we give that plan up. He told us that there was only one way to get an appointment in Washington, and that was through a lady lobbyist. He gave us the address of one he recommended, a Mrs Avery, who, he said, was high up in sociable and diplomatic rings and circles.

'The next morning at ten o'clock me and Andy called at her hotel, and was shown up to her reception room.

'This Mrs Avery was a solace and a balm to the eyesight. She had hair the colour of the back of a twenty-dollar gold certificate, blue eyes and a system of beauty that would make the girl on the cover of a July magazine look like a cook on a Monongahela coal barge.

'She had on a low-necked dress covered with silver spangles, and diamond rings and ear-bobs. Her arms was bare; and she was using a desk telephone with one hand, and drinking tea with the other.

'"Well, boys," says she after a bit, "what is it?"

'I told her in as few words as possible what we wanted for Bill, and the price we could pay.

'"Those western appointments," says she, "are easy. Le'me see, now," says she, "who could put that through for us? No use fooling with Territorial delegates. I guess," says she, "that Senator Sniper would be about the man. He's from somewhere in the West. Let's see how he stands on my private menu card." She takes some papers out of a pigeon-hole with the letter "S" over it.

'"Yes," says she, "he's marked with a star; that means 'ready to serve'. Now, let's see. 'Age 55; married twice; Presbyterian, likes blondes, Tolstoi, poker and stewed terrapin; sentimental at third bottle of wine.' Yes," she goes on, "I am sure I can have your friend, Mr Bummer, appointed Minister of Brazil."

'"Humble," says I. "And United States Marshal was the berth."

'"Oh, yes," says Mrs Avery. "I have so many deals of this sort I sometimes get them confused. Give me all the memoranda you have of the case, Mr Peters, and come back in four days. I think it can be arranged by then."

'So me and Andy goes back to our hotel and waits. Andy walks up and down and chews the left end of his moustache.

'"A woman of high intellect and perfect beauty is a rare thing, Jeff," says he.

'"As rare," says I, "as an omelet made from the eggs of the fabulous bird known as the epidermis," says I.

'"A woman like that," says Andy, "ought to lead a man to the highest position of opulence and fame."

'"I misdoubt," says I, "if any woman ever helped a man to secure a job any more than to have his meals ready promptly and spread a report that the other candidate's wife had once been a shoplifter. They are no more adapted for business and politics," says I, "than Algernon Charles Swinburne is to be floor manager at one of Chuck Connor's annual balls. I know," says I to Andy, "that sometimes a woman seems to step out into the kalsomine light as the chargé d'affaires of her man's political job. But

209

how does it come out? Say, they have a neat little berth somewhere as foreign consul of record to Afghanistan or lock-keeper on the Delaware and Raritan Canal. One day this man finds his wife putting on her overshoes and three months' supply of birdseed into the canary's cage. 'Sioux Falls?' he asks with a kind of hopeful light in his eye. 'No, Arthur,' says she, 'Washington. We're wasted here,' says she. 'You ought to be Toady Extraordinary to the Court of St Bridget or Head Porter of the Island of Porto Rico. I'm going to see about it.'"

'"Then this lady," I says to Andy, "moves against the authorities at Washington with her baggage and munitions, consisting of five dozen indiscriminating letters written to her by a member of the Cabinet when she was 15; a letter of introduction from King Leopold to the Smithsonian Institution and a pink silk costume with canary-coloured spats.

'"Well, and then what?" I goes on. "She has the letters printed in the evening papers that match her costume, she lectures at an informal tea given in the palm room of the B. & O. depot and then calls on the President. The ninth Assistant Secretary of Commerce and Labour, the first aide-de-camp of the Blue Room and an unidentified coloured man are waiting there to grasp her by the hands – and feet. They carry her out to SWB street and leave her on a cellar door. That ends it. The next time we hear of her she is writing postal cards to the Chinese Minister asking him to get Arthur a job in a tea store."

'"Then," says Andy, "you don't think Mrs Avery will land the Marshalship for Bill?"

'"I do not," says I. "I do not wish to be a sceptic, but I doubt if she can do as well as you and me could have done."

'"I don't agree with you," says Andy; "I'll bet you she does. I'm proud of having a higher opinion of the talent and the powers of negotiation of ladies."

'We was back at Mrs Avery's hotel at the time she appointed. She was looking pretty and fine enough, as far as that went, to make any man let her name every officer in the country. But I hadn't much faith in looks, so I was certainly surprised when she pulls out a document with the great seal of the United States on it, and "William Henry Humble" in a fine, big hand on the back.

'"You might have had it the next day, boys," says Mrs Avery, smiling. "I hadn't the slightest trouble in getting it," says she. "I just asked for it, that's all. Now, I'd like to talk to you a while," she goes on, "but I'm awfully busy, and I know you'll excuse me. I've got an Ambassadorship, two Consulates and a dozen other minor applications to look after. I can hardly find time to sleep at all. You'll give my compliments to Mr Humble when you get home, of course."

'Well, I handed her the $500, which she pitched into her desk drawer without counting. I put Bill's appointment in my pocket and me and

Andy made our adieux.

'We started back for the Territory the same day. We wired Bill: "Job landed; get the tall glasses ready," and we felt pretty good.

'Andy joshed me all the way about how little I knew about women.

'"All right," says I. "I'll admit that she surprised me. But it's the first time I ever knew one of 'em to manipulate a piece of business on time without getting it bungled up in some ways," says I.

'Down about the edge of Arkansas I got to Bill's appointment and looked it over, and then I handed it to Andy to read. Andy read it, but didn't add any remarks to my silence.

'The paper was for Bill, all right, and a genuine document, but it appointed him postmaster of Dade City, Fla.

'Me and Andy got off the train at Little Rock and sent Bill's appointment to him by mail. Then we struck northeast towards Lake Superior.

'I never saw Bill Humble after that.'

Without the Option

P.G. WODEHOUSE

THE EVIDENCE WAS ALL IN. The machinery of the law had worked without a hitch. And the beak, having adjusted a pair of pince-nez which looked as though they were going to do a nose dive any moment, coughed like a pained sheep and slipped us the bad news. 'The prisoner, Wooster,' he said – and who can paint the shame and agony of Bertram at hearing himself so described? – 'will pay a fine of five pounds.'

'Oh, rather!' I said. 'Absolutely! Like a shot!'

I was dashed glad to get the thing settled at such a reasonable figure. I gazed across what they call the sea of faces till I picked up Jeeves, sitting at the back. Stout fellow, he had come to see the young master through his hour of trial.

'I say, Jeeves,' I sang out, 'have you got a fiver? I'm a bit short.'

'Silence!' bellowed some officious blighter.

'It's all right,' I said; 'just arranging the financial details. Got the stuff, Jeeves?'

'Yes, sir.'

'Good egg!'

'Are you a friend of the prisoner?' asked the beak.

'I am in Mr Wooster's employment, Your Worship, in the capacity of gentleman's personal gentleman.'

'Then pay the fine to the clerk.'

'Very good, Your Worship.'

The beak gave a coldish nod in my direction, as much as to say that they might now strike the fetters from my wrists; and having hitched up the pince-nez once more, proceeded to hand poor old Sippy one of the nastiest looks ever seen in Bosher Street Police Court.

'The case of the prisoner Leon Trotzky – which,' he said, giving Sippy the eye again, 'I am strongly inclined to think an assumed and fictitious name – is more serious. He has been convicted of a wanton and violent assault upon the police. The evidence of the officer has proved that the prisoner struck him in the abdomen, causing severe internal pain, and in other ways interfered with him in the execution of his duties. I am aware that on the night following the annual aquatic contest between the Universities of Oxford and Cambridge a certain licence is traditionally granted by the authorities, but aggravated acts of ruffianly hooliganism like that of the prisoner Trotzky cannot be overlooked or palliated. He will serve a sentence of thirty days in the Second Division without the option of a fine.'

'No, I say – here – hi – dash it all!' protested poor old Sippy.

'Silence!' bellowed the officious blighter.

'Next case,' said the beak. And that was that.

The whole affair was most unfortunate. Memory is a trifle blurred; but as far as I can piece together the facts, what happened was more or less this:

Abstemious cove though I am as a general thing, there is one night in the year when, putting all other engagements aside, I am rather apt to let myself go a bit and renew my lost youth, as it were. The night to which I allude is the one following the annual aquatic contest between the Universities of Oxford and Cambridge; or, putting it another way, Boat-Race Night. Then, if ever, you will see Bertram under the influence. And on this occasion, I freely admit, I had been doing myself rather juicily, with the result that when I ran into old Sippy opposite the Empire I was in quite fairly bonhomous mood. This being so, it cut me to the quick to perceive that Sippy, generally the brightest of revellers, was far from being his usual sunny self. He had the air of a man with a secret sorrow.

'Bertie,' he said as we strolled along towards Piccadilly Circus, 'the heart bowed down by weight of woe to weakest hope will cling.' Sippy is by way of being an author, though mainly dependent for the necessaries of life on subsidies from an old aunt who lives in the country, and his conversation often takes a literary turn. 'But the trouble is that I have no hope to cling to, weak or otherwise. I am up against it, Bertie.'

'In what way, laddie?'

'I've got to go tomorrow and spend three weeks with some absolutely dud – I will go further – some positively scaly friends of my Aunt Vera. She has fixed the thing up, and may a nephew's curse blister every bulb in her garden.'

'Who are these hounds of hell?' I asked.

'Some people named Pringle. I haven't seen them since I was ten, but I remember them at that time striking me as England's premier warts.'

'Tough luck. No wonder you've lost your morale.'

'The world,' said Sippy, 'is very grey. How can I shake off this awful depression?'

It was then that I got one of those bright ideas one does round about 11.30 on Boat-Race Night.

'What you want, old man,' I said, 'is a policeman's helmet.'

'Do I, Bertie?'

'If I were you, I'd just step straight across the street and get that one over there.'

'But there's a policeman inside it. You can see him distinctly.'

'What does that matter?' I said. I simply couldn't follow his reasoning.

Sippy stood for a moment in thought.

'I believe you're absolutely right,' he said at last. 'Funny I never thought of it before. You really recommend me to get that helmet?'

'I do, indeed.'

'Then I will,' said Sippy, brightening up in the most remarkable manner.

So there you have the posish, and you can see why, as I left the dock a free man, remorse gnawed at my vitals. In his twenty-fifth year, with life opening out before him and all that sort of thing, Oliver Randolph Sipperley had become a jailbird, and it was all my fault. It was I who had dragged that fine spirit down into the mire, so to speak, and the question now arose, What could I do to atone?

Obviously the first move must be to get in touch with Sippy and see if he had any last messages and what not. I pushed about a bit, making inquiries, and presently found myself in a little dark room with whitewashed walls and a wooden bench. Sippy was sitting on the bench with his head in his hands.

'How are you, old lad?' I asked in a hushed, bedside voice.

'I'm a ruined man,' said Sippy, looking like a poached egg.

'Oh, come,' I said, 'it's not so bad as all that I mean to say, you had the swift intelligence to give a false name. There won't be anything about you in the papers.'

'I'm not worrying about the papers. What's bothering me is, how can I go and spend three weeks with the Pringles, starting today, when I've got to sit in a prison cell with a ball and chain on my ankle?'

'But you said you didn't want to go.'

'It isn't a question of wanting, fathead. I've got to go. If I don't my aunt will find out where I am. And if she finds out that I am doing thirty days, without the option, in the lowest dungeon beneath the castle moat – well, where shall I get off?'

I saw his point.

'This is not a thing we can settle for ourselves,' I said gravely. 'We must put our trust in a higher power. Jeeves is the man we must consult.'

And having collected a few of the necessary data, I shook his hand, patted him on the back and tooled off home to Jeeves.

'Jeeves,' I said, when I had climbed outside the pick-me-up which he had thoughtfully prepared against my coming, 'I've got something to tell you; something important; something that vitally affects one whom you have always regarded with – one whom you have always looked upon – one whom you have – well, to cut a long story short, as I'm not feeling quite myself – Mr Sipperley.'

'Yes, sir?'

'Jeeves, Mr Souperly is in the sip.'

'Sir?'

'I mean, Mr Sipperley is in the soup.'

'Indeed, sir?'

'And all owing to me. It was I who, in a moment of mistaken kindness, wishing only to cheer him up and give him something to occupy his mind, recommended him to pinch that policeman's helmet.'

'Is that so, sir?'

'Do you mind not intoning the responses, Jeeves?' I said. 'This is a most complicated story for a man with a headache to have to tell, and if you interrupt you'll make me lose the thread. As a favour to me, therefore, don't do it. Just nod every now and then to show that you're following me.'

I closed my eyes and marshalled the facts.

'To start with then, Jeeves, you may or may not know that Mr Sipperley is practically dependent on his Aunt Vera.'

'Would that be Miss Sipperley of the Paddock, Beckley-on-the-Moor, in Yorkshire, sir?'

'Yes. Don't tell me you know her!'

'Not personally, sir. But I have a cousin residing in the village who has some slight acquaintance with Miss Sipperley. He has described her to me as an imperious and quick-tempered old lady ... But I beg your pardon, sir, I should have nodded.'

'Quite right, you should have nodded. Yes, Jeeves, you should have nodded. But it's too late now.'

I nodded myself. I hadn't had my eight hours the night before, and what you might call a lethargy was showing a tendency to steal over me from time to time.

'Yes, sir?' said Jeeves.

'Oh – ah – yes,' I said, giving myself a bit of a hitch up. 'Where had I got to?'

'You were saying that Mr Sipperley is practically dependent upon Miss Sipperley, sir.'

'Was I?'

'You were, sir.'

'You're perfectly right; so I was. Well, then you can readily understand, Jeeves, that he has got to take jolly good care to keep in with her. You get that?'

Jeeves nodded.

'Now mark this closely: The other day she wrote to old Sippy, telling him to come down and sing at her village concert. It was equivalent to a royal command, if you see what I mean, so Sippy couldn't refuse in so many words. But he had sung at her village concert once before and had got the bird in no uncertain manner, so he wasn't playing any return dates. You follow so far, Jeeves?'

Jeeves nodded.

'So what did he do, Jeeves? He did what seemed to him at the moment a rather brainy thing. He told her that, though he would have been delighted to sing at her village concert, by a most unfortunate chance an editor had commissioned him to write a series of articles on the colleges of Cambridge and he was obliged to pop down there at once and would be away for quite three weeks. All clear up to now?'

Jeeves inclined the coconut.

'Whereupon, Jeeves, Miss Sipperley wrote back, saying that she quite realized that work must come before pleasure – pleasure being her loose way of describing the act of singing songs at the Beckley-on-the-Moor concert and getting the laugh from the local toughs; but that, if he was going to Cambridge, he must certainly stay with her friends, the Pringles, at their house just outside the town. And she dropped them a line telling them to expect him on the twenty-eighth, and they dropped another line saying right-ho, and the thing was settled. And now Mr Sipperley is in the jug, and what will be the ultimate outcome or upshot? Jeeves, it is a problem worthy of your great intellect. I rely on you.'

'I will do my best to justify your confidence, sir.'

'Carry on, then. And meanwhile pull down the blinds and bring a couple more cushions and heave that small chair this way so that I can put my feet up, and then go away and brood and let me hear from you in - say, a couple of hours, or maybe three. And if anybody calls and wants to see me, inform them that I am dead.'

'Dead, sir?'

'Dead. You won't be so far wrong.'

It must have been well towards evening when I woke up with a crick in my neck but otherwise somewhat refreshed. I pressed the bell.

'I looked in twice, sir,' said Jeeves, 'but on each occasion you were asleep and I did not like to disturb you.'

'The right spirit, Jeeves ... Well?'

'I have been giving close thought to the little problem which you indicated, sir, and I can see only one solution.'

'One is enough. What do you suggest?'

'That you go to Cambridge in Mr Sipperley's place, sir.'

I stared at the man. Certainly I was feeling a good deal better than I had been a few hours before; but I was far from being in a fit condition to have rot like this talked to me.

'Jeeves,' I said sternly, 'pull yourself together. This is mere babble from the sickbed.'

'I fear I can suggest no other plan of action, sir, which will extricate Mr Sipperley from his dilemma.'

'But think! Reflect! Why, even I, in spite of having had a disturbed night and a most painful morning with the minions of the law, can see that the scheme is a loony one. To put the finger on only one leak in the thing, it isn't me these people want to see; it's Mr Sipperley. They don't know me from Adam.'

'So much the better, sir. For what I am suggesting is that you go to Cambridge, affecting actually to be Mr Sipperley.'

This was too much.

'Jeeves,' I said, and I'm not half sure there weren't tears in my eyes, 'surely you can see for yourself that this is pure banana oil. It is not like you to come into the presence of a sick man and gibber.'

'I think the plan I have suggested would be practicable, sir. While you were sleeping, I was able to have a few words with Mr Sipperley, and he informed me that Professor and Mrs Pringle have not set eyes upon him since he was a lad of ten.'

'No, that's true. He told me that. But even so, they would be sure to ask him questions about my aunt – or rather his aunt. Where would I be then?'

'Mr Sipperley was kind enough to give me a few facts respecting Miss Sipperley, sir, which I jotted down. With these, added to what my cousin has told me of the lady's habits, I think you would be in a position to answer any ordinary question.'

There is something dashed insidious about Jeeves. Time and again since we first came together he has stunned me with some apparently drivelling suggestion or scheme or ruse or plan of campaign, and after about five minutes has convinced me that it is not only sound but fruity. It took nearly a quarter of an hour to reason me into this particular one, it being considerably the weirdest to date; but he did it. I was holding out pretty firmly, when he suddenly clinched the thing.

'I would certainly suggest, sir,' he sad, 'that you left London as soon as possible and remained hid for some little time in some retreat where you would not be likely to be found.'

'Eh? Why?'

'During the last hours Mrs Spenser has been on the telephone three times, sir, endeavouring to get into communication with you.'

'Aunt Agatha!' I cried, paling beneath my tan.

'Yes, sir. I gathered from her remarks that she had been reading in the evening paper a report of this morning's proceedings in the police court.'

I hopped from the chair like a jack rabbit of the prairie. If Aunt Agatha was out with her hatchet, a move was most certainly indicated.

'Jeeves,' I said, 'this is a time for deeds, not words. Pack – and that right speedily.'

'I have packed, sir.'

'Find out when there is a train for Cambridge.'

'There is one in forty minutes, sir.'

'Call a taxi.'

'A taxi is at the door, sir.'
'Good!' I said. 'Then lead me to it.'

The Maison Pringle was quite a bit of a way out of Cambridge, a mile or two down the Trumpington Road; and when I arrived everybody was dressing for dinner. So it wasn't till I had shoved on the evening raiment and got down to the drawing-room that I met the gang.

'Hullo-ullo!' I said, taking a deep breath and floating in.

I tried to speak in a clear and ringing voice, but I wasn't feeling my chirpiest. It is always a nervous job for a diffident and unassuming bloke to visit a strange house for the first time; and it doesn't make the thing any better when he goes there pretending to be another fellow. I was conscious of a rather pronounced sinking feeling, which the appearance of the Pringles did nothing to allay.

Sippy had described them as England's premier warts, and it looked to me as if he might be about right. Professor Pringle was a thinnish, baldish, dyspeptic-lookingish cove with an eye like a haddock, while Mrs Pringle's aspect was that of one who had had bad news round about the year 1900 and never really got over it. And I was just staggering under the impact of these two when I was introduced to a couple of ancient females wth shawls all over them.

'No doubt you remember my mother?' said Professor Pringle mournfully, indicating Exhibit A.

'Oh – ah!' I said, achieving a bit of a beam.

'And my aunt,' sighed the prof, as if things were getting worse and worse.

'Well, well, well!' I said, shooting another beam in the direction of Exhibit B.

'They were saying only this morning that they remembered you,' groaned the prof, abandoning all hope.

There was a pause. The whole strength of the company gazed at me like a family group out of one of Edgar Allan Poe's less cheery yarns, and I felt my *joie de vivre* dying at the roots.

'I remember Oliver,' said Exhibit A. She heaved a sigh. 'He was such a pretty child. What a pity! What a pity!'

Tactful, of course, and calculated to put the guest completely at his ease.

'I remember Oliver,' said Exhibit B, looking at me in much the same way as the Bosher Street beak had looked at Sippy before putting on the black cap. 'Nasty little boy! He teased my cat.'

'Aunt Jane's memory is wonderful, considering that she will be eighty-seven next birthday,' whispered Mrs Pringle with mournful pride.

'What did you say?' asked the Exhibit suspiciously.

'I said your memory was wonderful.'

'Ah!' the dear old creature gave me another glare. I could see that no beautiful friendship was to be looked for by Bertram in this quarter. 'He chased my Tibby all over the garden, shooting arrows at her from a bow.'

At this moment a cat strolled out from under the sofa and made for me with its tail up. Cats always do take to me, which made it all the sadder that I should be saddled with Sippy's criminal record. I stooped to tickle it under the ear, such being my invariable policy, and the Exhibit uttered a piercing cry.

'Stop him! Stop him!'

She leaped forward, moving uncommonly well for one of her years, and having scooped up the cat, stood eyeing me with bitter defiance, as if daring me to start anything. Most unpleasant.

'I like cats,' I said feebly.

It didn't go. The sympathy of the audience was not with me. And conversation was at what you might call a low ebb, when the door opened and a girl came in.

'My daughter Heloise,' said the prof moodily, as if he hated to admit it.

I turned to mitt the female, and stood there with my hand out, gaping. I can't remember when I've had such a nasty shock.

I suppose everybody has had the experience of suddenly meeting somebody who reminded them frightfully of some fearful person. I mean to say, by way of an example, once when I was golfing in Scotland I saw a woman come into the hotel who was the living image of my Aunt Agatha. Probably a very decent sort, if I had only waited to see, but I didn't wait. I legged it that evening, utterly unable to stand the spectacle. And on another occasion I was driven out of a thoroughly festive night club because the head waiter reminded me of my Uncle Percy.

Well, Heloise Pringle, in the most ghastly way, resembled Honoria Glossop.

I think I may have told you before about this Glossop scourge. She was the daughter of Sir Roderick Glossop, the loony doctor, and I had been engaged to her for about three weeks, much against my wishes, when the old boy most fortunately got the idea that I was off my rocker and put the bee on the proceedings. Since then the mere thought of her had been enough to make me start out of my sleep with a loud cry. And this girl was exactly like her.

'Er – how are you?' I said.

'How do you do?'

Her voice put the lid on it. It might have been Honoria herself talking. Honoria Glossop has a voice like a lion tamer making some authoritative announcement to one of the troupe, and so had this girl. I backed away convulsively and sprang into the air as my foot stubbed itself against something squashy. A sharp yowl rent the air, followed by an indignant cry, and I turned to see Aunt Jane, on all fours, trying to put things right with the cat, which had gone to earth under the sofa. She gave me a look, and I could see that her worst fears had been realized.

At this juncture dinner was announced – not before I was ready for it.

'Jeeves,' I said, when I got him alone that night, 'I am no faint heart, but I am inclined to think that this binge is going to prove a shade above the odds.'

'You are not enjoying your visit, sir?'

'I am not, Jeeves. Have you seen Miss Pringle?'

'Yes, sir, from a distance.'

'The best way to see her. Did you observe her keenly?'

'Yes, sir.'

'Did she remind you of anybody?'

'She appeared to me to bear a remarkable likeness to her cousin, Miss Glossop, sir.'

'Her cousin! You don't mean to say she's Honoria Glossop's cousin!'

'Yes, sir. Mrs Pringle was a Miss Blatherwick – the younger of two sisters, the older of whom married Sir Roderick Glossop.'

'Great Scott! That accounts for the resemblance.'

'Yes, sir.'

'And what a resemblance, Jeeves! She even talks like Miss Glossop.'

'Indeed, sir? I have not yet heard Miss Pringle speak.'

'You have missed little. And what it amounts to, Jeeves, is that, though nothing will induce me to let old Sippy down, I can see that this visit is going to try me high. At a pinch, I could stand the prof and wife. I could even make the effort of a lifetime and bear up against Aunt Jane. But to expect a man to mix daily with the girl Heloise – and to do it, what is more, on lemonade, which is all there was to drink at dinner – is to ask too much of him. What shall I do, Jeeves?'

'I think that you should avoid Miss Pringle's society as much as possible.'

'The same great thought had occurred to me,' I said.

It is all very well, though, to talk airily about avoiding a female's society; but when you are living in the same house with her, and she doesn't want to avoid you, it takes a bit of doing. It is a peculiar thing in life that the people you most particularly want to edge away from always seem to cluster round like a poultice. I hadn't been twenty-four hours in the place before I perceived that I was going to see a lot of this pestilence.

She was one of those girls you're always meeting on the stairs and in passages. I couldn't go into a room without seeing her drift in a minute later. And if I walked in the garden she was sure to leap out at me from a laurel bush or the onion bed or something. By about the tenth day I had begun to feel absolutely haunted.

'Jeeves,' I said, 'I have begun to feel absolutely haunted.'

220

'Sir?'

'This woman dogs me. I never seem to get a moment to myself. Old Sippy was supposed to come here to make a study of the Cambridge colleges, and she took me round about fifty-seven this morning. This afternoon I went to sit in the garden, and she popped up through a trap and was in my midst. This evening she cornered me in the morning-room. It's getting so that, when I have a bath, I wouldn't be a bit surprised to find her nestling in the soap dish.'

'Extremely trying, sir.'

'Dashed so. Have you any remedy to suggest?'

'Not at the moment, sir. Miss Pringle does appear to be distinctly interested in you, sir. She was asking me questions this morning respecting your mode of life in London.'

'What?'

'Yes, sir.'

I stared at the man in horror. A ghastly thought had struck me. I quivered like an aspen.

At lunch that day a curious thing had happened. We had just finished mangling the cutlets and I was sitting back in my chair, taking a bit of an easy before being allotted my slab of boiled pudding, when, happening to look up, I caught the girl Heloise's eye fixed on me in what seemed to me a rather rummy manner. I didn't think much about it at the time, because boiled pudding is a thing you have to give your undivided attention to if you want to do yourself justice; but now, recalling the episode in the light of Jeeves's words, the full sinister meaning of the thing seemed to come home to me.

Even at the moment, something about that look had struck me as oddly familiar, and now I suddenly saw why. It had been the identical look which I had observed in the eye of Honoria Glossop in the days immediately preceding our engagement – the look of a tigress that has marked down its prey.

'Jeeves, do you know what I think?'

'Sir?'

I gulped slightly.

'Jeeves,' I said, 'listen attentively. I don't want to give the impression that I consider myself one of those deadly coves who exercise an irresistible fascination over one and all and can't meet a girl without wrecking her peace of mind in the first half-minute. As a matter of fact, it's rather the other way with me, for girls on entering my presence are mostly inclined to give me the raised eyebrow and the twitching upper lip. Nobody, therefore, can say that I am a man who's likely to take alarm unnecessarily. You admit that, don't you?'

'Yes, sir.'

'Nevertheless, Jeeves, it is a known scientific fact that there is a particular style of female that does seem strangely attracted to the sort of fellow I am.'

'Very true, sir.'

'I mean to say, I know perfectly well that I've got, roughly speaking, half the amount of brain a normal bloke ought to possess. And when a girl comes along who has about twice the regular allowance, she too often makes a bee line for me with the love light in her eyes. I don't know how to account for it, but it is so.'

'It may be Nature's provision for maintaining the balance of the species, sir.'

'Very possibly. Anyway, it has happened to me over and over again. It was what happened in the case of Honoria Glossop. She was notoriously one of the brainiest women of her year at Girton, and she just gathered me in like a bull pup swallowing a piece of steak.'

'Miss Pringle, I am informed, sir, was an even more brilliant scholar than Miss Glossop.'

'Well, there you are! Jeeves, she looks at me.'

'Yes, sir?'

'I keep meeting her on the stairs and in passages.'

'Indeed, sir?'

'She recommends me books to read, to improve my mind.'

'Highly suggestive, sir.'

'And at breakfast this morning, when I was eating a sausage, she told me I shouldn't, as modern medical science held that a four-inch sausage contained as many germs as a dead rat. The maternal touch, you understand; fussing over my health.'

'I think we may regard that, sir, as practically conclusive.'

I sank into a chair, thoroughly pipped.

'What's to be done, Jeeves?'

'We must think, sir.'

'You think. I haven't the machinery.'

'I will most certainly devote my very best attention to the matter, sir, and will endeavour to give satisfaction.'

Well, that was something. But I was ill at ease. Yes, there is no getting away from it, Bertram was ill at ease.

Next morning we visited sixty-three more Cambridge colleges, and after lunch I said I was going to my room to lie down. After staying there for half an hour to give the coast time to clear, I shoved a book and smoking materials in my pocket, and climbing out of a window, shinned down a convenient waterpipe into the garden. My objective was the summer-house, where it seemed to me that a man might put in a quiet hour or so without interruption.

It was extremely jolly in the garden. The sun was shining, the crocuses were all to the mustard and there wasn't a sign of Heloise Pringle anywhere. The cat was fooling about on the lawn, so I chirruped to it and it gave a low gargle and came trotting up. I had just got it in my arms and was scratching it under the ear when there was a loud shriek from above, and there was Aunt Jane half out of the window. Dashed disturbing.

'Oh, right-ho,' I said.

I dropped the cat, which galloped off into the bushes, and dismissing the idea of bunging a brick at the aged relative, went on my way, heading for the shrubbery. Once safely hidden there, I worked round till I got to the summer-house. And, believe me, I had hardly got my first cigarette nicely under way when a shadow fell on my book and there was young Sticketh-Closer-Than-a-Brother in person.

'So there you are,' she said.

She seated herself by my side, and with a sort of gruesome playfulness jerked the gasper out of the holder and heaved it through the door.

'You're always smoking,' she said, a lot too much like a lovingly chiding young bride for my comfort. 'I wish you wouldn't. It's so bad for you. And you ought not to be sitting out here without your light overcoat. You want someone to look after you.'

'I've got Jeeves.'

She frowned a bit.

'I don't like him,' she said.

'Eh? Why not?'

'I don't know. I wish you would get rid of him.'

My flesh absolutely crept. And I'll tell you why. One of the first things Honoria Glossop had done after we had become engaged was to tell me she didn't like Jeeves and wanted him shot out. The realization that this girl resembled Honoria not only in body but in blackness of soul made me go all faint.

'What are you reading?'

She picked up my book and frowned again. The thing was one I had brought down from the old flat in London, to glance at in the train – a fairly zippy effort in the detective line called *The Trail of Blood*. She turned the pages with a nasty sneer.

'I can't understand you liking nonsense of this —' She stopped suddenly. 'Good gracious!'

'What's the matter?'

'Do you know Bertie Wooster?'

And then I saw that my name was scrawled right across the title page, and my heart did three back somersaults.

'Oh – er – well – that is to say – well, slightly.'

'He must be a perfect horror. I'm surprised that you can make a friend of him. Apart from anything else, the man is practically an imbecile. He was engaged to my Cousin Honoria at one time, and it was broken off because he was next door to insane. You should hear my Uncle Roderick talk about him!'

I wasn't keen.

'Do you see much of him?'

'A goodish bit.'

'I saw in the paper the other day that he was fined for making a disgraceful disturbance in the street.'

'Yes, I saw that.'

She gazed at me in a foul, motherly way.

'He can't be a good influence for you,' she said. 'I do wish you would drop him. Will you?'

'Well –' I began. And at this point old Cuthbert, the cat, having presumably found it a bit slow by himself in the bushes, wandered in with a matey expression on his face and jumped on my lap. I welcomed him with a good deal of cordiality. Though but a cat, he did make a sort of third at this party; and he afforded a good excuse for changing the conversation.

'Jolly birds, cats,' I said.

She wasn't having any.

'Will you drop Bertie Wooster?' she said, absolutely ignoring the cat *motif*.

'It would be so difficult.'

'Nonsense! It only needs a little willpower. The man surely can't be so interesting a companion as all that. Uncle Roderick says he is an invertebrate waster.'

I could have mentioned a few things that I thought Uncle Roderick was, but my lips were sealed, so to speak.

'You have changed a great deal since we last met,' said the Pringle disease reproachfully. She bent forward and began to scratch the cat under the other ear. 'Do you remember, when we were children together, you used to say that you would do anything for me?'

'Did I?'

'I remember once you cried because I was cross and wouldn't let you kiss me.'

I didn't believe it at the time, and I don't believe it now. Sippy is in many ways a good deal of a chump, but surely even at the age of ten he cannot have been such a priceless ass as that. I think the girl was lying, but that didn't make the position of affairs any better. I edged away a couple of inches and sat staring before me, the old brow beginning to get slightly bedewed.

And then suddenly – well, you know how it is, I mean. I suppose everyone has had that ghastly feeling at one time or another of being urged by some overwhelming force to do some absolutely blithering act. You get it every now and then when you're in a crowded theatre, and something seems to be egging you on to shout 'Fire!' and see what happens. Or you're talking to someone and all at once you feel, 'Now, suppose I suddenly biffed this bird in the eye!'

Well, what I'm driving at is this, at this juncture, with her shoulder squashing against mine and her black hair tickling my nose, a perfectly loony impulse came sweeping over me to kiss her.

'No, really?' I croaked.

'Have you forgotten?'

She lifted the old onion and her eyes looked straight into mine. I could feel myself skidding. I shut my eyes. And then from the doorway there spoke the most beautiful voice I had ever heard in my life:

'Give me that cat!'

I opened my eyes. There was good old Aunt Jane, that queen of her sex, standing before me, glaring at me as if I were a vivisectionist and she had surprised me in the middle of an experiment. How this pearl among women had tracked me down I don't know, but there she stood, bless her dear, intelligent old soul, like the rescue party in the last reel of a motion picture.

I didn't wait. The spell was broken and I legged it. As I went, I heard that lovely voice again.

'He shot arrows at my Tibby from a bow,' said this most deserving and excellent octogenarian.

For the next few days all was peace. I saw comparatively little of Heloise. I found the strategic value of that waterpipe outside my window beyond praise. I seldom left the house now by any other route. It seemed to me that, if only the luck held like this, I might after all be able to stick this visit out for the full term of the sentence.

But meanwhile, as they say in the movies –

The whole family appeared to be present and correct as I came down to the drawing-room a couple of nights later. The Prof, Mrs Prof, the two Exhibits and the girl Heloise were scattered about at intervals. The cat slept on the rug, the canary in its cage. There was nothing, in short, to indicate that this was not just one of our ordinary evenings.

'Well, well, well!' I said cheerily. 'Hullo-ullo-ullo!'

I always like to make something in the nature of an entrance speech, it seeming to me to lend a chummy tone to the proceedings.

The girl Heloise looked at me reproachfully.

'Where have you been all day?' she asked.

'I went to my room after lunch.'

'You weren't there at five.'

'No. After putting in a spell of work on the good old colleges I went for a stroll. Fellow must have exercise if he means to keep fit.'

'*Mens sana in corpore sano,*' observed the prof.

'I shouldn't wonder,' I said cordially.

At this point, when everything was going as sweet as a nut and I was feeling on top of my form, Mrs Pringle suddenly soaked me on the base of the skull with a sandbag. Not actually, I don't mean. No, no. I speak figuratively, as it were.

'Roderick is very late,' she said.

You may think it strange that the sound of that name should have sloshed into my nerve centres like a half-brick. But, take it from me, to a man who has had any dealings with Sir Roderick Glossop there is only one Roderick in the world – and that is one too many.

'Roderick?' I gurgled.

'My brother-in-law, Sir Roderick Glossop, comes to Cambridge tonight,' said the prof. 'He lectures at St Luke's tomorrow. He is coming here to dinner.'

And while I stood there, feeling like the hero when he discovers that he is trapped in the den of the Secret Nine, the door opened.

'Sir Roderick Glossop,' announced the maid or some such person, and in he came.

One of the things that get this old crumb so generally disliked among the better element of the community is the fact that he has a head like the dome of St Paul's and eyebrows that want bobbing or shingling to reduce them to anything like reasonable size. It is a nasty experience to see this bald and bushy bloke advancing on you when you haven't prepared the strategic railways in your rear.

As he came into the room I backed behind a sofa and commended my soul to God. I didn't need to have my hand read to know that trouble was coming to me through a dark man.

He didn't spot at first. He shook hands with the prof and wife, kissed Heloise and waggled his head at the Exhibits.

'I fear I am somewhat late,' he said. 'A slight accident on the road, affecting what my chauffeur termed the –'

And then he saw me lurking on the outskirts and gave a startled grunt, as if I hurt him a good deal internally.

'This –' began the prof, waving in my direction.

'I am already acquainted with Mr Wooster.'

'This,' went on the prof, 'is Miss Sipperley's nephew, Oliver. You remember Miss Sipperley?'

'What do you mean?' barked Sir Roderick. Having had so much to do with loonies has given him a rather sharp and authoritative manner on occasion. 'This is that wretched young man, Bertram Wooster. What is all this nonsense about Olivers and Sipperleys?'

The prof was eyeing me with some natural surprise. So were the others. I beamed a bit weakly.

'Well, as a matter of fact –' I said.

The prof was wrestling with the situation. You could hear his brain buzzing.

'He said he was Oliver Sipperley,' he moaned.

'Come here!' bellowed Sir Roderick. 'Am I to understand that you have inflicted yourself on this household under the pretence of being the nephew of an old friend?'

It seemed a pretty accurate description of the facts.

'Well – er – yes,' I said.

Sir Roderick shot an eye at me. It entered the body somewhere about the top stud, roamed around inside for a bit and went out at the back.

'Insane! Quite insane, as I knew from the first moment I saw him.'

'What did he say?' asked Aunt Jane.

'Roderick says this young man is insane,' roared the prof.

'Ah!' said Aunt Jane, nodding. 'I thought so. He climbs down waterpipes.'

'Does what?'

'I've seen him – ah, many a time!'

Sir Roderick snorted violently.

'He ought to be under proper restraint. It is abominable that a person in his mental condition should be permitted to roam the world at large. The next stage may quite easily be homicidal.'

It seemed to me that, even at the expense of giving old Sippy away, I must be cleared of this frightful charge. After all, Sippy's number was up anyway.

'Let me explain,' I said. 'Sippy asked me to come here.'

'What do you mean?'

'He couldn't come himself, because he was jugged for biffing a cop on Boat-Race Night.'

Well, it wasn't easy to make them get the hang of the story, and even when I'd done it it didn't seem to make them any chummier towards me. A certain coldness about expresses it, and when dinner was announced I counted myself out and pushed off rapidly to my room. I could have done with a bit of dinner, but the atmosphere didn't seem just right.

'Jeeves,' I said, having shot in and pressed the bell, 'we're sunk.'

'Sir?'

'Hell's foundations are quivering and the game is up.'

He listened attentively.

'The contingency was one always to have been anticipated as a possibility, sir. It only remains to take the obvious step.'

'What's that?'

'Go and see Miss Sipperley, sir.'

'What on earth for?'

'I think it would be judicious to apprise her of the facts yourself, sir, instead of allowing her to hear of them through the medium of a letter from Professor Pringle. That is to say, if you are still anxious to do all in your power to assist Mr Sipperley.'

'I can't let Sippy down. If you think it's any good –'

'We can but try it, sir. I have an idea, sir, that we may find Miss Sipperley disposed to look leniently upon Mr Sipperley's misdemeanour.'

'What makes you think that?'

'It's just a feeling that I have, sir.'

'Well, if you think it would be worth trying – How do we get there?'

'The distance is about a hundred and fifty miles, sir. Our best plan would be to hire a car.'

'Get it at once,' I said.

The idea of being a hundred and fifty miles away from Heloise Pringle, not to mention Aunt Jane and Sir Roderick Glossop, sounded about as good to me as anything I had ever heard.

The Paddock, Beckley-on-the-Moor, was about a couple of parasangs from the village, and I set out for it next morning, after partaking of a hearty breakfast at the local inn, practically without a tremor. I suppose when a fellow has been through it as I had in the last two weeks his system becomes hardened. After all, I felt, whatever this aunt of Sippy's might be like, she wasn't Sir Roderick Glossop, so I was that much on velvet from the start.

The Paddock was one of those medium-sized houses with a goodish bit of very tidy garden and a carefully rolled gravel drive curving past a shrubbery that looked as if it had just come back from the dry cleaner – the sort of house you take one look at and say to yourself, 'Somebody's aunt lives there.' I pushed on up the drive, and as I turned the bend I observed in the middle distance a woman messing about by a flower-bed with a trowel in her hand. If this wasn't the female I was after, I was very much mistaken, so I halted, cleared the throat and gave tongue.

'Miss Sipperley?'

She had had her back to me, and at the sound of my voice she executed a sort of leap or bound, not unlike a barefoot dancer who steps on a tin-tack halfway through the Vision of Salome. She came to earth and goggled at me in a rather goofy manner. A large, stout female with a reddish face.

'Hope I didn't startle you,' I said.

'Who are you?'

'My name's Wooster. I'm a pal of your nephew, Oliver.'

Her breathing had become more regular.

'Oh?' she said. 'When I heard your voice I thought you were someone else.'

'No, that's who I am. I came up here to tell you about Oliver.'

'What about him?'

I hesitated. Now that we were approaching what you might call the nub, or crux, of the situation, a good deal of my breezy confidence seemed to have slipped from me.

'Well, it's rather a painful tale, I must warn you.'

'Oliver isn't ill? He hasn't had an accident?'

She spoke anxiously, and I was pleased at this evidence of human feeling. I decided to shoot the works with no more delay.

'Oh, no, he isn't ill,' I said; 'and as regards having accidents, it depends on what you call an accident. He's in chokey.'

'In what?'

'In prison.'

'In prison!'

'It was entirely my fault. We were strolling along on Boat-Race Night and I advised him to pinch a policeman's helmet.'

'I don't understand.'

'Well, he seemed depressed, don't you know; and rightly or wrongly, I thought it might cheer him up if he stepped across the street and collared a policeman's helmet. He thought it a good idea, too, so he started doing it, and the man made a fuss and Oliver sloshed him.'

'Sloshed him?'

'Biffed him – smote him a blow – in the stomach.'

'My nephew Oliver hit a policeman in the stomach?'

'Absolutely in the stomach. And next morning the beak sent him to the bastille for thirty days without the option.'

I was looking at her a bit anxiously all this while to see how she was taking the thing, and at this moment her face seemed suddenly to split in half. For an instant she appeared to be all mouth, and then she was staggering about the grass, shouting with laughter and waving the trowel madly.

It seemed to me a bit of luck for her that Sir Roderick Glossop wasn't on the spot. He would have been sitting on her head and calling for the strait-waistcoat in the first half-minute.

'You aren't annoyed?' I said.

'Annoyed?' She chuckled happily. 'I've never heard such a splendid thing in my life.'

I was pleased and relieved. I had hoped the news wouldn't upset her too much, but I had never expected it to go with such a roar as this.

'I'm proud of him,' she said.

'That's fine.'

'If every young man in England went about hitting policemen in the stomach, it would be a better country to live in.'

I couldn't follow her reasoning, but everything seemed to be all right; so after a few more cheery words I said goodbye and legged it.

'Jeeves,' I said when I got back to the inn, 'everything's fine. But I am far from understanding why.'

'What actually occurred when you met Miss Sipperley, sir?'

'I told her Sippy was in the jug for assaulting the police. Upon which she burst into hearty laughter, waved her trowel in a pleased manner and said she was proud of him.'

'I think I can explain her apparently eccentric behaviour,' sir. I am informed that Miss Sipperley has had a good deal of annoyance at the hands of the local constable during the past two weeks. This has doubtless resulted in a prejudice on her part against the force as a whole.'

'Really? How was that?'

'The constable has been somewhat overzealous in the performance of his duties, sir. On no fewer than three occasions in the last ten days he has served summonses upon Miss Sipperley – for exceeding the speed limit in her car; for allowing her dog to appear in public without a collar; and for failing to abate a smoky chimney. Being in the nature of an autocrat, if I may use the term, in the village, Miss Sipperley has been accustomed to do these things in the past with impunity, and the constable's unexpected zeal has made her somewhat ill-disposed to policemen as a class and consequently disposed to look upon such assaults as Mr Sipperley's in a kindly and broadminded spirit.'

I saw his point.

'What an amazing bit of luck, Jeeves!'

'Yes, sir.'

'Where did you hear all this?'

'My informant was the constable himself, sir. He is my cousin.'

I gaped at the man. I saw, so to speak, all.

'Good Lord, Jeeves! You didn't bribe him?'

'Oh, no, sir. But it was his birthday last week, and I gave him a little present. I have always been fond of Egbert, sir.'

'How much?'

'A matter of five pounds, sir.'

I felt in my pocket.

'Here you are,' I said. 'And another fiver for luck.'

'Thank you very much, sir.'

'Jeeves,' I said, 'you move in a mysterious way your wonders to perform. You don't mind if I sing a bit, do you?'

'Not at all, sir,' said Jeeves.

Top of the League

A.G. MACDONELL

On his return from the trenches in 1918 Donald Cameron decides to leave his rural home at Balspindie in the Scottish highlands, deciding to seek fame and fortune as a writer in London. A chance reunion with an ex-army friend, Davies, leads to Donald's first commission – to write a book on England and the English seen through the eyes of a Scotsman. After several months of exhausting but fruitless research Donald is becoming desperate. . . .

IN THE MIDDLE OF AUGUST, Davies telephoned to Donald and asked him to come round to the office in Henrietta Street and report progress.

Donald was frankly depressed, and he said so. 'I'm out of my depth,' he said. 'My feet aren't on the ground.'

Davies laughed. He found his young friend's perplexities amusing.

'I didn't imagine you'd find it very easy,' he said. 'But don't forget what I told you in that infernal pillbox, years ago. I've got a sort of instinctive notion that the English character —'

'There's no such thing,' interrupted Donald. 'They're all different.'

'That the English character,' went on Davies firmly, 'is based fundamentally upon kindliness and poetry. Just keep that notion in mind, whether you agree with it or not. And now listen to me, I've got a job for you.'

'What sort of a job?' inquired Donald suspiciously.

'A private-secretaryship.'

Donald's face fell. 'But I want to write things. I don't think I want —'

'Of course you want to write things, you young donkey. And I'm trying to help you. What I'm offering to you is the private-secretaryship to an English politician – English, mind you – and it's only temporary. The man in question is a very old friend of mine, and his permanent fellow has gone down with scarlet fever.'

'But Parliament isn't sitting,' began Donald.

'There's a little Mr Know-all,' replied Davies pleasantly. 'It hadn't escaped my notice that Parliament isn't sitting. But my friend has just been appointed to the British delegation that is going to the Assembly of the League of Nations at Geneva in a fortnight, and he wants someone to go with him, and hold his hat and coat. Would you care to take it on? All expenses and a fiver a week.'

'For how long?'

'For a month. He might give you a very good notion of the Englishman as an internationalist.'

Donald sprang to his feet.

'Of course!' he exclaimed. 'What a fool I am! And how kind you are! You really are most awfully kind,' he added naïvely.

Mr Davies was pleased.

'That's capital,' he said. 'My friend's name is Sir Henry Wootton, and he's the Conservative member for East Something-or-Other. You'll find him in Vacher's. I'll give you a card to him and I'll ring him up and tell him you're coming to see him. He's a very decent fellow. Apart from that, I won't say another word about him so as not to prejudice you one way or the other. Goodbye and good luck. Come and see me when you get back.'

Sir Henry Wootton was a nice, cheerful, elderly buck of about seventy, and he lived in a large house in Queen's Gate. He had a rosy face, a large white moustache, and blue eyes, and his manners were old-fashioned in their perfection. He received Donald in a rather impressive library, lined with books on all sides. But the impressiveness wore off after a bit, for the books were not the books of a reader, but more like the reference section of a public library or a dusty corridor in a West End Club. The *Dictionary of National Biography* stretched out its interminable array; above it was an old edition of the *Encyclopaedia Britannica*. The *Annual Register* occupied shelf after shelf. Bailey's *Guide to the Turf*, Hansard's *Parliamentary Debates*, the *Gentleman's Magazine*, huge bound volumes of the *Illustrated London News*, the *Field*, *Country Life*, *Horse and Hound*, and other periodicals of bygone ages stood massively, leathery, shoulder to shoulder, rather like the massive, prosperous years of Victorianism which they recorded in their pages. They belonged to a period of the life of England in which there was time not only to read the five-hour speeches of long-dead Chancellors, but to reread them in after-years out of leather-bound collections, a period in which a gentleman had leisure for the pursuit of the gentlemanly pastimes.

Sir Henry belonged to that period. He had driven his coach-and-six to the Derby. He had been taken, as a boy, to see Lord Frederick Beauclerk play a single-wicket match at Lord's; he had seen Jem Mace box; he had damned Oscar Wilde's eyes on the steps of the Athenaeum; he had borrowed money from Sam Lewis to back Ormonde with; he had worshipped the Jersey Lily from afar, and the lesser ladies of *Florodora* and *The Geisha* from a little nearer, and a lot of ladies in Paris and Venice from much closer still. And, on inheriting the baronetcy, he had given up all these things and gone into politics. It was the traditional finish to the life of a traditional English gentleman, and Sir Henry was in the tradition.

The beginning of his political life was a welter of right-minded hatred of Mr Lloyd George and his anarchistic theories about land and money. The middle period was a glow of right-minded adoration of Mr Lloyd George and his magnificence as an organizer of victory; while the closing phase of Sir Henry's career at St Stephen's was untinged with hatreds or adorations. He had outlived the passions and had glided into a serene tranquillity. He did not understand in the least what had happened to the world or was likely to happen, but he was perfectly happy and perfectly willing to play any part that might be allotted to him. He was an admirable Chairman of Commissions to inquire into things of which he had not known the existence; he did not approve in theory of such things as the Irish Treaty, or votes for young ladies of twenty-one, or supertax, but as they had come and were obviously going to stay, he was quite willing to support them in practice. He liked the older members of the Conservative Party because at least ninety per cent of them were lifelong friends; he liked the 'young chaps' because they were the type that would have ridden straight, if hunting hadn't become so damned prohibitive, and would have chased the girls of *Florodora* and *The Geisha* if they weren't buckling down so damned well to the business of running the country; he liked the handful of Radicals in the House, because they were mostly brainy chaps and he admired brains; he liked the Socialists because they got so angry, and that made him laugh. In fact, he liked everyone except 'those damned turncoats' who jumped about from Party to Party like cats in search of jobs. Sir Henry could not stand them at any price, and said so repeatedly and, for his voice was naturally a rather loud one, loudly.

This, then, was the gentleman who welcomed Donald with old-fashioned politeness into his musty, dusty, leathery library.

'I'll tell you what it is, Cameron,' he said, after the usual courtesies had been exchanged, and butler had brought in a couple of glasses of sherry and a biscuit jar (in Sir Henry's life ceremonial 'Misters' played as small a part as Christian names); 'I don't really want a secretary in the proper sense of the word. I'm not going to make speeches with figures and facts and all that sort of rubbish in them. I'm just going to stick to generalities. The truth of the matter is that I don't know much about this League, and I don't know why the PM wants me to go. But he's asked me, and so of course, I'm going. I'm all in favour of peace myself, as every sane man is, but I've got a sort of notion that the best way to keep the peace is the good old British way of building a thumping great fleet and letting the dagoes do what they damned well like, eh? After all, it worked in the past, so why not now? However, I'm told that's all wrong in these modern times, and so I expect it is. They tell me that this League is the dodge now, and if that's so, I'm all in favour of it. Do you see what I mean?'

'Yes, sir,' replied Donald. So far he had found little difficulty in following the thread of Sir Henry's discourse.

'I don't run down the League just because it's new,' went on Sir Henry. 'If we've got to love the black man like a brother, I'm quite prepared to do it. At present I draw the line at loving him like a brother-in-law, but I expect that'll come later. Now your job at Geneva, if you agree to take it on, will be more like a cross between a valet and a friend. I mean you'll have to find my hat for me, and you'll have to keep me posted up with the sporting news from home, and you'll have to see that there's a taxi for me when I want one, and that I don't run out of whisky in the evenings, and all that sort of thing. Do you feel like taking it on for a month?'

'I should be delighted,' replied Donald.

'Splendid. We leave on Friday morning. You'd better run round to the Foreign Office and fix up about passports and so on. And you'd better see if you can find out what this League does, and how it works, and all that sort of thing.'

Donald found it very difficult at Geneva to keep his mind concentrated upon his task. There was so much that was new to be seen, heard, tasted, drunk, and done. With delegates of more than fifty nations concentrated into one town, or worse, into one small quarter of one town, it was almost impossible to remember that he was engaged upon a specific job – the study, at close quarters and at first hand, of the Representatives of England, at work upon international politics. They were, after all, well worth studying. For the English, whatever may be said against their home politics, or their climate, or their cooking, or their love-making, or their art, or their sport, have proved themselves over and over again throughout the centuries the masters of international diplomacy and foreign affairs. A glance at the history of the world shows how the enemies of England have always collapsed unexpectedly and mysteriously, whether owing to the sudden uprising of a southerly gale to drive invading galleons from Gravelines to the Pentland Firth, or owing to a trivial miscalculation which isolated the wing of an army in the obscure Danubian village of Blindheim, or owing to a Spanish ulcer, or to the sinking of a *Lusitania*, and it cannot be supposed that these incidents were all fortuitous. In the same way a glance at the geography of the world shows that in the days of sailing-ships every convenient port somehow or other fell into the hands of the English, except Walfish Bay and Pondicherry; that in the days of coal, every coaling-station was English; that in the days of oil, the only oil-wells that did not already belong to people who wanted selfishly to keep them for themselves, became English; that in 1920 even Walfish Bay, useless as it had become, went the same way as all the rest for the sake of the principle, leaving only Pondicherry as a sort of joke; and that the last scramble, the scramble for aerodromes, fell flat because every reasonably smooth island was already in English hands, except one a good deal north of Siberia, called Wrangel Island, and another in the South Seas called Johnson Island. These two alone were left out by English diplomacy: the first because it is so cold that petrol, oil, and water immediately freeze on arriving there, thus rendering it comparatively unfit for aeronautical manœuvres; and the other, Johnson Island, because, after a volley of notes and threats to the Norwegian Government – which also laid claim to it – the English Intelligence Service somehow ferreted out the fact that the disputed island had not been sighted since its first discovery, sixty-eight years earlier, by a dipsomaniacal Australian skipper, who had noted it down in his log as appearing on the horizon between two pale-pink lizards in yellow breeches and deer-stalkers; and that no one knew in the least where it was. The English Foreign Office immediately despatched a most cordial Note to the Norwegian Government relinquishing all claims to Johnson Island, not as a matter of international right and wrong, but as a graceful compliment to the King of Norway, whose birthday was due in a few weeks' time. Meanwhile the English Admiralty marked Johnson Island on its charts as 'disappeared in unrecorded land-subsidence,' and two years later, the Air Force, hearing the news, provisionally deleted it from its official list of aerodromes.

Donald ought, therefore, to have found no difficulty in concentrating upon the most fascinating of human spectacles, Experts at Work. The English had proved themselves for hundreds of years the Heads of the Profession, and here they were again, at the very centre of the international world, using all their unrivalled skill for the still further betterment of their Empire.

But there were many distractions. The streets were crowded with strange sights. Abyssinians in great blue robes and wearing great black beards swung proudly along the boulevards; Chinese and Japanese and Siamese and Cochinese and Cingalese and Tonkinese and Annamese moved inscrutably hither and thither. Frenchmen chattered. Australians in big hats strode. Sinn Fein ex-gunmen, now Ministers of State, sat in cafés and told witty stories. Albanians, ill at ease without their habitual arsenal of firearms, scowled at Yugoslavs. South Americans abounded, dark men with roving eyes and a passion for kissing typists in lifts. Maharajahs who were descended from ten thousand gods walked as if they were conscious of their ancestry. Newsboys, usually well over eighty years of age, sold papers written in every conceivable language but mainly in the language of the Middle-Western States of the United States; and everywhere pattered private secretaries, racing hither and thither, always in a hurry, always laden with papers, and always just managing to snatch a moment to exchange the latest gossip with each other as they sped by.

In strange contrast to these active young men was the vast, amorphous mass of American tourists who never had anything to do. They eddied about the streets in aimless shoals, like lost mackerel, pointing out celebrities to each other and always getting them wrong; taking endless photographs of obscure Genevese citizens in mistake for German Chancellors or Soviet Observers, and pretending that they had important luncheon-dates. Geneva during September had become as much a pilgrimage for Wyoming, Nebraska, and Boston, to name only three of the main pilgrim-exporting centres, as the Colosseum, the Venus de Milo, the outside of Mr Beerbohm's villa at Rapallo, or the fields at St Mihiel where the German Imperial Army met its first, its only, and its final defeat.

Nor was life in the streets the only distraction. There was the International Club, for instance, where a gentleman in a white coat, called Victor, performed prodigies of activity in the mixing of Bronxes, Gin-Slings, John Collinses, and Brandy St Johns, leaping to and fro, like a demented preacher, for bottles, sugar, lemons, cherries, and straws. His clients were mostly journalists, and very swagger journalists at that. They were not the type which runs round feverishly trying to pick up news. They did not carry notebooks in their hip pockets. They did not pester statesmen for interviews. What they did was to play billiards all day in the Club, calling upon the services of Mr Victor from time to time, until a message arrived giving the hour at which the French Foreign Minister, or the German Foreign Minister, was ready to receive them and answer questions. Occasionally the British Foreign Minister received them, but his receptions were not nearly so popular as those of his two colleagues, for the Frenchman could usually be relied upon for several calculated indiscretions, while the German could always be relied upon for free Munich beer. The Englishman, on the other hand, was both discreet and temperate.

There was also the great building of the Secretariat itself, in which the permanent officials were always ready to welcome visitors at any hour during the day. There was the lake, blue, clear, like a polished aquamarine, translucent, exquisite, studded with far-off brick-red sails of barges and white butterfly yachts, and defended by the everlasting snows of Mont Blanc and the Dent du Midi. Boats could be hired for sailing on the lake, the bathing was warm and luxurious, and on the far side were restaurants, where a man might dine with a lovely lady and see what could be done in the way of wooing by the light of Orion upon dark waters and the sound of little murmurous waves. And anyone who failed to advance his suit in those little lake-side restaurants might just as well reconcile himself at once to a long life of dreary celibacy.

In addition to all these attractions there were the dancing-halls and the cabarets and the cafés in the Old Town, especially the one that wasn't actually the one that Lenin and Trotsky used to frequent in the old days and is now demolished, but wasn't far off, and the Kursaal, and the lounges of the big hotels and the cinemas.

Yes, Geneva was full of distractions for even the keenest of students of international affairs and English policy, and, after the first week of preliminaries, Donald had to make a stern resolution to attend to business and eschew frivolities.

Sir Henry Wootton was thoroughly enjoying himself, and had already devoted several evenings to the discussion of a lot of urgent international business at one of the lake-side restaurants with the permanent deputy-chief of the Exchange-of-Municipal-Experience Section of the Secretariat. The permanent deputy-chief looked very fetching in black velvet and a picture hat, and Sir Henry was as sorry as his secretary when the time came for the application of noses to grindstones.

The normal procedure of the Assembly was as follows. The first week was devoted to speech-making on any subject under the sun by any delegate who wanted to get his name into print in the newspapers of his native country. Nobody listened to them, not even the reporters of the native newspapers, for they had received typewritten copies of the speech which affected them, six or seven hours before it was delivered.

After this week of oratory had been completed, the Assembly split itself up into six Committees, three of which were presided over by an English, French, and German president, two by South Americans, and one by an Asiatic. On this occasion the two South Americans were Panama and Paraguay; the Asiatic was Caspia. But the procedure had to be somewhat modified, as at first no South American delegates were available, for the following rather singular and quite exceptional reason. The second week of the Assembly happened to coincide with the fourth session of the Permanent Committee for the Suppression of Obscene Photographs, Post Cards, Magazines, Advertisements, and Publications in General, and by a curious coincidence all the South Americans, including Cuba, San Domingo, and Haiti – indeed, headed by San Domingo and Haiti, with Cuba well in the running for a place – decided to attend the meetings of the Committee. Fortunately for the work of the Assembly, the sessions of the Permanent Committee for the Suppression of Obscene Photographs, Post Cards, Magazines, Advertisements, and Publications in General came to an abrupt halt on the second day, the entire collection of specimens of the literature in question, so laboriously collected over a long period by the Secretariat, having been pinched by the delegates.

Sir Henry was assigned by the Earl of Osbaldestone, Britain's senior delegate, to the Committee for the Abolition of Social Abuses, and he despatched Donald first to the Secretariat for documents, which would tell him what exactly the Abuses were, and then to the Staff of Foreign Office experts for information about the British Official Policy which Sir Henry was to expound and advocate.

Donald had no difficulty about the documents. There were sheaves of them, printed and typed, records of past Conferences, verbatim minutes of Committees, draft resolutions, amendments to draft resolutions, alterations to amendments of draft resolutions, cancellations of alterations, copies of speeches, and Press reports from publications as far divided, geographically and politically, as the *Singapore Hardware and Allied Trades Independent*, the *Santiago de Chile Indigo Exporters' Quarterly*, *The Times*, *Der Wienerwurst und Schnitzeller Tages-Zeitung* of Rothenburg-am-Tauber, a matrimonial journal called *The Link*, the *Manchester Guardian*, *Who's Who in Cochin-China*, and the *Irish Free State Union of Sewage-Inspectors' Annual Report*.

Donald hired two taxis and filled one up to the roof with the necessary documents and directed the man to drive to Sir Henry's hotel, while he himself went in the other.

After a couple of hours spent in sorting, sifting, and arranging, Donald discovered the crucial sheet of paper on which was printed the agenda of the Commission. It appeared that the two main Abuses at which Sir Henry was due to launch himself were the Illicit Traffic in Synthetic Beer, and the existence in certain countries of Houses of Ill-Repute, discreetly called Licensed Establishments, and Donald set off on his second mission – to obtain the Official Policy on these two matters.

The Foreign Office experts occupied the whole of the second floor of the hotel, and Donald doubtfully entered a sitting-room from which issued a rattle of typewriters, and on the door of which was pinned a label which said, rather surprisingly, 'Chancery.' He was instantly abashed at finding himself in the midst of a perfect vision of beauty and elegance. On all sides radiant young ladies, obviously straight from the establishments of Poirot, Paquin, or Molyneux, were whacking away with dainty fingers at typewriting machines. The air was full of incense. Blood rushed to Donald's head. His eyes went dim. The room darkened. A golden-haired Aphrodite slid up to him but he could not see her. He wanted to fly but his legs would not move. He perspired vehemently, and longed for the quiet midden at the Mains of Balspindie.

After what seemed five or six hours, a vision of blue eyes and golden hair swam out of the mist before him and he stammered a vague and halting statement of his requirements, dropping his hat twice during the recital and, on the second occasion, clutching wildly at the Aphrodite's silken ankle as he groped for it. The goddess was quite unperturbed by the sudden grasp. Lady Secretaries at international conferences which are attended by South Americans quickly get accustomed to almost anything. Nervous Englishmen, or Scotsmen, are child's-play to those who can, with deftness and dignity, handle a Venezuelan.

As soon as Donald had released his grip upon her ankle, had retrieved his hat, and had embarked upon a flood of apologies, she cut him short with kindly firmness, and led him through the roomful of beauty to an inner sanctum into which she pushed him with the words, 'You want Mr Carteret-Pendragon.'

The inner sanctum was a strange contrast to the outer room. It was very large, being one of the largest sitting-rooms in the hotel and seldom occupied during the other months of the year except by Nebraskans and Maharajahs, and was furnished tastefully in green, gold, and marble. There were probably more than one thousand gold tassels on the curtains alone, a source of legitimate pride to the management.

Three young men were sitting in complete silence at three tables, marble-topped and gilt-legged. None of them looked up as Donald came in, and after the golden Venus had closed the door with a snap, a deep, religious soundlessness fell upon the place, as in a cathedral upon a summer's afternoon.

Donald choked down a nervous cough and waited. At last one of the young men laid down his pen, leant back in his chair and said, 'Well?'

'Mr Carteret-Pendragon?'

'That is my name, sir.'

'I am Sir Henry Wootton's private secretary,' began Donald. 'My name is Cameron —'

'How-do-you-do. My name is Carteret-Pendragon. Let me introduce Mr Carshalton-Stanbury, and this is Mr Woldingham-Uffington.'

The two young men got up and bowed gravely and sat down again and went on with their work. Donald noticed that all three were wearing Old Etonian ties.

'It's about Sir Henry and the Social Abuses Commission,' said Donald.

'Sit down,' said Mr Carteret-Pendragon. He was a young man of about thirty with beautiful fair hair, parted at the side and flat and very shiny, a razor-like crease down his grey trousers, pale-yellow horn-rimmed spectacles, and a dark-red carnation in his buttonhole. Mr Carshalton-Stanbury's hair was black, his horn-rims dappled, and his carnation vermilion. Mr Woldingham-Uffington's hair, horn-rims, and carnation were all yellow.

'Sir Henry wants to know what line he is to take about the traffic in Synthetic Beer,' said Donald.

Mr Carteret-Pendragon wrinkled his snow-white brow.

'I don't think I quite follow,' he said in some perplexity.

'Sir Henry thinks that he will probably have to make a speech about it, you see,' explained Donald.

'In a sense, yes,' replied Mr Carteret-Pendragon, 'and in another sense, no. It will,' he added, as if clarifying the position, 'of course, be expected of him.'

'And he wants to know what to say.'

'Oh! The usual things,' said Mr Carteret-Pendragon easily. He went on, checking off the points on his fingers: 'Devotion of British Commonwealth of Free Nations to ideals of League, nation of peace-lovers, all must cooperate, wonderful work of League, praise of the Secretariat, economy in League expenditure, a word about Woodrow Wilson, and a tribute to the French.'

He picked up a document, and began to study it as if the interview had been brought to a conclusion that was satisfactory to everyone.

'But why a tribute to the French?' asked Donald in surprise.

'It's the usual way to finish off a speech here. It does no harm and the French like it.'

'But what about the Synthetic Beer?'

'What about it?' said Mr Carteret-Pendragon in a rather tired voice.

'I mean, what is our policy?'

At the word 'policy' the other two diplomatists started as if they had suddenly been confronted with a rattlesnake, and all three stared at Donald.

'Policy?' repeated Mr Carteret-Pendragon in bewilderment, and Mr Carshalton-Stanbury and Mr Woldingham-Uffington echoed the word and gazed vaguely round the room, like people who have lost something which might turn up unexpectedly at any moment – a dog, for example, or a small child.

'Policy?' repeated Mr Carteret-Pendragon in a firmer voice. He had quicker wits than the other two, and had grasped what this queer youth in the lounge-suit and no buttonhole was talking about.

'My dear sir,' he went on indulgently, 'we don't have policies about things. We leave all that to the dagoes. It keeps them out of mischief.'

'But don't we – don't you – doesn't Great Britain take an independent line about anything?'

'Whatever for?' inquired Mr Carteret-Pendragon, and the other two murmured the words 'independent line,' like men in a maze.

'We are here to preserve balances,' went on the diplomat. 'Our task is to maintain equilibriums – equilibria, I ought to say,' he corrected himself with a small cough. 'After all, there are the proportions, when all is said and done. One must have a sense of equipoise.'

'Naturally,' murmured the other two, hitching up their beautiful trousers about a centimetre and a half in complete unison.

'But how does anything get settled?' inquired Donald, feeling remarkably foolish in the presence of these sophisticated men of the great world.

'Oh, they get settled all right – if not now, at some other time, and if not at Geneva, then in London. It's all a matter of tact. When in doubt agree with the Frenchman. Or if you prefer it, disagree with the Italian. It's all one.'

'And what about brothels? What do we say about them?'

'At the last six Assemblies we've simply said that we don't know what they are. All you have to do is to say it again.' ___

Mr Carteret-Pendragon pondered a moment and then added, 'Broadly speaking, you are fairly safe to take as a generalization, that so far as Organized Vice is concerned, we might, as an Empire, be reasonably described as being more or less against it.'

The interview was now definitely at an end, and Donald went out, feeling that he had gained some sort of insight, at first hand, into the subtle diplomacy which had spread the Union Jack upon all the potential aerodromes of the world. He could see that the genius was there, though he could not have explained for the life of him how it worked. But, of course, that was the genius of it.

The outer room was a dull and drab place as he passed through it. For it was by now past 12 o'clock and Beauty had gone off to lunch, leaving only a memory and a fragrance.

The President of the Committee for the Suppression of Social Abuses was the senior Caspian delegate, and he was enabled to carry through the sections on the agenda which dealt with the traffic in dangerous drugs with great expedition, being himself a lifelong addict to heroin, which he injected subcutaneously into his arm, just as Sherlock did, with a silver hypodermic syringe, encrusted with carved turquoises. His expert knowledge enabled him to correct several of the delegates when their rhetoric about the dismal after-effects of drugging carried them out of the sphere of reality into the sphere of imagination. It was the President also who threw a great deal of cold water upon the fervour of the Swiss representative, when that gentleman was affirming with a vast amount of eloquence that Switzerland had entirely extirpated the villainous crew of drug-traffickers from her free and snowy soil. For, having only that very morning run out of his indispensable heroin, the President had ap-proached a gendarme, courteously touched his red fez and inquired whether there was a drug-seller in the vicinity. The gendarme, according to the President, had courteously saluted and replied, 'Does your Excellency perceive that house along the street with pink shutters and an advertisement for the Sun Insurance Company above its door? Your Excellency does? Good. That is the only house in this vicinity that I know of, at which drugs are not procurable.'

But when the drug sections of the agenda had been satisfactorily dealt with and the consideration of a number of important resolutions postponed until the following year, the President's efficiency fell off considerably. This was partly owing to his lack of interest in the subjects, and partly that, between injections, he was inclined to drop off for forty winks. This habit led to one very unfortunate incident.

The item on the agenda which was being discussed was the advisability of compiling a register of deaths from bubonic plague in the ports of Macao, Bangkok, Wei-hai-Wei, and one or two fishing harbours at the southern end of the island of Formosa, and the Yugoslav delegate, having caught the President's eye just before the latter fell into a quiet snooze, delivered a slashing harangue. He stated, with all the emphasis at his command, that while approving in principle of the register of deaths from bubonic plague, for his Government yielded to none in its loyal adherence to all measures for the pacific betterment of humanity, at the same time he felt that he ought to draw the attention of the Committee to the barbarous conduct of the Hungarian Army in Yugoslavia during the Great War. The Hungarian delegate protested warmly, but the President, who was dreaming of the Mahometan Paradise, only smiled sweetly, and the Yugoslav continued.

'Libraries, often containing as many as sixty or seventy books,' he cried, 'were burnt. Castles were razed to the ground. Pictures were stolen, including a whole set of reproductions of the works of Rubens in the house of a baron; statues were broken; photogravures slashed; trees cut down, gardens destroyed; women raped —'

'What did you say?' exclaimed the Costa Rican delegate, waking up sharply.

'Women raped,' repeated the Yugoslav firmly.

'Mr President,' cried the senior Guatemalan, leaping up in great excitement, 'I beg to move the following resolution: that this Commission reaffirms its unshakable loyalty to the League of Nations, expresses its sincere sympathies for the sufferings of the kingdom of the Serb-Croat-Slovenes, and warmly invites the delegate of that kingdom to submit photographs of the atrocities to which he has alluded.'

'Mr President,' cried the delegate of San Salvador, 'I beg to second that resolution.'

'Agreed, agreed!' shouted an enthusiastic chorus of Latin-American voices.

The President, who had just reached the Seventh Heaven, nodded and smiled. The Yugoslav burst into tears of emotion. The New Zealander called across to the South African, 'For God's sake, let's go and have one. These swobs make me sick,' and the two stalwart Colonials marched out, followed hastily by the Australian.

It was some moments before the Yugoslav, mastering his manly sobs, was able to thank the honourable delegates of Guatemala and San Salvador. He held up a huge book.

'This book contains photographs,' he said, 'of the ruined castles of my unhappy country.'

'Only the castles?' asked the Venezuelan hopefully.

'Good God!' cried the Yugoslav. 'Isn't that enough for you?'

'No!' replied the Latin-Americans in chorus.

The representative of the kingdom of the Serb-Croat-Slovenes was so disgusted by this infidelity that he addressed himself sulkily to the question on the agenda, the bubonic plague in the Far East. Unfortunately the President, awaking at that moment, injected a dose of heroin into his arm and briskly ruled the speaker out of order, and the Commission broke up in confusion.

But the important Commission was the one devoted to Disarmament. All the senior delegates were represented upon it, and Donald stood in a crowd upon the steps of the Secretariat one morning and watched them arrive. The Frenchmen drove up in four magnificent Delage cars with the Tricolor on the radiators; the Spaniards were in Hispano-Suizas, for to the ignorant world the Hispano is even more Spanish than its name; the Italians in Isotta-Fraschinis, with their secretaries in Fiats; the Belgians in Minervas; while the Germans outdid everyone in vast silver Mercédès cars, driven by world-famous racing-drivers. The United States official Observers were mostly in Packards, Chryslers, Graham-Paiges, Willys-Knights, Buicks, Oldsmobiles, and Stutzes, and the Earl of Osbaldestone and his two chief colleagues came in a four-wheel cab, and his secretaries, Mr Carteret-Pendragon, Mr Carshalton-Stanbury, and Mr Woldingham-Uffington, walked.

Fortunately the prestige of British motor manufacturers was well maintained by the eleven Rolls-Royces, with real tortoiseshell bodies and gold bonnets, specially brought over from England by the Right Honourable Lieutenant-General the Maharajah of Hyderadore.

Donald attended several of the debates of the Disarmament Commission and listened to a masterly speech, lasting nearly an hour and three-quarters, in which the Earl of Osbaldestone explained that Great Britain had no special views on the burning question of the reduction and limitation of the output of nails for the horseshoes of cavalry horses, and to the superb oration by the French Foreign Minister which proved, to the complete satisfaction of Poland, Roumania, Czechoslovakia, and Yugoslavia, that a reduction of cavalry horseshoe-nails would be to France the equivalent of the withdrawal from the Vosges, the surrender of Metz, and the abandonment of conscription. His peroration, ending with the immortal words, 'The France of Charlemagne, of Gambetta, of Boulanger, the France of the 22nd of October, the France of the 18th of November, and the France of the 4th of March, is built upon the nails of her immortal horses,' drew thunders of applause.

He was followed by a Roumanian lady who descanted a good deal upon the beauties of dawn coming over distant mountaintops, and whose hand was admiringly kissed at the end of her speech by numbers of swarthy delegates, and she was followed by a small Lithuanian who pointed out in a squeaky voice that the whole question of horseshoes, and nails for horseshoes, was inextricably bound up with the act of dastardly brigandage by which Poland had stolen the ancient Lithuanian capital of Vilna. At this point an unseemly commotion was caused by a loud burst of laughter from a group consisting of the South African representative, the second Indian delegate, and a United States Observer, to whom the Foreign Minister of the Irish Free State had just whispered a vulgar story. The Vice-Chairman, a courtly Chinese, saved the situation by springing to his feet and saying, in slow but perfect French, 'Honourable gentlemen and ladies of the Commission, of which I have the honour unworthily to act as Vice-Chairman, I would crave the permission of you all to put the following consideration before you. The hour is now a quarter to 2, and we have laboured long and earnestly this morning in the cause that we all have at heart, and I would put it to you, in all deference and submission, that the time is at hand when we must decide whether to adjourn now for midday refreshment and resume our task, our so important task, with redoubled vigour later in the day, or whether to continue without rest or interval until we have settled this problem while it is fresh in our minds. I submit, most honourable ladies and gentlemen of the Commission, that we should now come to a decision upon the matter. I will ask the most honourable interpreter to render into English the poor observations which I have had the honour to address to you.'

He bowed with old-world grace to right and to left and sat down. The interpreter, a rosy youth whose knowledge of languages was only equalled by the profundity of his thirst, sprang to his feet eagerly and said in a loud voice, 'The Vice-Chairman says that if we don't stop now we'll be late for lunch,' and snapping an elastic band round his notebook, he thrust it under his arm and walked out of the room. There was helpless pause for a moment or two, and then the delegates, in ones and twos, headed by the British Dominions, streamed out into the corridor.

The third week of the Assembly was a dull week for Donald and also for Sir Henry Wootton. Sir Henry had made his two speeches and had found no difficulty in keeping to the lines laid down for him by Mr Carteret-Pendragon. Indeed, his two speeches were so very like each other, and were so carefully phrased in order to avoid giving the impression that Great Britain took any very strong interest in anything, that by a secretarial error the speech against the traffic in Synthetic Beer was printed in the section of the official report relating to Houses of Ill-Repute, and vice versa, and no one noticed that anything was wrong.

But after the two speeches had been delivered there was nothing more to be done.

Donald found that the other private secretaries attached to the delegation were in the same position. Their chiefs had each made their two speeches and their work was finished.

The fourth and last week was a little better, as there was a general inclination to return to lunch-parties, bathing, yachting, and discreet little dinners by starlight. Peacemakers, no less than warriors, need relaxation.

During this last week, part of Donald's duties was to entertain Sir Henry Wootton's sister and brother-in-law, Mr and Mrs Fielding, who were visiting Geneva to watch the League at work. Mr Fielding, a man of about sixty, who looked like a farmer and talked almost as charmingly and learnedly as the great Mr Charles Ossory himself, took a great fancy to Donald, and, by some mysterious process of unobtrusive questioning, succeeded in extracting from him the secret of his book about England.

Mr Fielding was both sympathetic and enthusiastic, and insisted that Donald should visit them in their Buckinghamshire home later in the year.

'No foreigner can understand England, Cameron,' he said, 'until he's seen Buckinghamshire.'

The final sessions of the Assembly were held. The last item on the agenda, the election of the Council, was taken, and a six-hour ballot resulted in the re-election of the entire Council with the exception that San Domingo took the place of Haiti. The last speeches were made. The last tributes to the peaceful ideals of France were paid by the Foreign Ministers of Poland, Roumania, Czechoslovakia, and Yugoslavia, and the delegates slipped away. The tumult and the oratory died.

Donald, sitting in his sleeper in the Paris express as it pulled out of Bellegarde, the Swiss-French frontier station, ran over in his mind the result of the four weeks' entertainment at which he had assisted, and checked off on a sheet of paper the results that had been achieved. He was flabbergasted to discover that there was hardly a man, woman, or child on the surface of the globe whose lives would not be affected for the better by the plans laid, schemes evolved or furthered, and measures taken during those four weeks. But how these results had been achieved, and when, and by whom, he was utterly unable to say. He was also utterly unable to detect how the English had gone about their inscrutable and mysterious paths their wonders to perform. In his complete bafflement he could only fall back upon the old truism, *ars est celare artem*, and conclude, as the world for centuries has concluded, that in the realms of international affairs the English are the supreme artists.

The Yahi-Bahi Oriental Society of Mrs Rasselyer-Brown

STEPHEN LEACOCK

MRS RASSELYER-BROWN lived on Plutoria Avenue in a vast sandstone palace, in which she held those fashionable entertainments which have made the name of Rasselyer-Brown what it is. Mr Rasselyer-Brown lived there also.

The exterior of the house was more or less a model of the façade of an Italian palazzo of the sixteenth century. If one questioned Mrs Rasselyer-Brown at dinner in regard to this (which was only a fair return for drinking five-dollar champagne) she answered that the façade was *cinquecentisti*, but that it reproduced also the Saracenic mullioned window of the Siennese School. But if the guest said later in the evening to Mr Rasselyer-Brown that he understood that his house was *cinquecentisti*, he answered that he guessed it was. After which remark and an interval of silence Mr Rasselyer-Brown would probably ask the guest if he was dry.

So from that one can tell exactly the sort of people the Rasselyer-Browns were.

In other words, Mr Rasselyer-Brown was a severe handicap to Mrs Rasselyer-Brown. He was more than that; the word isn't strong enough. He was, as Mrs Rasselyer-Brown herself confessed to her confidential circle of three hundred friends, a drag. He was also a tie, and a weight, and a burden, and, in Mrs Rasselyer-Brown's religious moments, a crucifix. Even in the early years of their married life, some twenty or twenty-five years ago, her husband had been a drag on her by being in the coal and wood business. It is hard for a woman to have to realize that her husband is making a fortune out of coal and wood and that people know it. It ties one down. What a woman wants most of all – this, of course, is merely a quotation from Mrs Rasselyer-Brown's own thoughts as expressed to her three hundred friends – is room to expand, to grow. The hardest thing in the world is to be stifled: and there is nothing more stifling than a husband who doesn't know a Giotto from a Carlo Dolci, but who can distinguish nut coal from egg and is never asked to dinner without talking about the furnace.

These, of course, were early trials. they had passed to some extent, or were, at any rate, garlanded with the roses of time.

But the drag remained.

246

Even when the retail coal and wood stage was long since over, it was hard to have to put up with a husband who owned a coal mine and who bought pulp forests instead of illuminated missals of the twelfth century. A coal mine is a dreadful thing at a dinner-table. It humbles one so before one's guests.

It wouldn't have been so bad – this Mrs Rasselyer-Brown herself admitted – if Mr Rasselyer-Brown *did* anything. This phrase should be clearly understood. It meant if there was any one thing that he *did*. For instance, if he had only *collected* anything. Thus, there was Mr Lucullus Fyshe, who made sodawater, but at the same time everybody knew that he had the best collection of broken Italian furniture on the continent; there wasn't a sound piece among the lot.

And there was the similar example of old Mr Feathertop. He didn't exactly *collect* things; he repudiated the name. He was wont to say, 'Don't call me a collector; I'm *not*. I simply pick things up. Just where I happen to be, Rome, Warsaw, Bucharest, anywhere' – and it is to be noted what fine places these are to happen to be. And to think that Mr Rasselyer-Brown would never put his foot outside of the United States! Whereas Mr Feathertop would come back from what he called a run to Europe, and everybody would learn in a week that he had picked up the back of a violin in Dresden (actually discovered it in a violin shop), and the lid of an Etruscan kettle (he had lighted on it, by pure chance, in a kettle shop in Etruria), and Mrs Rasselyer-Brown would feel faint with despair at the nonentity of her husband.

So one can understand how heavy her burden was.

'My dear,' she often said to her bosom friend, Miss Snagg, 'I shouldn't mind things so much' (the things she wouldn't mind were, let us say, the two million dollars of standing timber which Brown Limited, the ominous business name of Mr Rasselyer-Brown, were buying that year) 'if Mr Rasselyer-Brown *did* anything. But he does *nothing*. Every morning after breakfast off to his wretched office, and never back till dinner, and in the evening nothing but his club, or some business meeting. One would think he would have more ambition. How I wish I had been a man.'

It was certainly a shame.

So it came that, in almost everything she undertook, Mrs Rasselyer-Brown had to act without the least help from her husband. Every Wednesday, for instance, when the Dante Club met at her house (they selected four lines each week to meditate on, and then discussed them at lunch), Mrs Rasselyer-Brown had to carry the whole burden of it – her very phrase, 'the whole burden' – alone. Anyone who has carried four lines of Dante through a Moselle lunch knows what a weight it is.

In all these things her husband was useless, quite useless. It is not right to be ashamed of one's husband. And to do her justice, Mrs Rasselyer-Brown always explained to her three hundred intimates that she was *not* ashamed of him; in fact, that she *refused* to be. But it was hard to see him brought into comparison at their own table with superior men. Put him, for instance, beside Mr Sikleigh Snoop, the sex-poet, and where was he? Nowhere. He couldn't even understand what Mr Snoop was saying. And when Mr Snoop would stand on the hearthrug with a cup of tea balanced in his hand, and discuss whether sex was or was not the dominant note in Botticelli, Mr Rasselyer-Brown would be skulking in a corner in his illfitting dress-suit. His wife would often catch with an agonized ear such scraps of talk as, 'When I was first in the coal and wood business,' or, 'It's a coal that burns quicker than egg, but it hasn't the heating power of nut,' or even in a low undertone the words, 'If you're feeling *dry* while he's reading ——' And this at a time when everybody in the room ought to have been listening to Mr Snoop.

Nor was even this the whole burden of Mrs Rasselyer-Brown. There was another part of it which was perhaps more *real*, though Mrs Rasselyer-Brown herself never put it into words. In fact, of this part of her burden she never spoke, even to her bosom friend Miss Snagg; nor did she talk about it to the ladies of the Dante Club, nor did she make speeches on it to the members of the Women's Afternoon Art Society, nor to the Monday Bridge Club.

But the members of the Bridge Club and the Art Society and the Dante Club all talked about it among themselves.

Stated very simply, it was this: Mr Rasselyer-Brown drank.

It was not meant that he was a drunkard or that he drank too much, or anything of that sort. He drank. That was all.

There was no excess about it. Mr Rasselyer-Brown, of course, began the day with an eye-opener – and after all, what alert man does not wish his eyes well open in the morning? He followed it usually just before breakfast with a bracer – and what wiser precaution can a business man take than to brace his breakfast? On his way to business he generally had his motor stopped at the Grand Palaver for a moment, if it was a raw day, and dropped in and took something to keep out the damp. If it was a cold day he took something to keep out the cold, and if it was one of those clear, sunny days that are so dangerous to the system he took whatever the bartender (a recognized health expert) suggested to tone the system up. After which he could sit down in his office and transact more business, and bigger business, in coal, charcoal, wood, pulp, pulp-wood, and woodpulp, in two hours than any other man in the business could in a week. Naturally so. For he was braced, and propped, and toned up, and his eyes had been opened, and his brain cleared, till outside of very big business indeed few men were on a footing with him.

In fact, it was business itself which had compelled Mr Rasselyer-Brown to drink. It is all very well for a junior clerk on twenty dollars a week to do his work on sandwiches and malted milk. In big business it is not possible. when a man begins to rise in business, as Mr Rasselyer Brown had begun twenty-five years ago, he finds that if he wants to succeed he must cut malted milk clean out. In any position of responsibility a man has got to drink. No really big deal can be put through without it. If two keen men, sharp as flint, get together to make a deal in which each intends to outdo the other, the only way to succeed is for them to adjourn to some such place as the luncheon-room of the Mausoleum Club and both get partially drunk. This is what is called the personal element in business. And, beside it, plodding industry is nowhere.

Most of all do these principles hold true in such manly out-of-door enterprises as the forest and timber business, where one deals constantly with chief rangers, and pathfinders, and wood-stalkers, whose very names seem to suggest a horn of whisky under a hemlock tree.

But – let it be repeated and carefully understood – there was no excess about Mr Rasselyer-Brown's drinking. Indeed, whatever he might be compelled to take during the day, and at the Mausoleum Club in the evening, after his return from his club at night Mr Rasselyer-Brown made it a fixed rule to take nothing. He might, perhaps, as he passed into the house, step into the dining-room and take a very small drink at the sideboard. But this he counted as part of the return itself, and not after it. And he might, if his brain were over-fatigued, drop down later in the night in his pyjamas and dressing-gown when the house was quiet, and compose his mind with a brandy and water, or something suitable to the stillness of the hour, but this was not really a drink. Mr Rasselyer-Brown called it a *nip*; and of course any man may need a *nip* at a time when he would scorn a drink.

But after all, a woman may find herself again in her daughter. There, at least, is consolation. For, as Mrs Rasselyer-Brown herself admitted, her daughter Dulphemia was herself again. There were, of course, differences, certain differences of face and appearance. Mr Snoop had expressed this fact exquisitely when he said that it was a difference between a Burne-Jones and a Dante Gabriel Rossetti. But even at that the mother and daughter were so alike that people, certain people, were constantly mistaking them on the street. And as everybody that mistook them was apt to be asked to dine on five-dollar champagne there was plenty of temptation towards error.

There is no doubt that Dulphemia Rasselyer-Brown was a girl of remarkable character and intellect. So is any girl who has beautiful golden hair parted in thick bands on her forehead, and deep blue eyes soft as an Italian sky.

Even the oldest and most serious men in town admitted that in talking to her they were aware of a grasp, a reach, a depth that surprised them.

Thus old Judge Longerstill, who talked to her at dinner for an hour on the jurisdiction of the Interstate Commerce Commission, felt sure, from the way in which she looked up in his face at intervals and said, 'How interesting!', that she had the mind of a lawyer. And Mr Brace, the consulting engineer, who showed her on the tablecloth at dessert with three forks and a spoon the method in which the overflow of the spillway of the Gatun Dam is regulated, felt assured, from the way she leaned her face on her hand sideways and said, 'How extraordinary!' that she had the brain of an engineer. Similarly foreign visitors to the social circles of the city were delighted with her. Viscount FitzThistle, who explained to Dulphemia for half an hour the intricacies of the Irish situation, was captivated at the quick grasp she showed by asking him at the end, without a second's hesitation, 'And which are the Nationalists?'

This kind of thing represents female intellect in its best form. Every man that is really a man is willing to recognize it at once.

As to the young men, of course they flocked to the Rasselyer-Brown residence in shoals. There were batches of them every Sunday afternoon at five o'clock, encased in long black frock-coats, sitting very rigidly in upright chairs, trying to drink tea with one hand. One might see athletic young college men of the football team trying hard to talk about Italian music; and Italian tenors from the Grand Opera doing their best to talk about college football. There were young men in business talking about art, and young men in art talking about religion, and young clergymen talking about business. Because, of course, the Rasselyer-Brown residence was the kind of cultivated home where people of education and taste are at liberty to talk about things they don't know, and to utter freely ideas that they haven't got. It was only now and again, when one of the professors from the college across the avenue came booming into the room, that the whole conversation was pulverized into dust under the hammer of accurate knowledge.

This whole process was what was called, by those who understood such things, a *salon*. Many people said that Mrs Rasselyer-Brown's afternoons at home were exactly like the delightful *salons* of the eighteenth century: and whether the gatherings were or were not *salons* of the eighteenth century, there is no doubt that Mr Rasselyer-Brown, under whose care certain favoured guests dropped quietly into the back alcove of the dining-room, did his best to put the gathering on a par with the best saloons of the twentieth.

Now it so happened that there had come a singularly slack moment in the social life of the city. The Grand Opera had sung itself into a huge deficit and closed. There remained nothing of it except the efforts of a committee of ladies to raise enough money to enable Signor Puffi to leave town, and the generous attempt of another committee to gather funds in order to keep Signor Pasti in the city. Beyond this, opera was dead, though the fact that the deficit was nearly twice as large as it had been the year before showed that public interest in music was increasing. It was indeed a singularly trying time of the year. It was too early to go to Europe, and too late to go to Bermuda. It was too warm to go south, and yet still too cold to go north. In fact one was almost compelled to stay at home – which was dreadful.

As a result Mrs Rasselyer-Brown and her three hundred friends moved backward and forward on Plutoria Avenue, seeking novelty in vain. They washed in waves of silk from tango teas to bridge afternoons. They poured in liquid avalanches of colour into crowded receptions, and they sat in glittering rows and listened to lectures on the enfranchisement of the female sex. But for the moment all was weariness.

Now it happened, whether by accident or design, that just at this moment of general *ennui* Mrs Rasselyer-Brown and her three hundred friends first heard of the presence in the city of Mr Yahi-Bahi, the celebrated oriental mystic. He was so celebrated that nobody even thought of asking who he was or where he came from. They merely told one another, and repeated it, that he was *the* celebrated Yahi-Bahi. They added for those who needed the knowledge that the name was pronounced Yahhy-Bahhy, and the doctrine taught by Mr Yahi-Bahi was Boohooism. This latter, if anyone inquired further, was explained to be a form of Shoodooism, only rather more intense. In fact, it was esoteric – on receipt of which information everybody remarked at once how infinitely superior the oriental peoples are to ourselves.

Now as Mrs Rasselyer-Brown was always a leader in everything that was done in the best circles on Plutoria Avenue, she was naturally among the first to visit Mr Yahi-Bahi.

'My dear,' she said, in describing afterwards her experience to her bosom friend, Miss Snagg, 'it was *most* interesting. We drove away down to the queerest part of the city, and went to the strangest little house imaginable, up the narrowest stairs one ever saw – quite Eastern, in fact, just like a scene out of the Koran.'

'How fascinating!' said Miss Snagg. But as as matter of fact, if Mr Yahi-Bahi's house had been inhabited, as it might have been, by a street-car conductor or a railway brakesman, Mrs Rasselyer-Brown wouldn't have thought it in any way peculiar or fascinating.

'It was all hung with curtains inside,' she went on, 'with figures of snakes and Indian gods, perfectly weird.'

'And did you see Mr Yahi-Bahi?' asked Miss Snagg.

'Oh no, my dear. I only saw his assistant, Mr Ram Spudd; such a queer little round man, a Bengalee, I believe. He put his back against a curtain and spread out his arms sideways and wouldn't let me pass. He said that Mr Yahi-Bahi was in meditation and mustn't be disturbed.'

'How delightful!' echoed Miss Snagg.

But in reality Mr Yahi-Bahi was sitting behind the curtain eating a ten-cent can of pork and beans.

'What I like most about Eastern people,' went on Mrs Rasselyer-Brown, 'is their wonderful delicacy of feeling. After I had explained about my invitation to Mr Yahi-Bahi to come and speak to us on Boohooism, and was going away, I took a dollar bill out of my purse and laid it on the table. You should have seen the way Mr Ram Spudd took it. He made the deepest salaam and said, "Isis guard you, beautiful lady." Such perfect courtesy, and yet with the air of scorning the money. As I passed out I couldn't help slipping another dollar into his hand, and he took it as if utterly unaware of it, and muttered, "Osiris keep you, O flower of women!" And as I got into the motor I gave him another dollar and he said, "Isis and Osiris both prolong your existence, O lily of the rice-field"; and after he had said it he stood beside the door of the motor and waited without moving till I left. He had such a strange, rapt look, as if he were still expecting something!'

'How exquisite!' murmured Miss Snagg. It was her business in life to murmur such things as this for Mrs Rasselyer-Brown. On the whole, reckoning Grand Opera tickets and dinners, she did very well out of it.

'Is it not?' said Mrs Rasselyer-Brown. 'So different from our men. I felt so ashamed of my chauffeur, our new-man, you know; he seemed such a contrast beside Ram Spudd. The rude way in which he opened the door, and the rude way in which he climbed on to his own seat, and the *rudeness* with which he turned on the power – I felt positively ashamed. And he so managed it – I am sure he did it on purpose – that the car splashed a lot of mud over Mr Spudd as it started.'

Yet, oddly enough, the opinion of other people on this new chauffeur, that of Miss Dulphemia Rasselyer-Brown herself, for example, to whose service he was specially attached, was very different.

The great recommendation of him in the eyes of Miss Dulphemia and her friends, and the thing that gave him a touch of mystery, was – and what higher qualification can a chauffeur want? – that he didn't look like a chauffeur at all.

'My dear Dulphie,' whispered Miss Philippa Furlong, the rector's sister (who was at that moment Dulphemia's second self), as they sat behind the new chauffeur, 'don't tell me that he is a chauffeur, because he *isn't*. He can chauffe, of course, but that's nothing.'

For the new chauffeur had a bronzed face, hard as metal, and a stern eye; and when he put on a chauffeur's overcoat somehow it seemed to turn into a military greatcoat; and even when he put on the round cloth cap of his profession it was converted straightway into a military shako. And by Miss Dulphemia and her friends it was presently reported – or was invented – that he had served in the Philippines; which explained at once the scar upon his forehead, which must have been received at Iloilo, or Huila-Huila, or some other suitable place.

But what affected Miss Dulphemia Rasselyer-Brown herself was the splendid rudeness of the chauffeur's manner. It was so different from that of the young men of the *salon*. Thus, when Mr Sikleigh Snoop handed her into the car at any time he would dance about saying, 'Allow me,' and, 'Permit me,' and would dive forward to arrange the robes. But the Philippine chauffeur merely swung the door open and said to Dulphemia, 'Get in,' and then slammed it.

This, of course, sent a thrill up the spine and through the imagination of Miss Dulphemia Rasselyer-Brown, because it showed that the chauffeur was a gentleman in disguise. She thought it very probable that he was a British nobleman, a younger son, very wild, of a ducal family; and she had her own theories as to why he had entered the service of the Rasselyer-Browns. To be quite candid about it, she expected that the Philippine chauffeur meant to elope with her, and every time he drove her from a dinner or a dance she sat back luxuriously, wishing and expecting the elopement to begin.

But for the time being the interest of Dulphemia, as of everybody else that was anybody at all, centred round Mr Yahi-Bahi and the new cult of Boohooism.

After the visit of Mrs Rasselyer-Brown a great number of ladies, also in motors, drove down to the house of Mr Yahi-Bahi. and all of them, whether they saw Mr Yahi-Bahi himself or his Bengalee assistant, Mr Ram Spudd, came back delighted.

'Such exquisite tact!' said one. 'Such delicacy! As I was about to go I laid a five-dollar gold piece on the edge of the little table. Mr Spudd scarcely seemed to see it. He murmured, "Osiris help you!" and pointed to the ceiling. I raised my eyes instinctively, and when I lowered them the money had disappeared. I think he must have caused it to vanish.'

'Oh, I'm sure he did,' said the listener.

Others came back with wonderful stories of Mr Yahi-Bahi's occult powers, especially his marvellous gift of reading the future.

Mrs Buncomhearst, who had just lost her third husband – by divorce – had received from Mr Yahi-Bahi a glimpse into the future that was almost uncanny in its exactness. She had asked for a divination, and Mr Yahi-Bahi had effected one by causing her to lay six ten-dollar pieces on the table arranged in the form of a mystic serpent. Over these he had bent and peered deeply, as if seeking to unravel their meaning, and finally he had given her the prophecy, 'Many things are yet to happen before others begin.'

'How *does* he do it?' asked everybody.

As a result of all this it naturally came about that Mr Yahi-Bahi and Mr

Ram Spudd were invited to appear at the residence of Mrs Rasselyer-Brown; and it was understood that steps would be taken to form a special society, to be known as the Yahi-Bahi Oriental Society.

Mr Sikleigh Snoop, the sex-poet, was the leading spirit in the organization. He had a special fitness for the task: he had actually resided in India. In fact, he had spent six weeks there on a stopover ticket of a round-the-world 635-dollar steamship pilgrimage; and he knew the whole country from Jehumbapore in Bhootal to Jehumbalabad in the Carnatic. So he was looked upon as a great authority on India, China, Mongolia, and all such places, by the ladies of Plutoria Avenue.

Next in importance was Mrs Buncomhearst, who became later, by a perfectly natural process, the president of the society. She was already president of the Daughters of the Revolution, a society confined exclusively to the descendants of Washington's officers and others; she was also president of the Sisters of England, an organization limited exclusively to women born in England and elsewhere; of the Daughters of Kossuth, made up solely of Hungarians and friends of Hungary and other nations; and of the Circle of Franz Joseph, which was composed exclusively of the partisans, and others, of Austria. In fact, ever since she had lost her third husband, Mrs Buncomhearst had thrown herself – that was her phrase – into outside activities. Her one wish was, on her own statement, to lose herself. So very naturally Mrs Rasselyer-Brown looked at once to Mrs Buncomhearst to preside over the meetings of the new society.

The large dining-room at the Rasselyer-Browns' had been cleared out as a sort of auditorium, and in it some fifty or sixty of Mrs Rasselyer-Brown's more intimate friends had gathered. The whole meeting was composed of ladies, except for the presence of one or two special cases. There was, of course, little Mr Spillikins, with his vacuous face and football hair, who was there, as everybody knew, on account of Dulphemia; and there was old Judge Longerstill, who sat leaning on a gold-headed stick with his head sideways, trying to hear some fraction of what was being said. He came to the gathering in the hope that it would prove a likely place for seconding a vote of thanks and saying a few words – half an hour's talk, perhaps – on the constitution of the United States. Failing that, he felt sure that at least someone would call him 'this eminent old gentleman,' and even that was better than staying at home.

But for the most part the audience was composed of women, and they sat in a little buzz of conversation waiting for Mr Yahi-Bahi.

'I wonder,' called Mrs Buncomhearst from the chair, 'if some lady would be good enough to write minutes? Miss Snagg, I wonder if you would be kind enough to write minutes? Would you?'

'I shall be delighted,' said Miss Snagg, 'but I'm afraid there's hardly time to write them before we begin, is there?'

'Oh, but it would be all right to write them *afterwards*,' chorused several ladies who understood such things; 'it's quite often done that way.'

'And I should like to move that we vote a constitution,' said a stout lady with a double eye-glass.

'Is that carried?' said Mrs Buncomhearst. 'All those in favour please signify.'

Nobody stirred.

'Carried,' said the president. 'And perhaps you would be good enough, Mrs Fyshe,' she said, turning towards the stout lady, 'to *write* the constitution.'

'Do you think it necessary to *write* it?' said Mrs Fyshe. 'I should like to move, if I may, that I almost wonder whether it is necessary to write the constitution – unless, of course, anybody thinks that we really ought to.'

'Ladies,' said the president, 'you have heard the motion. All those against it ——'

There was no sign.

'All those in favour of it ——'

There was still no sign.

'Lost,' she said.

Then, looking across at the clock on the mantelpiece, and realizing that Mr Yahi-Bahi must have been delayed and that something must be done, she said:

'And now, ladies, as we have in our midst a most eminent gentleman who probably has thought more deeply about constitutions than ——'

All eyes turned at once towards Judge Longerstill, but as fortune had it at this very moment Mr Sikleigh Snoop entered, followed by Mr Yahi-Bahi and Mr Ram Spudd.

Mr Yahi-Bahi was tall. His drooping oriental costume made him taller still. He had a long brown face and liquid brown eyes of such depth that when he turned them full upon the ladies before him a shiver of interest and apprehension followed in the track of his glance.

'My dear,' said Miss Snagg afterwards, 'he seemed simply to see right through us.'

This was correct. He did.

Mr Ram Spudd presented a contrast to his superior. He was short and round, with a dimpled mahogany face, and eyes that twinkled in it like little puddles of molasses. His head was bound in a turban and his body was swatched in so many bands and sashes that he looked almost circular. The clothes of both Mr Yahi-Bahi and Ram Spudd were covered with the mystic signs of Buddha and the seven serpents of Vishnu.

It was impossible, of course, for Mr Yahi-Bahi or Mr Ram Spudd to address the audience. Their knowledge of English was known to be too slight for that. Their communications were expressed entirely through the medium of Mr Snoop, and even he explained afterwards that it was very difficult. The only languages of India which he was able to speak, he said, with any fluency were Gargamic and Gumaic, both of these being old Dravidian dialects with only two hundred and three words in each, and hence in themselves very difficult to converse in. Mr Yahi-Bahi answered in what Mr Snoop understood to be the Iramic of the Vedas, a very rich language, but one which unfortunately he did not understand. The dilemma is one familiar to all oriental scholars.

All of this Mr Snoop explained in the opening speech which he proceeded to make. And after this he went on to disclose, amid deep interest, the general nature of the cult of Boohooism. He said that they could best understand it if he told them that its central doctrine was that of Bahee. Indeed, the first aim of all followers of the cult was to attain to Bahee. Anybody who could spend a certain number of hours each day, say sixteen, in silent meditation on Boohooism would find his mind gradually reaching a condition of Bahee. The chief aim of Bahee itself was sacrifice: a true follower of the cult must be willing to sacrifice his friends, or his relatives, and even strangers, in order to reach Bahee. In this way one was able fully to realize oneself and enter into the Higher Indifference. Beyond this, further meditation and fasting – by which was meant living solely on fish, fruit, wine, and meat – one presently attained to complete Swaraj or Control of Self, and might in time pass into the absolute Nirvana, or the Negation of Emptiness, the supreme goal of Boohooism.

As a first step to all this, Mr Snoop explained, each neophyte or candidate for holiness must, after seaching his own heart, send ten dollars to Mr Yahi-Bahi. Gold, it appeared, was recognized in the cult of Boohooism as typifying the three chief virtues, whereas silver or paper money did not; even national banknotes were only regarded as *dô*, or a halfway palliation; and outside currencies such as Canadian or Mexican bills were looked upon as entirely *boo*, or contemptible. The oriental view of money, said Mr Snoop, was far superior to our own, but it also might be attained by deep thought, and, as a beginning, by sending ten dollars to Mr Yahi-Bahi.

After this Mr Snoop, in conclusion, read a very beautiful Hindu poem, translating it as he went along. It began 'O cow standing beside the Ganges, and apparently without visible occupation,' and it was voted exquisite by all who heard it. The absence of rhyme and the entire removal of ideas marked it as far beyond anything reached as yet by occidental culture.

When Mr Snoop had concluded, the president called upon Judge Longerstill for a few words of thanks, which he gave, followed by a brief talk on the constitution of the United States.

After this the society was declared constituted, Mr Yahi-Bahi made four salaams, one to each point of the compass, and the meeting dispersed.

And that evening, over fifty dinner tables, everybody discussed the nature of Bahee, and tried in vain to explain it to men too stupid to understand.

Now it so happened that on the very afternoon of this meeting at Mrs Rasselyer-Brown's, the Philippine chauffeur did a strange and peculiar thing. He first asked Mr Rasselyer-Brown for a few hours' leave of absence to attend the funeral of his mother-in-law. This was a request which Mr Rasselyer-Brown, on principle, never refused to a man-servant.

Whereupon, the Philippine chauffeur, no longer attired as one, visited the residence of Mr Yahi-Bahi. He let himself in with a marvellous little key which he produced from a very wonderful bunch of such. He was in the house for nearly half an hour, and when he emerged the notebook in his breast pocket, had there been an eye to read it, would have been seen to be filled with stranger details in regard to oriental mysticism than even Mr Yahi-Bahi had given to the world. So strange were they that before the Philippine chauffeur returned to the Rasselyer-Brown residence he telegraphed certain and sundry parts of them to New York. But why he should have addressed them to the head of a detective bureau instead of to a college of oriental research it passes the imagination to conceive. But as the chauffeur duly reappeared at motor-time in the evening the incident passed unnoticed.

It is beyond the scope of the present narrative to trace the progress of Boohooism during the splendid but brief career of the Yahi-Bahi Oriental Society. There could be no doubt of its success. Its principles appealed with great strength to all the more cultivated among the ladies of Plutoria Avenue. There was something in the oriental mysticism of its doctrines which rendered previous belief stale and puerile. The practice of the sacred rites began at once. The ladies' counters of the Plutorian banks were inundated with requests for ten-dollar pieces in exchange for banknotes. At dinner in the best houses nothing was eaten except a thin soup (or *brû*), followed by fish, succeeded by meat or by game, especially such birds as are particularly pleasing to Buddha, as the partridge, the pheasant, and the woodcock. After this, except for fruits and wine, the principle of Swaraj, or denial of self, was rigidly imposed. Special oriental dinners of this sort were given, followed by listening to the reading of oriental poetry, with closed eyes and with the mind as far as possible in a state of Stoj, or Negation of Thought.

By this means the general doctrine of Boohooism spread rapidly.

Indeed, a great many of the members of the society soon attained to a state of Bahee, or the Higher Indifference, that it would have been hard to equal outside of Juggapore or Jumbumbabad. For example, when Mrs Buncomhearst learned of the remarriage of her second husband – she had lost him three years before, owing to a difference of opinion on the emancipation of women – she shewed the most complete Bahee possible. And when Miss Snagg learned that her brother in Venezuela had died – a very sudden death brought on by drinking rum for seventeen years – and had left her ten thousand dollars, the Bahee which she exhibited almost amounted to Nirvana.

In fact, the very general dissemination of the oriental idea became more and more noticeable with each week that passed. Some members attained to so complete a Bahee, or Higher Indifference, that they even ceased to attend the meetings of the society; others reached a Swaraj, or Control of Self, so great that they no longer read its pamphlets; while others again actually passed into Nirvana, or Complete Negation of Self, so rapidly that they did not even pay their subscriptions.

But features of this sort, of course, are familiar wherever a successful occult creed makes its way against the prejudices of the multitude.

The really notable part of the whole experience was the marvellous demonstration of occult power which attended the final séance of the society, the true nature of which is still wrapped in mystery.

For some weeks it had been rumoured that a very special feat or demonstration of power by Mr Yahi-Bahi was under contemplation. In fact, the rapid spread of Swaraj and of Nirvana among the members rendered such a feat highly desirable. Just what form the demonstration would take was for some time a matter of doubt. It was whispered at first that Mr Yahi-Bahi would attempt the mysterious Eastern rite of burying Ram Spudd alive in the garden of the Rasselyer-Brown residence and leaving him there in a state of Stoj, or Suspended Inanition, for eight days. But this project was abandoned, owing to some doubt, apparently, in the mind of Mr Ram Spudd, as to his astral fitness for the high state of Stoj necessitated by the experiment.

At last it became known to the members of the Poosh, or Inner Circle, under the seal of confidence, that Mr Yahi-Bahi would attempt nothing less than the supreme feat of occultism, namely, a reincarnation, or more correctly a reastralization, of Buddha.

The members of the Inner Circle shivered with a luxurious sense of mystery when they heard of it.

'Has it ever been done before?' they asked of Mr Snoop.

'Only a few times,' he said; 'once, I believe, by Jambum, the famous Yogi of the Carnatic: once, perhaps twice, by Boohoo, the founder of the sect. But it is looked upon as extremely rare. Mr Yahi tells me that the great danger is that, if the slightest part of the formula is incorrectly observed, the person attempting the astralization is swallowed up into nothingness. However, he declares himself willing to try.'

The séance was to take place at Mrs Rasselyer-Brown's residence, and was to be at midnight.

'At midnight!' said each member in surprise. And the answer was, 'Yes, at midnight. You see, midnight here is exactly midday in Allahabad in India.'

This explanation was, of course, ample. 'Midnight,' repeated everybody to everybody else, 'is exactly midday in Allahabad.' That made things perfectly clear. Whereas if midnight had been midday in Timbuctoo the whole situation would have been different.

Each of the ladies was requested to bring to the séance some ornament of gold; but it must be plain gold, without any setting of stones.

It was known already that, according to the cult of Boohooism, gold, plain gold, is the seat of the three virtues — beauty, wisdom, and grace. Therefore, according to the creed of Boohooism, anyone who has enough gold, plain gold, is endowed with these virtues and is all right. All that is needed is to have enough of it; the virtues follow as a consequence.

But for the great experiment the gold used must not be set with stones, with the one exception of rubies, which are known to be endowed with the three attributes of Hindu worship — modesty, loquacity, and pomposity.

In the present case as it was found that a number of ladies had nothing but gold ornaments set with diamonds, a second exception was made; especially as Mr Yahi-Bahi, on appeal, decided that diamonds, though less pleasing to Buddha than rubies, possessed the secondary Hindu virtues of divisibility, movability, and disposability.

On the evening in question the residence of Mrs Rasselyer-Brown might have been observed at midnight wrapped in utter darkness. No lights were shown. A single taper, brought by Ram Spudd from the Taj Mahal, and resembling in its outer texture those sold at the five-and-ten store near Mr Spudd's residence, burned on a small table in the vast dining-room. The servants had been sent upstairs and expressly enjoined to retire at half-past ten. Moreover, Mr Rasselyer-Brown had had to attend that evening, at the Mausoleum Club, a meeting of the trustees of the Church of St Asaph, and he had come home at eleven o'clock, as he always did after diocesan work of this sort, quite used up; in fact, so fatigued that he had gone upstairs to his own suite of rooms sideways, his knees bending under him. So utterly used up was he with his church work that, as far as any interest in what might be going on in his own residence, he had attained to a state of Bahee, or Higher Indifference, that even Buddha might have envied.

The guests, as had been arranged, arrived noiselessly and on foot. All motors were left at least a block away. They made their way up the steps of the darkened house, and were admitted without ringing, the door opening silently in front of them. Mr Yahi-Bahi and Mr Rum Spudd, who had arrived on foot carrying a large parcel, were already there, and were behind a screen in the darkened room, reported to be in meditation.

At a whispered word from Mr Snoop, who did duty at the door, all furs and wraps were discarded in the hall and laid in a pile. then the guests passed silently into the great dining-room. There was no light in it except the dim taper which stood on a little table. On this table each guest, as instructed, laid an ornament of gold, and at the same time was uttered in a low voice the word 'Ksvoo.' This means, 'O Buddha, I herewith lay my unworthy offering at thy feet; take it and keep it for ever.' It was explained that this was only a form.

'What is he doing?' whispered the assembled guests as they saw Mr Yahi-Bahi pass across the darkened room and stand in front of the sideboard.

'Hush!' said Mr Snoop; 'he's laying the propitiatory offering for Buddha.'

'It's an Indian rite,' whispered Mrs Rasselyer-Brown.

Mr Yahi-Bahi could be seen dimly moving to and fro in front of the sideboard. There was a faint clinking of glass.

'He has to set out a glass of Burmese brandy, powdered over with nutmeg and aromatics,' whispered Mrs Rasselyer-Brown. 'I had the greatest hunt to get it all for him. He said that nothing but Burmese brandy would do, because in the Hindu religion the god can only be invoked with Burmese brandy, or, failing that, Hennessy's with three stars, which is not entirely displeasing to Buddha.'

'The aromatics,' whispered Mr Snoop, 'are supposed to waft a perfume or incense to reach the nostrils of the god. The glass of propitiatory wine and the aromatic spices are mentioned in the Vishnu-Buddayat.'

Mr Yahi-Bahi, his preparations completed, was now seen to stand in front of the sideboard bowing deeply four times in an oriental salaam. The light of the single taper had by this time burned so dim that his movements were vague and uncertain. His body cast great flickering shadows on the half-seen wall. From his throat there issued a low wail in which the word wah! wah! could be distinguished.

The excitement was intense.

'What does "wah" mean?' whispered Mr Spillikins.

'Hush!' said Mr Snoop; 'it means, "Oh Buddha, wherever thou art in thy lofty Nirvana, descend yet once in astral form before our eyes!"'

Mr Yahi-Bahi rose. He was seen to place one finger on his lips, and then, silently moving across the room, he disappeared behind the screen. Of what Mr Ram Spudd was doing during this period there is no record. It was presumed that he was still praying.

The stillness was now absolute.

'We must wait in perfect silence,' whispered Mr Snoop from the extreme tips of his lips.

Everybody sat in strained intensity, silent, looking towards the vague outline of the sideboard.

The minutes passed. No one moved. All were spellbound in expectancy.

Still the minutes passed. The taper had flickered down till the great room was almost in darkness.

Could it be that by some neglect in the preparations, the substitution perhaps of the wrong brandy, the astralization could not be effected?

But no.

Quite suddenly, it seemed, everybody in the darkened room was aware of a *presence*. That was the word as afterwards repeated in a hundred confidential discussions. A *presence*. One couldn't call it a body. It wasn't. It was a figure, an astral form, a presence.

'Buddha!' they gasped as they looked at it.

Just how the figure entered the room the spectators could never afterwards agree. Some thought it appeared through the wall, deliberately astralizing itself as it passed through the bricks. Others seemed to have seen it pass in at the further door of the room, as if it had astralized itself at the foot of the stairs in the back of the hall outside.

Be that as it may, there it stood before them, the astralized shape of the Indian deity, so that to every lip there rose the half-articulated word, 'Buddha'; or at least to every lip except that of Mrs Rasselyer-Brown. From her there came no sound.

The figure as afterwards described was attired in a long *shirâk*, such as is worn by the Grand Lama of Tibet, and resembling, if the comparison were not profane, a modern dressing-gown. the legs, if one might so call them, of the apparition were enwrapped in loose punjahamas, a word which is said to be the origin of the modern pyjamas; while the feet, if they were feet, were encased in loose slippers.

Buddha moved slowly across the room. Arrived at the sideboard the astral figure paused, and even in the uncertain light Buddha was seen to raise and drink the propitiatory offering. That much was perfectly clear. Whether Buddha spoke or not is doubtful. Certain of the spectators thought that he said, '*Must a fagotnit*,' which is Hindustani for 'Blessings on this house.' To Mrs Rasselyer-Brown's distracted mind it seemed as if Buddha said, 'I must have forgotten it.' But this wild fancy she never breathed to a soul.

Silently Buddha recrossed the room, slowly wiping one arm across his mouth after the Hindu gesture of farewell.

For perhaps a full minute after the disappearance of Buddha not a soul moved. Then quite suddenly Mrs Rasselyer-Brown, unable to stand the tension any longer, pressed an electric switch and the whole room was flooded with light.

There sat the affrighted guests staring at one another with pale faces.

But, to the amazement and horror of all, the little table in the centre stood empty – not a single gem, not a fraction of the gold that had lain upon it was left. All had disappeared.

The truth seemed to burst upon everyone at once. There was no doubt of what had happened.

The gold and the jewels had been deastralized. Under the occult power of the vision they had been demonetized, engulfed into the astral plane alone with the vanishing Buddha.

Filled with the sense of horror still to come, somebody pulled aside the little screen. They fully expected to find the lifeless bodies of Mr Yahi-Bahi and the faithful Ram Spudd. What they saw before them was more dreadful still. The outer oriental garments of the two devotees lay strewn upon the floor. The long sash of Yahi-Bahi and the thick turban of Ram Spudd were side by side near them; almost sickening in its repulsive realism was the thick black head of hair of the junior devotee, apparently torn from his scalp as if by lightning and bearing a horrible resemblance to the cast-off wig of an actor.

The truth was too plain.

'They are engulfed!' cried a dozen voices at once.

It was realized in a flash that Yahi-Bahi and Ram Spudd had paid the penalty of their daring with their lives. Through some fatal neglect, against which they had fairly warned the participants of the séance, the two orientals had been carried bodily into the astral plane.

'How dreadful!' murmured Mr Snoop. 'We must have made some awful error.'

'Are they deastralized?' murmured Mrs Buncomhearst.

'Not a doubt of it,' said Mr Snoop.

And then another voice in the group was heard to say, 'We must hush it up. We *can't* have it known!'

On which a chorus of voices joined in, everybody urging that it must be hushed up.

'Couldn't you try to reastralize them?' said somebody to Mr Snoop.

'No, no,' said Mr Snoop, still shaking. 'Better not try to. We must hush it up if we can.'

And the general assent to this sentiment showed that, after all, the principles of Bahee, or Indifference to Others, had taken a real root in the society.

'Hush it up,' cried everybody, and there was a general move towards the hall.

'Good heavens!' exclaimed Mrs Buncomhearst; 'our wraps!'

'Deastralized!' said the guests.

There was a moment of further consternation as everybody gazed at the spot where the illfated pile of furs and wraps had lain.

'Never mind,' said everybody, 'let's go without them – don't stay. Just think if the police should ——'

And at the word police, all of a sudden there was heard in the street the clanging of a bell and the racing gallop of the horses of the police patrol waggon.

'The police!' cried everybody. 'Hush it up! Hush it up!'

For of course the principles of Bahee are not known to the police.

In another moment the door bell of the house rang with a long and violent peal, and in a second, as it seemed, the whole hall was filled with bulky figures uniformed in blue.

'It's all right, Mrs Rasselyer-Brown,' cried a loud, firm voice from the sidewalk. 'We have them both. Everything is here. We got them before they'd gone a block. But if you don't mind, the police must get a couple of names for witnesses in the warrant.'

It was the Philippine chauffeur. But he was no longer attired as such. He wore the uniform of an inspector of police, and there was the metal badge of the Detective Department now ostentatiously outside his coat.

And beside him, one on each side of him, there stood the deastralized forms of Yahi-Bahi and Ram Spudd. They wore long overcoats, doubtless the contents of the magic parcel, and the Philippine chauffeur had a grip of iron on the neck of each as they stood. Mr Spudd had lost his oriental hair, and the face of Mr Yahi-Bahi, perhaps in the struggle which had taken place, had been scraped white in patches.

They were making no attempt to break away. Indeed, Mr Spudd, with that complete Bahee, or Submission to Fate, which is attained only by long service in state penitentiaries, was smiling and smoking a cigarette.

'We were waiting for them,' explained a tall police officer to the two or three ladies who now gathered round him with a return of courage. 'They had the stuff in a handcart and were pushing it away. The chief caught them at the corner, and rang the patrol from there. You'll find everything all right, I think, ladies,' he added, as a burly assistant was seen carrying an armload of furs up the steps.

Somehow many of the ladies realized at that moment what cheery, safe, reliable people policemen in blue are, and what a friendly, familiar shelter they offer against the wiles of oriental occultism.

'Are they old criminals?' someone asked.

'Yes, ma'am. They've worked this same thing in four cities already, and both of them have done time, and lots of it. They've only been out six months. No need to worry over them,' he concluded with a shrug of the shoulders.

So the furs were restored and the gold and the jewels parcelled out among the owners, and in due course Mr Yahi-Bahi and Mr Ram Spudd were lifted up into the patrol waggon, where they seated themselves with a composure worthy of the best traditions of Jehumbabah and Bahoola-pore. In fact, Mr Spudd was heard to address the police as 'boys,' and to remark that they had 'got them good' that time.

So the séance ended and the guests vanished, and the Yahi-Bahi Society terminated itself without even a vote of dissolution.

And in all the later confidential discussions of the episode only one point of mysticism remained. After they had time really to reflect on it, free from all danger of arrest, the members of the society realized that on one point the police were entirely off the truth of things. For Mr Yahi-Bahi, whether a thief or not, and whether he came from the Orient, or, as the police said, from Missouri, had actually succeeded in reastralizing Buddha.

Nor was anyone more emphatic on this point than Mrs Rasselyer-Brown herself.

'For after all,' she said, 'if it was not Buddha, who was it?'

And the question was never answered.

Body and Soul

ALAN COREN

'The smile of Marabel Morgan is the smile of the Total Woman. In London to launch her book The Total Woman, *Mrs Morgan runs Total Woman Inc, a marriage enrichment course which she started in America. Thousands of women have now followed her advice. "Call your husband at the office to say: Hurry home, I crave your body," she suggests, adding that she often meets hers at the door freshly bubble-bathed and wearing only babydoll pyjamas and white boots, causing him to drop his briefcase and chase her round the table.'* – Evening Standard

IT HAD NOT BEEN THE best of mornings for Mr Dennis Belwether.

It rarely was.

In the dark ruin of his lower lumbar regions, a worn disc throbbed evilly, while in his left knee the shredded cartilage tweaked an agonizing descant; nor could he be entirely certain that an arch had not fallen inside a shoe that seemed uncharacteristically full of lumps.

At forty-seven, he reflected, there was a limit to the number of times a man could jump off a wardrobe with impunity. His furred tongue went to his upper plate for the hundredth probe that morning, stencilling the expensive crack: how could he tell his dentist that he had done it when, as he sprinted from the shower, the spike on his *Pickelhauber* had struck the bedroom lintel with a judder that had set his wife's bra-bells jangling fifteen feet away?

He took off his glasses, their ear-pieces still bent from incautious passion, and stared at the thick blue folder labelled Phillimore Holdings which had lain on his desk for three days now, awaiting his deliberations, while the fox-faced executives over at Phillimore paced the Wilton and snapped their pencils and shrieked down the telephone at his boss.

Who had been, Belwether said to himself, remarkably reasonable. Coming into Belwether's office the previous afternoon and finding his employee's wispy head flat on the Phillimore file, snoring, Mr Soames had merely shaken Belwether gently from a dream of flat-chested twinsets toasting crumpets and, as Belwether lifted his pale cheek with its serried dents of Phillimore ring-binding to the painful light, said:

'Why not tell me about it, old chap? Is it a woman?'

To which Belwether had merely blinked wretchedly, a blink being the gesture that occupies the neutral ground between nod and shake; for it *was* a woman, and then again, it wasn't.

But how could one explain that?

'You don't want to chuck away a quarter-century of exemplary double-entry on some bit of teenage stuff from the typing-pool, old chap,' continued Mr Soames, not unkindly. 'There'll be an eight-day chiming bracket clock waiting for you in 1995, you know. Would you jeopardize that for the fleeting joy of how's-your-father?'

He had, it seemed to Belwether, almost patted his shoulder before leaving. The thought filled him with gloomy guilt, again, as he remembered. Mr Soames had offered himself as confidant and priest, almost a friend, just short of a father, and he, Belwether, had merely blinked, rejecting the offered ear, leaving himself adrift and comfortless. All over the world, men were this very moment sitting down together at quiet tables in a thousand bars, to share anaesthetizing drinks and friendly bags of cheesy things while each told the other of his sexual peccadilloes and disillusionments, of the wives who hadn't been feeling well lately and the nymphets ravenous for an experienced touch.

But to whom could Belwether go, and with what? What friendship, indeed, even if he had the time to form one, could withstand such ridicule?

He opened the Phillimore file for the twentieth time, and fought to focus his tired eyes on the reeling columns. He reached for his calculator. He unscrewed his pens, one green, one red, one black. The telephone rang.

'It's your wife,' said his secretary, and flipped the switch.

'How many times have I told you,' hissed Belwether into the mouthpiece, 'never to ring me at the office?'

'I crave your body,' murmured Felicity Belwether.

'There's a meeting,' cried Belwether, 'at half-past....'

'Passion,' groaned Felicity Belwether, 'billows through me like waves rolling towards the beach, hungry to dash themselves against the rocks. I am lying here clad only in a peep-hole bra and waders, my Dennis!'

'You may not appreciate it, Felicity, but Mr Cattermole of Phillimore Holdings, one of the foremost....'

'I have put your long sideburns out ready, my darling,' breathed his wife, 'and your busby has just come back from the cleaners. It will be the matter of a moment for you to jump into your clogs.'

'Oh, God,' muttered Belwether. He put down the receiver. He closed the Phillimore folder. He put the top back on his pens.

The typing pool watched him slink out, limping alternately as he favoured disc and knee.

'Tell Mr Soames I have to see a client,' he murmured automatically, as the door sighed shut behind him.

'*His* age.' said a secretary, studding a cat's eye deftly into her leather bolero, 'bleeding obscene.'

On the Xerox machine, the girl running off eight hundred copies of a Starsky and Hutch poster paused briefly.

'He's probably off up the Jacey,' she said. 'They got *Chinese Emmanuelle in Chains* and *Suburban Tongue*. All he's fit for.'

'Seen his eyes?' inquired a telephonist, breaking off her conversation to her Melbourne boyfriend. 'Don't half stand out. All them little veins.'

'They go like that,' said the tea-girl, adroitly slipping a two-pound jar of Nescafé into her Fiorucci holdall. 'It's a side-effect. I seen about it in the *Sun*.'

'Serves him bleeding right,' said the secretary. '*His* age.'

On the drizzled street, Dennis Belwether waited for a Number Eleven. It being only noon, none came. He stared into the buslessness, feeling the rain go down under his collar and the wind go up his trousers. He was starting a cold, of that there was little doubt. It would turn bronchial, the way it invariably did, but who would distil the Friar's Balsam, who pour out the Medinite, who tuck him in and tiptoe about the premises, bearing succulent trays of this and that, silencing children? The last time he had had 'flu, Felicity, driven near-insensate by his presence in the daytime bed, had insisted upon hurling herself on him with merciless regularity, in a variety of foreign uniforms, an activity which, in his enfeebled state, he had been powerless to discourage.

Nor had he ever been able to explain to his two children why, on their return from school, their mother was to be found blacked up and with a feather in her ginger wig, running round the house dressed only in the battle blouse of an Israeli paratrooper.

It would be even worse this time, with his back trouble on top of everything else. She had already shown signs of inordinate interest in the possibility of home traction, and there had been many a lip-smacking suggestion tht such games as Nurse And Orthopaedic Patient might soon sneak into Felicity Belwether's illimitable repertoire.

As he stood there, chilled, with the drizzle hardening to sleet and the only refuge from it the voracious premises of 14, Acacia Crescent, old longings stirred within the ravaged frame of Dennis Belwether. They had been stirring more and more regularly in recent months, and he entertained them with less and less shame: he had only one life, he would argue, and had he not passed forty-seven years of it as a faithful husband, and was that not better than par for the course? Was he to go to the long pine box having known only one woman? Was he, too, not as entitled to the free expression of his romantic imagination as Felicity, and could he be blamed if he sought that expression elsewhere than at 14, Acacia Crescent?

Not for the first time, his fingers trembled over the scribbled page at the back of his pocket diary. A blob of sleet fell on it, but fortunately did not disturb the inky number dictated so long ago by Mr Brill of Small Accounts, who had once, in a unique unguarded moment, revealed to him that Mrs Brill had a habit of springing out of cupboards at him, dressed in nothing but angora mittens, which had precipitated Mr Brill's early retirement.

Dennis Belwether looked again at Brill's legacy.

There was a telephone booth across the road.

I will give the bus until I count to fifty, he said to himself.

It did not come. He crossed the road, dialled without thinking, pressed in his hot coin.

When he rang the bell, two flights up above a Greek Street massage parlour, the door was answered by a middle-aged woman in a beige cardigan, grey lisle stockings, worn felt slippers, heavy tweed skirt, and a hairnet.

'Miss Desiree La Biche?' he inquired nervously. 'I rang earlier. Dennis.'

She looked at him over her bifocals.

'I suppose you didn't remember to bring the sprouts?' she said.

'Sprouts?' he said.

'You'll forget your own head one of these days, Dennis,' she said. 'Come in, don't stand there dripping, I just done that step.'

He went inside. The little corridor smelt of boiled cabbage and Johnson's Pride; a black-and-white dog came up and licked his hand.

'We'll have to take him down and get him wormed,' said Desiree La Biche, 'one of these days. You're always promising.'

'There's never the time,' he replied automatically, following her into a small living-room and sitting down in front of the television set.

'Ten pounds,' said Desiree La Biche.

He sprang up, fumbled for the notes.

'Sorry,' he said, 'almost forgot, ha-ha-ha!'

She put the money on the mantelpiece, under the clock.

'Price of things these days,' she said, 'I was only saying to Mrs Thing this morning, Dennis and me are going to have to give up meat altogether, I said. I know what you mean, she said, I just paid a pound for twelve ounces of ox liver. What? I said, a *pound*, I said. Without a word of a lie, she said. What do you think of that, Dennis?'

'Er, remarkable,' replied Belwether, sitting down again.

'Remarkable, remarkable, that's all you ever say, just so long as you've got your television, personally I don't know what you see in it, lot of rubbish, sit there stuck in front of it, never take me out no more, I was only saying yesterday down the launderette to Mrs, oh, you know, big woman, funny ears, got a son Norman in the navy, no, I tell a lie, army, anyway, what I said was....'

As Desiree La Biche droned on, Dennis Belwether felt a delightful numbness seep into his tired limbs, felt the monotonous voice grow distant, felt the evening paper she had put in his lap slip to the floor. He eased his feet from his shoes; he unbuttoned his waistcoat; he let his head fall back against the antimacassar, and let his mind, for the precious half-hour it had been allotted, drift away into luxurious nothingness.

The Brief Engagement of Lupin Pooter

GEORGE & WEEDON GROSSMITH

Mr Charles Pooter and his wife Carrie live in a newly-acquired well-to-do residence in suburban Holloway with their only son Lupin. After the annual family summer holiday to Margate, Mr Pooter sets himself to tackling the problem of finding a suitable job for his son. But Lupin appears far from ready to 'settle down' and there is a series of disturbing shocks in store for poor Mr P., as he records in his meticulously-kept diary....

August 22.
Home, sweet Home again! Carrie bought some pretty blue-wool mats to stand vases on. Fripps, Janus and Co. write to say they are sorry they have no vacancy among their staff of clerks for Lupin.

August 23.
I bought a pair of stags' heads made of plaster-of-Paris and coloured brown. They will look just the thing for our little hall, and give it style; the heads are excellent imitations. Poolers and Smith are sorry they have nothing to offer Lupin.

August 24.
Simply to please Lupin, and make things cheerful for him, as he is a little down, Carrie invited Mrs James to come up from Sutton and spend two or three days with us. We have not said a word to Lupin, but mean to keep it as a surprise.

August 25.
Mrs James of Sutton, arrived in the afternoon, bringing with her an enormous bunch of wild flowers. The more I see of Mrs James the nicer I think she is, and she is devoted to Carrie. She went into Carrie's room to take off her bonnet, and remained there nearly an hour talking about dress. Lupin said he was not a bit surprised at Mrs James's *visit*, but was surprised at *her*.

August 26, Sunday.
Nearly late for church, Mrs James having talked considerably about

what to wear all the morning. Lupin does not seem to get on very well with Mrs James. I am afraid we shall have some trouble with our next-door neighbours who came in last Wednesday. Several of their friends, who drive up in dog-carts, have already made themselves objectionable.

An evening or two ago I had put on a white waistcoat for coolness, and while walking past with my thumbs in my waistcoat pockets (a habit I have), one man, seated in the cart, and looking like an American, commenced singing some vulgar nonsense about '*I had thirteen dollars in my waistcoat pocket.*' I fancied it was meant for me, and my suspicions were confirmed; for while walking round the garden in my tall hat this afternoon a 'throw-down' cracker was deliberately aimed at my hat, and exploded on it like a percussion cap. I turned sharply, and am positive I saw the man who was in the cart retreating from one of the bedroom windows.

August 27.
Carrie and Mrs James went off shopping, and had not returned when I came back from the office. Judging from the subsequent conversation, I am afraid Mrs James is filling Carrie's head with a lot of nonsense about dress. I walked over to Gowing's and asked him to drop in to supper, and make things pleasant.

Carrie prepared a little extemporized supper, consisting of the remainder of the cold joint, a small piece of salmon (which I was to refuse, in case there was not enough to go round), and a blancmange and custards. There was also a decanter of port and some jam puffs on the sideboard. Mrs James made us play rather a good game of cards, called 'Muggins,' To my surprise, in fact disgust, Lupin got up in the middle, and, in a most sarcastic tone, said: 'Pardon me, this sort of thing is too fast for me. I shall go and enjoy a quiet game of marbles in the back garden.'

Things might have become rather disagreeable but for Gowing (who seems to have taken to Lupin) suggesting they should invent games. Lupin said: 'Let's play "monkeys."' He then led Gowing all round the room, and brought him in front of the looking-glass. I must confess I laughed heartily at this. I was a little vexed at everybody subsequently laughing at some joke which they did not explain, and it was only on going to bed I discovered I must have been walking about all the evening with an antimacassar on one button of my coat-tails.

August 28.
Found a large brick in the middle bed of geraniums, evidently come from next door. Pattles and Pattles can't find a place for Lupin.

August 29.
Mrs James is making a positive fool of Carrie. Carrie appeared in a new

dress like a smock-frock. She said 'smocking' was all the rage. I replied it put me in a rage. She also had on a hat as big as a kitchen coal-scuttle, and the same shape. Mrs James went home, and both Lupin and I were somewhat pleased – the first time we have agreed on a single subject since his return. Merkins and Son write they have no vacancy for Lupin.

October 30.

I should very much like to know who has wilfully torn the last five or six weeks out of my diary. It is perfectly monstrous! Mine is a large scribbling diary, with plenty of space for the record of my everyday events, and in keeping up that record I take (with much pride) a great deal of pains.

I asked Carrie if she knew anything about it. She replied it was my own fault for leaving the diary about with a charwoman cleaning and the sweeps in the house. I said that was not an answer to my question. This retort of mine, which I thought extremely smart, would have been more effective had I not jogged my elbow against a vase on a table temporarily placed in the passage, knocked it over, and smashed it.

Carrie was dreadfully upset at this disaster, for it was one of a pair of vases which cannot be matched, given to us on our wedding-day by Mrs Burtsett, an old friend of Carrie's cousins, the Pommertons, late of Dalston. I called to Sarah, and asked her about the diary. She said she had not been in the sitting-room at all; after the sweep had left, Mrs Birrell (the charwoman) had cleaned the room and lighted the fire herself. Finding a burnt piece of paper in the grate, I examined it, and found it was a piece of my diary. So it was evident someone had torn my diary to light the fire. I requested Mrs Birrell to be sent to me tomorrow.

October 31.

Received a letter from our principal, Mr Perkupp, saying that he thinks he knows of a place at last for our dear boy Lupin. This, in a measure, consoles me for the loss of a portion of my diary; for I am bound to confess the last few weeks have been devoted to the record of disappointing answers received from people to whom I have applied for appointments for Lupin. Mrs Birrell called, and, in reply to me, said: 'She never *see* no book, much less take such a liberty as *touch* it.'

I said I was determined to find out who did it, whereupon she said she would do her best to help me; but she remembered the sweep lighting the fire with a bit of the *Echo*. I requested the sweep to be sent to me tomorrow. I wish Carrie had not given Lupin a latchkey; we never seem to see anything of him. I sat up till past one for him, and then retired tired.

November 1.

My entry yesterday about 'retired tired,' which I did not notice at the time, is rather funny. If I were not so worred just now, I might have had a little joke about it. The sweep called, but had the audacity to come up to the hall-door and lean his dirty bag of soot on the doorstep. He, however, was so polite, I could not rebuke him. He said Sarah lighted the fire. Unfortunately, Sarah heard this, for she was dusting the banisters, and she ran down, and flew into a temper with the sweep, causing a row on the front doorsteps, which I would not have had happen for anything. I ordered her about her business, and told the sweep I was sorry to have troubled him; and so I was, for the doorsteps were covered with soot in consequence of his visit. I would willingly give ten shillings to find out who tore my diary.

November 2.

I spent the evening quietly with Carrie, of whose company I never tire. We had a most pleasant chat about the letters on 'Is Marriage a Failure?' It has been no failure in our case. In talking over our own happy experiences, we never noticed that it was past midnight. We were startled by hearing the door slam violently. Lupin had come in. He made no attempt to turn down the gas in the passage, or even to look into the room where we were, but went straight up to bed, making a terrible noise. I asked him to come down for a moment, and he begged to be excused, as he was 'dead beat,' an observation that was scarcely consistent with the fact that, for a quarter of an hour afterwards, he was positively dancing in his room, and shouting out, 'See me dance the polka!' or some such nonsense.

November 3.

Good news at last. Mr Perkupp has got an appointment for Lupin, and he is to go and see about it on Monday. Oh, how my mind is relieved! I went to Lupin's room to take the good news to him, but he was in bed, very seedy, so I resolved to keep it over till the evening.

He said he had last night been elected a member of an Amateur Dramatic Club, called the 'Holloway Comedians'; and, though it was a pleasant evening, he had sat in a draught, and got neuralgia in the head. He declined to have any breakfast, so I left him.

In the evening I had up a special bottle of port, and, Lupin being in for a wonder, we filled our glasses, and I said: 'Lupin my boy, I have some good and unexpected news for you. Mr Perkupp has procured you an appointment!' Lupin said: 'Good biz!' and we drained our glasses.

Lupin then said: 'Fill up the glasses again, for I have some good and unexpected news for you.'

I had some slight misgivings, and so evidently had Carrie, for she said:

'I hope we shall think it good news.'

Lupin said: 'Oh, it's all right! *I'm engaged to be married!*'

November 5, Sunday

Carrie and I troubled about that mere boy Lupin getting engaged to be married without consulting us or anything. After dinner he told us all about it. He said the lady's name was Daisy Mutlar, and she was the nicest, prettiest, and most accomplished girl he ever met. He loved her the moment he saw her, and if he had to wait fifty years he would wait, and he knew she would wait for him.

Lupin further said, with much warmth, that the world was a different world to him now, – it was a world worth living in. He lived with an object now, and that was to make Daisy Mutlar – Daisy Pooter, and he would guarantee she would not disgrace the family of the Pooters. Carrie here burst out crying, and threw her arms round his neck, and in doing so upset the glass of port he held in his hand all over his new light trousers.

I said I had no doubt we should like Miss Mutlar when we saw her, but Carrie said she loved her already. I thought this rather premature, but held my tongue. Daisy Mutlar was the sole topic of conversation for the remainder of the day. I asked Lupin who her people were, and he replied: 'Oh, you know Mutlar, Williams and Watts.' I did not know, but refrained from asking any further questions at present, for fear of irritating Lupin.

November 6.

Lupin went with me to the office, and had a long conversation with Mr Perkupp, our principal, the result of which was that he accepted a clerkship in the firm of Job Cleanands and Co., Stock and Share Brokers. Lupin told me, privately, it was an advertising firm, and he did not think much of it. I replied: 'Beggars should not be choosers;' and I will do Lupin the justice to say, he looked rather ashamed of himself.

In the evening we went round to the Cummings', to have a few fireworks. It began to rain, and I thought it rather dull. One of my squibs would not go off, and Gowing said: 'Hit it on your boot, boy; it will go off then.' I gave it a few knocks on the end of my boot, and it went off with one loud explosion, and burnt my fingers rather badly. I gave the rest of the squibs to the little Cummings' boy to let off.

Another unfortunate thing happened, which brought a heap of abuse on my head. Cummings fastened a large wheel set-piece on a stake in the ground by way of a grand finale. He made a great fuss about it; said it cost seven shillings. There was a little difficulty in getting it alight. At last it went off; but after a couple of slow revolutions it stopped. I had my stick with me, so I gave it a tap to send it round, and, unfortunately, it fell off the stake on to the grass. Anybody would have thought I had set the house on fire from the way in which they stormed at me. I will never join in any more firework parties. It is a ridiculous waste of time and money.

November 7.
Lupin asked Carrie to call on Mrs Mutlar, but Carrie said she thought Mrs Mutlar ought to call on her first. I agreed with Carrie, and this led to an argument. However, the matter was settled by Carrie saying she could not find any visiting cards, and we must get some more printed, and when they were finished would be quite time enough to discuss the etiquette of calling.

November 8.
I ordered some of our cards at Black's, the stationer's. I ordered twenty-five of each, which will last us for a good long time. In the evening, Lupin brought in Frank Mutlar, Miss Mutlar's brother. He was rather a gawky youth, and Lupin said he was the most popular and best amateur in the club, referring to the 'Holloway Comedians.' Lupin whispered to us that if we could only 'draw out' Frank a bit, he would make us roar with laughter.

At supper, young Mutlar did several amusing things. He took up a knife, and with the flat part of it played a tune on his cheek in a wonderful manner. He also gave an imitation of an old man with no teeth, smoking a big cigar. The way he kept dropping the cigar sent Carrie into fits.

In the course of conversation, Daisy's name cropped up, and young Mutlar said he would bring his sister round to us one evening – his parents being rather old-fashioned, and not going out much. Carrie said we would get up a little special party. As young Mutlar showed no inclination to go, and it was approaching eleven o'clock, as a hint I reminded Lupin that he had to be up early tomorrow. Instead of taking the hint, Mutlar began a series of comic imitations. He went on for an hour without cessation. Poor Carrie could scarcely keep her eyes open. At last she made an excuse, and said 'Goodnight.'

Mutlar then left, and I heard him and Lupin whispering in the hall something about the 'Holloway Comedians,' and to my disgust, although it was past midnight, Lupin put on his hat and coat, and went out with his new companion.

November 9.
My endeavours to discover who tore the sheets out of my diary still fruitless. Lupin has Daisy Mutlar on the brain, so we see little of him, except that he invariably turns up at meal times. Cummings dropped in.

November 10.
Lupin seems to like his new berth – that's a comfort. Daisy Mutlar the sole topic of conversation during tea. Carrie almost as full of it as Lupin. Lupin informs me, to my disgust, that he has been persuaded to take part in the forthcoming performance of the 'Holloway Comedians.' He says he is to play Bob Britches in the farce, *Gone to my Uncle's*; Frank Mutlar is going to play old Musty. I told Lupin pretty plainly I was not in the least degree interested in the matter, and totally disapproved of amateur theatricals. Gowing came in the evening.

November 11.
Returned home to find the house in a most disgraceful uproar. Carrie, who appeared very frightened, was standing outside her bedroom while Sarah was excited and crying. Mrs Birrell (the charwoman), who had evidently been drinking, was shouting at the top of her voice that she was 'no thief, that she was a respectable woman, who had to work hard for her living, and she would smack anyone's face who put lies into her mouth.' Lupin, whose back was towards me, did not hear me come in. He was standing between the two women, and, I regret to say, in his endeavour to act as peacemaker, he made use of rather strong language in the presence of his mother; and I was just in time to hear him say: 'And all this fuss about the loss of a few pages from a rotten diary that wouldn't fetch three-halfpence a pound!' I said, quietly: 'Pardon me, Lupin, that is a matter of opinion; and as I am master of this house, perhaps you will allow me to take the reins.'

I ascertained that the cause of the row was, that Sarah had accused Mrs Birrell of tearing the pages out of my diary to wrap up some kitchen fat and leavings which she had taken out of the house last week. Mrs Birrell had slapped Sarah's face, and said she had taken nothing out of the place, as there was 'never no leavings to take.' I ordered Sarah back to her work, and requested Mrs Birrell to go home. When I entered the parlour Lupin was kicking his legs in the air, and roaring with laughter.

November 12, Sunday.
Coming home from church Carrie and I met Lupin, Daisy Mutlar, and her brother. Daisy was introduced to us, and we walked home together, Carrie walking on with Miss Mutlar. We asked them in for a few minutes, and I had a good look at my future daughter-in-law. My heart quite sank. She is a big young woman, and I should think at least eight years older than Lupin. I did not even think her good-looking. Carrie asked her if she could come in on Wednesday next with her brother to meet a few friends. She replied that she would only be too pleased.

November 13.

Carrie sent out invitations to Gowing, the Cummings, to Mr and Mrs James (of Sutton), and Mr Stillbrook. I wrote a note to Mr Franching, of Peckham. Carrie said we may as well make it a nice affair, and why not ask our principal, Mr Perkupp? I said I feared we were not quite grand enough for him. Carrie said there was 'no offence in asking him.' I said: 'Certainly not,' and I wrote him a letter. Carrie confessed she was a little disappointed with Daisy Mutlar's appearance, but thought she seemed a nice girl.

November 14.

Everybody so far has accepted for our quite grand little party for tomorrow. Mr Perkupp, in a nice letter which I shall keep, wrote that he was dining in Kensington, but if he could get away, he would come up to Holloway for an hour. Carrie was busy all day, making little cakes and open jam puffs and jellies. She said she felt quite nervous about her responsibilities tomorrow evening. We decided to have some light things on the table, such as sandwiches, cold chicken and ham, and some sweets, and on the sideboard a nice piece of cold beef and a Paysandu tongue for the more hungry ones to peg into if they liked.

Gowing called to know if he was to put on 'swallow-tails' tomorrow. Carrie said he had better dress, especially as Mr Franching was coming, and there was a possibility of Mr Perkupp also putting in an appearance.

Gowing said: 'Oh, I only wanted to know; for I have not worn my dress-coat for some time, and I must send it to have the creases pressed out.'

After Gowing left, Lupin came in, and in his anxiety to please Daisy Mutlar, carped at and critized the arrangements, and, in fact, disapproved of everything, including our having asked our old friend Cummings, who, he said, would look in evening-dress like a greengrocer engaged to wait, and who must not be surprised if Daisy took him for one.

I fairly lost my temper, and said: 'Lupin, allow me to tell you Miss Daisy Mutlar is not the Queen of England. I gave you credit for more wisdom than to allow yourself to be inveigled into an engagement with a woman considerably older than yourself. I advise you to think of carning your living before entangling yourself with a wife whom you will have to support, and, in all probability, her brother also, who appeared to be nothing but a loafer.'

Instead of receiving this advice in a sensible manner, Lupin jumped up and said: 'If you insult the lady I am engaged to, you insult me. I will leave the house and never darken your doors again.'

He went out of the house, slamming the hall-door. But it was all right. He came back to supper, and we played Bézique till nearly twelve o'clock.

November 15.

A red-letter day. Our first important party since we have been in this house. I got home early from the City. Lupin insisted on having a hired waiter, and stood a half-dozen of champagne. I think this an unnecessary expense, but Lupin said he had had a piece of luck, having made three pounds out of a private deal in the City. I hope he won't gamble in his new situation. The supper-room looked so nice, and Carrie truly said: 'We need not be ashamed of its being seen by Mr Perkupp, should he honour us by coming.'

I dressed early in case people should arrive punctually at eight o'clock, and was much vexed to find my new dress-trousers much too short. Lupin, who is getting beyond his position, found fault with my wearing ordinary boots instead of dress-boots.

I replied satirically: 'My dear son, I have lived to be above that sort of thing.'

Lupin burst out laughing, and said: 'A man generally was above his boots.'

This may be funny, or it may *not*; but I was gratified to find he had not discovered the coral had come off one of my studs. Carrie looked a picture, wearing the dress she wore at the Mansion House. The arrangement of the drawing-room was excellent. Carrie had hung muslin curtains over the folding-doors, and also over one of the entrances, for we had removed the door from its hinges.

Mr Peters, the waiter, arrived in good time, and I gave him strict orders not to open another bottle of champagne until the previous one was empty. Carrie arranged for some sherry and port wine to be placed on the drawing-room sideboard, with some glasses. By-the-by, our new enlarged and tinted photographs look very nice on the walls, especially as Carrie had arranged some Liberty silk bows on the four corners of them.

The first arrival was Gowing, who, with his usual taste, greeted me with: 'Hulloh, Pooter, why your trousers are too short!'

I simply said: 'Very likely, and you will find my temper "*short*" also.'

He said: 'That won't make your trousers longer, Juggins. You should get your missus to put a flounce on them.'

I wonder I waste my time entering his insulting observations in my diary.

The next arrivals were Mr and Mrs Cummings. The former said: 'As you didn't say anything about dress, I have come "half-dress."' He had on a black frockcoat and white tie. The James', Mr Merton, and Mr Stillbrook arrived, but Lupin was restless and unbearable till his Daisy Mutlar and Frank arrived.

Carrie and I were rather startled at Daisy's appearance. She had a bright crimson dress on, cut very low in the neck. I do not think such a style modest. She ought to have taken a lesson from Carrie, and covered her shoulders with a little lace. Mr Nackles, Mr Sprice-Hogg and his four daughters came; so did Franching, and one or two of Lupin's new friends, members of the 'Holloway Comedians.' Some of these seemed rather theatrical in their manner, especially one, who was posing all the evening, and leant on our little round table and cracked it. Lupin called him 'our Henry,' and said he was 'our lead at the HC's and was quite as good in that department as Frank Mutlar was as the low-comedy merchant. All this is Greek to me.

We had some music, and Lupin, who never left Daisy's side for a moment, raved over her singing of a song, called 'Some Day.' It seemed a pretty song, but she made such grimaces, and sang, to my mind, so out of tune, I would not have asked her to sing again; but Lupin made her sing four songs right off, one after the other.

At ten o'clock we went down to supper, and from the way Gowing and Commings ate you would have thought they had not had a meal for a month. I told Carrie to keep something back in case Mr Perkupp should come by mere chance. Gowing annoyed me very much by filling a large tumbler of champagne, and drinking it straight off. He repeated this action, and made me fear our half-dozen of champagne would not last out. I tried to keep a bottle back, but Lupin got hold of it, and took it to the side-table with Daisy and Frank Mutlar.

We went upstairs, and the young fellows began skylarking. Carrie put a stop to that at once. Stillbrook amused us with a song, 'What have you done with your Cousin John?' I did not notice that Lupin and Frank had disappeared. I asked Mr Watson, one of the Holloways, where they were, and he said: 'It's a case of "Oh, what a surprise!"'

We were directed to form a circle – which we did. Watson then said: 'I have much pleasure in introducing the celebrated Blondin Donkey.' Frank and Lupin then bounded into the room. Lupin had whitened his face like a clown, and Frank had tied round his waist a large hearthrug. He was supposed to be the donkey, and he looked it. They indulged in a very noisy pantomime, and we were all shrieking with laughter.

I turned round suddenly, and then I saw Mr Perkupp standing halfway in the door, he having arrived without our knowing it. I beckoned to Carrie, and we went up to him at once. He would not come right into the room. I apologized for the foolery, but Mr Perkupp said: 'Oh, it seems amusing.' I could see he was not a bit amused.

Carrie and I took him downstairs, but the table was a wreck. There was not a glass of champagne left – not even a sandwich. Mr Perkupp said he required nothing, but would like a glass of seltzer or soda water. The last syphon was empty. Carrie said: 'We have plenty of port wine left.' Mr Perkupp said with a smile: 'No, thank you. I really require nothing, but I am most pleased to see you and your husband in your own home. Goodnight, Mrs Pooter – you will excuse my very short stay, I know.' I went with him to his carriage, and he said: 'Don't trouble to come to the office till twelve tomorrow.'

I felt despondent as I went back to the house, and I told Carrie I thought the party was a failure. Carrie said it was a great success, and I was only tired, and insisted on my having some port myself I drank two glasses, and felt much better, and we went into the drawing-room, where they had commenced dancing. Carrie and I had a little dance, which I said reminded me of old days. She said I was a spooney old thing.

November 16.

Woke about twenty times during the night, with terrible thirst. Finished off all the water in the bottle, as well as half that in the jug. Kept dreaming also, that last night's party was a failure, and that a lot of low people came without invitation, and kept chaffing and throwing things at Mr Perkupp till at last I was obliged to hide him in the box-room (which we had just discovered), with a bath-towel over him. It seems absurd now, but it was painfully real in the dream. I had the same dream about a dozen times.

Carrie annoyed me by saying: 'You know champagne never agrees with you.' I told her I had only a couple of glasses of it, having kept myself entirely to port. I added that good champagne hurt nobody, and Lupin told me he had only got it from a traveller as a favour, as that particular brand had been entirely bought up by a West-End club.

I think I ate too heartily of the 'side dishes,' as the waiter called them. I said to Carrie: 'I wish I had put those "side dishes" *aside.*' I repeated this, but Carrie was busy, packing up the teaspoons we had borrowed of Mrs Cummings for the party. It was just half-past eleven, and I was starting for the office, when Lupin appeared, with a yellow complexion, and said: "Hulloh! Guv, what priced head have you this morning?" I told him he might just as well speak to me in Dutch. He added: 'When I woke this morning, my head was as big as Baldwin's balloon.' On the spur of the moment I said the cleverest thing I think I have ever said; viz.: 'Perhaps that accounts for the para*shooting* pains.' We all three roared.

November 17.

Still feel tired and headachy! In the evening Gowing called, and was full of praise about our party last Wednesday. He said everything was done beautifully, and he enjoyed himself enormously. Gowing can be a very nice fellow when he likes, but you never know how long it will last. For instance, he stopped to supper, and seeing some *blancmange* on the table, shouted out, while the servant was in the room: 'Hulloh! The remains of Wednesday?'

November 18.

Woke up quite fresh after a good night's rest, and feel quite myself again. I am satisfied a life of going-out and Society is not a life for me; we therefore declined the invitation which we received this morning to Miss Bird's wedding. We only met her twice at Mrs James', and it means a present. Lupin said: 'I am with you for once. To my mind a wedding's a very poor play. There are only two parts in it – the bride and bridegroom. The best man is only a walking gentleman. With the exception of a crying father and a snivelling mother, the rest are *supers* who have to dress well and have to *pay* for their insignificant parts in the shape of costly presents.' I did not care for the theatrical slang, but thought it clever, though disrespectful.

I told Sarah not to bring up the *blancmange* again for breakfast. It seems to have been placed on our table at every meal since Wednesday. Cummings came round in the evening, and congratulated us on the success of our party. He said it was the best party he had been to for many a year; but he wished we had let him know it was full dress, as he would have turned up in his swallow-tails. We sat down to a quiet game of dominoes, and were interrupted by the noisy entrance of Lupin and Frank Mutlar. Cummings and I asked them to join us. Lupin said he did not care for dominoes, and suggested a game of 'Spoof.' On my asking if it required counters, Frank and Lupin in measured time said: 'One, two, three; go! Have you an estate in Greenland?' It was simply Greek to me, but it appears it is one of the customs of the 'Holloway Comedians' to do this when a member displays ignorance.

In spite of my instructions, that *blancmange* was brought up again for supper. To make matters worse, there had been an attempt to disguise it, by placing it in a glass dish with jam round it. Carrie asked Lupin if he would have some, and he replied: 'No second-hand goods for me, thank you.' I told Carrie, when we were alone, if that *blancmange* were placed on the table again I should walk out of the house.

November 19, Sunday.

A delightful quiet day. In the afternoon Lupin was off to spend the rest of the day with the Mutlars. He departed in the best of spirits, and Carrie said: 'Well, one advantage of Lupin's engagement with Daisy is that the boy seems happy all day long. That quite reconciles me to what I must confess seems an imprudent engagement.'

Carrie and I talked the matter over during the evening, and agreed that it did not always follow that an early engagement meant an unhappy marriage. Dear Carrie reminded me that we married early, and with the exception of a few trivial misunderstandings, we had never had a really serious word. I could not help thinking (as I told her) that half the pleasures of life were derived from the little struggles and small privations that one had to endure at the beginning of one's married life. Such struggles were generally occasioned by want of means, and often helped to make loving couples stand together all the firmer.

Carrie said I had expressed myself wonderfully well, and that I was quite a philosopher.

We are all vain at times, and I must confess I felt flattered by Carrie's little compliment. I don't pretend to be able to express myself in fine language, but I feel I have the power of expressing my thoughts with simplicity and lucidness. About nine o'clock, to our surprise, Lupin entered, with a wild, reckless look, and in a hollow voice, which I must say seemed rather theatrical, said: 'Have you any brandy?' I said: 'No; but here is some whisky.' Lupin drank off nearly a wine-glassful without water, to my horror.

We all three sat reading in silence till ten, when Carrie and I rose to go to bed. Carrie said to Lupin: 'I hope Daisy is well?'

Lupin, with a forced careless air that he must have picked up from the 'Holloway Comedians,' replied: 'Oh, Daisy? You mean Miss Mutlar. I don't know whether she is well or not, but please *never to mention her name again in my presence.*'

'Absolutely Ghastly'

H.E. BATES

The Larkins – Pop, Ma and their six children – have lured Mr Charlton, a young tax inspector, away from his official duties, welcoming him into the ample bosom of their family. One day Pop offers the use of his paddock to 'do-gooding' spinster, Miss Pilchester, for the charity gymkhana. Overwhelmed by his generosity (and delighted by his flirtatiousness), she accepts, little suspecting the chaos into which this will lead her....

ON THE DAY OF THE PONY gymkhana Mr Charlton was up at half past four. The morning was humid, dreamy, and overcast with low mist on the river. Pop, who had already been up an hour, giving swill to pigs and fodder to the Jersey cow, and was now staunching back the first pangs of hunger with a few slices of bread and Cheddar cheese doused half an inch thick with tomato-ketchup, said he thought 'the wevver looked a little bit thick in the clear' but otherwise, with luck, it ought to be all right by noon.

Mr Charlton breakfasted on two lean pork cutlets, some scrambled eggs cooked by Mariette, fried potatoes, and four halves of tomato.

'In the old days,' said Pop, whose estimation of Mr Charlton rose almost every time he talked to him, especially on occasions like coming down to breakfast at a good time and getting outside a reasonable amount of food, 'my Dad used to tell me that they always had beer for breakfast. Like a glass o' beer?'

Mr Charlton thanked him and said he didn't think he would. Mariette had just made tea.

'Well, I think I will,' Pop said. 'I don't think a lot o' tea is all that good for you.'

Pop, after pouring himself a Dragon's Blood, had much the same breakfast as Mr Charlton, except that there was a lot more of it and that his plate was gay with mustard, ketchup, and two kinds of Worcester sauce. Mariette, who looked pretty and fresh in dark green slacks and a pale yellow shirt blouse, said she was so excited she could hardly eat but nevertheless managed two eggs and bacon, a pint of milk, and four slices of bread.

Ma was not down yet but had sent word that as the day was going to be a long one she was having a lay-in, which meant she would be down by half past six.

Towards the end of breakfast Pop turned to Mr Charlton, who had not been able to keep his eyes off Mariette for more than two seconds since she had come into the kitchen tying up her hair with a thin emerald ribbon, and said:

'Are you two going to feed and water the donkeys? I've got forty thousand jobs to do and Miss Pilchester'll be here by six.'

Mr Charlton said of course they would feed the donkeys and helped himself to a fifth slice of bread and covered it half an inch thick with fresh Jersey butter made by Ma. Pop watched this process with immense admiration, telling himself he had never seen such a change in a man's health as he had witnessed in three weeks in Mr Charlton.

Mr Charlton was still on sick leave.

'Oh! those sweet donkeys,' Mariette said.

The donkeys that she and Mr Charlton were going to feed were not the rest of the Larkin household but four animals Pop had secured for racing. Pop thought that gymkhanas were sometimes inclined to be on the dull side, what he called 'a bit horseface like – so many folks with long faces you can't very often tell the mares from some of the old women' – and that therefore something was needed to enliven the customary round of trotting, riding, leading rein, jumping, bending, and walk, trot, canter, and run.

This was why he had thought of the donkeys and why, later on in the day, he thought of introducing a few private harmless jokes of his own. What these were he was keeping to himself; but he had not forgotten the one about putting a firework under Miss Pilchester.

To his grievous disappointment the committee had turned down his offer of fireworks. It might well be, they had pointed out, that a few ponies would be late leaving the ground and that some fireworks would in any case go off early and the ponies be distressed. Pop saw the reason in this but if there was going to be one firework and only one it was, he was determined, going to be Miss Pilchester's.

'What time is the cocktail party, Pop?' Mr Charlton said.

Pop was delighted that Mr Charlton now called him Pop.

'Ma thinks eight o'clock would be the perfick time.'

'What a day,' Mariette said. 'All this and cocktails too.'

She went on to confess that she had never been to a cocktail party and Pop said:

'Come to that neither have I. Neither has Ma.'

'What do people normally drink at cocktail parties?' Mariette said.

'Cocktails,' Mr Charlton said slyly and before he could move she gave him a swift playful cuff, exactly like that of a dark soft kitten, across the head.

'Not at this one you don't,' Pop said.

Both Mariette and Mr Charlton were too excited to remember that the whole question of what was drunk at cocktail parties had been discussed a week before.

Since Pop had been unable to indulge himself with fireworks he and Ma had decided that there must, if possible, be something in their place. A cocktail party, Pop said, would be the perfick answer. Ma agreed, but said they ought to keep it very select if possible. Not more than thirty people, she thought at the outside: mostly the committee and their families and of course nice people like the Miss Barnwells and the Luffingtons and the Brigadier. And what about eats?

Neither Pop nor Ma had any idea what you ate at cocktail parties; therefore Mr Charlton was consulted.

'Canapés, vol-au-vents, pistachios, and that sort of thing,' Mr Charlton said.

A lot more marks for Mr Charlton, Pop thought, as once again he heard words he had never even heard on television.

'You mean nuts and things?' Ma said. 'They won't keep anybody alive very long. I'd better cook a ham.'

Pop warmly agreed; the ham was firmly decided upon. Ma could cut plenty of the thinnest white and brown sandwiches, with nice Jersey butter. And what else?

Mariette said she thought small pieces of cold sardine on toast would be nice. 'They're absolutely marvellous hot too,' Mr Charlton said and got himself still more marks by also suggesting small squares of toast with hot Welsh rarebit, chicken sandwiches, and little sausages on sticks.

Most of this, to Pop, seemed rather light, unsatisfying fare.

'We want to give 'em enough,' he said. 'We don't want 'em to think we're starving 'em. What about a leg o' pork?'

To his disappointment Mr Charlton said he rather ruled out the leg of pork.

'All right,' Pop said. 'What about drinks?'

Pop was all for making plenty of Rolls-Royces and that sort of thing, good, strong ones, together with two new ones he had recently tried out from *The Guide to Better Drinking*: Red Bull and Ma Chérie. Red Bull was a blinder. That would curl their hair.

Mr Charlton said he thought it made it so much simpler if you stuck to two, or at the outside, three good drinks: say sherry, port, and gin-and-french. He suggested the port in case the evening was cool.

He got no marks this time. Pop thought it was all about as dull as flippin' ditchwater. With sudden enthusiasm he said:

'What about champagne?'

Both Ma and Mariette said they adored champagne. That was a brilliant idea. Something extra nice always happened, Mariette said, when you had champagne, and it seemed to Pop that he saw her exchange with Mr Charlton an intimate glance of secret tenderness that left him baffled and unsatisfied. Couldn't be nothing in the wind?

'Well, champagne it is then!' Pop said. 'Might as well do the thing properly.'

Here Mr Charlton remarked with tact that since not everybody liked champagne it might be just as well to have some other drink in reserve.

'I'll make a few hair-curlers,' Pop said. 'Red Bull – remember that one? – and Ma Chérie.'

Mr Charlton remembered Red Bull. It had rammed him one evening after a hardish day in the strawberry field. It was not inaptly named.

It was half past five before Mr Charlton and Mariette got up at last from breakfast and went across the yard to feed the donkeys. The four little donkeys had been tied up in the stable that Pop had built with his eye on the day when all the family, with the possible exception of Ma, would have a pony or a horse to ride. That would be the day. Two donkeys had been hired by Pop; two had been brought over by their owners the previous night. Three more, it was hoped, were still to come.

As soon as Mariette and himself were in the half-dark stable, among the donkeys, Mr Charlton took her quickly in his arms and kissed her. His arms and hands, as they tenderly touched her face, breasts, and shoulders, were as brown as her own.

Mariette laughed, trembling, and said she'd hardly been able to wait for that one, the first, the loveliest of the day. Mr Charlton, with something like ecstasy, said he hadn't been able to wait either. He could hardly wait for anything. Above all he could hardly wait for the afternoon. 'Nor me,' Mariette said and held her body out to him again.

Quietly, as the second kiss went on, the donkeys stirred about the stable, swishing tails, restless. Hearing them, Mariette partly broke away from Mr Charlton and said with half-laughing mouth:

'I suppose there's a first time for everything. I've never been kissed among donkeys before.'

Quick as a swallow himself, Mr Charlton answered. It was the answer of a man sharpened by three weeks in the strawberry field, living with the Larkins, and using his loaf.

'Wait till the cocktail party,' he said.

It was almost half past ten before Miss Pilchester fell bodily out of the taxi she had hired in desperation, four hours late, to bring her to the meadow. Pop, who was helping the Brigadier to string up gay lines of square and triangular flags about and among the tents, stared in stupefaction at a figure that might have been that of a tired and collapsing mountaineer descending from a peak. Miss Pilchester was armed with shooting stick, rolled mackintosh, a leather holdall containing a spare cardigan, her lunch and a red vacuum flask, an attaché case containing the judging lists, *The Times*, several books, and a basket of pot-eggs. The pot-eggs, evidently brought for use in some pony event or other, rolled about the squatting Miss Pilchester exactly as if, in a sudden over-spasm of broodiness, she had laid them all herself.

It was all absolutely ghastly, but both Pop and the Brigadier were too stupefied to go over and pick up either Miss Pilchester or the eggs; and Pop, for once, was utterly without words. It was the Brigadier who spoke for him.

'Good God, Larkin,' he said, 'Edith must be either tight or egg-bound.'

Five minutes later Miss Pilchester, the great organizer, was at her work. This was all done, as the Brigadier himself pointed out, at a half canter. With indecisive excitement Miss Pilchester rushed from tent to tent, inquiring if someone had seen this, somebody that, had the caterers arrived, and above all wasn't it ghastly?

The caterers had been on the field since seven o'clock; all of them had knocked off for tea. Where, then, was the loudspeaker for announcements? Hadn't that arrived? It had arrived and Miss Pilchester tripped over two lines of its wires. Cancelled entries – were there any cancelled entries? – all entries, she wailed, should have been cancelled by nine o'clock.

It was now, the Brigadier was heard to point out dryly, half past ten.

Where then, Miss Pilchester wanted to know, were the donkeys? Were the donkeys here?

'Some donkeys', the Brigadier was heard to remark, 'have been here all night,' but the remark was lost on Miss Pilchester, who rushed away to inquire if the ladies' conveniences had been installed. 'They are most important,' she said and disappeared into a far tent as if feeling it suddenly necessary to prove it for herself.

At half-past eleven the sun broke through, beginning to dry at last the heavy dew on the grass, the trees of the bluebell wood, and the hedgerows. From the completely windless river the last transparent breaths of mist began to rise. A few water-lilies were in bud, heads rising above wet leaves, and they looked like pipes, gently smoking.

It was then discovered that Miss Pilchester had completely forgotten to meet a London train, as she had faithfully promised, at ten forty-five. The train was bringing a judge who had, in counties west of London, a great reputation for judging such things as The Horse of the Year Show. The committee had specially asked for him.

Now Ma came hurrying from the house to say she'd had a bulldog on the phone. 'And *did* he bark. And *oh!* the language.'

'Why the 'ell couldn't he come by car?' Pop said.

'Said he flipping well couldn't afford one under this flipping government.'

'*We must do something!*' Miss Pilchester said. 'It's absolutely ghastly!'

'Mariette and Mr Charlton can fetch him in the station-wagon,' Pop said. 'They've got to collect more champagne anyway. Ma don't think we've got enough.'

'Champagne? What champagne? Who ordered champagne?'

'I did.'

'Not for this show?'

'Cocktail party,' Pop said. 'Me and Ma. Instead of the fireworks tonight. You got your invite, didn't you? Mariette and Mr Charlton sent all the invites out.'

The word fireworks dragged Miss Pilchester back to Pop's side like a struggling dog on a lead.

'Now you will promise, won't you, no fireworks?'

'No fireworks,' Pop said.

Miss Pilchester, remembering Pop's delicate investigation of her knee in the Rolls, the velvety battering ram of the kiss that, as Ma had predicted, had made her sleep so much more sweetly, now permitted herself the luxury of a half-smile, the first of her hurried day.

'I know you. Sometimes you're more than naughty.'

Sun twinkled on Pop's eyes, lighting up the pupils in a face that otherwise remained as dead as a dummy.

'Not today though,' Pop said. 'Got to behave today.'

'And promise no fireworks?'

'No fireworks.'

'Not one?'

'Not one,' Pop said and fixed his eyes on the hem of her skirt as she rushed away to attend once again to the matter of the ladies' conveniences, which were not quite what she had hoped they would be. It was a matter of some delicacy.

As she disappeared Pop reminded the Brigadier of how he had said Miss Pilchester was a splendid organizer and all that.

The Brigadier was more than kind: 'Well, in her own sweet way I suppose she is. Fact is, I suppose, she's the only one who can spare the time. Nobody else has the time.'

That was it. Nobody had the time. In the crushing, rushing pressure of modern life nobody, even in the country, had the time.

A few moments later the Brigadier glanced hurriedly at his watch, saw it was after twelve o'clock and said he must rush back for a bite of cold. Pop begged him to come to the beer-tent for a quick snifter before he went but the Brigadier was firm. Nellie would be waiting. He was going to be adamant this time.

Pop, watching him depart with bemused admiration, remembered that word. The Brigadier had one shoe-lace missing and had replaced it with packing string. His hair badly needed cutting at the back, and his shirt collar was, if anything, more frayed than before. But the word adamant shone from him to remind Pop once again of all those wonderful fellers who could use these startling words. He envied them very much.

Going to the beer-tent he found that the bulldog of a judge had arrived and was drinking with two members of the committee, Jack Woodley and Freda O'Connor. The judge was a squat ebullient man in a bowler hat. With Woodley, a ruddy, crude, thick-lipped man who was wearing a yellow waistcoat under his hacking jacket, he kept up a constant braying duet, swaying backwards and forwards, waving a pint mug of beer. Woodley was evidently telling smoke-room stories, at the same time gazing with rough interest at the notorious O'Connor bosom, which protruded by several white marble inches above a low yellow sweater. The coarser the stories the more the O'Connor bosom seemed to like them. Like a pair of bellows, its splendid heaving mass pumped air into the hearty organ of her voice, setting the air about her ringing.

All three ignored Pop and he knew why. He and Ma hadn't invited them to the cocktail party. Not caring, he said in a loud voice, 'How's everybody? Fit as fleas?' as he went past them. Nobody answered, but Pop didn't care. He believed in treating everybody alike, fleas or no fleas.

Glass of beer in hand, he found a companion some moments later in Sir George Bluff-Gore, who owned a large red-brick Georgian mansion that was too expensive to keep up. He and his wife somehow pigged it out in a keeper's cottage instead. Bluff-Gore, yellowish, funereal, stiff, and despondent, had the face of a pall bearer cramped by indigestion. He was not the sort of man you could slap on the back to wish him well.

Nevertheless Pop did so.

Bluff-Gore, recoiling with dejection, managed to say that it was nice of Larkin to invite him and Lady Rose to this cocktail party. They didn't get out much.

'More the merrier,' Pop said and then remembered that the Bluff-Gores had a daughter – Rosemary, he thought her name was – a big puddeny girl with sour eyes and a blonde fringe, whom he had sometimes seen riding at meetings or pony gymkhanas with Mariette. He wondered where she was; he hadn't seen her lately.

'Hope the daughter's coming too?' he said. 'Welcome.'

'Rosemary? Afraid not. Lives in London now.'

'Oh?' Pop said. 'Doing what? Working?'

With increasing gloom Bluff-Gore gazed at the grass of the beer-tent and thought of his only daughter, who had suddenly decided for some utterly unaccountable reason to give up a perfectly sound, happy, normal home to go and paint in Chelsea. It had practically broken her mother's heart; it was utterly unaccountable.

'Gone over to art,' he said.

It was as if he spoke of some old despicable enemy and Pop could only say he hoped it would turn out well.

Drinking again, deciding that art could only be some man or other that

289

Rosemary had run off with, he suddenly switched the subject, charging the unready Bluff-Gore with a startling question.

'When are you going to sell Bluff Court, Sir George?'

Bluff-Gore looked white. For some moments he could find no suitable words with which to tell Pop that he had no intention of selling his house, Bluff Court, even though it was far too large to live in. Bluff Court had sixty rooms, an entire hamlet of barns, dairies, and stables, half a mile of greenhouses and potting sheds and an orangery where, for fifty years, no oranges had grown. You needed a hundred tons of coal to heat it every winter and eighteen gardeners to keep the place tidy and productive in summer. You needed to keep twenty servants to wait on you and another twenty to wait on them. It was dog eat dog. You couldn't get the servants anyway and you couldn't have afforded to pay them if you could.

But to give it up, to sell it, even though you hadn't a bean, was unthinkable. It was a monstrous idea; it simply couldn't be entertained. Among its miles of neglected beeches, elms, and oaks, Bluff Court must and would stand where it did. It might be that one day it would be possible to let it to one of those stockbroker chaps who played at farming, made colossal losses but in the end came out on the right side because they got it out of taxes. Everybody was doing it and it was all perfectly legitimate, they said. It just showed, of course, what the country was coming to. It was grim. No wonder everybody you met was worried stiff. The country was committing suicide. 'What makes you think I have any intention of selling Bluff Court?'

'Well, you don't live in the damn thing,' Pop said, straight as a bird, 'do you? And never will do if you ask me.'

Bluff-Gore indicated with funereal acidity that he was, in fact, not asking him.

'Damn silly,' Pop said. He started to say that it was like having a car you never rode in and then decided on a more illuminating, more contemporary metaphor and said: 'Like having a television set you never look at.'

The illustration was, however, lost on Sir George, who had no television set.

'There are certain aspects other than material', he said, 'that have to be borne in mind.'

Pop said he couldn't think for the life of him what they were, and Bluff-Gore looked at the perky, side-lined face with tolerant irony and an oysterish half-smile.

'You were not thinking of buying the place, by any chance, were you?'

'Course I was.' The gentry were, Pop thought, really half-dopes sometimes. 'What d'ye think I asked you for?'

The oysterish smile widened a little, still ironically tolerant, for the next question.

'And what would you do with it, may I ask?'

'Pull the flippin' thing down.' Pop gave one of his piercing, jolly shouts of laughter. 'What else d'ye think?'

'Good God.'

By now Bluff-Gore was whiter than ever. The eyes themselves had become oysters, opaque, sightless jellies, wet with shock, even with a glint of tears.

'Lot o' good scrap there,' Pop said. 'Make you a good offer.'

Bluff-Gore found himself quite incapable of speaking; he could only stare emptily and with increasing dejection at the grass of the beer-tent, as if mourning for some dear, unspoken departed.

'Cash,' Pop said. 'Ready as Freddy – why don't you think it over?'

Laughing again, he made a final expansive swing of his beer-mug, drawing froth, and left the speechless, sightless Bluff-Gore standing dismally alone.

Outside, in the meadow now gay with strung flags of yellow, scarlet, blue, and emerald, the tents and the marquees standing about the new green grass like white haystacks, Pop found the sun now shining brilliantly. Over by the river, well away from the ring, Mariette was having a practice canter. She had changed already into her yellow shirt and jodhpurs and her bare head was like a curly black kitten against the far blue sky. Mr Charlton was in attendance and suddenly Pop remembered the little matter of the baby. He supposed she wouldn't have to ride much longer and he wondered mildly if Mr Charlton knew. He'd forgotten about that.

Suddenly, from far across the meadow, he heard a rousing, familiar sound. It was Ma beating with a wooden spoon on a big jam-saucepan.

It was time to eat. It was hot in the midday sun and there was a scent of bruised grass in the air.

'Perfick,' Pop thought. 'Going to be a stinger. Going to be a wonderful afternoon.'

All afternoon Mr Charlton watched Mariette taking part in the riding and jumping events she had chosen. Once again, as she took her pony faultlessly through the walk, trot, canter, and run, he could hardly believe in that astral delicious figure, yellow, fawn, and black on its bay pony. Impossible almost to believe that it was the girl who had undressed him on the billiard table, scratched the eyes out of Pauline Jackson, and worked with him in the strawberry field. Once again she looked so perfectly aristocratic that she might have been the niece of Lady Planson-Forbes and he had never been so happy in his life as he watched her.

Ma was happy too. Who wouldn't be? All the children were properly dressed for the occasion, wearing riding habits, jodhpurs, and proper riding caps, even though only Mariette and Montgomery were going to ride. Each of them went about sucking enormous pink and yellow ice-creams; and the twins, who took so much after Ma, had large crackling bags of popcorn and potato crisps.

Nor were there any flies on Ma. She was wearing a silk costume in very pale turquoise, with slightly darker perpendicular stripes. She had chosen a rather large dark blue straw hat that shaded her face nicely and, as the milliner had predicted, 'helped to balance her up a bit'. Her shoes were also blue, almost the colour of her hat, and her hair had been permed into stiffish little waves. The only thing that really bothered her was her turquoise rings. They had started to cut into her fingers again. She would have to have them off.

Beside her the Brigadier's sister looked, as she always did, in her beige shantung and pink cloche hat, like a clothes peg with a thimble perched on top of it.

'Not going in for this 'ere ladies' donkey Derby, are you?' Ma said. Her body quivered with resonant, jellying laughter.

An invitation to strip down to the bare bosom could hardly have brought less response from the sister of the Brigadier.

'I think Miss Pilchester's going in,' Ma said. 'Anyway Pop's trying to persuade her to.'

The ladies' donkey Derby was a late, inspired idea of Pop's. He had managed to persuade the committee that they owed it to him in return for the field. He had also found a silver cup. He had once bought it at a sale, thinking it would be nice to stand on the sideboard. It was engraved with the details of an angling competition, but Pop didn't think it mattered all that much.

While Ma wandered about with the children and Mr Charlton watched the various events, listening with pride every time the loud-speakers spoke the name of Miss Mariette Larkin, Pop was spending some time behind the beer-tent, trying to induce Miss Pilchester to ride in the donkey Derby.

'I honestly couldn't. It would be absolutely ghastly.'

'I thought you liked a bit o' fun?'

'I think you are trying to be very naughty.'

Irresistible though Miss Pilchester always found him, she could not help thinking that this afternoon, in the brilliant sun, Pop looked even more so. He was wearing a suit of small, smart brown-and-white checks, an orange-brown tie, and a new brown Edwardian cap. Like Ma, he compared very favourably with other people: with, for instance, the Brigadier, who was wearing a snuff-coloured sports jacket patched at the elbows with brown leather, his washed-out University tie, and a pair of crumpled corduroys the colour of a moulting stoat.

For the second or third time Pop urged Miss Pilchester to be a sport.

'Just one more rider to make up the seven.'

'Who else is riding? I have never even ridden a donkey in my life before.'

'All girls of your age.'

Miss Pilchester darted one of her rapid glances at Pop. The cast of suspicion died in her eye as she saw the brown new cap. How well it suited him.

'What about that time I took you home in the Rolls?'

'What about it?'

'Best kiss I've had for a long time.'

'You make me feel shy!' Miss Pilchester said.

'Beauty,' Pop said. 'Haven't been able to forget it.'

Miss Pilchester hadn't been able to forget it either; she had even wondered if it might ever be repeated.

'I admitted it was far from unpleasant, but what has it to do with the donkey Derby?'

Pop started to caress the outer rim of Miss Pilchester's thigh. With upsurgent alarm Miss Pilchester felt an investigating finger press a suspender button.

'People will be looking!'

'Coming to the cocktail party?'

'I think so. Yes, I am.'

'Repeat performance tonight at the cocktail party. Promise.'

'I know those promises. They're like pie-crust!'

At four o'clock Miss Pilchester was ready to ride in the ladies' donkey Derby.

A quarter of an hour before that Montgomery and Mr Charlton had ridden in the men's donkey Derby. Most of the donkeys, including Mr Charlton's, had had to be started with carrots and the race had been won by a pale sagacious animal named Whiskey Johnny, who didn't need any carrots. Mr Charlton had ridden three yards and then fallen off. His mount had instantly bolted, ending up in stirring style far beyond the tea-tent, by the river, where already a few lovers, bored by the events and stimulated by a warm afternoon of entrancing golden air, were embracing in the long grasses by the bank, profitably dreaming out the day in a world of rising fish, wild irises, and expanding water-lily blooms.

When Pop went to collect the animal, which was called Jasmine, he found it staring with detached interest at a soldier and a passionate, well-formed young blonde, both of whom were oblivious, in the grasses, of the presence of watchers. Jasmine, Pop thought, seemed so interested in what was going on that after being led away some paces she turned, pricked up her ears and looked around, rather as if she wanted to come back and see it all again.

After all this Pop selected Jasmine for Miss Pilchester to ride. The animal stood dangerously still at the starting point, in stubborn suspense, while Pop gave earnest antepost advice to Miss Pilchester, who sat astride.

'Hang on with your knees. Don't let go. Hang on tight. Like grim death.'

Miss Pilchester, already looking like grim death, gave a hasty glance round at the other competitors, dismayed to find them all young, effervescent girls of sixteen or seventeen. She herself felt neither young nor effervescent and the donkey was horribly hairy underneath her calves.

'Don't mind them, Edith. Don't look at them. Look straight ahead — straight as you can go. Hang on like grim death.'

Miss Pilchester became vaguely aware of carrots, in orange arcs, being waved in all directions. A few animals trotted indifferently up the track, between shrieking, cheering rows of spectators. One trotted at incautious speed for thirty yards or so and then, as if inexpicably bored about something, turned and came back. Another sidled to the side of the track and leaned against a post, allowing itself to be stroked by various children, including Victoria and the twins. Two girls fell off, screaming, and there were gay momentary glimpses of black and apricot lingerie.

Jasmine stood fast. 'Git up, old gal!' Pop said, and started to push her. 'Git up there, Jasmine!' Pop put his weight against her rump and heaved. Nothing happened, and it seemed as if Jasmine had sunk her feet into the ground.

It was all absolutely ghastly, Miss Pilchester was just thinking when over the loudspeaker a voice started up an announcement about Anne Fitzgerald, aged three, who had lost her mother. Would Mrs Fitzgerald please —

The loudspeaker gave a few snappy barks. Jasmine cocked her ears and broke through with frenzy the final waving arcs of carrots, leaving Pop on the ground and everybody scattered.

Miss Pilchester, as Pop had so earnestly and correctly advised, hung on firmly and desperately with her knees, just like grim death, and in thirty seconds Jasmine was back at the river, once more staring into the world of grasses, water-lilies, irises, and a soldier's summer love.

Half-dismounting, half-falling, a dishevelled and demoralized Miss Pilchester stood staring too. It was all absolutely and utterly ghastly and it only made things worse when the soldier, disturbed in the middle of his technique, look up calmly and said:

'Why don't you go away, Ma? Both of you. You *and* your sister.'

Tom Edison's Shaggy Dog

KURT VONNEGUT JR

TWO OLD MEN SAT ON A park bench one morning in the sunshine of Tampa, Florida – one trying doggedly to read a book he was plainly enjoying while the other, Harold K. Bullard, told him the story of his life in the full, round, head tones of a public address system. At their feet lay Bullard's Labrador retriever, who further tormented the aged listener by probing his ankles with a large, wet nose.

Bullard, who had been, before he retired, successful in many fields, enjoyed reviewing his important past. But he faced the problem that complicates the lives of cannibals – namely: that a single victim cannot be used over and over. Anyone who had passed the time of day with him and his dog refused to share a bench with them again.

So Bullard and his dog set out through the park each day in quest of new faces. They had had good luck this morning, for they had found this stranger right away, clearly a new arrival in Florida, still buttoned up tight in heavy serge, stiff collar and necktie, and with nothing better to do than read.

'Yes,' said Bullard, rounding out the first hour of his lecture, 'made and lost fortunes in my time.'

'So you said,' said the stranger, whose name Bullard had neglected to ask. 'Easy, boy. No, no, no, boy,' he said to the dog, who was growing more aggressive toward his ankles.

'Oh? Already told you that, did I?' said Bullard.

'Twice.'

'Two in real estate, one in scrap iron, and one in oil and one in trucking.'

'So you said.'

'I did? Yes, I guess I did. Two in real estate, one in scrap iron, one in oil, and one in trucking. Wouldn't take back a day of it.'

'No, I suppose not,' said the stranger. 'Pardon me, but do you suppose you could move your dog somewhere else? He keeps —'

'Him?' said Bullard, heartily. 'Friendliest dog in the world. Don't need to be afraid of him.'

'I'm not afraid of him. It's just that he drives me crazy, sniffing at my ankles.'

'Plastic,' said Bullard, chuckling.

'What?'

'Plastic. Must be something plastic on your garters. By golly, I'll bet it's those little buttons. Sure as we're sitting here, those buttons must be plastic. That dog is nuts about plastic. Don't know why that is, but he'll sniff it out and find it if there's a speck around. Must be a deficiency in his diet, though, by gosh, he eats better than I do. Once he chewed up a whole plastic humidor. Can you beat it? *That's* the business I'd go into now, by glory, if the pill rollers hadn't told me to let up, to give the old ticker a rest.'

'You could tie the dog to that tree over there,' said the stranger.

'I get so darn' sore at all the youngsters these days!' said Bullard. 'All of 'em mooning around about no frontiers any more. There never have been so many frontiers as there are today. You know what Horace Greeley would say today?'

'His nose is wet,' said the stranger, and he pulled his ankles away, but the dog humped forward in patient pursuit. 'Stop it, boy!'

'His wet nose shows he's healthy,' said Bullard. '"Go plastic, young man!" That's what Greeley'd say. "Go atom, young man!"'

The dog had definitely located the plastic buttons on the stranger's garters and was cocking his head one way and another, thinking out ways of bringing his teeth to bear on those delicacies.

'Scat!' said the stranger.

'"Go electronic, young man!"' said Bullard. 'Don't talk to me about no opportunity any more. Opportunity's knocking down every door in the country, trying to get in. When I was young, a man had to go out and find opportunity and drag it home by the ears. Nowadays —'

'Sorry,' said the stranger, evenly. He slammed his book shut, stood and jerked his ankle away from the dog. 'I've got to be on my way. So good day, sir.'

He stalked across the park, found another bench, sat down with a sigh and began to read. His respiration had just returned to normal, when he felt the wet sponge of the dog's nose on his ankles again.

'Oh – it's you!' said Bullard, sitting down beside him. 'He was tracking you. He was on the scent of something, and I just let him have his head. What'd I tell you about plastic?' He looked about contentedly. 'Don't blame you for moving on. It was stuffy back there. No shade to speak of and not a sign of a breeze.'

'Would the dog go away if I bought him a humidor?' said the stranger.

'Pretty good joke, pretty good joke,' said Bullard, amiably. Suddenly he clapped the stranger on his knee. 'Sa-ay, you aren't in plastics, are you? Here I've been blowing off about plastics, and for all I know that's your line.'

'My line?' said the stranger crisply, laying down his book. 'Sorry – I've never had a line. I've been a drifter since the age of nine, since Edison set up his laboratory next to my home, and showed me the intelligence analyzer.'

'Edison?' said Bullard. 'Thomas Edison, the inventor?'

'If you want to call him that, go ahead,' said the stranger.

'If I *want* to call him that?' – Bullard guffawed – 'I guess I just will! Father of the light bulb and I don't know what all.'

'If you want to think he invented the light bulb, go ahead. No harm in it.' The stranger resumed his reading.

'Say, what is this?' said Bullard, suspiciously. 'You pulling my leg? What's this about an intelligence analyzer? I never heard of that.'

'Of course you haven't,' said the stranger. 'Mr Edison and I promised to keep it a secret. I've never told anyone. Mr Edison broke his promise and told Henry Ford, but Ford made him promise not to tell anybody else – for the good of humanity.'

Bullard was entranced. 'Uh, this intelligence analyzer,' he said, 'it analyzed intelligence, did it?'

'It was an electric butter churn,' said the stranger.

'Seriously now,' Bullard coaxed.

'Maybe it *would* be better to talk it over with someone,' said the stranger. 'It's a terrible thing to keep bottled up inside me, year in and year out. But how can I be sure that it won't go any further?'

'My word as a gentleman,' Bullard assured him.

'I don't suppose I could find a stronger guarantee than that, could I?' said the stranger, judiciously.

'There is no stronger guarantee,' said Bullard, proudly. 'Cross my heart and hope to die!'

'Very well.' The stranger leaned back and closed his eyes, seeming to travel backwards through time. He was silent for a full minute, during which Bullard watched with respect.

'It was back in the fall of eighteen seventy-nine,' said the stranger at last, softly. 'Back in the village of Menlo Park, New Jersey. I was a boy of nine. A young man we all thought was a wizard had set up a laboratory next door to my home, and there were flashes and crashes inside, and all sorts of scary goings-on. The neighborhood children were warned to keep away, not to make any noise that would bother the wizard.

'I didn't get to know Edison right off, but his dog Sparky and I got to be steady pals. A dog a whole lot like yours, Sparky was, and we used to wrestle all over the neighborhood. Yes, sir, your dog is the image of Sparky.'

'Is that so?' said Bullard, flattered.

'Gospel,' replied the stranger. 'Well, one day Sparky and I were wrestling around, and we wrestled right up to the door of Edison's laboratory. The next thing I knew, Sparky had pushed me in through the door, and bam! I was sitting on the laboratory floor, looking up at Mr

Edison himself.'

'Bet he was sore,' said Bullard, delighted.

'You can bet I was scared,' said the stranger. 'I thought I was face to face with Satan himself. Edison had wires hooked to his ears and running down to a little black box in his lap! I started to scoot, but he caught me by the collar and made me sit down.

'"Boy," said Edison, "it's always darkest before the dawn. I want you to remember that."

'"Yes, sir," I said.

'"For over a year, my boy," Edison said to me, "I've been trying to find a filament that will last in an incandescent lamp. Hair, string, splinters – nothing works. So while I was trying to think of something else to try, I started tinkering about with another idea of mine, just letting off steam. I put this together," he said, showing me the little black box. "I thought maybe intelligence was just a certain kind of electricity, so I made this intelligence analyzer here. It works! You're the first one to know about it, my boy. But I don't know why you shouldn't be. It will be your generation that will grow up in the glorious new era when people will be as easily graded as oranges."'

'I don't believe it!' said Bullard.

'May I be struck by lightning this very instant!' said the stranger. 'And it did work, too. Edison had tried out the analyzer on the men in his shop, without telling them what he was up to. The smarter a man was, by gosh, the farther the needle on the indicator in the little black box swung to the right. I let him try it on me, and the needle just lay where it was and trembled. But dumb as I was, then is when I made my one and only contribution to the world. As I say, I haven't lifted a finger since.'

'Whadja do?' said Bullard, eagerly.

'I said, "Mr Edison, sir, let's try it on the dog." And I wish you could have seen the show that dog put on when I said it! Old Sparky barked and howled and scratched to get out. When he saw we meant business, that he wasn't going to get out, he made a beeline right for the intelligence analyzer and knocked it out of Edison's hands. But we cornered him, and Edison held him down while I touched the wires to his ears. And would you believe it, that needle sailed clear across the dial, way past a little red pencil mark on the dial face!'

'The dog busted it,' said Bullard.

'"Mr Edison, sir," I said, "what's that red mark mean?"

'"My boy," said Edison, "it means that the instrument is broken, because that red mark is me."'

'I'll say it was broken,' said Bullard.

The stranger said gravely, 'But it wasn't broken. No, sir. Edison checked the whole thing, and it was in apple-pie order. When Edison told me that, it was then that Sparky, crazy to get out, gave himself away.'

'How?' said Bullard, suspiciously.

'We really had him locked in, see? There were three locks on the door – a hook and eye, a bolt, and a regular knob and latch. That dog stood up, unhooked the hook, pushed the bolt back and had the knob in his teeth when Edison stopped him.'

'No!' said Bullard.

'Yes!' said the stranger, his eyes shining. 'And then is when Edison showed me what a great scientist he was. He was willing to face the truth, no matter how unpleasant it might be.

'"So!" said Edison to Sparky. "Man's best friend, Huh? Dumb animal, huh?"'

'That Sparky was a caution. He pretended not to hear. He scratched himself and bit fleas and went around growling at rat-holes – anything to get out of looking Edison in the eye.

'"Pretty soft, isn't it, Sparky?" said Edison. "Let somebody else worry about getting food, building shelters and keeping warm, while you sleep in front of a fire or go chasing after the girls or raise hell with the boys. No mortgages, no politics, no war, no work, no worry. Just wag the old tail or lick a hand, and you're all taken care of."

'"Mr Edison," I said, "do you mean to tell me that dogs are smarter than people?"

'"Smarter?" said Edison. "I'll tell the world! And what have I been doing for the past year? Slaving to work out a light bulb so dogs can play at night!"

'"Look, Mr Edison," said Sparky, "why not —"'

'Hold on!' roared Bullard.

'Silence!' shouted the stranger, triumphantly. '"Look, Mr Edison," said Sparky, "why not keep quiet about this? It's been working out to everybody's satisfaction for hundreds of thousands of years. Let sleeping dogs lie. You forget all about it, destroy the intelligence analyzer, and I'll tell you what to use for a lamp filament."'

'Hogwash!' said Bullard, his face purple.

The stranger stood. 'You have my solemn word as a gentleman. That dog rewarded *me* for my silence with a stockmarket tip that made me independently wealthy for the rest of my days. And the last words that Sparky ever spoke were to Thomas Edison. "Try a piece of carbonized cotton thread," he said. Later, he was torn to bits by a pack of dogs that had gathered outside the door, listening.'

The stranger removed his garters and handed them to Bullard's dog. 'A small token of esteem, sir, for an ancestor of yours who talked himself to death. Good day.' He tucked his book under his arm and walked away.

The Idol's Eye

S.J. PERELMAN

I HAD BEEN WEEKENDING with Gabriel Snubbers at his villa, 'The Acacias,' on the edge of the Downs. Gabriel isn't seen about as much as he used to be; one hears that an eccentric aunt left him a tidy little sum and the lazy beggar refuses to leave his native haunts. Four of us had cycled down from London together: Gossip Gabrilowitsch, the Polish pianist; Downey Couch, the Irish tenor; Frank Falcovsky, the Jewish prowler, and myself, Clay Modelling. Snubbers, his face beaming, met us at the keeper's lodge. His eyes were set in deep rolls of fat for our arrival, and I couldn't help thinking how well they looked. I wondered whether it was because his daring farce, *Mrs Stebbins' Step-Ins*, had been doing so well at the Haymarket.

'Deuced decent of you chaps to make this filthy trip,' he told us, leading us up the great avenue of two stately alms toward the house. 'Rum place, this.' A surprise awaited us when we reached the house, for the entire left wing had just burned down. Snubbers, poor fellow, stared at it a bit ruefully, I thought.

'Just as well. It was only a plague-spot,' sympathized Falcovsky. Snubbers was thoughtful.

'D'ye know, you chaps,' he said suddenly, 'I could swear an aunt of mine was staying in that wing.' Falcovsky stirred the ashes with his stick and uncovered a pair of knitting needles and a half-charred corset.

'No, it must have been the other wing,' dismissed Snubbers. 'How about a spot of whisky and soda?' We entered and Littlejohn, Snubbers' man, brought in a spot of whisky on a piece of paper which we all examined with interest. A splendid fire was already roaring in the middle of the floor to drive out the warmth.

'Soda?' offered Snubbers. I took it to please him, for Gabriel's cellar was reputedly excellent. A second later I wished that I had drunk the cellar instead. Baking soda is hardly the thing after a three-hour bicycle trip.

'You drank that like a little soldier,' he complimented, his little button eyes fastened on me. I was about to remark that I had never drunk a little soldier, when I noticed Littlejohn hovering in the doorway.

'Yes, that will be all,' Snubbers waved, 'and, oh, by the way, send up to London tomorrow for a new wing, will you?' Littlejohn bowed and left, silently, sleekly Oriental.

'Queer cove, Littlejohn,' commented Snubbers. 'Shall I tell you a story?' He did, and it was one of the dullest I have ever heard. At the end of it Falcovsky grunted. Snubbers surveyed him suspiciously.

'Why, what's up, old man?' he queried.

'What's up? Nothing's up,' snarled Falcovsky. 'Can't a man grunt in front of an open fire if he wants to?'

'But. . . .' began Snubbers.

'But nothing,' Falcovsky grated. 'You haven't lived till you've grunted in front of an open fire. Just for that – grunt, grunt, grunt,' and he grunted several times out of sheer spite. The baking soda was beginning to tell on Snubbers.

'Remarkable thing happened the other day,' he began. 'I was pottering about in the garden. . . .'

'Why must one always potter around in a garden?' demanded Couch. 'Can't you potter around in an armchair just as well?'

'I did once,' confessed Snubbers moodily, revealing a whitish scar on his chin. 'Gad, sir, what a wildcat she was!' He chewed his wad of carbon paper reminiscently. 'Oh, well, never mind. But as I was saying – I was going through some of my great-grandfather's things the other day. . . .'

'What things?' demanded Falcovsky.

'His bones, if you must know,' Snubbers said coldly. 'You know, Great-grandfather died under strange circumstances. He opened a vein in his bath.'

'I never knew baths had veins,' protested Gabrilowitsch.

'I never knew his great-grandfather had a ba – ' began Falcovsky derisively. With a shout Snubbers threw himself on Falcovsky. It was the signal for Pandemonium, the upstairs girl, to enter and throw herself with a shout on Couch. The outcome of the necking bee was as follows: Canadians 12, Visitors 9. Krebs and Vronsky played footie, subbing for Gerber and Weinwald, who were disabled by flying antipasto.

We were silent after Snubbers had spoken; men who have wandered in far places have an innate delicacy about their great-grandfathers' bones. Snubbers' face was a mask, his voice a harsh whip of pain in the stillness when he spoke again.

'I fancy none of you knew my great-grandfather,' he said slowly. 'Before your time, I daresay. A rare giant of a man with quizzical eyes and a great shock of wiry red hair, he had come through the Peninsular Wars without a scratch. Women loved this impetual Irish adventurer who would rather fight than eat and vice versa. The wars over, he turned toward cookery, planning to devote his failing years to the perfection of the welsh rarebit, a dish he loved. One night he was chafing at The Bit, a tavern in Portsmouth, when he overheard a chance remark from a brawny gunner's mate in his cups. In Calcutta the man had heard native tales of a mysterious idol, whose single eye was a flawless ruby.

'"Topscuttle my bamberger, it's the size of a bloomin' pigeon's egg!"
spat the salt, shifting his quid to his other cheek. "A bloomin' rajah's
ransom and ye may lay to that, mateys!"

'The following morning the *Maid of Hull*, a frigate of the line mounting
thirty-six guns, out of Bath and into bed in a twinkling, dropped
downstream on the tide, bound out for Bombay, object matrimony. On
her as passenger went my great-grandfather, an extra pair of nankeen
pants and a dirk his only baggage. Fifty-three days later in Poona, he was
heading for the interior of one of the Northern states. Living almost
entirely on cameo brooches and the few ptarmigan which fell to the
ptrigger of his pfowlingpiece, he at last sighted the towers of Ishpeming,
the Holy City of the Surds and Cosines, fanatic Mohammedan warrior
sects. He disguised himself as a beggar and entered the gates.

'For weeks my great-grandfather awaited his chance to enter the
temple of the idol. They were changing the guard one evening when he
saw it. One of the native janissaries dropped his knife. My great-
grandfather leaped forward with cringing servility and returned it to him,
in the small of his back. Donning the soldier's turban, he quickly slipped
into his place. Midnight found him within ten feet of his prize. Now came
the final test. He furtively drew from the folds of his robes a plate of curry,
a dish much prized by Indians, and set it in a far corner. The guards
rushed upon it with bulging squeals of delight. A twist of his wrist and the
gem was his. With an elaborately stifled yawn, my great-grandfather left
under pretense of going out for a glass of water. The soldiers winked slyly
but when he did not return after two hours, their suspicions were
aroused. They hastily made a canvass of the places where water was
served and their worst fears were realized. The ruby in his burnoose,
Great-grandfather was escaping by fast elephant over the Khyber Pass.
Dockside loungers in Yarmouth forty days later stared curiously at a
mammoth of a man with flaming red hair striding toward the Bull and
Bloater Tavern. Under his belt, did they but only know it, lay the Ruby
Eye.

'Ten years to that night had passed, and my great-grandfather, in
seclusion under this very roof, had almost forgotten his daring escapade.
Smoking by the fireplace, he listened to the roar of the wind and reviewed
his campaigns. Suddenly he leaped to his feet – a dark face had vanished
from the window. Too late my great-grandfather snatched up powder
and ball and sent a charge hurtling into the night. The note pinned to the
window drained the blood from his face.

'It was the first of a series. Overnight his hair turned from rose-red to
snow-white. And finally, when it seemed as though madness were to rob
them of their revenge, *they came.*'

Snubbers stopped, his eyes those of a man who had looked beyond life
and had seen things best left hidden from mortal orbs. Falcovsky's hand

was trembling as he pressed a pinch of snuff against his gums.

'You – you mean?' he quavelled.

'Yes.' Snubbers' voice had sunk to a whisper. 'He fought with the strength of nine devils, but the movers took away his piano. You see,' he added very gently, 'Great-grandfather had missed the last four instalments.' Gabrilowitsch sighed deeply and arose, his eyes fixed intently on Snubbers.

'And – and the ruby?' he asked softly, his delicate fingers closing around the fire-tongs.

'Oh, *that*,' shrugged Snubbers, 'I just threw that in to make it interesting.'

We bashed in his conk and left him to the vultures.

The Morning After

KINGSLEY AMIS

Jim Dixon, a history lecturer at a northern university, is invited for an 'arty weekend' by his insufferable senior professor, Welch. Dixon disgraces himself the first evening by being rude to the professor's son, Bertrand, and then going out to the pub to get drunk. Climbing back into the house, he finds himself in the bedroom of his depressive 'girlfriend', Margaret, just recovering from a breakdown and attempted suicide. To his drink-befuddled mind it seems that she welcomes his advances, but he soon discovers his mistake and stumbles unsteadily back to his own room....

DIXON WAS ALIVE AGAIN. Consciousness was upon him before he could get out of the way; not for him the slow, gracious wandering from the halls of sleep, but a summary, forcible ejection. He lay sprawled, too wicked to move, spewed up like a broken spider-crab on the tarry shingle of the morning. The light did him harm, but not as much as looking at things did; he resolved, having done it once, never to move his eyeballs again. A dusty thudding in his head made the scene before him beat like a pulse. His mouth had been used as a latrine by some small creature of the night, and then as its mausoleum. During the night, too, he'd somehow been on a cross-country run and then been expertly beaten up by secret police. He felt bad.

He reached out for and put on his glasses. At once he saw that something was wrong with the bedclothes immediately before his face. Endangering his chance of survival, he sat up a little, and what met his bursting eyes roused to a frenzy the timpanist in his head. A large, irregular area of the turned-back part of the sheet was missing; a smaller but still considerable area of the turned-back part of the blanket was missing; an area about the size of the palm of his hand in the main part of the top blanket was missing. Through the three holes, which appropriately enough, had black borders, he could see a dark brown mark on the second blanket. He ran a finger round a bit of the hole in the sheet, and when he looked at his finger it bore a dark-grey stain. That meant ash; ash meant burning; burning must mean cigarettes. Had this cigarette burnt itself out on the blanket? If not, where was it now? Nowhere on the bed; nor in it. He leaned over the side, gritting his teeth; a sunken brown channel, ending in a fragment of discoloured paper, lay across a light patch in the pattern of a valuable-looking rug. This made him feel very unhappy, a feeling sensibly increased when he looked at the bedside table. This was marked by two black, charred grooves, greyish and shiny in parts, lying at right angles and stopping well short of the ashtray, which held a single used match. On the table were two unused matches; the remainder lay with the empty cigarette packet on the floor. The bakelite mug was nowhere to be seen.

Had he done all this himself? Or had a wayfarer, a burglar, camped out in his room? Or was he the victim of some Horla fond of tobacco? He thought that on the whole he must have done it himself, and wished he hadn't. Surely this would mean the loss of his job, especially if he failed to go to Mrs Welch and confess what he'd done, and he knew already that he wouldn't be able to do that. There was no excuse which didn't consist of the inexcusable: an incendiary was no more pardonable when revealed as a drunkard as well – so much of a drunkard, moreover, that obligations to hosts and fellow-guests and the counter-attraction of a chamber-concert were as nothing compared with the lure of the drink. The only hope was that Welch wouldn't notice what his wife would presumably tell him about the burning of the bedclothes. But Welch had been known to notice things, the attack on his pupil's book in that essay, for example. But that had really been an attack on Welch himself; he couldn't much care what happened to sheets and blankets which he wasn't actually using at the time. Dixon remembered thinking on an earlier occasion that to yaw drunkenly round the Common Room in Welch's presence screeching obscenities, punching out the window-panes, fouling the periodicals, would escape Welch's notice altogether, provided his own person remained inviolate. The memory in turn reminded him of a sentence in a book of Alfred Beesley's he'd once glanced at: 'A stimulus cannot be received by the mind unless it serves some need of the organism.' He began laughing, an action he soon modified to a wince.

He got out of bed and went into the bathroom. After a minute or two he returned, eating toothpaste and carrying a safety-razor blade. He started carefully cutting round the edges of the burnt areas of the bedclothes with the blade. He didn't know why he did this, but the operation did seem to improve the look of things: the cause of the disaster wasn't so immediately apparent. When all the edges were smooth and regular, he knelt down slowly, as if he'd all at once become a very old man, and shaved the appropriate part of the rug. The debris from these modifications he stuffed into his jacket pocket, thinking that he'd have a bath and then go downstairs and phone Bill Atkinson and ask him to come through with his message about the senior Dixons a good deal earlier than had been arranged. He sat on the bed for a moment to recover from his vertiginous exertions with the rug, then, before he could rise, somebody, soon identifiable as male, came into the bathroom next door. He heard the clinking of a plug-chain, then the swishing of tap-water. Welch, or his son, or Johns was about to take a bath. Which one it was was soon settled by the upsurge of a deep, untrained voice into song. The piece was recognizable to Dixon as some skein of untiring facetiousness by filthy Mozart. Bertrand was surely unlikely to sing anything at all, and Johns made no secret of his indifference to anything earlier than Richard Strauss. Very slowly, like a forest giant under the axe, Dixon heeled over sideways and came to rest with his hot face on the pillow.

This, of course, would give him time to collect his thoughts, and that, of course, was just what he didn't want to do with his thoughts; the longer he could keep them apart from one another, especially the ones about Margaret, the better. For the first time he couldn't avoid imagining what she'd say to him, if indeed she'd say anything, when he next saw her. He pushed his tongue down in front of his lower teeth, screwed up his nose as tightly as he could, and made gibbering motions with his mouth. How long would it be before he could persuade her first to open, then to empty, her locker of reproaches, as preliminary to the huge struggle of getting her to listen to his apologies? Desperately he tried to listen to Welch's song, to marvel at its matchless predictability, its austere, unswerving devotion to tedium; but it didn't work. Then he tried to feel pleased about the acceptance of his article, but all he could remember was Welch's seeming indifference on hearing the news and his injunction, so exasperatingly like Beesley's, to 'get a definite date from him, Dixon, otherwise it's not much ... not much ...' He sat up and by degrees worked his feet to the floor.

There was an alternative to the Atkinson plan; the simpler, nicer one of clearing out at once without a word to anybody. That wouldn't really do, though, unless he cleared out as far as London. What was going on in London now? He began to take off his pyjamas, deciding to omit his bath. Those wide streets and squares would be deserted at this time, except for a few lonely, hurrying figures; he could revisualize it all from remembering a weekend leave during the war. He sighed; he might as well be thinking of Monte Carlo or Chinese Turkestan; then, jigging on the rug with one foot out of, the other still in, his pyjamas, thought of nothing but the pain that slopped through his head like water into a sand-castle. He clung to the mantelpiece, nearly displacing the squatting Oriental, crumpling like a shot film-gunman. Had Chinese Turkestan its Margarets and Welches?

Some minutes later he was in the bathroom. Welch had left grime round the bath and steam on the mirror. After a little thought, Dixon stretched out a finger and wrote 'Ned Welch is a Soppy Fool with a Fase like A Pigs Bum' in the steam; then he rubbed the glass with a towel and looked at himself. He didn't look too bad, really; anyway, better than he felt. His hair, however, despite energetic brushing helped out by the use of a water-soaked nail-brush, was already springing away from his scalp. He considered using soap as a pomatum, but decided against it, having in the past several times converted the short hairs at the sides and back of his head into the semblance of duck-plumage by this expedient. His glasses seemed more goggle-like than usual. As always, though, he looked healthy and, he hoped, honest and kindly. He'd have to be content with that.

He was all ready to slink down to the phone when, returning to the bedroom, he again surveyed the mutilated bedclothes. They looked in some way unsatisfactory; he couldn't have said how. He went and locked the outer bathroom door, picked up the razor-blade, and began again on the circumferences of the holes. This time he made jagged cuts into the material, little inlets from the great missing areas. Some pieces he almost severed. Finally he held the blade at right angles and ran it quickly round the holes, roughening them up. He stood back from his work and decided the effect was perceptibly better. The disaster now seemed much less obviously the work of man and might, for a few seconds, be put down to some fulminant dry-rot or the ravages of a colony of moths. He turned the rug round so that the shaven burn, without being actually hidden by a nearby chair, was none the less not far from it. He was considering taking the bedside table downstairs and later throwing it out of the bus on his journey back when a familiar voice came into aural range singing in a way that suggested head-wagging jollity. It grew in volume, like the apprehension of something harmful or awful, until the locked bathroom door began to be shaken and its handle to be rattled. The singing stopped, but the rattling went on, was joined by kicking, even momentarily replaced by the thudding of what must be a shoulder. Welch hadn't thought in advance that the bathroom might bear signs of occupation by another when he wanted to get back into it himself (why, in any case, did he want to get back into it?), nor did he soon realize it now. After trying several manoeuvres to replace his first vain rattling of the handle, he returned his attention to a vain rattling of the handle. There was a final orgasm of shakings, knockings, thuddings, and rattlings, then footsteps and a door closed.

With tears of rage in his eyes, Dixon left the bedroom, first unintentionally treading on and shattering the bakelite mug, which must have rolled out from under something into his path. Downstairs, he looked at the hall clock – twenty past eight – and went into the drawing-room, where the phone was. It was a good job that Atkinson got up early on Sundays to go out for the papers. He'd be able to catch him easily before he went. He picked up the phone.

What gave him most trouble during the next twenty-five minutes was giving vent to his feelings without hurting his head too much. Nothing whatever came out of the receiver during that time except the faint sea-shell whispering. As he sat on the arm of a leather-covered armchair, putting his face through all its permutations of loathing, the whole household seemed to spring into activity around him. Footsteps walked the floor above his head; others descended the stairs and entered the breakfast-room; still others came from the back of the house and also entered the breakfast-room; far off a vacuum-cleaner whined; a cistern flushed; a door banged; a voice called. When it sounded as if a posse was being assembled immediately outside the drawing-room door, he hung up and left, his bottom aching from its narrow seat, his arm aching from rattling the receiver-rest.

Breakfast technics at the Welches', like many of their ways of thought, recalled an earlier epoch. The food was kept on the sideboard in what Dixon conjected were chafing-dishes. The quantity and variety of this food recalled in turn the fact that Mrs Welch supplemented Welch's professorial salary with a good-sized income of her own. Dixon had often wondered how Welch had contrived to marry money; it could hardly have been due to any personal merit, real or supposed, and the vagaries of Welch's mind could leave no room there for avarice. Perhaps the old fellow had had when younger what he now so demonstrably lacked: a way with him. In spite of the ravages wrought by his headache and his fury, Dixon felt happier as he wondered what foods would this morning afford visible proof of the Welches' prosperity. He went into the breakfast-room with the bedclothes and Margaret a long way from the foreground of his mind.

The only person in the room was the Callaghan girl, sitting behind a well-filled plate. Dixon said good morning to her.

'Oh, good morning.' Her tone was neutral, not hostile.

He quickly decided on a bluff, speak-my-mind approach as the best cloak for rudeness, past or to come. One of his father's friends, a jeweller, had got away with conversing almost entirely in insults for the fifteen years Dixon had known him, merely by using this simple device. Deliberately intensifying his northern accent, Dixon said: 'Afraid I got off on the wrong foot with you last night.'

She looked up quickly, and he saw with bitterness how pretty her neck was. 'Oh ... that. I shouldn't worry too much about it if I were you. I didn't show up too well myself.'

'Nice of you to take it like that,' he said, remembering that he'd already had one occasion to use this phrase to her. 'Very bad manners it was on my part, anyway.'

'Well, let's forget it, shall we?'

'Glad to; thanks very much.'

There was a pause, while he noted with mild surprise how much and how quickly she was eating. The remains of a large pool of sauce were to be seen on her plate beside a diminishing mound of fried egg, bacon, and tomatoes. Even as he watched she replenished her stock of sauce with a fat scarlet gout from the bottle. She glanced up and caught his look of interest, raised her eyebrows, and said, 'I'm sorry, I like sauce; I hope you don't mind,' but not convincingly, and he fancied she blushed.

'That's all right,' he said heartily; 'I'm fond of the stuff myself.' He pushed aside his bowl of cornflakes. They were of a kind he didn't like: malt had been used in their preparation. A study of the egg and bacon and tomatoes opposite him made him decide to postpone eating any himself. His gullet and stomach felt as if they were being deftly sewn up as he sat. He poured and drank a cup of black coffee, then refilled his cup.

'Aren't you going to have any of this stuff?' the girl asked.

'Well, not yet, I don't think.'

'What's the matter? Aren't you feeling so good?'

'No, not really, I must admit. Bit of a headache, you know.'

'Oh, then you did go to the pub, like that little man said – what was his name?'

'Johns,' Dixon said, trying to suggest by his articulation of the name the correct opinion of its bearer. 'Yes, I did go to the pub.'

'You had a lot, did you?' In her interest she stopped eating, but still gripped her knife and fork, her fists resting on the cloth. He noticed that her fingers were square-tipped, with the nails cut quite close.

'I suppose I must have done, yes,' he replied.

'How much did you have?'

'Oh, I never count them. It's a bad habit, is counting them.'

'Yes, I dare say, but how many do you think it was? Roughly.'

'Ooh ... seven or eight, possibly.'

'Beers, that is, is it?'

'Good Lord, yes. Do I look as if I can afford spirits?'

'Pints of beer?'

'Yes.' He smiled slightly, thinking she didn't seem such a bad sort after all, and that the slight blueness of the whites of her eyes helped to give her her look of health. He changed his mind abruptly about the first of these observations, and lost interest in the second, when she replied:

'Well, if you drink as much as that you must expect to feel a bit off colour the next day, mustn't you?' she drew herself upright in her seat in a schoolmarmy attitude.

He remembered his father, who until the war had always worn stiff white collars, being reproved by the objurgatory jeweller as excessively 'dignant' in demeanour. This etymological sport expressed for Dixon exactly what he objected to in Christine. He said rather coldly: 'Yes, I must, mustn't I?' It was an idiom he'd caught from Carol Goldsmith. Thinking of her made him think, for the first time that morning, of the embrace he'd witnessed the night before, and he realized that it had its bearing on this girl as well as on Goldsmith. Well, she could obviously take care of herself.

'Everybody was wondering where you'd got to,' she said.

'I've no doubt they were. Tell me: how did Mr Welch react?'

'What, to finding out you'd probably gone to the pub?'

'Yes. Did he seem irritated at all?'

'I really have no idea.' Conscious, possibly, that this must sound rather bald, she added: 'I don't know him at all, you see, and so I couldn't really tell. He didn't seem to notice much, if you see what I mean.'

Dixon saw. He felt too that he could tackle the eggs and bacon and tomatoes now, so went to get some and said: 'Well, that's a relief, I must say. I shall have to apologize to him, I suppose.'

'It might be a good idea.'

She said this in a tone that made him turn his back for a moment at the sideboard and made his Chinese mandarin's face, hunching his shoulders a little. He disliked this girl and her boyfriend so much that he couldn't understand why they didn't dislike each other. Suddenly he remembered the bedclothes; how could he have been such a fool? He couldn't possibly leave them like that. He must do something else to them. He must get up to his room quickly and look at them and see what ideas their physical presence suggested. 'God,' he said absently; 'oh, my God,' then, pulling himself together: 'I'm afraid I shall have to dash off now.'

'Have you got to get back?'

'No, I'm not actually going until ... No, I mean there's ... I've got to go upstairs.' Realizing that this was a poor exit-line, he said wildly, still holding a dish-cover: 'There's something wrong with my room, something I must alter.' He looked at her and saw her eyes were dilated. 'I had a fire last night.'

'You lit a fire in your bedroom?'

'No, I didn't light it purposely, I lit it with a cigarette. It caught fire on its own.'

Her expression changed again. 'Your bedroom caught fire?'

'No, only the bed. I lit it with a cigarette.'

'You mean you set fire to your bed?'

'That's right.'

'With a cigarette? Not meaning to? Why didn't you put it out?'

'I was asleep. I didn't know about it till I woke up.'

'But you must have ... Didn't it burn you?'

He put the dish-cover down. 'It doesn't seem to have done.'

'Oh, that's something, anyway.' She looked at him with her lips pressed firmly together, then laughed in a way quite different from the way she'd laughed the previous evening; in fact, Dixon thought, rather unmusically. A blonde lock came away from the devotedly-brushed hair and she smoothed it back. 'Well, what are you going to do about it?'

310

'I don't know yet. I must do something, though.'

'Yes, I quite agree. You'd better start on it quickly, hadn't you, before the maid goes round?'

'I know. But what can I do?'

'How bad is it?'

'Bad enough. There are great pieces gone altogether, you see.'

'Oh. Well, I don't really know what to suggest without seeing it. Unless you ... no; that wouldn't help.'

'Look, I suppose you wouldn't come up and ...?'

'Have a look at it?'

'Yes. Do you think you could?'

She sat up again and thought. 'Yes, all right. I don't guarantee anything, of course.'

'No, of course not.' He remembered with joy that he still had some cigarettes left after last night's holocaust. 'Thanks very much.'

They were moving to the door when she said: 'What about your breakfast?'

'Oh, I shall have to miss that. There's not time.'

'I shouldn't if I were you. They don't give you much for lunch here, you know.'

'But I'm not going to wait till ... I mean there isn't much time to ... Wait a minute.' He darted back to the sideboard, picked up a slippery fried egg and slid it into his mouth whole. She watched him with folded arms and a blank expression. Chewing violently, he doubled up a piece of bacon and crammed it between his teeth, then signalled he was ready to move. Intimations of nausea circled round his digestive system.

They went in file through the hall and up the stairs. The ocarina-like notes of a recorder playing a meagre air were distantly audible; perhaps Welch had breakfasted in his room. Dixon found, with a pang of relief, that he could open the bathroom door.

The girl looked sternly at him. 'What are we going in here for?'

'My bedroom's on the far side of this.'

'Oh, I see. What a curious arrangement.'

'I imagine old Welch had this part of the house built on. It's better like this than having the bathroom on the far side of a bedroom.'

'I suppose so. My goodness, you certainly have gone to town, haven't you?' She went forward and fingered the sheet and blankets like one shown material in a shop. 'But this doesn't look like a burn; it looks as if it's been cut with something.'

'Yes, I ... cut the burnt bits off with a razor-blade. I thought it would look better than just leaving it burnt.'

'Why on earth did you do that?'

'I can't really explain. I just thought it would look better.'

'Mm. And did all this come from one cigarette?'

'That I don't know. Probably.'

'Well, you must have been pretty far gone not to . . . And the table too. And the rug. You know, I don't know that I ought to be a party to all this.' She grinned, which made her look almost ludicrously healthy, and revealed at the same time that her front teeth were slightly irregular. For some reason this was more disturbing to his equanimity than regularity could possibly have been. He began to think he'd noticed quite enough things about her now, thank you. Then she drew herself up and pressed her lips together, seeming to consider. 'I think the best thing would be to remake the bed with all this mess at the bottom, out of sight. We can put the blanket that's only scorched – this one – on top; it'll probably be almost all right on the side that's underneath now. What about that? It's a pity there isn't an eiderdown.'

'Yes. Sounds all right to me, that. They're bound to find it when they strip the bed, though, aren't they?'

'Yes, but they probably won't connect it with smoking, especially after what you did with your razor-blade. And after all, you wouldn't have put your head right down the bottom of the bed to smoke, would you?'

'That's a point, of course. We'd better get on with it, then?'

He heaved the bed away from the wall, while she watched with arms folded, then they both set about the unmaking and remaking. The vacuum-cleaner could now be heard quite close at hand, drowning Welch's recorder. As they worked, Dixon studied the Callaghan girl, despite his determination to notice nothing more about her, and saw with fury that she was prettier than he'd thought. He found himself wanting to make the kind of face or noise he was accustomed to make when entrusted with a fresh ability-testing task by Welch, or seeing Michie in the distance, or thinking about Mrs Welch, or being told by Beesley something Johns had said. He wanted to implode his features, to crush air from his mouth, in a way and to a degree that might be set against the mess of feelings she aroused in him: indignation, grief, resentment, peevishness, spite, and sterile anger, all the allotropes of pain. The girl was doubly guilty, first of looking like that, secondly of appearing in front of him looking like that. Run-of-the-mill queens of love – Italian film-actresses, millionaires' wives, girls on calendars – he could put up with; more than that, he positively liked looking at them. But this sort of thing he'd as soon not look at at all. He remembered seeing in a book once that some man who claimed to have love well weighed up – someone like Plato or Rilke – had said that it was an emotion quite different in kind, not just degree, from ordinary sexual feelings. Was it love, then, that he felt for girls like this one? No emotion he'd experienced or could imagine came anything like so close, to his way of thinking; but apart from the dubious support of Plato or Rilke he had all the research on the subject against him there. Well, what was it if it wasn't love? It didn't seem like desire;

when the last corner was tucked in and he joined her on her side of the bed, he was strongly tempted to put his hand out and lay it on one of those full breasts, but this action, if performed, would have appeared as natural to him, as unimportant and unobjectionable, as reaching out to take a large ripe peach from a fruit-dish. No, all this, whatever it was or was called, was something nothing could be done about.

'There, I think that looks very nice,' the girl said. 'You couldn't guess what was underneath it all if you didn't know, could you?'

'No, and thanks very much for the idea and the help.'

'Oh, that's all right. What are you going to do with the table?'

'I've been thinking about that. There's a little junk-room at the end of the passage, full of broken furniture and rotting books and things; they sent me up there yesterday to fetch a music-stand or whatever they call the things. That room's the place for this table, behind an old screen with French courtiers painted on it – you know, floppy hats and banjos. If you'll go and see whether the coast's clear, I'll rush along there with it now.'

'Agreed. I must say that's an inspiration. With the table out of the way nobody'll connect the sheets with smoking. They'll think you tore them with your feet, in a nightmare or something.'

'Some nightmare, to get through two blankets as well.'

She looked at him open-mouthed, then began to laugh. She sat down on the bed but immediately jumped up again as if it were once more on fire. Dixon began laughing too, not because he was much amused but because he felt grateful to her for her laughter. They were still laughing a minute later when she beckoned to him from outside the bathroom door, when he ran out on to the landing with the table, and when Margaret suddenly flung open the door of her bedroom and saw them.

'What do you imagine you're up to, James?' she asked.

'We're just ... I'm just ... I was just getting rid of this table, as a matter of fact,' Dixon said, looking from one woman to the other.

The Callaghan girl made an extraordinarily loud snorting noise of incompetently-suppressed laughter. Margaret said: 'Just what is all this nonsense?'

'It isn't nonsense, Margaret, I assure you. I've ...'

'If anybody minds me saying so,' the girl interrupted him, 'I think we'd better get rid of the table first and explain the whys and wherefores afterwards, don't you?'

'That's right,' Dixon said, put his head down, and ran up the passage. In the junk-room he nudged aside an archery target, making his crazy-peasant face at it – what flaring imbecilities must it have witnessed? – and dumped the table behind the screen. Next, he unrolled a handy length of

313

mouldering silk and spread it over the table-top; then arranged upon the cloth thus provided two fencing foils, a book called *The Lesson of Spain*, and a Lilliputian chest-of-drawers no doubt containing sea-shells and locks of children's hair; finally propped up against this display a tripod meant for some sort of telescopic or photographic tomfoolery. The effect, when he stepped back to look, was excellent; no observer could doubt that these objects had lived together for years in just this way. He smiled, shutting his eyes for a moment before slopping back into the world of reality.

Margaret was waiting for him at the threshold of her room. One corner of her mouth was drawn in in a way he knew well. The Callaghan girl had gone.

'Well, what was all that about, James?'

He shut the door and began to explain. As he talked, his incendiarism and the counter-measures adopted struck him for the first time as funny. Surely Margaret, especially since she wasn't personally implicated, must find them funny too; they formed the sort of story she liked. He said as much at the end of his account.

Without changing her expression, she dissented. 'I could see you and that girl were finding it all pretty funny, though.'

'Well, why shouldn't we have found it funny?'

'No reason at all; it's nothing to do with me. The whole thing just strikes me as rather silly and childish, that's all.'

He said effortfully: 'Now look, Margaret: I can quite see why it looked like that to you. But don't you see? the whole point is that naturally I didn't mean to burn that bloody sheet and so on. Once I'd done it, though, I'd obviously got to do something about it, hadn't I?'

'You couldn't have gone to Mrs Welch and explained, of course.'

'No, "of course" is right, I couldn't have. I'd have been out of my job in five minutes.' He produced and lit cigarettes for the two of them, trying to remember whether Bertrand's girl had said anything about owning up to Mrs Welch. He didn't think she had, which was odd in a way.

'You'll be out in less time than that if she ever finds that table.'

'She won't find it,' he said irritably, beginning to pace up and down the room.

'What about that sheet? You say it was Christine Callaghan's idea to remake the bed?'

'Well, what about it? And what about the sheet?'

'You seem to have got on a good deal better with her than you did last night.'

'Yes, that's good, isn't it?'

'Incidentally I thought she was abominably rude just now.'

'How do you mean?'

'Barging in and sending you off with that table like that.'

Stung with this reflection on his dignity, Dixon said: 'You've got this "rude" business on the winkle, Margaret. She was absolutely right: one of the Welches might have turned up at any moment. And if anyone barged in, it was you, not her.' He began regretting this speech well before it was over.

She stared at him with her mouth a little open, then whipped abruptly round away from him. 'I'm sorry, I won't barge in again.'

'Now, Margaret, you know I didn't mean it like that; don't be ridiculous. I was only....'

In a high voice, kept steady only by obvious effort, she said: 'Please go.'

Dixon fought hard to drive away the opinion that, both as actress and as scriptwriter, she was doing rather well, and hated himself for failing. Trying to haul urgency into his tone, he began: 'You mustn't take it like that. It was a bloody stupid thing to say, on my part, I admit. I didn't mean you actually barged in, in that way, of course I didn't. You must see....'

'Oh, I see all right, James. I see perfectly.' This time her voice was flat. She wore a sort of arty get-up of multi-coloured shirt, skirt with fringed hem and pocket, low-heeled shoes, and wooden beads. The smoke from her cigarette curled up, blue and ashy in a sunbeam, round her bare forearm. Dixon moved closer and saw that her hair had been recently washed; it lay in dry lustreless wisps on the back of her neck. In that condition it struck him as quintessentially feminine, much more feminine than the Callaghan girl's shining fair crop. Poor old Margaret, he thought, and rested his hand, in a gesture he hoped was solicitous, on her nearer shoulder.

Before he could speak she'd shaken his hand off, moved over to the window, and begun to talk in a strain that marked the opening, he soon realized, of a totally new phase of the scene they were evidently having. 'Get away. How dare you. Stop pushing and pulling me about. Who do you think you are? You haven't even had the grace to apologize for last night. You behaved disgracefully. I hope you realize you absolutely stank of beer. I've never given you the least impression ... Whatever made you think you could get away with that sort of thing? What the hell do you take me for? It isn't as if you didn't know what I've had to put up with, all these last weeks. It's intolerable, absolutely intolerable. I won't stand for it. You must have known how I've been feeling.'

She went on like this while Dixon looked her in the eyes. His panic mounted in sincerity and volume. Her body moved jerkily about; her head bobbed from side to side on its rather long neck, shaking the wooden beads about on the multi-coloured shirt. He found himself thinking that the whole arty get-up seemed oddly at variance with the way she was acting. People who wore clothes of that sort oughtn't to mind things of this sort, certainly not as much as Margaret clearly minded this thing. It was surely wrong to dress, and to behave most of the time, in a way that was so un-prim when you were really so proper all of the time. But then, with Catchpole at any rate, she hadn't been proper all of the time, had she? But of course it was all wrong to think like this, very bad, in fact, to allow his irritation with some of the things about her to do what it always did, to obscure what was most important: she was a neurotic who'd recently taken a bad beating. Yes, she was right really, though not in the way she meant. He had behaved badly, he had been inconsiderate. He'd better devote all his energy to apologizing. He booted out of his mind the reflection, derived apparently from nowhere, that in spite of her emotion she seemed well able to keep her voice down.

'I was thinking only yesterday afternoon about the relationship we'd been building up, how valuable it was, something really good. But that was silly, wasn't it? I was dead wrong, I....'

'No, you're dead wrong now, you were right then,' he broke in. 'These things don't stop just like that, you know; human beings aren't as simple as that, they're not like machines.'

He went on like this while she looked him in the eyes. The rotten triteness of his words seemed, if anything, to help him to meet her gaze. She stood with one leg partly crossed over the other in her favourite attitude, no doubt designed to show off her legs, for they were good, her best feature. At one point she moved slightly so that her spectacles caught the light and prevented him seeing where she was looking. The eeriness of this disconcerted him a good deal, but he soldiered pluckily on to his objective, the promise or avowal, not yet in sight, which would end this encounter, bring some respite from the trek away from honesty. Boots, boots, boots, boots, marching up and down again.

After a while she was no more than implacably annoyed; then annoyed; then sullen and monosyllabic. 'Oh James,' she said at last, smoothing her hair with a convex palm; 'do let's stop this for now. I'm tired, I'm terribly tired, I can't go on any more. I'm going back to bed; I couldn't manage to sleep much last night. I just want to be left alone. Try to understand.'

'What about your breakfast?'

'I don't want any. It'll be over by now, anyway. And I don't want to have to talk to anybody.' She sank on to the bed and closed her eyes. 'Just leave me alone.'

'Are you sure you'll be all right?'

She said 'Oh yes' on a great sigh. 'Please.'

'Don't forget what I said.'

When no reply came, he went quietly out and into his bedroom, where he lay on the bed smoking a cigarette and reflecting, to small purpose, on the events of the last hour. Margaret he succeeded in putting from his mind almost at once; it was all very complicated, but then it had always

been that, and he'd hated what she'd said to him and what he'd said to
her, but then he'd been bound to do that. How well, really, the Callaghan
girl had behaved, in spite of her stand-offishness at times, and how sound
her suggestion had been. That, and her laughing fit, proved that she
wasn't as 'dignant' as she looked. He remembered uneasily the awful
glow of her skin, the distressing clarity of her eyes, the immoderate
whiteness of those slightly irregular teeth. Then he cheered up a little as
he put it to himself that her attachment to Bertrand was a fair guarantee
of her being really very nasty. Yes, Bertrand; he must either make peace
with him or keep out of his way. Keeping out of his way would almost
certainly be better; he could combine it with keeping out of Margaret's
way. If Atkinson phoned punctually he'd be out of the house in well
under the hour.

He put out his cigarette in the ashtray, taking twenty or thirty seconds
over the job, then went and had a shave. Some time later a loud baying
bawl of 'Dixon' brought him to the stairhead. 'Somebody want me?' he
roared.

'Telephone. Dixon. Dixon. Telephone.'

In the drawing-room, Bertrand was sitting with his parents and his
girl. He pointed to the phone with his big head, then went on listening to
his father, who, canted over in his chair like a broken robot, was saying
spleneticially: 'In children's art, you see, you get what you might call a
clarity of vision, a sort of thinking in terms of the world as it appears, you
see, not as the adult knows it to be. Well, this this '

'That you, Jim?' said Atkinson's cruel voice. 'How are things at
Barnum and Bailey's?'

'All the better for hearing your voice, Bill.'

While Atkinson, unexpectedly garrulous, described a case he'd been
reading about in the *News of the World*, asked Dixon's opinion on a clue in
its prize crossword, and made an impracticable suggestion for the
entertainment of the company at the Welches', Dixon watched the
Callaghan girl listening to something Bertrand was explaining about art.
She was sitting bolt upright in her chair, her lips compressed, wearing, he
noticed for the first time, exactly what she'd been wearing the previous
evening. Everything about her looked severe, and yet she didn't mind
sheets and charred table-tops, and Margaret did. this girl hadn't minded
fried eggs eaten with the fingers, either. It was a puzzle.

Raising his voice a little, Dixon said: 'Well, thanks very much for
ringing, Bill. Apologize to my parents, will you, and tell them I'll be back
as soon as I can?'

'Tell Johns from me where to put his oboe before you go.'

'I'll do my best. Goodbye.'

'That's the real point about Mexican art, Christine,' Bertrand was
saying. 'Primitive technique can't have any virtue in itself, obviouslam.'

'No of course not; I see,' she said.

'I'm afraid I shall have to leave right away, Mrs Welch,' Dixon said. 'That phone call ...'

They all looked round at him, Bertrand impatiently, Mrs Welch censoriously, Welch with incomprehension, Bertrand's girl without curiosity. Before Dixon could begin to explain, Margaret walked in through the open door, followed by Johns. Her recovery from prostrating fatigue had been rapid; had Johns somehow assisted it?

'A-ah,' Margaret said. It was her usual greeting to a roomful of people; a long, exhaled, downward glissando. 'Hallo, everybody.'

Those already in the room began moving uneasily about in response to this. Welch and Bertrand began talking simultaneously, Mrs Welch looked rapidly to and fro between Dixon and Margaret, Johns hung whey-faced at the threshold. When Welch, still talking, sprang ataxically from his chair towards Johns, Dixon, finding his own chance to talk about to lapse, moved forward. He heard Welch use the phrase 'figured bass'. He coughed, then said loudly and with unforeseen hoarseness: 'I'm afraid I've got to be off now. My parents have come to see me unexpectedly.' He paused, to give room for any cries of protest and regret. When none came, he hurried on: 'Thank you very much for putting me up, Mrs Welch; I've enjoyed myself very much. And now I'm afraid I really must be off. Goodbye, all.'

Avoiding Margaret's eye, he walked through the silence and out of the door. Apart from making him feel he might die or go mad at any moment, his hangover had vanished. Johns grinned at him as he passed.

A Visit to Niagara

MARK TWAIN

NIAGARA FALLS IS A MOST enjoyable place of resort. The hotels are excellent, and the prices not at all exorbitant. The opportunities for fishing are not even equalled elsewhere. Because, in other localities, certain places in the streams are much better than others; but at Niagara one place is just as good as another, for the reason that the fish do not bite anywhere, and so there is no use in your walking five miles to fish, when you can depend on being just as unsuccessful nearer home. The advantages of this state of things have never heretofore been properly placed before the public.

The weather is cool in summer, and the walks and drives are all pleasant and none of them fatiguing. When you start out to 'do' the Falls you first drive down about a mile, and pay a small sum for the privilege of looking down from a precipice into the narrowest part of the Niagara river. A railway 'cut' through a hill would be as comely if it had the angry river tumbling and foaming through its bottom. You can descend a staircase here a hundred and fifty feet down, and stand at the edge of the water. After you have done it, you will wonder why you did it; but you will then be too late.

The guide will explain to you, in his blood-curdling way, how he saw the little steamer, *Maid of the Mist*, descend the fearful rapids – how first one paddle-box was out of sight behind the raging billows, and then the other, and at what point it was that her smokestack toppled overboard, and where her planking began to break and part asunder – and how she did finally live through the trip, after accomplishing the incredible feat of travelling seventeen miles in six minutes, or six miles in seventeen minutes, I have really forgotten which. But it was very extraordinary, anyhow. It is worth the price of admission to hear the guide tell the story nine times in succession to different parties, and never miss a word or alter a sentence or a gesture.

Then you drive over the Suspension Bridge, and divide your misery between the chances of smashing down two hundred feet into the river below, and the chances of having the railway train overhead smashing down on to you. Either possibility is discomforting taken by itself, but mixed together, they amount in the aggregate to positive unhappiness.

On the Canada side you drive along the chasm between long ranks of photographers standing guard behind their cameras, ready to make an

319

ostentatious frontispiece of you and your decaying ambulance, and your solemn crate with a hide on it, which you are expected to regard in the light of a horse, and a diminished and unimportant background of sublime Niagara; and a great many people have the incredible effrontery or the native depravity to aid and abet this sort of crime.

Any day, in the hands of these photographers, you may see stately pictures of papa and mamma, Johnny and Bub and Sis, or a couple of country cousins, all smiling vacantly, and all disposed in studied and uncomfortable attitudes in their carriage, and all looming up in their awe-inspiring imbecility before the snubbed and diminished presentment of that majestic presence whose ministering spirits are the rainbows, whose voice is the thunder, whose awful front is veiled in clouds, who was monarch here dead and forgotten ages before this hackful of small reptiles was deemed temporarily necessary to fill a crack in the world's unnoted myriads, and will still be monarch here ages and decades of ages after they shall have gathered themselves to their blood relations, the other worms, and been mingled with the unremembering dust.

There is no actual harm in making Niagara a background whereon to display one's marvellous insignificance in a good strong light, but it requires a sort of superhuman self-complacency to enable one to do it.

When you have examined the stupendous Horseshoe Fall till you are satisfied you cannot improve on it, you return to America by the new Suspension Bridge, and follow up the back to where they exhibit the Cave of the Winds.

Here I followed instructions, and divested myself of all my clothing, and put on a waterproof jacket and overalls. This costume is picturesque, but not beautiful. A guide, similarly dressed, led the way down a flight of winding stairs, which wound and wound, and still kept on winding long after the thing ceased to be a novelty, and then terminated long before it had begun to be a pleasure. We were then well down under the precipice, but still considerably above the level of the river. We now began to creep along flimsy bridges of a single plank, our persons shielded from destruction by a crazy wooden railing, to which I clung with both hands – not because I was afraid, but because I wanted to. Presently the descent became steeper, and the bridge flimsier, and sprays from the American Fall began to rain down on us in fast-increasing sheets that soon became blinding, and after that our progress was mostly in the nature of groping. Now a furious wind began to rush out from behind the waterfall, which seemed determined to sweep us from the bridge, and scatter us on the rocks and among the torrents below. I remarked that I wanted to go home; but it was too late. We were almost under the monstrous wall of water thundering down from above, and speech was in vain in the midst of such a pitiless crash of sound.

In another moment the guide disappeared behind the deluge, and bewildered by the thunder, driven, helplessly by the wind, and smitten by the arrowy tempest of rain, I followed. All was darkness. Such a mad storming, roaring, and bellowing of warring wind and water never crazed my ears before. I bent my head, and seemed to receive the Atlantic on my back. The world seemed going to destruction. I could not see anything, the flood poured down so savagely. I raised my head, with open mouth, and the most of the American cataract went down my throat. If I had sprung a leak now, I had been lost. And at this moment I discovered that the bridge had ceased, and we must trust for a foothold to the slippery and precipitous rocks. I never was so scared before and survived it. But we got through at last, and emerged into the open day, where we could stand in front of the laced and frothy and seething world of descending water, and look at it. When I saw how much of it there was, and how fearfully in earnest it was, I was sorry I had gone behind it.

The noble Red Man has always been a friend and darling of mine. I love to read about him in tales and legends and romances. I love to read of his inspired sagacity, and his love of the wild free life of mountain and forest, and his general nobility of character, and his stately metaphorical manner of speech, and his chivalrous love for the dusky maiden, and the picturesque pomp of his dress and accoutrements. Especially the picturesque pomp of his dress and accoutrements. When I found the shops at Niagara Falls full of dainty Indian bead-work, and stunning moccasins, and equally stunning toy figures representing human beings who carried their weapons in holes bored through their arms and bodies, and had feet shaped like a pie, I was filled with emotion. I knew that now, at last, I was going to come face to face with the noble Red Man.

A lady clerk in a shop told me, indeed, that all her grand array of curiosities were made by the Indians, and that they were plenty about the Falls, and that they were friendly, and it would not be dangerous to speak to them. And sure enough, as I approached the bridge leading over to Luna Island, I came upon a noble Son of the Forest sitting under a tree, diligently at work on a bead reticule. He wore a slouch hat and brogans, and had a short black pipe in his mouth. Thus does the baneful contact with our effeminate civilization dilute the picturesque pomp which is so natural to the Indian when far removed from us in his native haunts. I addressed the relic as follows:—

'Is the Wawhoo-Wang-Wang of the Whack-a-Whack happy? Does the great Speckled Thunder sigh for the warpath, or is his heart contented with dreaming of the dusky maiden, the Pride of the Forest? Does the mighty Sachem yearn to drink the blood of his enemies, or is he satisfied to make bead reticules for the papooses of the paleface? Speak, sublime relic of bygone grandeur – venerable ruin, speak!'

The relic said —

'An' is it mesilf, Dennis Hooligan, that ye'd be takin' for a dirty Injin, ye drawlin', lantern-jawed, spider-legged divil! By the piper that played before Moses, I'll ate ye!'

I went away from there.

By and by, in the neighborhood of the Terrapin Tower, I came upon a gentle daughter of the aborigines in fringed and beaded buckskin moccasins and leggins, seated on a bench, with her pretty wares about her. She had just carved out a wooden chief that had a strong family resemblance to a clothes-pin, and was now boring a hole through his abdomen to put his bow through. I hesitated a moment, and then addressed her:

'Is the heart of the forest maiden heavy? Is the Laughing Tadpole lonely? Does she mourn over the extinguished council-fires of her race, and the vanished glory of her ancestors? Or does her sad spirit wander afar toward the hunting grounds whither her brave Gobbler-of-the-Lightning is gone? Why is my daughter silent? Has she aught against the paleface stranger?'

The maiden said —

'Faix, an' is it Biddy Malone ye dare to be callin' names? Lave this, or I'll shy your lean carcass over the cataract, ye sniveling blaggard!'

I adjourned from there also.

'Confound these Indians!' I said. 'They told me they were tame; but, if appearances go for anything, I should say they were all on the warpath.'

I made one more attempt to fraternize with them, and only one. I came upon a camp of them gathered in the shade of a great tree, making wampum and moccasins, and addressed them in the language of friendship:

'Noble Red Men, Braves, Grand Sachems, War Chiefs, Squaws, and High Muck-a-Mucks, the paleface from the land of the setting sun greets you! You, Beneficent Polecat – you, Devourer of Mountains – you, Roaring Thundergust – you, Bully Boy with a Glass eye – the paleface from beyond the great waters greets you all! War and pestilence have thinned your ranks, and destroyed your once proud nation. Poker and seven-up, and a vain modern expense for soap, unknown to your glorious ancestors, have depleted your purses. Appropriating, in your simplicity, the property of others, has gotten you into trouble. Misrepresenting facts, in your simple innocence, has damaged your reputation with the soulless usurper. Trading for forty-rod whisky, to enable you to get drunk and happy and tomahawk your familes, has played the everlasting mischief with the picturesque pomp of your dress, and here you are, in the broad light of the nineteenth century, gotten up like the ragtag and bobtail of the purlieus of New York. For shame! Remember your ancestors! Recall their mighty deeds! Remember Uncas! – and Red Jacket! – and Hole in the Day! – and Whoopdedoodledo! Emulate their achievements! Unfurl yourselves under my banner, noble savages, illustrious guttersnipes' —

'Down wid him!' 'Scoop the blaggard!' 'Burn him!' 'Hang him!' 'Dhround him!'

It was the quickest operation that ever was. I simply saw a sudden flash in the air of clubs, brickbats, fists, bead-baskets, and moccasins – a single flash, and they all appeared to hit me at once, and no two of them in the same place. In the next instant the entire tribe was upon me. They tore half the clothes off me; they broke my arms and legs; they gave me a thump that dented the top of my head till it would hold coffee like a saucer; and, to crown their disgraceful proceedings and add insult to injury, they threw me over the Niagara Falls, and I got wet.

About ninety or a hundred feet from the top, the remains of my vest caught on a projecting rock, and I was almost drowned before I could get loose. I finally fell, and brought up in a world of white foam at the foot of the Fall, whose celled and bubbly masses towered up several inches above my head. Of course I got into the eddy. I sailed round and round in it forty-four times – chasing a chip and gaining on it – each round trip a half mile – reaching for the same bush on the bank forty-four times, and just exactly missing it by a hair's-breadth every time.

At last a man walked down and sat down close to that bush, and put a pipe in his mouth, and lit a match, and followed me with one eye and kept the other on the match, while he sheltered it in his hands from the wind. Presently a puff of wind blew it out. The next time I swept around he said —

'Got a match?'

'Yes; in my other vest. Help me out, please.'

'Not for Joe.'

When I came round again, I said —

'Excuse the seemingly impertinent curiosity of a drowning man, but will you explain this singular conduct of yours?'

'With pleasure. I am the coroner. Don't hurry on my account. I can wait for you. But I wish I had a match.'

I said – 'Take my place, and I'll go and get you one.'

He declined. This lack of confidence on his part created a coldness between us, and from that time forward I avoided him. It was my idea, in case anything happened, to so time the occurrence as to throw my custom into the hands of the opposition coroner over on the American side.

At last a policeman came along, and arrested me for disturbing the peace by yelling at people on shore for help. The judge fined me, but I had the advantage of him. My money was with my pantaloons, and my pantaloons were with the Indians.

Thus I escaped. I am now lying in a very critical condition. At least I am lying anyway – critical or not critical. I am hurt all over, but I cannot tell the full extent yet, because the doctor is not done taking inventory. He will make out my manifest this evening. However, thus far he thinks only sixteen of my wounds are fatal. I don't mind the others.

Upon regaining my right mind, I said —

'It is an awful savage tribe of Indians that do the bead work and moccasins for Niagara Falls, doctor. Where are they from?'

'Limerick, my son.'

The Fiancé

NANCY MITFORD

Since the earliest days of her childhood, when her parents separated and went to live abroad, Fanny had lived with her aunt Emily during term time, spending her holidays at Alconleigh with her eccentric cousins, the Radletts. A sudden threat to this settled routine is posed by an extraordinary piece of news....

IT WAS AN ACCEPTED FACT at Alconleigh that Uncle Matthew loathed me. This violent, uncontrolled man, like his children, knew no middle course, he either loved or he hated, and generally it must be said, he hated. His reason for hating me was that he hated my father; they were old Eton enemies. When it became obvious, and obvious it was from the hour of my conception, that my parents intended to doorstep me, Aunt Sadie had wanted to bring me up with Linda. We were the same age, and it had seemed a sensible plan. Uncle Matthew had categorically refused. He hated my father, he said, he hated me, but, above all, he hated children, it was bad enough to have two of his own. (He evidently had not envisaged so soon having seven, and indeed both he and Aunt Sadie lived in a perpetual state of surprise at having filled so many cradles, about the future of whose occupants they seemed to have no particular policy.) So dear Aunt Emily, whose heart had once been broken by some wicked dallying monster, and who intended on this account never to marry, took me on and made a life's work of me, and I am very thankful that she did. For she believed passionately in the education of women, she took immense pains to have me properly taught, even going to live at Shenley on purpose to be near a good day school. The Radlett daughters did practically no lessons. They were taught by Lucille, the French governess, to read and write, they were obliged, though utterly unmusical, to 'practise' in the freezing ballroom for one hour a day each, their eyes glued to the clock, they would thump out the 'Merry Peasant' and a few scales, they were made to go for a French walk with Lucille on all except hunting days, and that was the extent of their education. Uncle Matthew loathed clever females, but he considered that gentlewomen ought, as well as being able to ride, to know French and play the piano. Although as a child I rather naturally envied them their freedom from thrall and bondage, from sums and science, I felt, nevertheless, a priggish satisfaction that I was not growing up unlettered, as they were.

Aunt Emily did not often come with me to Alconleigh. Perhaps she had an idea that it was more fun for me to be there on my own, and no doubt it was a change for her to get away and spend Christmas with the friends of her youth,and leave for a bit the responsibilities of her old age. Aunt Emily at this time was forty, and we children had long ago renounced on her behalf the world, the flesh, and the devil. This year, however, she had gone away from Shenley before the holidays began, saying that she would see me at Alconleigh in January.

One afternoon Linda called a meeting of the Hons. The Hons was the Radlett secret society, anybody who was not a friend to the Hons was a Counter-Hon, and their battle-cry was 'Death to the horrible Counter-Hons'. I was a Hon, since my father, like theirs, was a lord.

There were also, however, many honorary Hons: it was not necessary to have been born a Hon in order to be one. As Linda once remarked: 'Kind hearts are more than coronets, and simple faith than Norman blood.' I'm not sure how much we really believed this, we were wicked snobs in those days, but we subscribed to the general idea. Head of the hon. Hons was Josh, the groom, who was greatly beloved by us all and worth buckets of Norman blood; chief of the horrible Counter-Hons was Craven, the gamekeeper, against whom a perpetual war to the knife was waged. The Hons would creep into the woods, and hide Craven's steel traps, let out the chaffinches which, in wire cages without food or water, he used as bait for hawks, give decent burial to the victims of his gamekeeper's larder, and, before a meet of the hounds, unblock the earths which Craven had so carefully stopped.

The poor Hons were tormented by the cruelties of the countryside, while, to me, holidays at Alconleigh were a perfect revelation of beastliness. Aunt Emily's little house was in a village; it was a Queen Anne box; red brick, white panelling, a magnolia tree and a delicious fresh smell. Between it and the country were a neat little garden, an ironwork fence, a village green and a village. The country one then came to was very different from Gloucestershire, it was emasculated, sheltered, over-cultivated, almost a suburban garden. At Alconleigh the cruel woods crept right up to the house; it was not unusual to be awoken by the screams of a rabbit running in horrified circles round a stoat, by the strange and awful cry of the dog-fox, or to see from one's bedroom window a live hen being carried away in the mouth of a vixen; while the roosting pheasant and the waking owl filled every night with wild primeval noise. In the winter, when snow covered the ground, we could trace the footprints of many creatures. These often ended in a pool of blood, and mass of fur or feathers, bearing witness to successful hunting by the carnivores.

On the other side of the house, within a stone's throw, was the Home

Farm. Here the slaughtering of poultry and pigs, the castration of lambs and the branding of cattle took place as a matter of course, out in the open for whoever might be passing by to see. Even dear old Josh made nothing of firing, with red-hot irons, a favourite horse after the hunting season.

'You can only do two legs at a time,' he would say, hissing through his teeth as though one were a horse and he grooming one, 'otherwise they can't stand the pain.'

Linda and I were bad at standing pain ourselves, and found it intolerable that animals should have to lead such tormented lives and tortured deaths. (I still do mind, very much indeed, but in those days at Alconleigh it was an absolute obsession with us all.)

The humanitarian activities of the Hons were forbidden, on pain of punishment, by Uncle Matthew, who was always and entirely on the side of Craven, his favourite servant. Pheasants and partridges must be preserved, vermin must be put down rigorously, all except the fox, for whom a more exciting death was in store. Many and many a whacking did the poor Hons suffer, week after week their pocket-money was stopped, they were sent to bed early, given extra practising to do; nevertheless they bravely persisted with their discouraged and discouraging activities. Huge cases full of new steel traps would arrive periodically from the Army & Navy Stores and lie stacked until required round Craven's hut in the middle of the wood (an old railway carriage was his headquarters, situated, most inappropriately, among the primroses and blackberry bushes of a charming little glade); hundreds of traps, making one feel the futility of burying, at great risk to life and property, a paltry three or four. Sometimes we would find a screaming animal held in one; it would take all our reserves of courage to go up to it and let it out, to see it run away with three legs and a dangling mangled horror. We knew that it then probably died of blood-poisoning in its lair; Uncle Matthew would rub in this fact, sparing no agonizing detail of the long-drawn-out ordeal, but, though we knew it would be kinder, we could never bring ourselves to kill them; it was asking too much. Often, as it was, we had to go away and be sick after these episodes.

The Hons' meeting-place was a disused linen cupboard at the top of the house, small, dark, and intensely hot. As in so many country houses the central-heating apparatus at Alconleigh had been installed in the early days of the invention, at enormous expense, and was now thoroughly out of date. In spite of a boiler which would not have been too large for an Atlantic liner, in spite of the tons of coke which it consumed daily, the temperature of the living-rooms was hardly affected, and all the heat there was seemed to concentrate in the Hons' cupboard, which was always stifling. Here we would sit, huddled upon the slatted shelves, and talk for hours about life and death.

Last holidays our great obsession had been childbirth, on which entrancing subject we were informed remarkably late, having supposed for a long time that a mother's stomach swelled up for nine months and then burst open like a ripe pumpkin, shooting out the infant. When the real truth dawned upon us it seemed rather an anticlimax, until Linda produced, from some novel, and read out loud in ghoulish tones, the description of a woman in labour.

'Her breath comes in great gulps – sweat pours down her brow like water – screams as of a tortured animal rend the air – and can this face, twisted with agony, be that of my darling Rhona – can this torture-chamber really be our bedroom, this rack our marriage-bed? "Doctor, doctor," I cried, "do something" – I rushed out into the night – and so on.

We were rather disturbed by this, realizing that too probably we in our turn would have to endure these fearful agonies. Aunt Sadie, who had only just finished having her seven children, when appealed to, was not very reassuring.

'Yes,' she said, vaguely. 'It is the worst pain in the world. but the funny thing is, you always forget in between what it's like. Each time, when it began, I felt like saying, "Oh, now I can remember, stop it, stop it." And, of course, by then it was nine months too late to stop it.'

At this point Linda began to cry, saying how dreadful it must be for cows, which brought the conversation to an end.

It was difficult to talk to Aunt Sadie about sex; something always seemed to prevent one; babies were the nearest we ever got to it. She and Aunt Emily, feeling at one moment that we ought to know more, and being, I suspect, too embarrassed to enlighten us themselves, gave us a modern textbook on the subject.

We got hold of some curious ideas.

'Jassy,' said Linda one day, scornfully, 'is obsessed, poor thing, with sex.'

'Obsessed with sex!' said Jassy, 'there's nobody so obsessed as you, Linda. Why if I so much as look at a picture you say I'm a pygmalionist.'

In the end we got far more information out of a book called *Ducks and Duck Breeding*.

'Ducks can only copulate,' said Linda, after studying this for a while, 'in running water. Good luck to them.'

This Christmas Eve we all packed into the Hons' meeting-place to hear what Linda had to say – Louisa, Jassy, Bob, Matt, and I.

'Talk about back-to-the-womb,' said Jassy.

'Poor Aunt Sadie,' I said. 'I shouldn't think she'd want you all back in hers.'

'You never know. Now rabbits eat their children – somebody ought to explain to them how it's only a complex.'

'How can one *explain* to *rabbits*? That's what is so worrying about animals, they simply don't understand when they're spoken to, poor angels. I'll tell you what about Sadie though, she'd like to be back in one herself, she's got a thing for boxes and that always shows. Who else – Fanny, what about you?'

'I don't think I would, but then I imagine the one I was in wasn't very comfortable at the time you know, and nobody else has ever been allowed to stay there.'

'Abortions?' said Linda with interest.

'Well, tremendous jumpings and hot baths anyway.'

'How *do* you know?'

'I once heard Aunt Emily and Aunt Sadie talking about it when I was very little, and afterwards I remembered. Aunt Sadie said: "How does she manage it?" and Aunt Emily said; "Skiing, or hunting, or just jumping off the kitchen table."'

'You are so lucky, having wicked parents.'

This was the perpetual refrain of the Radletts, and, indeed, my wicked parents constituted my chief interest in their eyes – I was really a very dull little girl in other respects.

'The news I have for the Hons today,' said Linda, clearing her throat like a grown-up person, 'while of considerable Hon interest generally, particularly concerns Fanny. I won't ask you to guess, because it's nearly teatime and you never could, so I'll tell you straight out. Aunt Emily is engaged.'

There was a gasp from the Hons in chorus.

'Linda,' I said, furiously, 'you've made it up.' But I knew she couldn't have.

Linda brought a piece of paper out of her pocket. It was a half-sheet of writing-paper, evidently the end of a letter, covered with Aunt Emily's large babyish handwriting, and I looked over Linda's shoulder as she read it out:

'... not tell the children we're engaged, what d'you think darling, just at first? But then suppose Fanny takes a dislike to him, though I don't see how she could, but children are so funny, won't it be more of a shock? Oh, dear, I can't decide. Anyway, do what you think best, darling, we'll arrive on Thursday, and I'll telephone on Wednesday evening and see what's happening. All love from Emily.'

Sensation in the Hons' cupboard.

'But why?' I said, for the hundredth time.

Linda, Louisa, and I were packed into Louisa's bed, with Bob sitting on the end of it, chatting in whispers. These midnight talks were most strictly forbidden, but it was safer, at Alconleigh, to disobey rules during the early part of the night than at any other time in the twenty-four hours. Uncle Matthew fell asleep practically at the dinner-table. He would then doze in his business-room for an hour or so before dragging himself, in a somnambulist trance, to bed, where he slept the profound sleep of one who has been out of doors all day, until cockcrow the following morning, when he became very much awake. This was the time for his never-ending warfare with the housemaids over wood-ash. The rooms at Alconleigh were heated by wood fires, and Uncle Matthew maintained, rightly, that if these were to function properly, all the ash ought to be left in the fireplaces in a great hot smouldering heap. Every housemaid, however, for some reason (an early training with coal fires probably) was bent on removing this ash altogether. When shakings, imprecations, and being pounced out at by Uncle Matthew in his paisley dressing-gown at six a.m., had convinced them that this was not really feasible, they became absolutely determined to remove, by hook or by crook, just a little, a shovelful or so, every morning. I can only suppose they felt that they were asserting their personalities.

The result was guerrilla warfare at its most exciting. Housemaids are notoriously early risers, and can usually count upon three clear hours when a house belongs to them alone. But not at Alconleigh. Uncle Matthew was always, winter and summer alike, out of his bed by five a.m., and it was then his habit to wander about, looking like Great Agrippa in his dressing-gown, and drinking endless cups of tea out of a thermos flask, until about seven, when he would have his bath. Breakfast for my uncle, my aunt, family, and guests alike, was sharp at eight, and unpunctuality was not tolerated. Uncle Matthew was no respecter of other people's early morning sleep, and after five o'clock one could not count on any, for he raged round the house, clanking cups of tea, shouting at his dogs, roaring at the housemaids, cracking the stock whips which he had brought back from Canada on the lawn with a noise greater than gunfire, and all to the accompaniment of Galli Curci on his gramophone, an abnormally loud one, with an enormous horn, through which would be shrieked 'Una voce poco fà' – 'The Mad Song' from *Lucia* – Lo, here the gen-tel lar-ha-hark' – and so on, played at top speed, thus rendering them even higher and more screeching than they ought to be.

Nothing reminds me of my childhood days at Alconleigh so much as those songs. Uncle Matthew played them incessantly for years, until the spell was broken when he went all the way to Liverpool to hear Galli Curci in person. The disillusionment caused by her appearance was so great that the records remained ever after silent, and were replaced by the deepest bass voices that money could buy.

'Fearful the death of the diver must be,
Walking alone in the de-he-he-he-he-epths of the sea' or 'Drake is

going West, lads'.

These were, on the whole, welcomed by the family, as rather less
piercing at early dawn

'Why should she want to be married?'

'It's not as though she could be in love. She's forty.'

Like all the very young we took it for granted that making love is
child's play.

'How old do you suppose he is?'

'Fifty or sixty I guess. Perhaps she thinks it would be nice to be a
widow. Weeds, you know.'

'Perhaps she thinks Fanny ought to have a man's influence.'

'Man's influence!' said Louisa. 'I foresee trouble. Supposing he falls in
love with Fanny, that'll be a pretty kettle of fish, like Somerset and
Princess Elizabeth – he'll be playing rough games and pinching you in
bed, see if he doesn't.'

'Surely not, at his age.'

'Old men love little girls.'

'And little boys,' said Bob.

'It looks as if Aunt Sadie isn't going to say anything about it before
they come,' I said.

'There's nearly a week to go – she may be deciding. She'll talk it over
with Fa. Might be worth listening next time she has a bath. You can,
Bob.'

Christmas Day was spent, as usual at Alconleigh, between alternate
bursts of sunshine and showers. I put, as children can, the disturbing
news about Aunt Emily out of my mind, and concentrated upon
enjoyment. At about six o'clock Linda and I unstuck our sleepy eyes and
started on our stockings. Our real presents came later, at breakfast and
on the tree, but the stockings were wonderful *hors d'œuvre* and full of
treasures. Presently Jassy came in and started selling us things out of
hers. Jassy only cared about money because she was saving up to run
away – she carried her post office book about with her everywhere, and
always knew to a farthing what she had got. This was then translated by
a miracle of determination, as Jassy was very bad at sums, into so many
days in a bed-sittingroom.

'How are you getting on, Jassy?'

'My fare to London and a month and two days and an hour and a half
in a bed-sitter, with basin and breakfast.'

Where the other meals would come from was left to the imagination.
Jassy studied advertisements of bed-sitters in *The Times* every morning.
The cheapest she had found so far was in Clapham. So eager was she for
the cash that would transform her dream into reality, that one could be

certain of picking up a few bargains round about Christmas and her birthday. Jassy at this time was aged eight.

I must admit that my wicked parents turned up trumps at Christmas, and my presents from them were always the envy of the entire household. This year my mother, who was in Paris, sent a gilded bird-cage full of stuffed humming-birds which, when wound up, twittered and hopped about and drank at a fountain. She also sent a fur hat and a gold and topaz bracelet, whose glamour was enhanced by the fact that Aunt Sadie considered them unsuitable for a child, and said so. My father sent a pony and cart, a very smart and beautiful little outfit, which had arrived some days before, and been secreted by Josh in the stables.

'So typical of that damned fool Edward to send it here,' Uncle Matthew said, 'and give us all the trouble of getting it to Shenley. And I bet poor old Emily won't be too pleased. Who on earth is going to look after it?'

Linda cried with envy. 'It *is* unfair,' she kept saying, 'that you should have wicked parents and not me.'

We persuaded Josh to take us for a drive after luncheon. The pony was an angel and the whole thing easily managed by a child, even the harnessing. Linda wore my hat and drove the pony. We got back late for the Tree – the house was already full of tenants and their children; Uncle Matthew, who was struggling into his Father Christmas clothes, roared at us so violently that Linda had to go and cry upstairs, and was not there to collect her own present from him. Uncle Matthew had taken some trouble to get her longed-for dormouse and was greatly put out by this; he roared at everybody in turns, and ground his dentures. There was a legend in the family that he had already ground away four pairs in his rages.

The evening came to a climax of violence when Matt produced a box of fireworks which my mother had sent him from Paris. On the box they were called *pétards*. Somebody said to Matt: 'What do they do?' to which he replied: '*Bien, ça pète, quoi.*' This remark, overheard by Uncle Matthew, was rewarded with a first-class hiding, which was actually most unfair, as poor Matt was only repeating what Lucille had said to him earlier in the day. Matt however, regarded hidings as a sort of natural phenomenon, unconnected with any actions of his own, and submitted to them philosophically enough. I have often wondered since how it was that Aunt Sadie could have chosen Lucille, who was the very acme of vulgarity, to look after her children. We all loved her, she was gay and spirited and read aloud to us without cease, but her language really was extraordinary, and provided dreadful pitfalls for the unwary.

'*Qu'est-ce que c'est ce custard, qu'on fout partout?*'

I shall never forget Matt quite innocently making this remark in Fuller's at Oxford, where Uncle Matthew had taken us for a treat. The consequences were awful.

It never seemed to occur to Uncle Matthew that Matt could not know these words by nature, and that it would really have been more fair to check them at their source.

I naturally awaited the arrival of Aunt Emily and her future intended with some agitation. She was, after all, my real mother, and, greatly as I might hanker after that glittering evil person who bore me, it was to Aunt Emily that I turned for the solid, sustaining, though on the face of it uninteresting relationship that is provided by motherhood at its best. Our little household at Shenley was calm and happy and afforded an absolute contrast to the agitations and tearing emotions of Alconleigh. It may have been dull, but it was sheltering harbour, and I was always glad to get back to it. I think I was beginning dimly to realize how much it all centred upon me; the very time-table, with its early luncheon and high tea, was arranged to fit in with my lessons and bed-time. Only during those holidays when I went to Alconleigh did Aunt Emily have any life of her own, and even these breaks were infrequent, as she had an idea that Uncle Matthew and the whole stormy set-up there were bad for my nerves. I may not have been consciously aware of the extent to which Aunt Emily had regulated her existence round mine, but I saw, only too clearly, that the addition of a man to our establishment was going to change everything. Hardly knowing any men outside the family, I imagined them all to be modelled on the lines of Uncle Matthew, or of my own seldom seen, violently emotional papa, either of whom, plunging about in that neat little house, would have been sadly out of place. I was filled with apprehension, almost with horror, and, greatly assisted by the workings of Louisa's and Linda's vivid imaginations, had got myself into a real state of nerves. Louisa was now teasing me with the *Constant Nymph*. She read aloud the last chapters, and soon I was dying at a Brussels boarding-house, in the arms of Aunt Emily's husband.

On Wednesday Aunt Emily rang up Aunt Sadie, and they talked for ages. The telephone at Alconleigh was, in those days, situated in a glass cupboard halfway down the brilliantly lighted back passage; there was no extension, and eavesdropping was thus rendered impossible. (In later years it was moved to Uncle Matthew's business-room, with an extension, after which all privacy was at an end.) When Aunt Sadie returned to the drawing-room she said nothing except: 'Emily is coming tomorrow on the three-five. She sends you her love, Fanny.'

The next day we all went out hunting. The Radletts loved animals, they loved foxes, they risked dreadful beatings in order to unstop their earths, they read and cried and rejoiced over Reynard the Fox, in summer they got up at four to go and see the cubs playing in the pale-green light of the woods; nevertheless, more than anything in the world, they loved hunting. It was in their blood and bones and in my blood and bones, and nothing could eradicate it, though we knew it for a kind of original sin. For three hours that day I forgot everything except my body and my pony's body; the rushing, the scrambling, the splashing, struggling up the hills, sliding down them again, the tugging, the bucketing, the earth, and the sky. I forgot everything, I could hardly have told you my name. That must be the great hold that hunting has over people, especially stupid people; it enforces an absolute concentration, both mental and physical.

After three hours Josh took me home. I was never allowed to stay out long or I got tired and would be sick all night. Josh was out on Uncle Matthew's second horse; at about two o'clock they changed over, and he started home on the lathered, sweating first horse, taking me with him. I came out of my trance, and saw that the day, which had begun with brilliant sunshine, was now cold and dark, threatening rain.

'And where's her ladyship hunting this year?' said Josh, as we started on a ten-mile jog along Merlinford road, a sort of hog's back, more cruelly exposed than any road I have ever known, without a scrap of shelter or windscreen the whole of its fifteen miles. Uncle Matthew would never allow motorcars either to take us to the meet or to fetch us home; he regarded this habit as despicably soft.

I knew that Josh meant my mother. He had been with my grandfather when she and her sisters were girls, and my mother was his heroine, he adored her.

'She's in Paris, Josh.'

'In Paris – what for?'

'I suppose she likes it.'

'Ho,' said Josh, furiously, and we rode for about half a mile in silence. The rain had begun, a thin cold rain, sweeping over the wide views on each side of the road; we trotted along, the weather in our faces. My back was not strong, and trotting on a side-saddle for any length of time was agony to me. I edged my pony on to the grass, and cantered for a bit, but I knew how much Josh disapproved of this, it was supposed to bring the horses back too hot; walking, on the other hand, chilled them. It had to be jog, jog, back-breaking jog, all the way.

'It's my opinion,' said Josh at last, 'that her ladyship is wasted, downright wasted, every minute of her life that she's not on a 'oss.'

'She's a wonderful rider, isn't she?'

I had had all this before from Josh, many times, and could never have enough of it.

'There's no human being like her, that I've ever seen,' said Josh, hissing through his teeth. 'Hands like velvet, but strong like iron, and her seat – ! Now look at you, jostling about on that saddle, first here, then there – we shall have a sore back tonight, that's one thing certain we shall.'

334

'Oh, Josh – trotting. And I'm so tired.'

'Never saw her tired. I've seen 'er change 'osses after a ten-mile point, get on to a fresh young five-year-old what hadn't been out for a week – up like a bird – never know you had 'er foot in your hand, pick up the reins in a jiffy, catch up its head, and off over a post and rails and bucking over the ridge and furrow, sitting like a rock. Now his lordship (he meant Uncle Matthew) he can ride, I don't say the contrary, but look how he sends his 'osses home, so darned tired they can't drink their gruel. He can ride all right, but he doesn't study his 'oss. I never knew your mother bring them home like this, she'd know when they'd had enough, and then heads for home and no looking back. Mind you, his lordship's a great big man, I don't say the contrary, rides every bit of sixteen stone, but he has great big 'osses and half kills them, and then who has to stop up with them all night? Me!'

The rain was pouring down by now. An icy trickle was feeling its way past my left shoulder, and my right boot was slowly filling with water, the pain in my back was like a knife. I felt that I couldn't bear another moment of this misery, and yet I knew I must bear another five miles, another forty minutes. Josh gave me scornful looks as my back bent more and more double; I could see that he was wondering how it was that I could be my mother's child.

'Miss Linda,' he said, 'takes after her ladyship something wonderful.'

At last, at last, we were off the Merlinford road, coming down the valley into Alconleigh village, turning up the hill to Alconleigh house, through the lodge gates, up the drive, and into the stable yard. I got stiffly down, gave the pony to one of Josh's stable boys, and stumped away, walking like an old man. I was nearly at the front door before I remembered, with a sudden leap of my heart, that Aunt Emily would have arrived by now, with HIM. It was quite a minute before I could summon up enough courage to open the front door.

Sure enough, standing with their backs to the hall fire, were Aunt Sadie, Aunt Emily, and a small, fair, and apparently young man. My immediate impression was that he did not seem at all like a husband. He looked kind and gentle.

'Here is Fanny,' said my aunts in chorus.

'Darling,' said Aunt Sadie, 'can I introduce Captain Warbeck?'

I shook hands in the abrupt graceless way of little girls of fourteen, and thought that he did not seem at all like a captain either.

'Oh, darling, how wet you are. I suppose the others won't be back for ages – where have you come from?'

'I left them drawing the spinney by the Old Rose.'

Then I remembered, being after all a female in the presence of a male, how dreadful I always looked when I got home from hunting, splashed from head to foot, my bowler all askew, my hair a bird's nest, my stocking a flapping flag, and, muttering something, I made for the back stairs, towards my bath and my rest. After hunting we were kept in bed for at least two hours. Soon Linda returned, even wetter than I had been, and got into bed with me. She, too, had seen the Captain, and agreed that he looked neither like a marrying nor like a military man.

'Can't see him killing Germans with an entrenching tool,' she said, scornfully.

Much as we feared, much as we disapproved of, passionately as we sometimes hated Uncle Matthew, he still remained for us a sort of criterion of English manhood; there seemed something not quite right about any man who greatly differed from him.

'I bet Uncle Matthew gives him rat week,' I said, apprehensive for Aunt Emily's sake.

'Poor Aunt Emily, perhaps he'll make her keep him in the stables,' said Linda with a gust of giggles.

'Still, he looks rather nice to know, and, considering her age, I should think she's lucky to get anybody.'

'I can't wait to see him with Fa.'

However, our expectations of blood and thunder were disappointed, for it was evident at once that Uncle Matthew had taken an enormous fancy to Captain Warbeck. As he never altered his first opinion of people, and as his few favourites could commit nameless crimes without doing wrong in his eyes, Captain Warbeck was, henceforward, on a good wicket with Uncle Matthew.

'He's such a frightfully clever cove, literary you know, you wouldn't believe the things he does. He writes books and criticizes pictures, and whacks hell out of the piano, though the pieces he plays aren't up to much. Still, you can see what it would be like, if he learnt some of the tunes out of the *Country Girl*, for instance. Nothing would be too difficult for him, you can see that.'

At dinner Captain Warbeck sitting next to Aunt Sadie, and Aunt Emily next to Uncle Matthew, were separated from each other, not only by four of us children (Bob was allowed to dine down, as he was going to Eton next half), but also by pools of darkness. The dining-room table was lit by three electric bulbs hanging in a bunch from the ceiling and screened by a curtain of dark-red jap silk with a gold fringe. One spot of brilliant light was thus cast into the middle of the table, while the diners themselves, and their plates, sat outside it in total gloom. We all, naturally, had our eyes fixed upon the shadowy figure of the fiancé, and found a great deal in his behaviour to interest us. He talked to Aunt Sadie at first about gardens, plants, and flowering shrubs, a topic which was unknown at Alconleigh. The gardener saw to the garden, and that was that. It was quite half a mile from the house, and nobody went near it, except as a little walk sometimes in the summer. It seemed strange that a

man who lived in London should know the names, the habits, and the medicinal properties of so many plants. Aunt Sadie politely tried to keep up with him, but could not altogether conceal her ignorance, though she partly veiled it in a mist of absentmindedness.

'And what is your soil here?' asked Captain Warbeck.

Aunt Sadie came down from the clouds with a happy smile, and said, triumphantly, for here was something she did know, 'Clay.'

'Ah, yes,' said the Captain.

He produced a little jewelled box, took from it an enormous pill, swallowed it, to our amazement, without one sip to help it down, and said, as though to himself, but quite distinctly, 'Then the water here will be madly binding.'

When Logan, the butler, offered him shepherd's pie (the food at Alconleigh was always good and plentiful, but of the homely schoolroom description) he said, again so that one did not quite know whether he meant to be overheard or not, 'No, thank you, no twice-cooked meat. I am a wretched invalid, I must be careful, or I pay.'

Aunt Sadie, who so much disliked hearing about health that people often took her for a Christian Scientist, which, indeed, she might have become had she not disliked hearing about religion even more, took absolutely no notice, but Bob asked with interest, what it was that twice-cooked meat did to one.

'Oh, it imposes a most fearful strain on the juices, you might as well eat leather,' replied Captain Warbeck, faintly, heaping onto his plate the whole of the salad. He said, again in that withdrawn voice:

'Raw lettuce, antiscorbutic,' and, opening another box of even larger pills, he took two, murmuring, 'Protein.'

'How delicious your bread is,' he said to Aunt Sadie, as though to make up for his rudeness in refusing the twice-cooked meat. 'I'm sure it has the germ.'

'What?' said Aunt Sadie, turning from a whispered confabulation with Logan ('ask Mrs Crabbe if she could quickly make some more salad').

'I was saying that I feel sure your delicious bread is made of stone-ground flour, containing a high proportion of the germ. In my bedroom at home I have a picture of a grain of wheat (magnified, naturally) which shows the germ. As you know, in white bread the germ, with its wonderful health-giving properties, is eliminated – extracted, I should say – and put into chicken food. As a result the human race is becoming enfeebled, while hens grow larger and stronger with every generation.'

'So in the end,' said Linda, listening all agog, unlike Aunt Sadie, who had retired into a cloud of boredom, 'Hens will be Hons and Hons will be Hens. Oh, how I should love to live in a dear little Hon-house.'

'You wouldn't like your work,' said Bob. 'I once saw a hen laying an egg, and she had a most terrible expression on her face.'

'Only about like going to the lav,' said Linda.

'Now, Linda,' said Aunt Sadie, sharply, 'that's quite unnecessary. Get on with your supper and don't talk so much.'

Vague as she was, Aunt Sadie could not always be counted on to ignore everything that was happening about her.

'What were you telling me, Captain Warbeck, something about germs?'

'Oh, not germs — the germ —'

At this point I became aware that, in the shadows at the other end of the table, Uncle Matthew and Aunt Emily were having one of their usual set-tos, and that it concerned me. Whenever Aunt Emily came to Alconleigh these tussles with Uncle Matthew would occur, but, all the same, one could see that he was fond of her. He always liked people who stood up to him, and also he probably saw in her a reflection of Aunt Sadie, whom he adored. Aunt Emily was more positive than Aunt Sadie, she had more character and less beauty, and she was not worn out with childbirth, but they were very much sisters. My mother was utterly different in every respect, but then she, poor thing, was, as Linda would have said, obsessed with sex.

Uncle Matthew and Aunt Emily were now engaged upon an argument we had all heard many times before. It concerned the education of females.

Uncle Matthew: 'I hope poor Fanny's school (the word school pronounced in tones of withering scorn) is doing her all the good you think it is. Certainly she picks up some dreadful expressions there.'

Aunt Emily, calmly, but on the defensive: 'Very likely she does. She also picks up a good deal of education.'

Uncle Matthew: 'Education! I was always led to suppose that no educated person ever spoke of notepaper, and yet I hear poor Fanny asking Sadie for notepaper. What is this education? Fanny talks about mirrors and mantelpieces, handbags and perfume, she takes sugar in her coffee, has a tassel on her umbrella, and I have no doubt that, if she is ever fortunate enough to catch a husband, she will call his father and mother Father and Mother. Will the wonderful education she is getting make up to the unhappy brute for all these endless pinpricks? Fancy hearing one's wife talk about notepaper — the irritation!'

Aunt Emily: 'A lot of men would find it more irritating to have a wife who had never heard of George III. (All the same, Fanny darling, it is called writing-paper you know — don't let's hear any more about the note, please.) That is where you and I come in, you see, Matthew, home influence is admitted to be a most important part of education.'

Uncle Matthew: 'There you are —'

Aunt Emily: 'A most important, but not by any means the most important.'

Uncle Matthew: 'You don't have to go to some awful middle-class establishment to know who George III was. Anyway, who was he, Fanny?'

Alas, I always failed to shine on these occasions. My wits scattered to the four winds by my terror of Uncle Matthew, I said, scarlet in my face:

'He was king. He went mad.'

'Most original, full of information,' said Uncle Matthew, sarcastically. 'Well worth losing every ounce of feminine charm to find that out, I must say. Legs like gateposts from playing hockey, and the worst seat on a horse of any woman I ever knew. Give a horse a sore back as soon as look at it. Linda, you're uneducated, thank God, what have you got to say about George III?'

'Well,' said Linda, her mouth full, 'he was the son of poor Fred and the father of Beau Brummell's fat friend, and he was one of those vacillators you know. "I am his Highness's dog at Kew, pray tell me, sir, whose dog are you?"' she added, inconsequently. 'Oh, how sweet!'

Uncle Matthew shot a look of cruel triumph at Aunt Emily. I saw that I had let down the side and began to cry, inspiring Uncle Matthew to fresh bouts of beastliness.

'It's a lucky thing that Fanny will have £15,000 a year of her own,' he said, 'not to speak of any settlements the Bolter may have picked up in the course of her career. She'll get a husband all right, even if she does talk about lunch, and *envelope*, and put the milk in first. I'm not afraid of that, I only say she'll drive the poor devil to drink when she has hooked him.'

Aunt Emily gave Uncle Matthew a furious frown. She had always tried to conceal from me the fact that I was an heiress, and, indeed, I was one only until such time as my father, hale and hearty and in the prime of life, should marry somebody of an age to bear children. It so happened that, like the Hanoverian family, he cared for women only when they were over forty; after my mother had left him he had embarked upon a succession of middle-aged wives whom even the miracles of modern science were unable to render fruitful. It was also believed, wrongly, by the grown-ups that we children were ignorant of the fact that my mamma was called the Bolter.

'All this,' said Aunt Emily, 'is quite beside the point. Fanny may possibly, in the far future, have a little money of her own (though it is ludicrous to talk of £15,000). Whether she does, or does not, the man she marries may be able to support her – on the other hand, the modern world being what it is, she may have to earn her own living. In any case she will be a more mature, a happier, a more interested and interesting person if she –'

'If she knows that George III was a king and went mad.'

All the same, my aunt was right, and I knew it and she knew it. The

Radlett children read enormously by fits and starts in the library at Alconleigh, a good representative nineteenth-century library, which had been made by their grandfather, a most cultivated man. But, while they picked up a great deal of heterogeneous information, and gilded it with their own originality, while they bridged gulfs of ignorance with their charm and high spirits, they never acquired any habit of concentration, they were incapable of solid hard work. One result, in later life, was that they could not stand boredom. Storms and difficulties left them unmoved, but day after day of ordinary existence produced an unbearable torture of ennui, because they completely lacked any form of mental discipline.

As we trailed out of the dining-room after dinner, we heard Captain Warbeck say:

'No port, no, thank you. Such a delicious drink, but I must refuse. It's the acid from port that makes one so delicate now.'

'Ah – you've been a great port drinker, have you?' said Uncle Matthew.

'Oh, not me, I've never touched it. My ancestors –'

Presently, when they joined us in the drawing-room, Aunt Sadie said: 'The children know the news now.'

'I suppose they think it's a great joke,' said Davey Warbeck, 'old people like us being married.'

'Oh, no, of course not,' we said, politely, blushing.

'He's an extraordinary fella,' said Uncle Matthew, 'knows everything. He says those Charles II sugar casters are only a Georgian imitation of Charles II, just fancy, not valuable at all. Tomorrow we'll go round the house and I'll show you all our things and you can tell us what's what. Quite useful to have a fella like you in the family, I must say.'

'That will be very nice,' said Davey, faintly, 'and now I think, if you don't mind, I'll go to bed. Yes, please, early morning tea – so necessary to replace the evaporation of the night.'

He shook hands with us all, and hurried from the room, saying to himself: 'Wooing, so tiring.'

'Davey Warbeck is a Hon,' said Bob as we were all coming down to breakfast next day.

'Yes, he seems a terrific Hon,' said Linda, sleepily.

'No, I mean he's a real one. Look, there's a letter for him, The Hon. David Warbeck. I've looked him up, and it's true.'

Bob's favourite book at this time was Debrett, his nose was never out of it. As a result of his researches he was once heard informing Lucille that *'les origines de la famille Radlett sont perdues dans les brumes de l'antiquité.'*

'He's only a second son, and the eldest has got an heir, so I'm afraid Aunt Emily won't be a lady. And his father's only the second Baron,

created 1860, and they only start in 1720, before that it's a female line.'
Bob's voice was trailing off. 'Still –' he said.

We heard Davey Warbeck, as he was coming down the stairs, say to
Uncle Matthew:

'Oh no, that couldn't be a Reynolds. Prince Hoare, at his very worst, if
you're lucky.'

'Pig's thinkers, Davey?' Uncle Matthew lifted the lid of a hot dish.

'Oh, yes please, Matthew, if you mean brains. So digestible.'

'And after breakfast I'm going to show you our collection of minerals in
the north passage. I bet you'll agree we've got something worth having
there, it's supposed to be the finest collection in England – left me by an
old uncle, who spent his life making it. Meanwhile, what'd you think of
my eagle?'

'Ah, if that were Chinese now, it would be a treasure. But Jap I'm
afraid, not worth the bronze it's cast in. Cooper's Oxford, please, Linda.'

After breakfast we all flocked to the north passage, where there were
hundreds of stones in glass-fronted cupboards. Petrified this and
fossilized that, blue-john and lapis were the most exciting, large flints
which looked as if they had been picked up by the side of the road, the
least. Valuable, unique, they were a family legend. 'The minerals in the
north passage are good enough for a museum.' We children revered
them. Davey looked at them carefully, taking some over to the window
and peering into them. Finally, he heaved a great sigh and said:

'What a beautiful collection. I suppose you know they're all diseased?'

'Diseased?'

'Badly, and too far gone for treatment. In a year or two they'll all be
dead – you might as well throw the whole lot away.'

Uncle Matthew was delighted.

'Damned fella,' he said, 'nothing's right for him, I never saw such a
fella. Even the minerals have got foot-and-mouth, according to him.'

The Night the Bed Fell

JAMES THURBER

I SUPPOSE THAT THE high-water mark of my youth in Columbus, Ohio, was the night the bed fell on my father. It makes a better recitation (unless, as some friends of mine have said, one had heard it five or six times) than it does a piece of writing, for it is almost necessary to throw furniture around, shake doors, and bark like a dog, to lend the proper atmosphere and verisimilitude to what is admittedly a somewhat incredible tale. Still, it did take place.

It happened, then, that my father had decided to sleep in the attic one night, to be away where he could think. My mother opposed the notion strongly because, she said, the wooden bed up there was unsafe: it was wobbly and the heavy headboard would crash down on father's head in case the bed fell, and kill him. There was no dissuading him, however, and at a quarter past ten he closed the attic door behind him and went up the narrow twisting stairs. We later heard ominous creakings as he crawled into bed. Grandfather, who usually slept in the attic bed when he was with us, had disappeared some days before. (On these occasions he was usually gone six or eight days and returned growling and out of temper, with the news that the federal Union was run by a passel of blockheads and that the Army of the Potomac didn't have any more chance than a fiddler's bitch.)

We had visiting us at the time a nervous first cousin of mine named Briggs Beall, who believed that he was likely to cease breathing when he was asleep. It was his feeling that if he were not awakened every hour during the night, he might die of suffocation. He had been accustomed to setting an alarm clock to ring at intervals until morning, but I persuaded him to abandon this. He slept in my room and I told him that I was such a light sleeper that if anybody quit breathing in the same room with me, I would wake instantly. He tested me the first night – which I had suspected he would – by holding his breath after my regular breathing had convinced him I was asleep. I was not asleep, however, and called to him. This seemed to allay his fears a little, but he took the precaution of putting a glass of spirits of camphor on a little table at the head of his bed. In case I didn't arouse him until he was almost gone, he said, he would sniff the camphor, a powerful reviver. Briggs was not the only member of his family who had his crotchets. Old Aunt Melissa Beall (who could whistle like a man, with two fingers in her mouth) suffered under the premonition that she was destined to die on South High Street, because she had been born on South High Street and married on South High Street. Then there was Aunt Sarah Shoaf, who never went to bed at night without the fear that a burglar was going to get in and blow chloroform under her door through a tube. To avert this calamity – for she was in greater dread of anæsthetics than of losing her household goods – she always piled her money, silverware, and other valuables in a neat stack just outside her bedroom, with a note reading: 'This is all I have. Please take it and do not use your chloroform, as this is all I have.' Aunt Gracie Shoaf also had a burglar phobia, but she met it with more fortitude. She was confident that burglars had been getting into her house every night for forty years. The fact that she never missed anything was to her no proof to the contrary. She always claimed that she scared them off before they could take anything, by throwing shoes down the hallway. When she went to bed she piled, where she could get at them handily, all the shoes there were about her house. Five minutes after she had turned off the light, she would sit up in bed and say 'Hark!' Her husband, who had learned to ignore the whole situation as long ago as 1903, would either be sound asleep or pretend to be sound asleep. In either case he would not respond to her tugging and pulling, so that presently she would arise, tiptoe to the door, open it slightly and heave a shoe down the hall in one direction, and its mate down the hall in the other direction. Some nights she threw them all, some nights only a couple of pairs.

But I am straying from the remarkable incidents that took place during the night that the bed fell on father. By midnight we were all in bed. The layout of the rooms and the disposition of their occupants is important to an understanding of what later occurred. In the front room upstairs (just under father's attic bedroom) were my mother and my brother Herman, who sometimes sang in his sleep, usually 'Marching Through Georgia' or 'Onward, Christian Soldiers.' Briggs Beall and myself were in a room adjoining this one. My brother Roy was in a room across the hall from ours. Our bull terrier, Rex, slept in the hall.

My bed was an army cot, one of those affairs which are made wide enough to sleep on comfortably only by putting up, flat with the middle section, the two sides which ordinarily hang down like the sideboards of a drop-leaf table. When these sides are up, it is perilous to roll too far toward the edge, for then the cot is likely to tip completely over, bringing the whole bed down on top of one, with a tremendous banging crash. This, in fact, is precisely what happened, about two o'clock in the morning. (It was my mother who, in recalling the scene later, first referred to it as 'the night the bed fell on your father.')

Always a deep sleeper, slow to arouse (I had lied to Briggs), I was at first unconscious of what had happened when the iron cot rolled me onto the floor and toppled over on me. It left me still warmly bundled up and unhurt, for the bed rested above me like a canopy. Hence I did not wake up, only reached the edge of consciousness and went back. The racket, however, instantly awakened my mother, in the next room, who came to the immediate conclusion that her worst dread was realized: the big wooden bed upstairs had fallen on father. She therefore screamed, 'Let's go to your poor father!' It was this shout, rather than the noise of my cot falling, that awakened Herman, in the same room with her. He thought that mother had become, for no apparent reason, hysterical. 'You're all right, Mamma!' he shouted, trying to calm her. They exchanged shout for shout for perhaps ten seconds: 'Let's go to your poor father!' and 'You're all right!' That woke up Briggs. By this time I was conscious of what was going on, in a vague way, but did not yet realize that I was under my bed instead of on it. Briggs, awakening in the midst of loud shouts of fear and apprehension, came to the quick conclusion that he was suffocating and that we were all trying to 'bring him out'. With a low moan, he grasped the glass of camphor at the head of his bed and instead of sniffing it poured it over himself. The room reeked of camphor. 'Ugf, ahfg,' choked Briggs, like a drowning man, for he had almost succeeded in stopping his breath under the deluge of pungent spirits. He leaped out of bed and groped toward the open window, but he came up against one that was closed. With his hand, he beat out the glass, and I could hear it crash and tinkle on the alleyway below. It was at this juncture that I, in trying to get up, had the uncanny sensation of feeling my bed above me! Foggy with sleep, I now suspected, in my turn, that the whole uproar was being made in a frantic endeavour to extricate me from what must be an unheard-of and perilous situation. 'Get me out of this!' I bawled. 'Get me out!' I think I had the nightmarish belief that I was entombed in a mine. 'Gugh,' gasped Briggs, floundering in his camphor.

By this time my mother, still shouting, pursued by Herman, still shouting, was trying to open the door to the attic, in order to go up and get my father's body out of the wreckage. The door was stuck, however, and wouldn't yield. Her frantic pulls on it only added to the general banging and confusion. Roy and the dog were now up, the one shouting questions, the other barking.

Father, farthest away and soundest sleeper of all, had by this time been awakened by the battering on the attic door. He decided that the house was on fire. 'I'm coming, I'm coming!' he wailed in a slow, sleepy voice – it took him many minutes to regain full consciousness. My mother, still believing he was caught under the bed, detected in his 'I'm coming!' the mournful, resigned note of one who is preparing to meet his Maker. 'He's dying!' she shouted.

'I'm all right!' Briggs yelled to reassure her. 'I'm all right!' He still believed that it was his own closeness to death that was worrying mother. I found at last the light switch in my room, unlocked the door, and Briggs and I joined the others at the attic door. The dog, who never did like Briggs, jumped for him – assuming that he was the culprit in whatever was going on – and Roy had to throw Rex and hold him. We could hear father crawling out of bed upstairs, Roy pulled the attic door open, with a mighty jerk, and father came down the stairs, sleepy and irritable but safe and sound. My mother began to weep when she saw him. Rex began to howl. 'What in the name of God is going on here?' asked father.

The situation was finally put together like a gigantic jigsaw puzzle. Father caught a cold from prowling around in his bare feet but there were no other bad results. 'I'm glad,' said mother, who always looked on the bright side of things, 'that your grandfather wasn't here.'

An Italian's View of a New England Winter

JAMES M. BAILEY

THERE WAS A BURST IN A tin conductor leading from the roof of the house on the corner of Rose and Myrtle streets the other afternoon, and the water thus escaping ran across the walk. Toward night the weather stiffened up, and the loose water became a sheet of ice. About four o'clock the next morning there was a slight fall of snow. In the basement of the building an Italian gentleman has a fruit store. Shortly after six o'clock this morning he had his outside wares in a line of display. Peanuts being a specialty with him, two or three bushels of that article made a tempting pile on a large stand. While he was making this arrangement, a carpenter with a tool-box on his shoulder came around the corner, and, stepping on the concealed ice, immediately threw his tool-box into the street, got up himself, looked around to see what had happened, and then picked up his tools. This so amused the Italian that he felt obliged to rush into the shelter of the basement to conceal his delight. Had he been a native of this country, it might have suggested itself to him to sweep the thin guise of snow from the ice and to sprinkle salt or ashes upon it, but being a foreigner, and not very well acquainted with our language, he did not think of this, but, instead, he posted himself in a position to give him a good view of the corner, and patiently waited for developments. He saw them. If his object was to get an idea of the fullness and flexibility of the English language, he could not have possibly adopted a better course.

Scarcely had the carpenter gathered up his things and limped off, when a man smoking came hurrying along. When he reached the ice he suddenly turned part way round, bit a brier-wood pipe completely in twain, and slid on his breast off from the walk into the gutter. He got up, cautiously recovered his pipe, and melted away. The Italian shook all over.

Following closely after this mishap was a laborer with a dinner-kettle. When he touched the ice it was difficult for the fruit merchant to determine whether it was his feet or another part of his person – it was done so quick. The new-comer appeared to suddenly come apart and shut up at the middle, and in the same flash the tin pail described a circle of lightning rapidity, and was then slapped against the pavement with terrific force. At the same instant the Italian saw a piece of pie, several

346

half-slices of buttered bread, two hard-boiled eggs, a piece of cold beef, and a fork and spoon fly off in different directions, while a pint tin of coffee made its appearance, and emptied its contents in the prostrate man's lap. While this individual was getting up to his feet, and securing his pail and cutlery, the Italian managed to blend considerable instruction with the amusement.

Then there came a man with a board on his shoulder. He laid down on the board, with one of his hands under the board. Then he got up, and put the injured hand between his knees, where he pressed it tightly, while he used the most dreadful language the Italian ever heard; and he didn't hear it all either, being so convulsed with laughter as to necessarily divide his attention.

And thus the performance went on until after eight o'clock. Scarcely ten minutes elapsed between the acts. Sometimes a boy would be the hero, then again a couple of merchants, or perhaps somebody connected with a bank. Whoever it might be, he went down, and went down hard, and the Italian watched and improved his mind, and began to think that this country had its advantages as well as its disadvantages. It was eleven minutes past eight when the final catastrophe occurred. This was consummated in the person of a long slim man with a picture under his arm, and a very large woman carrying a basket. The long slim man was somewhat in advance. The Italian, being impressed with the conviction that something of an extraordinary nature was about to transpire, stared with fairly bulging eyes at the coming figure. No sooner did the tall slim man touch the treacherous spot, than the venturing foot kicked out most savagely at the atmosphere, and his body shot around like fireworks. The picture flew from his possession at the same moment, and being thus freed he made a spasmodic clutch with all his limbs at once for a place of refuge, and in a flash his legs whipped about a corner leg of the inoffensive peanut stand, and the great shining yellow pyramid followed him to the pavement. The horrified Italian, stunned for an instant by the enormity of the catastrophe, sought to plunge out to the rescue of his goods, but was too late. The fleshy woman, having rushed to the aid of the tall slim man, who was her husband, was caught herself by the subtle foe, and in her descent, which was by far the most vigorous of the series, she took in two-thirds of the peanuts; and the crash of the demolished fruit, as she pinned it to the walk, might have been heard four squares away.

The unhappy vender reached the place in time to be taken in himself, and the addition of one hundred and thirty pounds of macaroni-fed Italian added to the dismal proportions of the scene. How they got disentangled and on their feet, no one seems able to explain, but the result was reached amid an appalling uproar of Italian, English and feminine noises.

347

What a great matter a little fire kindleth! Ten cents' worth of salt would have saved all the misery and distress. As it is, Danbury has some twenty persons with damaged backs or legs, the owner of the building has four suits on hand for damages, the tall slim man and his wife are confined to their beds, and on Saturday last the Italian was morosely squatted alongside of the funnel of a steamer bound for Italy.

Acknowledgments

The Publishers would like to thank the following authors, publishers and others for their permission to reproduce the copyright material included in this volume:

Special Delivery by Richard Gordon. Reprinted from *Doctor in the House* by Richard Gordon by permission of the Author, the Publishers Michael Joseph Ltd and Curtis Brown Ltd, London.

When in Rome by Peter Ustinov. Reprinted from *Dear Me* by Peter Ustinov by permission of the Author and the Publishers William Heinemann Ltd and Little, Brown and Company in association with the Atlantic Monthly Press. Copyright © Pavor, SA, 1977.

Butch Minds the Baby by Damon Runyon. Reprinted from *Runyon on Broadway* by Damon Runyon by permission of the Publishers Constable Publishers and by special arrangement with Raoul Lionel Felder Esq. and the American Play Company. Copyright by Damon Runyon September 13th 1930. Renewed 1957 by Damon Runyon Jr and Mary Runyon McCann.

The Whore of Mensa by Woody Allen. Reprinted from *Without Feathers* by Woody Allen by permission of the Author and the Publishers Elm Tree Books and Random House, Inc. Copyright © 1974 by Woody Allen.

Introduction to Cold Comfort by Stella Gibbons. Reprinted from *Cold Comfort Farm* by Stella Gibbons by permission of Curtis Brown Ltd, London. Copyright of Stella Gibbons 1932.

A Day in the Life of a Milligan by Spike Milligan. Reprinted from *Puckoon* by Spike Milligan by permission of the Author and his Agent. Copyright © Spike Milligan, 1963.

Adventures of a YMCA Lad by H. L. Mencken. Reprinted from *The Vintage Mencken* by permission of the Publishers Alfred A. Knopf, Inc. Copyright 1943 by Alfred A. Knopf, Inc.

The House of Fahy by E. Œ. Somerville and M. Ross. Reprinted from *Some Experiences of an Irish RM* by Somerville and Ross by permission of John Farquharson Ltd.